Bradley G. Richardson's

Jobsmarts
for
Twentysomethings

Bradley Richardson was a sales and marketing executive in
the high-tech industry before he left to start his own training and consulting firm, The BGR Group. His work takes
him to corporations, conferences, and universities, where
he lectures students, recent graduates, and young professionals on how to search for jobs more creatively, what to expect during the first year on the job, and how to become
effective more quickly. He lives in Dallas, Texas, with his
wife.

Jobsmarts

for
Twentysomethings

■ ■ ■

Bradley G. Richardson

WITH CARTOONS BY R. J. Matson

VINTAGE BOOKS
A Division of Random House, Inc.   New York

A Vintage Original, April 1995
FIRST EDITION

Library of Congress Cataloging-in-Publication Data
Richardson, Bradley G.
Jobsmarts for twentysomethings / Bradley G. Richardson
p.   cm.
"A Vintage original."
Includes bibliographical references (p.)
ISBN 0-679-75717-1
1. Job hunting. 2. Vocational guidance. I. Title.
HF5382.7.R5517   1995
650.14—dc20   95-3941
CIP

Manufactured in the United States of America
10 9 8 7 6

"Great people are ordinary people with
extraordinary determination."
—Anonymous

This book is dedicated to my mother,
Judy Richardson,
who gave me the dream,
and to my wife,
Meredith,
who helped it come true.

CONTENTS

PART I
Training for the Race:
Preparing for Your Career

PART II
Entering the Race:
Finding a Job

PART III
Running the Race:
Succeeding on the Job

Appendices

APPENDIX A
What Can I Do? Industry Profiles
367

APPENDIX B
Resources
395

ACKNOWLEDGMENTS

This would not have been possible without so many people who have helped me, supported me, kicked me in the butt, and believed in me and the idea of *Jobsmarts*.

Meredith, my true companion, my wife, who has made both of my dreams come true. Bob Gordon, my mentor and role model, to whom I am eternally grateful for taking a chance on me and opening the doors. My mother, Judy Richardson, who has been my biggest fan and cheerleader. Eternal thanks to Donna Dever, who was the first one to see the proposal and who saw the possibilities and need for *Jobsmarts*—without her it would have been in the round file. My agent, Pam Bernstein, for believing in me. Marty Asher at Vintage Books, for taking a chance on me. Many thanks to Edward Kastenmeier, who saw the need for providing something positive for our generation and for remaining so calm while I was having a coronary over deadlines and for putting up with my stupid rookie questions. Jack and Jan Introligator, for taking me under their wing and making me family. Paige, my little sister I look up to. Jerry Bowles, for his guidance and help with the original proposal. Bette Scott and the CP&PS staff at the University of Oklahoma, for their helping me get my start as a speaker. Katy Barrett and the publicity staff at Vintage. The staff at Random House Audio. My new brothers Jimmy and Craig. Jack McClendon. Ken and Myra Evans. Grandma Owens. Joy and Jeff—thanks for the contracts and flu shots. Steve and Shana—thanks for hearing me kvetch. Greg Dial, a great friend. Beth Shilling. Eldra Gillman at CBS. Adam West, for all of his help and his printer. Phil Ramirez. Scott Brown. Don Phillips. Linda Penrod. And Herb Stokes.

I would also like to thank all of the people and companies I have interviewed and that have contributed in so many ways, including Tony Goode at EDS; Howie Schwab and Mike Tirico at ESPN; Anne Mintz and Amy Feldman at Forbes; Anthony Mark Hankins and Bruce Ackerman; Jonathan Zager of the *Maury Povich Show*; Scott Chesney, Eric Celeste, Wendy Kopp, Adrienne Taxon, Kate Caldwell, Stan Richards of the Richards Group; Lindsey Green of Deloitte & Touche; Glenn Solomon; Seth Grubstein; Cookie Lehman; Jeff Thompson; Amy Sussman; Richard Tass; Traci Parsons; Craig Obey; Elyse Cohn; Scott Leiberenz; Seretha Wilkinson; the college relations staff at Bank of America; and MetLife, Texas A&M University, the University of North Texas, Texas Tech University, and countless others.

Finally, to the writers, business people, and consultants I have had the pleasure and benefit of reading and learning from in my short career. I hope that I can help others as much as you have helped me.

Bradley G. Richardson
Dallas, Texas
April 1995

PREFACE

The experiences and stories that you will read about in the following pages have been taken from my own experience and that of countless other twenty-somethings around the country. In the course of writing this book, I met many people, some of whom asked that they not be identified by name. Note: These are usually those who have pulled the biggest "bonehead" moves. So, to honor their wishes, some names have been changed to protect the innocent, while others have been left in all their glory.

I wrote this because I couldn't find anything practical out there that wasn't written by someone my mom's age or a boomer trying way too hard to be cool, or that wasn't purely satirical fluff. I just got too sick of hearing that everyone in their twenties sits around in flannel shirts playing Sega and listening to Nirvana all day. I mean, for God's sake, I have only one flannel shirt. (Okay, I also have a Sega . . . but I hate Nirvana.) So I decided to write something that offers answers and is useful for people who really work for a living, or at least want to. You're going to enjoy reading this but, more important, you will walk away with something you can use every day in your professional career.

One final note before you begin. *This stuff really works!* Anyone beginning their career or changing jobs can tell you what a stressful period it is. Over the past twelve months, while I was writing this book, I was also living the Job-smarts experience. In less than a year, I changed careers, moved to another state, got married, started a company, and oh . . . I wrote a book. It was as if somebody upstairs was saying, "Okay, buddy, if you are going to write a book on this, you had better know your stuff." Well, I am here to tell you, the information given over the next few hundred pages is 100 percent road tested.

INTRODUCTION

The Situation

Let me paint a picture for you. You have just spent the past four years . . . okay, the past five years at an institution of higher learning. You have done one of the following: A) worked nights, weekends, summers, and most holidays trying to pay for school, only to end up in the unemployment line; B) accumulated debt up to your eyeballs with student loans and owe Uncle Sam your firstborn; or C) had your parents fork over $100,000 for your education only to have you move back home to become the resident expert on afternoon soaps.

Fact is, graduating from college these days does not exactly open the door to a world of opportunity, as it has in the past. More likely than not, the door is slammed in your face. This is supposed to be the time in your life when opportunities and choices lie ahead of you. The world is your oyster, right? But you don't have to have a 4.0 GPA to realize that today choices are limited for everyone, not just young adults. Read the headlines or watch the evening news to see how difficult things are for young people just starting out.

Even Top Grads Face Grim Job Market
        —*San Francisco Chronicle*
Career Prospects are Worst in Decades
        —*Wall Street Journal*
Grads Face Worst Job Market in 30 Years
        —*Atlanta Journal-Constitution*
Young Job Hunters Facing Stiff Competition in Weak Job Market
        —*Chicago Tribune*
Job Market Proves Unfriendly to Recent Grads
        —*CNN*

Fortune magazine recently displayed a graduate lamenting his employment situation on its cover. The caption read: "out of college, out of work."

The over 1.1 million graduates of this year's class are not only competing with each other, but with laid-off workers and peers who graduated one or two years ahead of them. It's discouraging to compete for an entry-level job with someone who has fifteen years of experience and is closer to your parents' age than to yours. Besides, you're not just competing with more than one million peers with undergraduate degrees; you have 79,000 MBAs and 42,000 law grads to contend with, as well. The numbers keep swelling, with the Class of '94 graduating more students than any other in U.S. history.

In the professional world, they call it "corporate shrinkage," "downsizing," "rightsizing," "restructuring," "staff reduction," etc. You get the picture. The demand is just not there for anyone, but especially not for new grads or young people without experience. During the past three years, corporations have cut recruiting of new graduates by 35 percent, according to an annual nationwide survey conducted by Michigan State University. Many schools claim that the number of employers visiting campuses has dropped as much as 60 percent since 1989.

The College Placement Council stated that this year college campuses had an average of 23 companies recruiting on campus. Eight years ago, the average was 42 companies per campus. Last year, for the first time in history, General Motors and Kodak conducted no campus recruiting.

It's not just campus recruiting; there are problems at the corporate level, too. The U.S. entered a recession in the summer of 1989. Depending on whom you talk to, we are either still in it or whatever progress we are making is creeping along at a snail's pace. Any growth in the economy has not been significant enough to change unemployment figures dramatically. Prior to this economic downturn, major companies were hiring new recruits in droves. Microsoft hired 2,000 graduates before the recession. Last year, they added 150. In the past, BankAmerica hired 200 business students for management training jobs. This year they will hire 25. In 1991, Frito-Lay hired 400 new grads. This year they will hire 100. Procter & Gamble, the company many graduates feel offers the ultimate Fortune 500 sales job, has cut this year's number of recruits by 20 percent.

The competition for these few openings is staggering. Even in what are considered "hot" or "growth" areas, such as high-tech, jobs are hard to come by. Intel, which makes microprocessor chips for computers, receives 20,000 résumés a year from college grads, for only 350 positions. Apple Computer receives 11,000 résumés annually for 100 entry-level jobs and 300 summer internships.

The unemployment rate among people in their twenties is outrageous, 11.6 percent—well above the national rate of 5.6 percent. Despite declining national unemployment figures, you still read about cutbacks and layoffs of thousands at a time. The unemployment figures can be deceiving, because they don't include people who have not filed for unemployment or who have given up or postponed their job search. The figures also do not account for "underemployment," or "McJobs," if you will. The Labor Department says that 35 percent of recent graduates are in jobs that don't require a degree— one in three. Temps & Co., a Washington, D.C.–based temporary service, claims that half of the 1,500 people it sends out per day are recent grads, making $5 to $6 per hour as file clerks or mail-room workers. There is a big difference between a job and a career. Douglas Coupland, in *Generation X*, coined the term "McJob," which is basically a nowhere, dead-end job, for little pay, with fewer benefits, which doesn't require the $100,000 degree you've earned. Believe me, it's not by design that there are so many bright young people stocking shelves at your local Gap or Tower Records.

By the year 2,000, the United States will produce an average of 914,000 jobs per year that require a college degree, according to the Labor Department, but there will be 1.32 million graduates each year competing for them. The Bureau of Labor Statistics claims that in the years between 1988 and 1992, the number of college students grew 11 times faster than the number of full-time, nonfarm jobs.

What about those who are lucky enough to land a job? Easy Street? No way! Companies no longer have the time or money to train people and allow them to grow into a position. They want immediate results. Roger Muller, Placement Director at Northwestern University's Kellogg School of Management, one of the top three MBA programs in the country, says, "If you're looking to bring someone in now, you're looking for someone who can bring value right away."

A common complaint from employers is that graduates have unrealistic expectations for their first jobs, as well as what they have to offer employers. The results of an annual survey of employers by Northwestern University found, "the number one weakness of college students is that they have unrealistic expectations. They are unfocused and unprepared." Patrick Sheetz, Placement Director of Michigan State University says, "A gap exists between the expectations of many MBA grads and reality." Ouch! As Garth from *Wayne's World* would say, "Live in the now."

The bottom line is . . . Things SUCK!!!

I don't mean to be a prophet of doom, but it's getting harder and harder for the average person to get a foot in the door and get ahead. Sure, there will always be a market for the 4.0 GPA, bilingual, well-connected activity kings and queens. But if you're not in that category, you now have two choices: A) believe the media, give up, move home, flip burgers, and collect hair nets and name tags like Wayne; or B) reassess your skills, refocus what you want to do, determine how you can add value to an employer, then position yourself to stand apart from the crowd.

I hope you chose B, because if you have, this book is for you.

WHY JOBSMARTS?

When I graduated from the University of Oklahoma five years ago, I wished that I had a big brother. Someone to sit me down and tell me about life. No, not a birds and bees type of talk (hopefully, I'd figured that out earlier in college), but someone who could have told me the real facts of life, how the world outside of my bubble for the past four—okay five—years, operated.

I wanted to know what the professors, counselors, and textbooks wouldn't tell me. Sure, classes could teach me management principles, and my career counselors could tell me how to write a résumé and not to pick my nose during an interview, but no one told me what really counts. I thought, What a joke; you spend tens of thousands of dollars on an education, yet they don't teach you about work. How do you find it and what it's like in the real world?

Every once in a while, we would have a guest speaker or I would read books about careers. Most of the time, the books were written by very successful people around my parents' age. They were so far removed from where I was at and often out of touch with people in their twenties. They had some good things to say, but there was something incongruous about a multimillionaire CEO with the corner office or a Ph.D. shrouded with degrees and thirty years my senior telling me about the struggles of just starting a career. Their concerns were just a little different from mine. I mean, they didn't have to worry about a 2.4 GPA and $20,000 in student loans to repay. These people had boats and mortgages and ate in fine restaurants. I had a used couch and a Volkswagen and could do wonders with ramen noodles and macaroni and cheese. We were not on the same playing field.

I wanted to hear it from someone in the trenches. Someone close to my age who still remembered, or was actually living the same struggles that I was about to face. Someone who would tell me what I needed to know and wouldn't sugarcoat it or give me a watered-down version.

You know—when you are an underclassman, and some older kid takes you under wing and shows you the ropes. That's my goal. To show you the ropes. That is the role I have taken with this book . . . that of a big brother. "Everything you've wanted to know about finding a job and getting a quick start in your career."

My background is probably not that different from most of yours. I was an average student at the University of Oklahoma, where I majored in communications, worked my way through school, and played on the tennis team. Until my junior year, I had little real work experience. It was about that time I realized that, while I thought I was a bright guy and would have no problem getting a job in sales or advertising, on paper it was a different story. I knew that I was much more capable than my résumé and grades indicated. I was not going to settle for being one of the thousands of "also-rans" who would take whatever they could find in the career planning office. So, I used much of what you will learn in the following chapters and aggressively marketed myself with a targeted plan. It paid off.

After several offers from around the country, I took a sales position with DataTimes, a small, aggressive high-tech company in Oklahoma City. It was an exciting opportunity to have a lot of responsibility right off the bat. I was attracted to the idea of being on the cutting edge of the "Information Age," the booming online information industry which is playing a part in developing the "Information Superhighway." I also saw the benefits of having ties with the company's owners, Dow Jones & Co. and Forbes 400 billionaire Ed Gaylord.

I began my career by traveling once a month to Cleveland and Cincinnati, new markets for our company. There I learned the ropes, by selling to major Fortune 500 companies, such as Goodyear and Procter & Gamble. While Cleveland may not sound like the most glamorous assignment in the world, it offered me a great place to learn and a chance to show what I could do. In my third month, I set the company sales record. After eleven months on the job, I was promoted to New York City, where I dealt with a diverse group of corporate and media clients, including IBM, Grey Advertising, Pepsi, Philip Morris, CBS, Time Warner, and MetLife. I learned a lot by getting to deal with top-level executives, and my exposure to a variety of industries made me a "jack of all trades." Meanwhile, because I was with a smaller company, I was given leadership responsibilities and opportunities to shine.

I was then promoted and from that time dealt exclusively with major accounts. A typical day included meeting with top executives at CBS or discussing information services at the headquarters of Major League Baseball (way before the strike). I even spent time with the guys at ESPN and on the set of *Inside Edition*. Back at the home office, I helped to create mentoring and continuing-education programs, and to develop new products and marketing strategies.

After a few years, I left DataTimes and spent a brief period as vice president of an interactive multimedia company before forming my own company. Today, at 28, I am president of The BGR Group, a training and consulting firm that works with corporations and colleges to incorporate *Jobsmarts* skills among their employees and students. I also conduct workshops and serve as a professional speaker and guest lecturer at colleges and universities around the country.

In my travels and dealings, I've made many contacts and kept extensive notes about what I and others have gone through in the beginning. I've spoken to many people, young and old, and asked them how they began their careers and obtained their "Jobsmarts." The results are what I will pass on to you in this book.

WHAT JOBSMARTS FOR TWENTYSOMETHINGS WILL TELL YOU

The Northwestern University Survey of employers mentioned earlier found recent grads to be lacking in knowledge of industries, companies, competitors, and the job market, and to have poor understanding of the work world. It also mentioned that we lack communication skills appropriate for business environments, are deficient in technical skills, and are poor in math, problem solving, leadership, creativity, time management, and reading skills. Whew . . . is that all they could find? (Actually, the list goes on for a while.)

Jobsmarts for Twentysomethings will help you gain the knowledge and skills that employers want in recent graduates and young adults.

This book is divided into three main sections and takes the approach of training for a race. After all, that is what you are about to enter—the rat race. Part I, Training for the Race, covers preparing and positioning yourself to be a marketable asset before you begin your career.

Part II, Entering the Race, is a comprehensive look at the job search process. This section covers where to find companies, where to get contacts and research information, how to get in the door, the importance of mentors and networking, résumés and creative search strategies, interviewing, and communication skills. It will also tell you what employers really look for and help you decide what you want from a career and company.

Part III, Running the Race, discusses everything that they don't tell you in school about the world of work. It includes: getting up to speed; identifying corporate norms and cultures; dealing with peer, team, and managerial relationships; creating value; organizing time, information, and yourself; communication skills; office politics; reviews and compensation; what really counts;

rookie mistakes; and ethics. It also addresses winning the race; what success is and how to keep it in perspective; how to stay focused; and how to enjoy yourself and have a life while working (it can be done).

Throughout the text will be "coaching," or advice from other highly successful people in their twenties who have "Jobsmarts." People such as Mike Tirico, 27, co-host of ESPN's SportCenter; Wendy Kopp, 27, founder of Teach for America; and 25-year-old fashion designer Anthony Mark Hankins, among others, will tell you how they got started and what they have learned along the way.

You are about to enter the next phase of your life. You have choices to make. What will it be? Do you want to start preparing and training so YOU can make the choices that will control your future, or do you want the choices to be made for you? Getting started in the '90s is a tough race for young people. If you want to succeed in today's economy, you need "Jobsmarts."

There is so much in the media today about "Twentysomethings," "Baby Busters," "Generation X," "13ers." Whatever you want to call them, the 47 million people in the United States between the ages of 18 and 29 are suddenly a major target for marketers, a misunderstood enigma to management, and the newest darlings of the media. All I know is that it's my group. I recently turned twenty-eight and I think part of the hype is on target and some of it's crap. The media is correct when it describes this generation as more individualistic and less driven than the yuppies before us.

With corporate restructuring, layoffs, and everyone from *Business Week* to Ross Perot telling us that ours is to be the first generation whose standard of living will be lower than that of our parents, one might not be willing to devote body and soul to the corporation. However, I don't believe the hype that everyone in his twenties is a cynical, unresponsive, unmotivated sloth who watches *Beavis & Butthead,* and listens to "grunge" rock.

There are plenty of talented young people who have real concerns, goals, and ambitions. I believe that it's still possible for a young person to succeed in today's economy . . . even without a 4.0 GPA. You don't have to be smarter to make it today, but you do have to work smarter. An Wang, founder of Wang Computer and most likely a 4.0 himself, said, "Success is more a function of consistent common sense than it's of genius." Common sense skills . . . "Jobsmarts," are what twentysomethings need to run in the rat race of the 90s.

Now, on your mark, get set . . . GO.

■ PART I ■

TRAINING FOR THE RACE:

PREPARING FOR YOUR CAREER

■1■

What Do You Really Want to Do?

To be or not to be . . . that is the question.
—Shakespeare

Let's face it, Shakespeare is wrong. The real question is, "What am I going to do with the rest of my life?" You may have already realized that, as you go down life's highway, there are several "big" questions that occur in a person's life.

Some questions, you ask yourself. These are usually the bigger philosophical questions, such as, Who am I? Why am I here? Is there a God? Why are cold-water faucets always on the right? Who invented liquid soap and why? You know, the real burning questions that gnaw at your soul.

The other questions are the ones that everyone asks you. These seem more mundane and trivial than the really "big" questions you asked yourself, but they are much more difficult to answer. Believe me, everybody asks. It could be a family member, a teacher, a friend, or some stranger in a store. It really doesn't matter who they are, they want to stick their noses in your business.

These questions start when you are very young and they have a recurring theme. When you are small, the interrogation begins innocently enough, "So, little camper, what do you want to be when you grow up?" At that age, it's pretty easy. There is no pressure. There are no limits. The world truly is your oyster. "I want to be a firefighter, a doctor, a cowboy/cowgirl, and if I have time, maybe I will be president." I always wanted to be an astronaut. Mostly because they got to drink Tang and eat those really cool spacefood sticks. You remember what it was like at that age. The answers came effortlessly. Later in life, that same simple question could make you sweat.

Let's fast-forward a few years to high school graduation. The same old aunt or uncle with warts and bad breath, the one who relentlessly grabbed your cheeks and embarrassed the hell out of you when you were a child, asks the same question, worded differently. "Where are you going to school? What are you going to study? What are you going to do with *that* degree?" OK, it's not just older relatives. Almost everyone asks you these questions. Each person is fully expecting an articulate, well-thought-out five-year plan.

Inside, you feel the pressure. All of these well-intentioned people asking the same questions over and over again. It's too much. By the time you graduate from college, you have years of pent-up angst and frustration from so many people probing, questioning, asking, "What are you going to do when you graduate?"

I'm waiting to watch on CNN how some recent graduate snaps like a disgruntled postal worker and goes on a six-state rampage, offing any poor soul who dares ask about her future career plans.

If you are like the majority of twentysomethings, you have panic attacks and wake up in cold sweats because you don't have a clear idea of what you want to do with your life, FEAR NOT. YOU ARE NOT ALONE. If you don't know what you are going to do, or even what you want to do, don't worry. Hardly anyone else knows for sure either.

Keys to Knowing What You Want

We envy people who seem to have a clear idea of what is in store for them. They know where they are going and what they will be doing. The reason for this envy is that we like security and despise uncertainty. Our society (our parents, in particular) expects us to know where we are going and to know precisely what lies ahead.

Oddly enough, the key to knowing what you want to do is *not* in having a detailed map of every step of your career path. Too many people start out by looking for a job description, "What am I going to do?" Instead, you should start by looking at three basic things:

- What do you like?
- What do you want from a career?
- What is available? What opportunities are out there?

It's easy to get tunnel vision when you are graduating or just starting a career. Your experience in the professional ranks is limited and your exposure to different industries or companies may be limited to those that recruited on campus or employers in your area. If you talked to seniors at my school, the University of Oklahoma, you would think that there were only two companies in the state: Phillips Petroleum and Kerr-McGee Petroleum. Why? Because they are the major Fortune 500 companies that everyone has heard of, and they recruit on campus.

People don't know what they want to do, simply because they aren't aware of what is out there. They don't know what they want, but they sure know what they don't want to do. Due to a lack of research and effort, or often by default, people limit their career opportunities to only those they have heard of or been trained for. There are careers you might be good at or enjoy, but you may not know such avenues exist.

Some see a limited number of choices before them because they have limited knowledge. For example, there is a lot more to the world of accounting and finance than being a banker, broker, or accountant. Those just happen to be the three most common or well-known careers in those professions. Others see their roadblocks in the form of limited access. You may think it would be great to work for a magazine, but you don't know how to get in the door, so you eliminate that option. Don't sell yourself short!

Put it on paper. The first step in determining what you want to do is to list on paper what you like and don't like. I know it's a cliche, but it works. The reason for these lists is so you can identify what you will be happy doing and will know what to look for. If you at least know what you like, you can identify whether or not a certain career can satisfy your needs. If you are happy and satisfied in a job, you will be successful in that job. This may seem very basic, but believe me there is something very powerful about putting it in writing. It will serve as a tool that you can refer back to and add to from time to time.

Make a list of every possible thing that you like and enjoy doing. No matter how stupid and mundane it is, put it down. Try to write things quickly, as soon as they pop into your head. If you hesitate and think about something too long, you are overanalyzing. Put down gut reactions.

Do you like to travel? Do you like to be outdoors? Do you like to research? Do you like to speak in front of people? Be honest with yourself. Think about the hard questions. What do you truly like and enjoy? When you are finished, do the same with the "Don't Like" side. After a while, you will go blank. If you can't think of any more, take a break and come back to it. You will be surprised by the number of responses that you list.

Picture yourself in your future career. What do you want from a career? Big money, respect, a corner office, and your own personal valet? Of course, sign me up. But beyond that, when you close your eyes and daydream, what do you see yourself doing? And don't tell me that you don't daydream because I know everyone at one time or another has dreamed of being a model, a movie star, or an athlete or thought, while singing in the car, that she was Whitney Houston.

While it may sound New Age and Zen-like, visualization is a tip that almost every successful athlete has used at one time or another. Before Hakeem Olajuwon or Patrick Ewing makes a free throw, before the ball leaves their hands, they visualize the ball going into the basket. Arnold Palmer or any professional golfer pictures the putt in the bottom of the cup, before his putter touches the ball.

Think about what you want from a career and picture yourself in that scenario. See yourself dealing with certain types of clients and people. Picture yourself in a certain atmosphere or environment. Visualize what you will wear, what type of meetings you will attend, what your title will be. See what would make you happy.

What is important to you? Using the same high-tech process, get a pen and paper and make one more list. What do you picture the characteristics or elements of your perfect job to be? This will become your "wish list" of what you want from a career. Remember your vision. Don't think in terms of job titles or what you want to do in a specific job. Put down how you want to be treated. How important are freedom and autonomy to you? Do you like working alone or in close contact with people? Is an impressive title important to you? Do you want a large or a small company? Do you work best in a loose or a rigid environment?

Another helpful tool used to discover what you like and want is aptitude testing. Granted, a sheet of paper and a pen are much cheaper than a testing service. However, if you have the means and are totally lost about what your interests or needs are, these people can help you identify your abilities and perhaps suggest a direction for you. Through various kinds of testing they can help you identify skills you may not be aware that you possess. There are several aptitude testing services around the country. They aren't cheap, but they provide a fantastic professional service.

Try Everything

Discovering what you like, or want to do, is only the first step. Now you know what to look for. The next step is to become aware of what is available to you.

How? Try to experience everything possible. Be open and let your mind soak up everything. Every experience you have, every person you meet, every company, career opportunity or idea that you read or hear about—take it in. Analyze all of these things. Determine what you like and don't like about each experience, summer job, etc.

Expand your boundaries. Look beyond what you currently know. This means exposing yourself to many different things. Exposure to different things will help give you a clearer picture of what you want, or want to run away from. Love it or hate it. That's OK. That's what it's for.

You're young. Now is the time to try everything. Hang out with people who have a different background, who think and dress differently than you do. Try different kinds of food, music, literature, experiences, and cultures. Go outside your frame of reference. Seek out people and professionals in areas you want to learn about or are not familiar with.

This is a great chance to see if something meets your criteria. You might not like everything you see or experience, but you will at least know about it. You may find that you have an interest in something that you were not aware of before. If you hate it, chalk it up to experience. You are a wiser, more worldly person for it. Plus you can gain some great party BS.

Expanding your horizons is a lot like trying a new cuisine. Yes, Chinese food. Have you ever met someone who was just a meat and potatoes person? She has never tried anything different. Then you take her to try Chinese food. She whines and moans the whole way to the restaurant. She doesn't want to try anything new. Ends up, she doesn't know what she is eating, but she loves it. She's hooked on Chinese food for life. My point being, you won't know what you like and dislike unless you give things a chance. So, think of life as a giant Chinese buffet.

Discovering that you don't like something can be just as effective as finding something that you do enjoy. Some people have an idea that they might like something, without having tried it or learned much about it. Perhaps you want to be in a certain field or profession but you aren't very familiar with it. You may only see or

> *Kathy graduated from the University of Connecticut law school with the idea of being in a family law practice. She wanted to help couples adopt children. Shortly after she started with a firm specializing in family law, she found that dealing with cute kids and happy couples was only a very small part of the job. There were foster-care cases, divorces, custody battles, and abuse cases. Kathy was depressed and saw how her "dream" job was not so dreamy. Kathy wished that she had known what was involved before she started. "I should have researched it more, or worked part time for free while I was in school. It would have been worth it to find out that I'm not cut out for family law."*

hear about the glamorous side of a business. Yet, once you try it or learn more, you realize it's not at all what you thought it would be. If you have a clear idea of what you like and dislike, you will know what to look for and be able to recognize appealing opportunities when they come your way.

It's not as if you graduate and suddenly one day you realize that, "I like books, I think my life's calling is to be an editor," so you become one. It's a gradual process. You are exposed to different elements of the profession. You will find yourself drawn to those activities you enjoy and are good at. Through that, you can gain practical experience or find your life's calling.

Keep your eyes open. Always be looking. Opportunities are not always clear-cut and they don't bite you on the leg. You must know what to look for so you can recognize it when it arrives.

There are plenty of people, in one career, who become exposed to another field or company. This exposure reveals to them that something else is out there. Often, they decide that that is what they want to do, and they change careers midstream.

The most important thing is to determine what you like and find something you enjoy. It may be cliche, but it's true. If you like what you are doing, you'll be good at it. If you love what you do, everything else, including the money and success, will follow.

Numerous CEOs and entrepreneurs claim to enjoy what they do so much they would do it for free. It doesn't seem like work to them. (However, I would like to see one of these seven-figure CEOs actually give up the bucks—Yeah, right!)

There is a great book about this subject, *Do What You Love, The Money Will Follow,* by Marsha Sinetar. I think that Marsha gives the secret of the book away in the title. It really is that simple. If you like what you do, it won't feel like work. When that happens, everything else falls into place.

Listen to Your Gut

Do what *you* want to do. No one else. Don't listen to what the newspapers or media say is the "hot" new career for this year or what majors are being hired. "Hot careers" generally aren't so hot by the time they make those lists, and besides, everybody flocks to them like lemmings.

Three years ago, applications to MBA programs were at an all-time high. MBAs were in demand and could command great starting salaries. Now, three years later, those who entered graduate school when the press said an MBA was a "must have," have found the market for MBAs has become soft. Only now is it beginning to pick up, marginally. But there is still a glut of over-priced MBAs on the market.

Don't let your parents guilt you into a career, either. Some parents or family members try to live vicariously through you. Your father might moan, "I should have been an accountant, and by God, you are going to be one. Don't break my heart." Well maybe not that much guilt, but you get the idea.

Cornell University asked notable alumni to offer advice to the graduating class of '94. Novelist Kurt Vonnegut responded, "What I have come to become has almost nothing to do with Cornell, where, on the bad advice of my brother and father, I was attempting and failing to become a biochemist."

He added that his subsequent experiences in life, "were freakish in the extreme . . . [and] mostly accidents. Hence, the advice I give myself at the age of 71 is the best advice I could have given myself when I first detrained at Cornell in 1940. Keep your hat on. We may end up miles from here."

▪2▪

Where Are You Going?

Goals and Direction

My goal is to have like . . . a career.
—Reality Bites

Most likely, you had little to do with setting any of your early goals: first words uttered, first steps, going to the bathroom by yourself, or crossing the street by yourself.

Parents, teachers, and gym coaches with beer guts and those oh-so-attractive polyester shorts tried to instill in us the importance of setting goals. I remember listening to my Coach Roach (yes, that was his real name). "Yew see here son, yew gotta have sumthin to work fur." Remember, I grew up in West Texas.

People have been harping at us about goals ever since we were knee-high. Win the Championship. Graduate. Get a job. I feel that the whole idea of "setting goals" is overplayed. The trouble is that people talk about goals all the time, but they don't tell you how to set them, use them, or achieve them properly. They don't even tell you why you need to set goals. Just that "everybody *needs* goals."

I'm not going to get into that. I don't want to insult anyone's intelligence or bore you. I'm going to assume that: A) You know what goals are; and B) You realize that goals are a good thing and that people need to set them.

Goals Are a Road Map

I'm going to give you an example of why you should set goals, in terms that everyone can understand—"cold, hard cash."

TAKING YOUR GAME TO THE NEXT LEVEL...

One year several decades ago, Yale University conducted a study of its graduating class. The study surveyed the graduating seniors and found that fewer than five percent had any type of written or stated goals. The study charted the progress of the group over their careers. Thirty years later, results showed that the members of the group who had taken time to write down their goals and target their future achievements possessed 90 percent of the wealth of the group.

Now of course this example is not meant to equate goals with money. Not at all. Not everyone wants or can have great financial wealth. For some, their goal may be to be vice president in a corporation or to have their own business. Others may want to have a beach house or to be able to work abroad. What the Yale study does show is that there are advantages to having a stated goal.

Writing your goals needs to become a habit. If you are going on a trip, you may not know how to get there. You may even get lost on the way. But if you know your final destination, where you want to be, you can become lost and still end up where you need to go. If you don't know where you are going and you get lost, you will surely wander around.

Goals help you to determine where you are going, so you can then develop a strategy that will take you there.

Be Committed

Make yourself accountable. In order for goals to be effective, you must be committed to them and to their completion. If you are not accountable, they are nothing more than empty words. Accountability begins with making your goals tangible.

Put your goals on paper. Putting them on paper makes them appear more real. They have made the big journey from your mind to something tangible that you can see in front of you. Goals that are written down have a better chance of being accomplished.

The second thing crucial to the completion of goals is to tell someone. I'm not talking about telling everyone in sight or blabbing to everyone what you want to do. Those who shoot their mouths off to anyone end up being known as talkers, not doers. You've met the kind, "All talk and no action."

By telling a close friend or someone special, you will give your goals substance. By telling another person about what you want to accomplish, you are not only accountable to yourself, but to that person, as well. When you've told someone about your goal, you are really committed to seeing it through to completion.

Some people are scared to tell another person about what they truly want, because it's not safe. They are afraid of failing and looking dumb. "If I don't tell anybody my goal, they won't know if I fail and I won't look dumb. I'll just tell them if I succeed." Sure it's safer, but it's wimpy and it's unlikely that you will succeed at an unstated goal.

The person you share your goals with is aware that you are trying for something. He will push you and help you. He will also bug you about it so you do it and you don't rest on your laurels. Peer pressure can be a great motivator.

When I first decided to write this book, I was hesitant to tell any of my friends or family what I wanted to do. When I finally did tell people that I was writing a book, I couldn't escape it. My secret was out and now I had to see it through to completion, or be known as a big talker. They would ask me all the time, "How is it coming? When will it be finished?" They hounded me, but it also pushed me when I was in a slump because there was no way in hell that I was going to face all of these people if I didn't do it.

Go for It

Set your goals high. High enough to be challenging and worth achieving. If you set your goals too low or accomplish things that aren't much of a stretch, you don't grow or advance. You improve by testing yourself. Push yourself to do something that you didn't think was possible, or that you have never done before.

But remember not to set your goals so high that they can't be reached, or that you are setting yourself up for failure. Be realistic in what you can achieve. Too many people make the mistake of setting goals that are so unrealistic that they are destined to fail. "I'm going to lose 20 pounds in two weeks." "Tomorrow, I'm going to start running five miles a day." When they inevitably fail, they feel more discouraged than before they set their goal.

Plan to Succeed

Talk about it. Tell people what you want to do. Don't talk around it—"Maybe I might want to try and work for a magazine someday." Acknowledge it.

Don't listen to anyone, including yourself, who says that you aren't capable, that your dream or goal is stupid, that it can't be done, that you don't have the right background, or that you can't make a living doing it. There are a million and one reasons why you can't do something. You should only be interested in the reasons why it's possible.

Many people have a habit of being their own worst critics, shooting down things that they want because they feel that others may think it's stupid or that they might look like a dork. Consequently, they discount their own wishes and don't give themselves credit. I know that ventures into touchy-feely sensitive person territory, but it's true.

Keep Score

Create goals that can be measured. It's rewarding to mark your progress. Have checkpoints along the way. These will help you see if you are on track or not. They can be a certain task or level of achievement, or accomplishing something by a certain time. As you complete a task or reach a goal, mark it on paper as completed.

Keep your goals visible and refer to them often. Seeing them written down and having them visible will serve as a constant reminder of what you are working for.

A good way to measure your goals is to break them up into various time increments.

Deadlines

Assign a target date or deadline to complete your tasks. Be realistic when you are setting your time frame. Many people are too optimistic about how long things will take them. They plan more activities than there are hours in the day. They couldn't possibly do everything they set out to do.

It doesn't do you any good to set a goal and then not give yourself enough time to complete it.

You should try always to reach your realistic deadline, but don't kill yourself if you don't make it. Goals are not intended to depress you or make you lose sleep and beat yourself up. If you don't meet a self-imposed deadline, take a look at why you did not meet it and set another. But don't make a habit of creating soft deadlines.

Always reevaluate and add to your goals. You can have several at once. They should reflect all parts and stages of your life, from the next stop ahead to way down the road.

Short-Term and Long-Term Goals

Short-term. Short-term goals are those that can be accomplished in a day, at the shortest, to a year, at the longest. Short-term goals are usually broken down into the following increments: the same or next day; week; month; quarter; six months; and year.

In almost every industry, the time frame of choice for goal setting, targets and forecasting is the quarter, or every three months. This is only twelve weeks, when you think about it. Not a lot of time, so get used to it.

Short-term goals can be measured easily and are important because they give you an instant feeling of accomplishment and motivation. You can constantly add to and modify short-term goals.

Long-term. Long-term goals are different. They give you something to focus on over the long haul. When someone asks about your long-term goals, you should be thinking next year, three years, five years, even ten years ahead.

Longer-term goals may have no definite time frame or deadline like short-range goals do, but they still need a general timetable. For example, you might say, "I'm going to have a six-figure job by the time I'm thirty," or "I'm going to move out of my parents' house by the time I'm thirty," whichever applies.

More often than not, long-range plans stay more constant because they project so far into the future.

Reward Yourself

Mark the progress as you reach certain milestones and reward yourself. Take a trip, buy a CD, have a beer. Rewarding yourself will make you feel as if you are really working for something and achieving something. If you finish ahead of schedule, mark it down on your calendar or paper. Put the date of completion down next to the deadline so you can see how you have succeeded.

Keep Your Goals Where You Can See Them

Your goals should be written in your DayTimer or on your calendar. Keep them on a bulletin board or marker board. Write them on a slip of paper and keep it with you. Anyplace where you can see them and they can serve as a constant reminder that you have a mission (should you choose to accept it) and a deadline.

ERIC CELESTE
Editor,
Weekly Alternative Newspaper
Age: 26

MANY PEOPLE WANT TO LIVE the life and experience the risk and excitement of a struggling young writer starting their own newspaper. At 26, Eric Celeste is taking such a chance by launching *The Met*, a weekly arts and entertainment tabloid. As Eric and I exit his offices on top of a local bar called The Elephant and go for $1 screwdrivers below, I realize that this would be a pretty cool life if you were a young writer fresh out of school. However, *The Met* is not your average entertainment rag that has band listings and bar specials. Almost 95 percent of the staff is under thirty, with professional writing backgrounds or investigative journalist experience, and are all very intelligent.

The Met is taking on the largest chain of alternative news weeklies in the country, and is doing so by targeting a younger au-

---

dience with good quality and informative journalism that has the right amount of jest and irreverence.

Eric Celeste is one of the founders and is the editor. His original goal was to become an actor. He had been involved with the theater for years, but when he transferred to Southern Methodist University he learned that most of his credits would not transfer. On to the next plan. "I took a writing class, and someone from the school newspaper came in to talk to us. They needed writers. I knew newspapers. I mean I had read them all my life, so why not?" Eric went to the school newspaper and offered to write a theater column. "As I am turning in my first piece to the editor, he is complaining because he can't find someone to cover a story that day before 3 p.m. I said I'm not doing anything." Eric got the assignment and made the deadline. The editor was impressed and gave Eric a job covering theater and news for his first year.

"I think I am the only person in the world who believed the deadlines they set were real. I would turn in my stories at 3 p.m. and everyone else would roll in around 8 p.m." Eric loved the writing. He changed his major and spent all of his time at the paper. "I learned about an internship at *American Way* magazine, the in-flight magazine for American Airlines, and got the job as fact checker. Again, I took my job much more seriously than anyone else, but it paid off. I was a pest and always asked for stuff to do and to sit in on meetings." Eric's big break came when he suddenly was asked to finish writing a story on which he had done the research and fact checking.

"While I was at *American Way*, I was still writing for the school paper. There was a lot of turmoil at SMU while I was there, and I became known as a troublemaker because I would write breaking stories. By the time I graduated, I had managed to piss off the president, the provost, and the dean. The Dean of Student Affairs called me a pest, which means I must have been doing something right."

In the meantime, Eric was learning practical skills in his job at the newspaper and at the magazine. "I learned how to prepare story queries and I was published more. We always used to make fun of the honors journalism students, because they never had jobs and were never forced to write under real conditions. The work experience was better than anything else I did."

When Eric was about to graduate, he was told that the only way he or anyone else was going to get a job at a newspaper was to go to a small town. "I was preparing to move to the suburbs to cover high school girls' water volleyball when I received a call from the wife of one of my professors. This woman was the writing coach for the *Dallas Morning News*. She told me that they had over 500 applicants for an internship for which I had not applied. There had been six months of weeding down and the job was to start next week. The person who was selected to work on the sports desk had dropped out, was I interested?" The woman had asked her husband if there were any bright students that he could recommend. It always helps to know someone and network.

Eric fumbled for a little bit, saying, "I have to check with my wife." The woman from the paper said, "I don't think you understand, this is the eighth largest media market in the country and I'm offering you a position." "OK, OK I'll take it."

"I stayed there until my internship was up and then moved to a magazine, where I reported to the managing editor. Several weeks after I arrived, 6 of the 36 employees were laid off, including the managing editor. I became de facto managing editor."

Eric did this while still honing his writing. One of his biggest lessons came when he pitched a story idea to do a feature on Dallas Cowboys MVP quarterback Troy Aikman. "Everyone thought, sure, what a great idea. Who should we get to write it? I was furious. Finally I laid my balls on the table and said, nobody can write this story like I can. I was so emotional. I was shaking." He was aggressive. The editor later told him that she was going to give the story to someone else, until Eric showed her how much he believed in himself and his abilities. For the next three months Eric hung out with Troy Aikman, getting to know him very well and writing a piece that would garner Eric his first cover story.

He then met a "wired and brilliant" 23-year-old who had an idea for an alternative newspaper. "This guy possessed maniacal commitment." Through connections and networking, the two were put together and Eric was wooed into running the new paper. "We raised money through a private offering, and used my connections to get the look and feel right."

Eric has learned that even a writer needs people skills. "The only way you will get your stories published is to learn to deal with other people. You can't ram your ideas down someone's throat. You have to compromise. I think that older people are intimidated and threatened by someone who is talented and young. There is nothing you can do except work with them. You can't be direct and tell them that they are wrong. You have to be subtle."

Eric has learned so much along the way in his short career; he tells his young writers he can save them thousands of dollars. "Journalism school won't teach you nearly as much as working. Work for free. Practical experience is the most valuable thing. Work your ass off and do a little extra. No one will ever ask you to work hard. Gain a reputation for working hard."

Eric is a hard worker. With a wife and a child, he is devoted to his family and to his work. "I could make three times what I do at this job, and I might someday, but I am committed to this right now." He says, "Make a commitment to what you want. If your goal is to make money, do it. If your goal is to have a nice life and enjoy all that you do, be committed to that."

▪3▪

Perception vs. Reality: Expectations

Toto, I don't think we're in Kansas anymore.
—Dorothy, from *The Wizard of Oz*

Things aren't always what they are cracked up to be. Take, for example, when you are set up on a date or you finally go out with someone you've had a crush on. Before the event, you may already have pictured in your mind how the evening will go, or whether or not you will have a good time. You may have decided that this person will be the "Hunk-O-Burnin'-Love" you have been looking for. As you may have noticed, things aren't always what you expect.

Life has been pretty good to you so far. No major curveballs, anyway. You can avoid a major one that stifles most people starting their careers by heeding the following advice: Keep your mind open and adapt. Things will not always be what you expect.

An annual survey of employers conducted by Northwestern University found the number one weakness of college students to be "unrealistic expectations." This is especially true regarding two areas: 1) lifestyle; and 2) where you really fit on the career food chain.

Everyone pays dues. Get this straight. I don't care how smart you are, what kinds of grades you made, who your daddy knows, or where you went to school—nobody, and I mean nobody, starts out at the top.

"I want to go into management," goes the mating call of thousands of recent graduates and students interviewing across the land. About this time, the interviewer might be saying in her mind, "Right. The only thing you have managed in four years is to get your ass out of bed and make it to class by noon, and you want to manage people with mortgages?"

Think about it. If you recently graduated, you are in your first full-time professional position or you have just completed your education. You have only limited knowledge of your company's products, facilities, marketing, clients, pricing, distribution, and the way they do business. And you want to have a management position over people with industry experience who are ten to twenty years older than you? I don't think so.

Realize that everybody pays their dues. David Geffen of Geffen Records—one of the most powerful men in the entertainment industry—started his career in the mail room. As did countless other successes. You have to understand the business before you can run it.

Eldra, who is in charge of internships and professional development for CBS News, says, "We have new graduates come in here every year, and they immediately expect to be in front of the camera. Every one of them thinks he or she is the next Dan Rather or Connie Chung. They are incensed when someone tells them to make copies. But around here, everybody pitches in and does everything. There are too many people who want to work here—and who are willing to do whatever it takes—to put up with prima donnas."

Taco Bell believes in starting from the ground floor. If you want to work in Taco Bell's corporate offices, regardless of whether you are in administration, marketing, or human resources, you will start out in the field through what is called "impact training." Yes, that means slapping beans on burritos. You spend a period of time in a store learning every phase of the business, so by the time you get to the corporate level, you know the company and products and you can successfully manage, market, etc., from experience.

Don't be upset because you won't have the corner office or sit next to Connie Chung every night. Use that time wisely by learning as much as you can. And do it with a smile.

Lifestyles of the Rich and Famous . . . Not

Another thing that can be discouraging is the lifestyle you will lead. Let's face it, even though you have been living on a paltry college budget, and you will be making a comparatively large sum of money, your quality of life will not skyrocket right off the bat.

You are in for two giant surprises regarding your finances. The first surprise comes when you get a job offer, and the second comes on getting your first paycheck. Most employers feel that the area where young adults are most clueless and out of touch is in regard to how much money they can expect to make, so it's not surprising that it's also the area recent grads are most disillusioned with when they enter the workforce.

I see many people become disappointed because they feel that they have not achieved a significant degree of success at a young age. Personally. Professionally. Financially. It's tough. Everyone wants to come out of school and have a good standard of living.

Many of us were accustomed to a certain quality of life and standard of living while we were growing up. If you were middle-class, you had a home and cars; the bills were paid; you may have even have taken vacations or belonged to a club. You were comfortable. The problem lies in that people expect the same standard of living in their twenties, and feel inadequate because they are unable to maintain the lifestyle they are accustomed to. It's tough paying all of your bills and still have a life, starting out. Life's pretty expensive.

It probably took your parents twenty years or more to get to where they are now. We weren't around or don't remember when our parents were our age and first starting out. How they struggled and saved, working their way up to the home and lifestyle that you enjoyed growing up. It doesn't happen overnight.

I've spoken with people around the country who at twenty-six or twenty-seven are disappointed because they expected to be driving a Lexus and to have a mortgage by that age. It used to be that owning a home was the "American Dream" for a family. Now, it seems that for many, owning a home and a top-of-the-line luxury car by age thirty is expected.

Bette Scott, of the Career Placement Center at the University of Oklahoma, tells of students who come in and unrealistically think that three years out of school they will be making $75,000 to $100,000 per year. I've got news for you. While it does happen, it's not very often.

There has been much talk about how young Americans are getting shortchanged by our government. Chances are pretty good that we will never see social security, be cheated out of decent health care, and be left to manage the deficit. Economic prognosticators are predicting a college education for our children will cost almost $250,000. Can you imagine if Mike Brady wanted to send Greg, Marcia, and the rest of the bunch to a private college. Face it—it just takes more money to live today, and it's only getting worse. It's expected that our generation will be the first whose standard of living is lower than that of our parents.

There seems to be a growing disparity between those who are living comfortably and those who are struggling to get by. The middle class seems to be shrinking each year and the college degree we once thought would be the ticket to a prosperous future is now the minimum price of admission to the cheap seats.

I don't want to rain on anybody's parade, but be realistic, not everyone will make a fortune. While the yuppies of the eighties were "upwardly mobile," we have the misfortune of starting out in a downward economic trend. Even the yuppies are now paying the fiddler, in this era of downsizing.

These new realities may force you to reassess your goals and lower your sights a little bit. Don't be discouraged if it doesn't come all at once. The quality of life and the things that you want will come if you give it time, work hard, and more important . . . work smart.

▪4▪

Skills That Will Set You Apart

Over one million people will graduate from U.S. colleges and universities this year. In total, there are over 48 million adults in their twenties. That makes for some stiff competition, no doubt. So, the question is: What separates the winners from the losers and the also-rans? What will it take for you to stand above the rest and succeed in your career?

Do you think that your degree, limited summer work experience, and charm will make you the most desirable employee in the world? It's not as if you wake up the morning after graduation and are transformed into this magnetic, super-marketable individual who's in demand.

The days of getting by on just your degree are over. You need to have a lot more than good grades, experience, and an impressive résumé to make it. There are certain skills that you won't find in class. You won't find them in the syllabus of life, and you must have them to make it today.

What is the difference between being just another employee and an exceptional performer? It takes being aware of and practicing several skills that are quite basic, but that are overlooked by the majority of people. Exceptional performers realize the following things . . .

C+ Doesn't Cut It in the Real World

I think that at one time or another almost everyone reading this book has done one or more of the following (ask yourself and answer truthfully): turned an assignment in late; pulled an all-nighter before an exam because you failed to open the book or go to class during the semester; borrowed or copied notes because you slept through class; done only what was required on the syllabus or just enough work to pass the class; or given a wordy bullshit blue book essay answer because you had no clue what you were talking about?

Whether it's one of the slip-ups mentioned above or something else, almost every one of us at some time in our young lives has done something "half-ass." Well, I've got news for you, the days of doing only what it takes to get by, or doing things less than 100 percent, are gone.

Think of business as a giant pass/fail class, and you can't fail. Passing is equivalent to an A, and anything less fails. You must be exceptional. Doing just enough to get by or only what is asked of you is a major reflection on your work. Keep that up and you won't get very far. You must go above and beyond.

You cannot afford to turn in late, incomplete, or sloppy work. You cannot afford not to return phone calls promptly. And you definitely can't afford to make excuses. These may seem like nitpicky or insignificant things to you, but they matter. Companies aren't looking for employees, they are looking for performers (and not the circus variety).

Some of you will be in a situation where you will be given assignments or told what tasks to complete. It's the self-motivated individuals who look for projects on their own, and don't always have to be told what to do, who are recognized first and viewed as exceptional.

If you do C+ or average work, it will indicate that you are an average performer, and average performers don't stay around companies very long. Employers realize that there are millions of young, educated, talented, and hungry people who need work. And if you think you are secure by only doing enough to get by and collecting a paycheck, you are sadly mistaken. You can bet employers know that the guy or girl with the English degree from Wake Forest, who is schlepping coffee at Starbucks or Java Joe's, would love to trade places with you. Everyone is expendable.

There is no place in your career for mediocrity, procrastination, sloppiness, or not paying attention to details. The competition is too tough. But more than that, there's also your professional reputation and responsibility to consider.

In school if you did an average job, or dropped the ball in some way (let's say you turned a project in late or incomplete), you were the only one whom it would affect. The most that was at stake was a grade, and while at the time that seems like an important thing, the stakes are much higher in business.

A similar faux pas in the professional world would not only cost you your reputation with employers and clients, but there would most likely be financial concerns depending on your efforts. You could have jeopardized a project or risked losing an important client. Other people might have depended on you. People with mortgages and families to support. C+ effort puts other people's livelihoods at risk. Your name would be mud.

I want you to understand I am talking about C+ EFFORT, not grades.

What makes an A+ performance? Doing more than is asked of you. Making the extra effort and seeing that the job is completed thoroughly. Taking the initiative and not waiting for someone to tell you what to do. And, most of all, doing it with a smile.

Now don't get depressed. I know it sounds hard-core, but it really isn't as bad as it sounds. Just realize that you have more responsibility to yourself, and to others, than you have had before.

Become a Renaissance Person

Have you ever met anyone who was one-dimensional? Someone who could only talk about one thing? She either knew sports, or computers, or another subject, like the back of her hand. However, ask her about anything outside her field of expertise and she either has no clue or flat out doesn't care.

The most successful people are those who are well-rounded and know a little bit about a lot of things. Having interest in or knowledge of a wide range of subjects makes you a more marketable and more interesting person. You will find that you can use your knowledge and experiences from different aspects of your life in your professional endeavors.

I can safely say that you won't always be surrounded by people whose thoughts and interests are exactly like yours. Having a unique hobby or special knowledge can be a valuable icebreaker at an interview or with a client. It also makes for great cocktail party fodder. When you have, and seek, knowledge of

Jeff, a Villanova graduate, tells of interviewing a candidate for a sales position who on the surface seemed to be all right. The candidate had a great résumé and good grades. It wasn't until Jeff met this person and asked about his interests that a disturbing pattern developed. Jeff asked what hobbies the candidate had and was told, "I like computers." "That's great," Jeff said, and they discussed computers for a little bit. Jeff then asked, "What other interests do you have, for example, hobbies or activities?" The candidate, proving to be the most boring individual on the planet, claimed, "Oh, nothing else really, I spend a great deal of time on my PC." Obviously.

Jeff decided to rephrase the question. "What do you do for fun in your spare time?" To which the candidate replied, "I do programming for my enjoyment." OK, now I'm sure that our friend was a blast at parties and a swell dancer if he wanted, but, for Pete's sake, get out of the house once in a while. Develop some interests. Whether it's computers, sports, music, or a fraternity or sorority, too much of one thing can be negative.

many different things, it makes you more interesting and able to appeal to and identify with a wider variety of people. As our world is becoming smaller and business more global, being able to talk intelligently about many different things will be crucial. In the course of your professional and personal life, it may prove to be a special advantage.

Have a general understanding of current events, different cultures, art, music, and food. You don't have to be a walking encyclopedia, a Cliff Claven know-it-all, or MacGyver, able to build a laser from a paper clip and chewing gum. But you should be able to demonstrate that your knowledge extends beyond Seinfeld quotes, cheap places to go after work, and ways to keep from doing laundry. (To which the answer is: buy more underwear.)

Become a World Citizen: Learn Another Language

I mentioned earlier how business is becoming more global. In the global marketplace, the most valuable asset you can have is to know a foreign language. Did you know that almost every country in Europe as well as most Asian countries make English a requirement for school children? It's amazing that people from other countries, especially Europeans, seem to know, at a minimum, two languages fluently and often many more. By understanding and speaking a foreign language you will have a distinct advantage when negotiating and dealing with foreign clients. It also gives you added respect when dealing with international clients.

Closer to home, it puts you ahead of other people when it comes to international assignments or opening new markets. More and more schools are requiring language studies as part of their degree plans. Many companies are recommending that candidates have language skills, or are looking more favorably upon those who do.

Which language do you choose? It really doesn't matter, although the most popular languages for business appear to be Japanese, Chinese, German, French, and one of the fastest growing languages, Spanish—which can give you an advantage in an increasingly bilingual society (ours).

Perhaps you are limited to spring-break Spanish. You can order a beer and find the bathroom, but that is about it. You can learn a language while in school or through a community program. You can even attend a special language school, such as Berlitz. There are also several fantastic tapes you can listen to in the car, as well.

Master Your Native Tongue

Success in business revolves around communication. Regardless of your profession or line of work, the better you communicate, the more success you will achieve. When it comes to your native tongue, nothing will discredit you faster and mark you as an unprofessional buffoon as poor grammar. This is the case for both written and verbal communication. And proper spelling is essential for business correspondence and proposals.

You can have the suit and the look, but if you open your mouth and you can't conjugate a verb, you might as well be naked. Nothing will get your résumé or letter thrown out more quickly than spelling and grammar mistakes. They are the number one thing that eliminates job candidates. That holds true for obtaining clients as well.

A client might see your proposal riddled with misspelled words and improper grammar, and wonder, "If they pay so little attention to their own work, what would they do with my business?" Everyone makes mistakes from time to time, but gross or frequent errors give the appearance either that you are not very bright, or that you don't pay attention to details and don't care enough to do the job properly.

Polish your grammar now. You may think that you are a poor speller. Great, so am I. This book had to be spell-checked thousands of times. The good news is there are tools to help you. There is no shame in asking for help or in using a crutch.

Always spell-check anything that you write. It's easy to miss things with the naked eye, because often you are too close to the writing. You know what you want to say, so when you proofread it you overlook the mistakes. It's a common phenomenon. If your document is on the computer, always use the spell-check program that comes with your word processor, but remember that spell-checkers don't catch words that are used improperly. Have someone proofread your work before sending an important document or letter. Also, make the five dollar investment and buy a spelling aid book. There are several out there, such as the *Word Book*, by Houghton Mifflin. Use it as a great reference tool. Also buy a style book, such as Strunk & White's *The Elements of Style* or *The Little Brown Book*, to check punctuation and grammar.

We are so used to speaking in relaxed English or slang that, sometimes, it's difficult to change gears. Make a conscious effort to clean up your speech and communicate more clearly. The only way to improve is to practice.

Become a "Wordsmith"

Grammar and spelling are only two of the elements crucial to having control of the language. Vocabulary is another. You may be saying, "Hey buddy, I scored a 700 on my SAT verbal, so back off." Well my well-versed friend, you will always be increasing your vocabulary. There are plenty of words that you run across every day that you don't know.

Think about how large our language is. There are several hundred thousand words in the English language—more than in most other languages. In conversation and writing there is a lot of opportunity for ambiguity.

This huge volume of words allows us to be more descriptive and to communicate more clearly and accurately. The larger your vocabulary, the more accurately and descriptively you will speak. You also appear more educated and professional. The higher in an organization you go, the better the vocabularies of the people in those positions.

How do you improve your vocabulary? Keep a notebook of words that you don't know. Whenever you are reading or hear one that you don't know, mark it in your notebook. Once a week or month, look them up and try using them in a conversation. You may feel funny at first, but keep trying. In a very short time you will find yourself using those words naturally, and understanding more. There are also plenty of vocabulary tapes and books available. If you think they are dorky, listen to them in your car when no one else is with you. Plus, there is nothing dorky about learning and improving yourself. Your friends may change their attitudes when you are moving up the career ladder and their professional vocabulary consists of "Paper or Plastic?"

Count Your Change

Remember when you skipped that 7:30 a.m. math class because you thought "There's no way that I'll ever use this stuff." Bubba, you were wrong. You will use math and numbers in some form or fashion in anything you do. I know people who planned their whole college careers or accepted certain positions so they would not have to deal with math. But what is the primary function and goal of any business? To make a profit. That means making money, and that you are dealing with numbers and math somehow, some way.

Depending on your profession, your need for advanced math will vary. Of course, accountants, bankers, brokers, and engineers are surrounded by numbers. Their careers depend on their mathematical proficiency. However, even if you are in sales or if you're an advertising executive, you will need to be comfortable working with and manipulating numbers. How?

For example, you will calculate budgets, targets, percentages, margins, loans, interest, billable hours, discounts, leases, expense reports, or net profits. There are any number of day-to-day calculations you may be asked to do, regardless of industry. But don't panic. These activities don't require your third-year calculus. Outside of the specialty fields mentioned above, business math is pretty basic. It just takes remembering some simple skills. Addition, subtraction, percentages, division, multiplication, averages, fractions, and decimals—if you like little things like money.

You would be surprised how many people forget their basic math skills. It's not because they are bad in math, but because these skills have not been used in a while. Just like any skill, if you don't practice or use it, it will deteriorate.

Warm up and practice your math skills. Keep them sharp. It's embarrassing to have to ask a coworker how to figure a discount for a client, or to determine your commission percentage.

Computer Skills

Information superhighway, the Internet, the Information Age. This is our world, our time. We were raised on this stuff. We are the computer-literate generation. We blow away our elders with our understanding of technology and computers.

And it's a good thing that we excel in this area, because the world keeps becoming more and more high-tech. The personal computer is only a little over ten years old. Today, over 85 percent of all offices in America have PCs. If you don't have at least a basic knowledge of computers and the basic applications programs, you might as well be using an abacus to do math and riding a horse to work, because you are behind the times. It seems you can't communicate, write a letter, or crunch numbers without a computer anymore. Alan Krueger, economics professor at Princeton, reports that those who use computers on the job earn 10 to 15 percent more than those who don't.

What is so funny is that those who are in a position of power in a company (generally older executives) are often incredible technophobes. Ernst & Young, the Big Six accounting firm, offers computer classes for partners that are held separately from those for the younger staffers. "They don't want to look silly," says Linda Belton of the L.A. office.

This technology gap offers you a great opportunity. If you are very computer-literate, you are ahead of the game. Use it to your advantage to be more efficient and to make yourself valuable.

What you need to know. If you don't have much experience using computers, I recommend that you do anything you can to learn about them ASAP. It's essential for getting a job at many companies. Don't be intimidated by computers. Computers today are easy to learn and use. Both Macintosh and Windows environments are graphical, with lots of pictures and icons to guide you. You also need to become familiar with, at minimum, a word processing package and spreadsheet program. The most common word processing programs are Microsoft

Word and WordPerfect. The spreadsheets you will find in most offices are either Microsoft Excel or Lotus 123. Once you have these mastered, you can move to e-mail, databases, and online services.

Where you can learn. If you are in school, go to your computer lab to practice. Look into what classes are offered, or have a friend show you the ropes. In most areas, community courses are offered to teach the basics of these programs. They are cheap and usually are one- or two-day classes taken at night or on weekends.

Take the time to learn how to type. In many jobs you will need to type and knowing how will help save you a lot of time. Using two fingers to hunt and peck will not cut it when you have a deadline and must produce an error-free document.

It doesn't happen overnight. Most of all, be patient when learning. Don't get frustrated and don't be afraid to try something on the machine. You aren't going to break it or screw anything up so badly that it can't be recovered. Just remember to save your work and always back it up. Once you get the hang of it, you won't know how you lived without it.

▪5▪

Getting the Experience

Employers Want

Experience Required
—Almost any want ad you read

It's a Catch 22. You need experience to land a job, but employers only want people with experience. So where do you get it? Many people find themselves in this dilemma.

A degree and great grades are no longer enough. Most companies are requiring some form of experience, either through an internship, co-op, summer job, or part-time work during the school year. Practical experience is what is in demand, not just mowing lawns, bartending, or working for your dad. Companies want experience and skills related to what you are being hired for, or at least experience that can be transferred.

Each year corporations spend billions of dollars training employees. Time spent training new employees is too valuable and costly for an employer to waste. According to *Fortune*, companies are less likely to take a chance on an unproven commodity. "They want recruits who can perform real work, even when they are in training."

What If You Have Never Worked?

If you are in a position where you have never worked or don't have any formal experience, don't lose hope. While practical work experience is preferred, you can certainly gain fantastic skills and experience from other activities.

Activities and groups. You can turn your experience in social, civic, and student activities into valuable experience that can be transferred to employers. In any of your activities, were you in charge of a staff, or did you manage other people? Did you organize, plan, and implement activities? Were you responsible for a budget or increasing sales, revenue, or attendance? Were you in charge of ticket sales for a particular event? Did you hold an office in student government, volunteer for Big Brothers/Big Sisters, or serve on a housing committee for your Greek organization? Did you help start a club, serve on a committee, or participate in an organization related to your major? Were you involved in sports? Some employers have a preference for people who have participated in sports, because they feel that such participation demonstrates discipline, leadership, and team skills. Any of these types of activities can give you experience and responsibility that can be used on the job.

Part-time work, even in an unrelated field, is desirable. One recruiter for a major bank says, "We don't even look at anyone without work experience. Now, it doesn't have to be bank experience—just something that shows they have worked before and at least understand responsibility and leadership." If you work in a bookstore, are you in charge of other employees or purchasing merchandise? This can be valuable to an employer.

You don't even have to have worked for someone else. Did you start a company or business while you were in school? Your entrepreneurial endeavors might have given you more relevant experience than someone who has worked for a company.

What if you have already graduated? Even if you are out of school and don't have any experience, don't give up. Experience is the one thing that you can always get more of. If you are at square one and have nothing you think can serve as experience, you may have to bite the bullet and take a temp position, work part time, or volunteer somewhere just to gain any type of work experience. While it may not be your number one choice, putting your major job search on hold for three to six months to gain some experience may make you more marketable in the long run. And if you get your foot in the door through a temp job and perform well, you may be offered a permanent position you'd enjoy.

Tangible results. In whatever you do (activities, internships, or jobs), make sure to accomplish tangible results and measure your performance. If you were responsible for ticket sales, by what percentage did you increase ticket sales? How many people were you in charge of? What was the dollar amount of inventory you ordered? What did you learn from this experience that can be useful to an employer? It's these things that employers are looking for from your experience. Remember, tangible results are what matter most to employers.

Where You Get It

There are a variety of internships that offer very useful work experience. Regardless of which you choose or have the opportunity to participate in, remember that experience is what you are after. Paid or unpaid, credit or no credit, don't let these factors prevent you from taking an internship. Those things don't matter as much as getting practical work experience that you can use later. It's worth the trade-off. You are after the experience and the networking contacts, and you want to see if you like a particular field.

A common method for gaining experience is through a formal internship program sponsored by your school or a company. Even if you are out of school you can still participate in an internship, or even create your own.

Internship programs. You generally can find out about formal internship programs by asking your professors or checking with the career planning and placement center at your school. Many companies have their own formal internships or development programs, which are independent of universities. You can contact companies directly for information on these programs. Many are advertised, but make sure to ask around. Connections are often how many of these corporate internships are discovered.

> *Sharon, from Kansas State University, thought that she wanted to be in television production, until she spent a summer working for a station. She thought it would be glamorous. Little did she know it required grueling hours and, as she says, "the people were caustic, they were under so much pressure all the time. I couldn't live that way."*

Formal internships serve as a great way for you to get a feel for the industry and see if it's right for you. You will be exposed to life on the job and day-to-day activities, and will become familiar with the culture.

For a company, internships can serve as a recruiting trip or a test drive. They can see if you are a star in the making. Many companies have offered permanent positions to their interns upon graduation. "It's a great way to try employees on for size and see if there is a fit," says one banking executive from Louisiana.

Formal internships, especially those through a company, are set up to expose you to different elements of the business. TBWA Advertising in New York offers a formal internship, where students get hands-on experience with a real client. Possibilities include conducting client meetings, as well as creating and pitching a proposal.

Co-ops. Formal co-op programs are another way to obtain practical experience. Co-ops differ from internships because they act more as a work-study program during the school year. You are paid and it's often part of your degree plan. Co-op programs can be found through your college or university. They have relationships with employers in the area and will make arrangements for you through the cooperative education or career planning department.

What to Get Out of It

Before you start an internship, co-op, or part-time position, decide on your own what you want to achieve. What do you hope to gain from this experience? Write down a few specific things that you want to learn about the company or industry. Decide that this is what you hope to learn from this experience, and seek it out. Have an agenda.

The number one thing that you want is experience that you can take to another employer. It's impressive to be able to say to an employer, "I have experience in this industry and can understand your business."

You are looking for more than résumé filler. You're looking for something that will make them sit up and take notice. Here are several tips that will help you to get the most out of your internship.

Talk to people. Don't just be a worker bee and junior peon afraid to talk to anyone. Talk to people who are higher up than yourself. Belly up to the boss. Introduce yourself to people around the office. In formal internships where there are several interns, they tend to travel in packs. It's fine to hang with your buddies, but they aren't going to be the ones who can recommend you for a job at the end of the summer. They are as powerless and clueless as you are. So hang out with them socially, but at work, branch out on your own. Don't be afraid to be aggressive and to introduce yourself.

Ask for things to do. Take charge and ask for more responsibility. Don't wait around until there is something to do. Volunteer for it. Nothing is beneath you. Making coffee or copies or walking the boss's dog. When asked to do something that you think is grunt work, do it with a smile and a grunt. Your professional reputation starts now. Your work ethic and attitude will be remembered, especially if you want a recommendation letter at the end of the summer. Show up on time and do the work that is asked of you, correctly.

Learn all you can about the industry. Don't be limited to what information you are told or are handed. Ask questions about the company, its competitors, and why they do something a certain way.

Look at documents. If you are told to copy something, look at what it is, unless, of course, it's marked confidential. You can learn a lot by looking at memos, letters, and other correspondence. If you are asked to type or copy something, make certain you look at what it is. By having contact with these and other documents, you can begin to understand how contracts look and are structured. You can learn the names of companies they deal with and who their clients are. You will become informed.

Get in the information loop. Being informed is a crucial part of career success. You are the low person on the totem pole. You are completely shut out of the information loop. This is true when you are an intern or part-timer, and also when you are beginning your career. Try anything you can to get into the information loop. You can get there simply by asking people questions. Ask someone about a deal that you heard of, or ask someone what they are responsible for and what they do. You might ask why the company markets a certain way.

Keep your ears open. Besides reading and asking, you should listen around the office. You can pick up a great deal about how a company really works and what is going on by paying attention to the impromptu meetings in the hallway or break room. You can find out what the people in the field think about a product, why a certain competitor is beating the company in the marketplace, what is good and bad about a certain product, who in the company is respected and who is not.

Be informed outside the office. Read company reports, news about the company and its competitors, press releases, and brochures—anything that will put you in the know, because you aren't going to be told everything you need to know. I'm not talking at all about being a snoopy, eavesdropping gossip, but simply be aware of what is around you.

Milk the fact that you are a student or intern. People will open up, tell you things and let you do things other employees might not be able to do, because you are viewed as nonthreatening. After all, they are thinking, "You aren't after my job, you're just a kid." Oddly enough, there is a lot a value in playing naive. "I don't get it, tell me more."

Being a student or part-timer can be a double-edged sword, though. On one hand, some people might not take you seriously. However, others will grant you access to things and share information with you, because they are willing to help a student. They think that you don't know anything and can't do any harm, so they are more open than they might be to a fellow employee.

Ask to attend interoffice and client meetings. Say that you want to observe. Don't be afraid to ask for things. You will be surprised by what people are willing to do for you because you are a student. Play to people's egos. People like to think of themselves as knowledgeable and love to tell others what they know. By simply asking to learn more you may be granted access to these situations, when more senior employees would not.

When you attend these meetings, soak up everything you can. Listen to what is being said, how they communicate and negotiate.

Don't burn any bridges. You want to gain experience, but these people can also serve as valuable contacts and references when you are seeking a permanent position. You don't want a potential employer to hear that you were lazy, showed up late for work, or couldn't get along with people.

In every office you will find your fair share of nice people and jerks. Don't let petty personality conflicts discount the experience you have worked so hard to get. No matter how badly you want to tell your boss or a jerky coworker to go to hell, don't do it.

Always, at the end of a position, ask your boss, supervisor, or head of the company to write a recommendation letter for you. You want to stay in contact with this person and use them as a contact for the future. Never, never burn any bridges.

Creating Your Own Internship

Plan ahead. If you want a job for the summer, the time to start looking is *not* April or May. You should start contacting companies and lay the groundwork in January or February. Try to beat the summer rush. Everybody will be trying to get part-time work or summer internships during that time. Companies often don't make decisions quickly, either. They do want to plan ahead, however. Get your name in early. If the company does not know what their summer or part-time staffing needs will be, at least your name will be fresh in their minds when they reach a decision.

How do you gain work experience if no formal program exists? Begin by making a list of the industries or fields that you are interested in learning more about or need experience in. Write down the names, addresses, and phone numbers of about ten to fifteen companies in your city or town in that field. Call and find out the president or CEO's name. Try to find out who the top person in the company is or at least the head of the particular area you would like to work in. For example, the vice president of Communications would be your contact if you were after a public relations or communications position.

Don't ask "who's in charge of your interns or summer jobs?" Many companies don't have formal programs and some smaller ones may not have thought of it or have not reached the size to warrant a program. If they don't have one, you have just blown your chance and will get shut down early. "Sorry, no internship program." Click.

When you reach someone in a position to make a decision, tell him that you are a student and are considering going into this particular field. In the course of your research you had come across his name and would like to meet with him to seek his advice and learn more about the industry. You want to see what it has to offer and learn more about it.

He may invite you to the office to meet with him or he may just want to see if you have any questions on the phone right then. In any case, tell him that you would like to be around his company and learn from the ground up. You need to get experience and want to see if you are making the right choice. "I would like to acquire experience in this field." You may get a response like, "We don't have interns, or we aren't hiring now." That's OK. Tell them, "I'm offering to work for you for free. I will do whatever you need around the office. I would like to be around and learn from the ground up. I will observe or do whatever is needed. You don't even have to pay me."

You may be saying to yourself. "Work for free! What, are you crazy?" Not at all. You are just getting in the door. Think of this. Many internships are unpaid anyway. There is a good chance, if you go in and do a great job, work your butt off, do whatever it takes, that within a few weeks they will pay you something. No one is so evil that they will see a student working hard, doing a good job, and not take care of them. Besides, you are after the experience. It's a great way to get in the door, even if they don't end up paying you.

> *Rachel, an Auburn University graduate, wanted to work at a museum. She had a contact with a curator there and got in touch with her. The curator told Rachel that nothing was available. Rachel called every week for six weeks, hounding this poor woman. "I will do anything. Bring me on and I will work for nothing." The curator took her up on it. For two months, Rachel went to work as if it were a regular full-time job. She took pride in her work and proved that she was capable. It got people's attention. After two months of working gratis, she was offered a full-time paid position.*

What a deal for the employer! It's risk-free and not threatening for the employer. They might not be hiring or able to bring on an employee, but who can turn down free labor? The company gets an eager, hardworking employee, and if it doesn't work out, what's the loss? Nothing . . . Zip . . . *Nada.*

Quality, Not Quantity

Employers are interested in the quality of your experience and what you can bring to the table, not the quantity. You have seen résumés that were pure filler and fluff. You may have known someone who once walked by a Marketing Club meeting and then listed on his résumé that he was chairman of the membership committee and past president.

It doesn't take a rocket scientist to read through that. You will find yourself squirming in your seat when a savvy interviewer asks specifically what you did on that committee and wants you to expand on your involvement. OOPS!

Try to vary your experience. I know you have to pay the bills, but try to have more than a steady track record of yard work or waitress gigs.

The bottom line is: Do something, anything. Have some type of position, job, or responsibility, paid, unpaid, credit, or none. It doesn't matter. Just get some experience.

▪ 6 ▪

It Really Is Who You Know:
Networking and Connections in
the Real World

Let's cut to the chase. The world revolves around relationships. It really is who you know. People want to do business with someone they know, or who comes recommended. It lends credibility. If someone you know and trust recommends you try a new restaurant, you are very likely to try it. It's as if they screened the restaurant for you and gave it the OK. It's the same way with people. Meeting someone through a referral or a contact is like a seal of approval. If you think that you will send your résumé to a company and, because of your sterling credentials alone, you will be plucked from the ranks, you are kidding yourself big-time.

Studies have indicated that up to 80 percent of all positions are obtained through networking and connections. Eighty percent! Like it or not, it's how the world operates. Contacts are everything.

You may be saying, "Oh great! My inner circle of movers and shakers consists of the guy who can get me free beer on Thursday nights, and my parents don't even know our neighbors. I'm completely screwed."

Before you picture yourself in polyester saying, "Would you like fries with that?" calm down. Even if your parents aren't connected outside of their bowling league, you are still in luck. I'm not talking about having connections that date back to Plymouth Rock. I mean meeting as many people as you possibly can, and establishing contacts or acquaintances. Whether you realize it or not, everyone has connections, or can easily start their own solid network.

Networking is an integral part of business. You need to begin establishing and cultivating your network now. Networking is a skill that will not only be critical to your job search, but will prove valuable for the rest of your career.

It's simply capitalizing on your human assets and using relationships and contacts for mutual benefit.

What If I'm Not Connected?

Are you still saying to yourself, "Hey, I don't know anybody"? Fear not. You probably already have a network in place but you don't know it. Establishing a network is very easy to do. You don't have to be a gregarious schmoozer to do it, either.

Everyone you meet is a potential contact (yes, the beer guy counts, too). A contact may be directly with a person, or indirectly, by way of an introduction or referral to a third party.

Do you have friends? I hope so. Do you go to class? Don't answer that. You have professors; you have parents and relatives.

Jason, at the University of Alabama, recalls telling a friend about his desire to work for a New York advertising agency, and how he wasn't having any luck getting in the door. His friend's roommate overheard the conversation and told Jason, "My uncle is a vice president at Young & Rubicam, I could call him for you, if you would like." Of course Jason said yes, jumping all over this opportunity. The roommate called his uncle and arranged an introduction and interview for Jason during spring break.

Believe it or not, your parents know more people than just your neighbors and their bowling buddies. They might have an attorney, a banker, an accountant, a doctor, or yes . . . even a bowling or golf buddy. And every one of them either has friends or knows people. You don't know who their circle of contacts consists of. You get the point. Maybe you have a roommate who has an uncle who knows the president of the company you want to work for. Everyone is a potential contact, because you don't know who they can put you in touch with.

You don't have to know a person intimately to consider him a contact.

How Do I Network?

Networking, as you saw by Jason's example, is rather painless. Often it's merely asking for an introduction. At this stage you are on the receiving end. Networking can also can also mean introducing business associates to one another, informing them of special helpful knowledge, or giving someone a business lead. Networking does not happen automatically. You must take the initiative in making contacts. If you need an introduction, ask for it. These things rarely fall into your lap unless people know that you are looking. Don't worry whether you will offend someone by asking. If they mind, they will let you know. They will tell you that they don't feel comfortable or that they can't help you. That's OK. No big deal. You never know unless you ask.

For the most part, people will want to help you, especially older people or professionals who are already established. They remember when they first got started and someone gave them a break or opened a door for them. Believe me, what goes around comes around, and they see it as a way of giving back. Your peers may feel more important if they are able to help you make contacts.

Simply tell people about yourself, what you want to do, and what you are working toward. You want to constantly have your name in front of people and be expanding your network. Tell people you are about to graduate, or that you are looking to enter a certain field. Bryan Tracy, author of *Maximum Achievement*, recommends telling anyone, even strangers, about your dreams and what you want to do, because you don't know if who you are talking to might be able to help you.

People in business always want to expand their networks and make more contacts. Don't think because you are young that you have nothing to offer a veteran business man or woman. Harvey MacKay and others recommend taking a millionaire to lunch. Try to establish contacts with successful business people or industry contacts now. The smart business person will make an effort and treat you well, even though she doesn't know you, for several reasons: You could be a client or customer, if not now, maybe someday; you could have something great to offer, a hot idea, and be a potential employee or partner; or maybe they realize you aren't a big wheel right now, but someday you might be pretty important. You are on your way up and they don't know who you may become.

Everyone is important. It pays to treat everyone with respect, and as if they are someone important. You never know when you may need somebody's assistance. Look at Bill Clinton. Most of his staff members are either childhood friends, college buddies, or people he met coming up the ladder. Think about it. The guy or girl dribbling next to you in class could be the leader of the free world someday.

Meredith had just graduated from Iowa State University with a masters degree in costume history. She wanted to work in a museum, but was having difficulty getting in any doors. She was at a friend's house lamenting her situation, when her friend's mother said, "Why don't we call Aunt Jackie?" The mother immediately picked up the phone and called Aunt Jackie, who happened to be one of their oldest family friends and who also held a position on the board of a university museum with a large costume collection. Introductions were made and Meredith was granted interviews and eventually secured a position with the university.

■ ■ ■

Michelle worked at J. Crew part-time while she went to school to study graphic design. She was personable and talked to many customers, often asking questions after she had helped them for a while. After asking one customer what he did for a living, she discovered that he owned a graphic design firm. She told him that she was in school and was graduating the next semester. He invited her to show him her work, and ended up offering Michelle a job when she graduated.

Give and Take

Never approach anyone with a "what can you do for me?" attitude. That is not what it's about.

Smart networkers are open to helping people and gaining new contacts because they know it comes back to them in spades. Before I moved to Dallas, I did not know anyone in the business community there. I decided to target over a hundred executives I wanted to meet. Some were in a field similar to mine, while others were merely influential people in the city. I did not know any of them. I wrote each a letter, which stated my background, that I was relocating to the city, and that I would like to meet with them to explore professional common interests and establish contacts in the area. Risky? What did I have to lose? It may sound like a crap shoot, but of the letters sent, over 40 percent of executives responded. I made fantastic contacts in the area. Some wanted to explore business opportunities and interest, while others simply wanted to meet and establish a contact out of curiosity. From that, many of these people introduced or referred me to other executives in the area, doubling my number of contacts. Why would executives care to do this when they don't know me from Troy Aikman? Because you can never know enough people. Just because someone gets you in a door or introduces you to someone doesn't mean that it's smooth sailing. You then have to perform on your own merits. Often it's only an introduction. Bob Gordon, of WABU television in Boston, says "I will help people make contacts and get in doors, but what they do after that is up to them." Gordon says that often people he recommends to associates, "work harder once they get in, because they want to prove that they are worth it and that they can do the job on their own merits. They also don't want to disappoint the person who referred them."

> *Linda, in Philadelphia, was a top sales executive with Digital Equipment before launching her own consulting firm. She is a wonderful networker. It seems she knows everyone. What is special about her, and one of the reasons for her success, is that anytime you talk to her, she always asks, "Is there anything I can do for you?"—and she means it. No matter who initiates the call, she sincerely wants to help you. If it's with a contact, an introduction, sharing industry information, or a referral, Linda delivers. Consequently, people want to know her, and approach her to share information. They know that if they give information to Linda they will get it back tenfold.*

Maintaining Your Network

Keeping your network intact takes work. You need to cultivate it and always keep adding to it. Keep it going and growing. Stay in touch with people on a somewhat regular basis, even if it's only through a brief note or phone call. Make sure that you contact them at least once a year, if not more. How do you possibly keep up with all of these people you are going to meet? Use progress reports.

A well-placed phone call also does wonders. You don't have to call every contact at once, but break it up so that you contact 25 percent of your network every quarter. When you notice special events, such as a promotion, a big deal, or new project for your contact or their company, drop them a note or call to congratulate them. It will mean a lot to that person and they will remember that you noticed. Surprisingly, not many people remember or acknowledge the little things, so those who do really stick out. Regardless of how you stay in touch, just keep your name fresh in their minds.

> *Cheryl, from Southern Methodist University, maintains her network by sending out yearly progress reports, alerting her contacts to her current status. She lets her contacts know if there are any new developments in her life, projects, promotions. She makes sure to include her current phone number and address. Christmas and holiday cards operate in the same fashion.*

Your Own Board of Directors: Mentors and Role Models

Most corporations have a board of directors. In many cases they are successful older or established professionals who can use their experience to advise and guide the direction of a company. For all practical purposes, you are a rookie professional. You need someone to serve as a professional coach or advisor. You can have this wisdom at your disposal by forming your own personal board of directors, or board of advisors. A group to serve as mentors, advisors, or coaches for your career.

A mentor is someone you can bounce ideas off. They are who you go to for advice or counsel. Anyone can be a mentor, a parent, boss, professor, family friend, or professional contact. Anyone who you respect and admire for their wisdom and success.

Companies pay consultants outrageous fees to dispense advice on managing their company. Think of yourself as a company, with your own personal staff of consultants that you can seek advice from and help manage your career (only, they're free).

They can save you a lot of heartache. Whenever you have a question, bounce it off one of your personal board members. Use their experience. Ask their advice when faced with a major decision or choice. See what they would do in certain situations. Learn from their mistakes and successes.

Never be afraid to ask for advice and help. The intelligent person is the one who can ask for help, and who knows his limitations. Save yourself some time and aggravation.

Choosing a mentor. In choosing mentors, pick successful people with diverse backgrounds. It's better to have more than one mentor. Try to give yourself a broad range of experience to choose from. Make sure that you value their opinion, and that you get along with them.

How does someone become your mentor? Simple . . . you ask them. You can make the relationship as formal or informal as you want. Sometimes it does not even have to be said, just understood. Anyone should be flattered that you thought enough of them to consult their expertise in certain matters. They will get as much out of helping you as you will benefit from their advice. As your career grows, you will add and change mentors in your roster, to reflect your current needs.

Role models. Besides mentors, you need role models, too. A role model is someone whom you admire and would like to pattern yourself after. It could be for her style, her track record, her success, or her integrity or ethics. The difference between a mentor and a role model is that you don't have to know a role model. It may be a successful leader in your chosen industry, an author, any leader. Harvey MacKay and Tom Peters are two of my role models. You need to select role models who reflect your professional and your personal life, as well. The same goes for choosing mentors. Have a balanced team.

It really works. I can't stress enough that connections are really how the world works. Let me tell you from experience that everything I just mentioned works. This book would never have been published if it were not for networking and telling people about my dreams.

I was having dinner one evening with a mentor of mine in Boston. I was telling him about my book idea. He said, "Show me your book proposal. I know some people in the publishing business." A week after he read my proposal, he called and said, "This is fantastic; it must be told. Do you want me to do something about it?" "YES!"

He sent my proposal to Donna Dever—a young woman whom he had worked with before—who was now the assistant to a literary agent. Donna, herself a twentysomething graduate from Hamilton College, loved the idea for the book and showed it to her boss, Pam Bernstein. Pam saw the potential in *Jobsmarts* and became my agent, which resulted in getting the book signed with Vintage. The rest is history.

You never know who you are talking to, so in the course of a conversation you may ask someone what they do or tell them about yourself. You may be surprised at the connections you can make.

I obtained one of my former positions through networking and connections. I was talking to a friend who happened to be a doctor. I was telling him of the career change I was looking to make. Two days later, he called, telling me that he had just talked with a patient of his who had just started a new firm. He introduced me to the patient, who ended up offering me the job.

Remember networking really is how the world works. You can never know enough people.

Phil had just graduated from law school at the University of Oklahoma. Despite his law degree, he was interested in pursuing a career with one of the major brokerage houses. Having no real connections to speak of, he took a chance. By using alumni records at his alma mater, he discovered that the chairman of the American Stock Exchange happened to be an O.U. alum.

Through the alumni directory, Phil obtained the chairman's address and FedExed a résumé and "Personal Press Kit" to him at his home. Phil was expecting to receive a canned response letter, if any response at all. Phil was shocked two days later when he heard personally from the chairman of the American Stock Exchange. The chairman called to tell Phil that he was coming to Houston, where Phil lived, to meet with the CEOs of the exchange-listed companies in the area. He asked Phil to meet him for breakfast during his visit. It was a long shot that paid off. That brief breakfast meeting led to the chairman, who is now the Ambassador to Mexico, making calls and writing letters for Phil to set up interviews with the major brokerage houses in New York.

ANTHONY MARK HANKINS
Fashion Designer
Age: 25

FOR MOST PEOPLE, being a fashion designer with your own private line created exclusively for one of the largest retailers in America, studying fashion in Paris with Yves St. Laurent as your personal mentor, and being profiled on the *Today Show* would be pretty remarkable achievements for someone who has been designing for eighteen years. It's even more remarkable when that person is a twenty-five-year-old African American male from the suburbs of New Jersey.

Anthony Mark Hankins found his calling at age 7, when he first designed and made a suit for his mother to wear to a wedding. This was not the ordinary rag that children make for their parents and that is politely put in a drawer. The youngest of seven children, Anthony displayed incredible talent at an early age. His mother was proud to wear his design to a wedding, where it received raves. He began to design and make dresses for other women in town.

Anthony has been working hard ever since that first creation. "My mother managed a Dunkin' Donuts, and my father was a Cuban immigrant. We all knew the value of hard work. I remember getting up at 4:30 in the morning to help Mom make donuts. I realize how much work it takes to make things happen."

Anthony says, "My twin sister was a tomboy, who loved to climb trees and play baseball, and here I was making dresses for my mom. She took us to a doctor and asked if this was normal. Luckily, the doctor said to leave us alone and to give the boy some material and the girl a baseball mitt." Anthony was truly supported and allowed to explore his talent. In high school, he designed band uniforms for school and prom dresses for friends.

Upon graduation, he attended the Pratt Institute in New York. There he showed great promise. He began networking with the faculty, and was able to get internships with Willi Smith and Homer Lane. "I did everything I could. I asked for extra work and learned everything possible. However, the funny thing about internships is that too many people go into them thinking, I am going to learn what I want. You will learn what they want you to learn."

At Homer Lane, Anthony met two women who came in for fittings. One was Maria Cuomo, Governor Mario Cuomo's daughter, and the other was Judith Agiston, who is now Anthony's publicist. "We hit it off. They asked more about me. It had been recommended that I go to Paris and study at the prestigious École de la Chambre Syndicale de la Couture Parisienne. The two ladies learned of this and agreed. Maria Cuomo asked if I could do a favor for her boyfriend, Kenneth Cole." Always the networker, Anthony said of course. "Any time the ladies came in, they would ask what I was doing to get to Paris. Maria gave me a list of people to contact. She said to tell these people my story." The list included people such as Calvin Klein, Victor Costa, and other heavy hitters. Word got out about Anthony. The *Today Show* did a piece on him. He was accepted to the school in Paris. A plane ticket arrived mysteriously and he was off.

"It all happened so quickly. When I arrived in Paris, the first thing I did was go to the House of St. Laurent. I stood there thinking it would be so wonderful to go inside. It was at that point, where I really believed and envisioned what I wanted to do. That bonding of belief and action is so important.

"The first day of school, I was nervous and worried about the tuition when I received a phone call from Yves St. Laurent's assistant, saying that they wanted to meet me. Would I come over? I met with St. Laurent and, in two hours, my school and living expenses were paid for and I had an internship with Yves St. Laurent."

After returning from Paris he went to work for Adrienne Vittadini and realized that he would never want to work on 7th Avenue. "It is so cutthroat and you have to deal with so much attitude. My early work ethic from my parents showed me I have to work for what I get. I'm not going to be a prima donna or a diva."

He then heard of an opening in quality assurance for JCPenney. A far cry from designing, but he wanted to learn more about the manufacturing end. He began as a field inspector. Yes, Inspector 12. "My friends were like, no way are you going to do that. Then I told them the salary, $28,000. A fortune for 7th Avenue. It was great because I learned all of the other elements of fashion and manufacturing. It really rounded out my education."

Initially, he did not tell JCPenney about his background as a couture designer. "I was completely overqualified. The only real qualification for the job was that I know how to drive, since the job was in Los Angeles." This was daunting for Anthony. "Being from the East Coast, I had never learned to drive. Learning to drive in LA is an experience, but I managed."

"I was dealing with all of the suppliers to JCPenney Fashions, working with them on their quality specifications. I was networking hard, too. I collected cards and told people what I was doing, and that I wanted to have my own design firm some day."

Anthony says that one of the most important things is to "network and let people know who you are." It was in LA that he had his idea to start an affordable line of clothing for women with urban style. He worked with a friend to prepare a customer profile and proposal. "It looked hot. I sent the proposal up through JCPenney, and some older people, trying to protect their turf, attempted to stand in my way. They said no to my idea. I said, 'What do you mean, no?' Anthony Mark Hankins doesn't take 'no' very easily."

Anthony says he has been treated differently by older people, because of his age. "There are so many older people who are territorial and who want to hold on to what they have. They will stand in front of a young person and block their way."

Anthony says, "I do what I think is right and don't take no for an answer." Anthony did not get discouraged. He took a different tack and befriended Bruce Ackerman, who was head of minority development at JCPenney. Bruce became a champion for the idea, and helped guide Anthony through the process of getting a line started and approved. Later, Bruce would become president of Anthony's design firm.

Anthony would not let anyone or anything stand in his way. He sold top executives on the idea, and produced the products in record time. In the over-ninety-year history of JCPenney, they had never had an in-store designer . . . until now. Anthony Mark Hankins designs are now found at over 324 stores nationwide. All of this in less than a three-year span.

The time eventually came for Anthony to leave JCPenney and operate his own design studio. He still has a contract with JCPenney, but he is free to call his shots.

"I will be branching out into other areas in the future, such as men's designs and home furnishings." Anthony also believes in giving back to his customers and to the community. "I represent the African American community, an underserved community, and I won't let anyone stand in my way of serving my customers and paving the way for other minorities."

Anthony Mark Hankins has taken charge of his career and created his own destiny. We can all learn from his advice for someone starting their career: "Don't let anyone stand in the way of your dream, and don't take no for an answer." Anthony says, "If we have a vision, we have to follow that vision."

■ PART II ■

ENTERING THE RACE:

FINDING A JOB

■ 7 ■

Success Doesn't Come
Looking for You

Just Do It
—Nike slogan

It's never too early to start planning your job search or career change. Today the average job search takes between four and nine months. The higher up the ladder you go, the longer it takes to find work. Finding executives who labor for six months to a year to find a job or make a career move has become commonplace.

If you are just beginning your career, you should start sending out résumés before March of your senior year. Today, many students start their career search even before their senior year.

Many people plan their job search around May or December, generally the months when people graduate. The problem with this is that companies often hire at times other than May or December.

Companies hire according to need. Their needs may not coincide with your graduation or when you are changing careers. Lay the groundwork ahead of time. Make people aware of your name and situation beforehand. Realize that it takes time and that contacts must be cultivated. When a need arises they will think of you, because you have been in contact repeatedly.

Companies can be incredibly slow-moving creatures. They are

great at putting you off. When it comes to our own needs, we can be impatient. "I want what I want and I want it now." Particularly when it comes to a decision about our careers. You wait to hear from an employer and think, "C'mon, this is my life, my career you're messing with. I need an answer now." Remember, your needs and time frame are a secondary concern to them. However, when the tables are turned and they need to fill a position, time is of the essence.

It's important to get a foot in the door ahead of time, so when they are ready to fill a position they know who you are and that you are available. Sure there is something to be said for being in the right place at the right time, but you also have a big hand in making sure you put yourself in the right place when the time comes.

The key is to be proactive. Take charge of your career. Companies *don't* come to you. They don't even know who you are. You must seek out employers and tell them about you. So get off the couch ASAP!

▪ 8 ▪

Go for It: Take Risks

You miss 100 percent of the shots you never take.
—Wayne Gretsky, professional hockey player,
a.k.a. "The Great One"

I've heard many successful people claim they would rather be lucky than smart, but luck and breaks don't always just happen. Thomas Jefferson once said, "The harder I work the luckier I get."

You make your own breaks. Some people are truly lucky, while others take the chances and risks to put themselves in situations where, with a little luck, there is a chance for success.

Take chances. Have no shame in seeking and asking for what you want and taking a chance to succeed. If you view yourself in a positive light, others will pick up on it. You will convey confidence, which is appealing to employers.

Don't sell yourself short or psyche yourself out by thinking that you are not capable of a position because of your major, grades, or experience. What is the worst thing that can happen if you try to get in the door and get shut down? Nothing. You are back to where you started. Pick yourself up and do it again. Have a thick skin and don't take rejection or negative criticism personally.

Aim high and take risks to get there. If you want to reach the fruit, you must climb out on a limb sometimes. Gamblers will tell you that you have to risk something to win. Taking a risk can be calling a company that you really want to work for. Often the worst thing that can happen is that you are told "no," or that your correspondence is put in the trash. Other situations offer a much larger risk.

You are young and have little to lose and everything to gain. It's not like you are in your fifties with a mortgage, a spouse, and a kid in college. Decide what risks you are willing to take and roll the dice.

> *Take Steve, for example. Steve grew up in Florida and graduated with an engineering degree from the University of South Florida. Upon graduation he was offered a position with Texas Instruments. This was great, except for the fact they wanted him to move halfway across the country to Texas. Steve had never been there in his life and didn't know a soul. Weighing the risk, Steve decided the potential reward was worth taking a chance on the prospect of starting a new life and career. He loaded up the U-Haul and trekked to Texas. Not knowing anybody in Texas, Steve managed to make a life for himself. Yet, had he never taken the chance, none of it would have happened to him.*

JEFF THOMPSON
President, Peripheral Outlet
Age: 22

JEFF THOMPSON IS PRESIDENT of his own computer company, which anticipates worldwide sales this year of between 20 and 30 million dollars. He was also named Young Entrepreneur of the Year by the U.S. Small Business Administration. He is not an Ivy Leaguer. He did not inherit the company, nor does he have a large trust fund. He does not live in New York, Los Angeles, or Chicago either. Jeff Thompson's little empire is headquartered in the small town of Ada, Oklahoma. Jeff is also a senior in college and only 22 years old.

At age 15, Jeff began buying computers out of the newspaper classifieds. He would clean the equipment, possibly adding a small upgrade, and sell the same computer back in the newspaper at a higher price. "It was simply a matter of buy low, sell high." After a year or so, he branched out nationally. "Gradually, I also moved into selling computer memory over the phone. That is the core business right now, selling computer memory all over the world." What began as a hobby, started with $2,500 saved from a paper route, has sprung into a true worldwide operation, with a sales force working around the clock selling to Eastern Europe, Holland, Russia, India, and Australia.

How does someone so young accomplish so much? Jeff sees himself as an entrepreneur and a salesman more than a computer person. "My age has not affected my business at all. Since our clients are all over the world, from the Czech Republic to India, I do almost all of my business over the phone. I worked very hard on my phone presence to sound more professional. No one knows how old I am until I meet them at a trade show or in person. By then, they are a satisfied customer."

As strange as it seems, Jeff has had a somewhat normal college experience, although, just as some athletes are given the hard sell by college recruiters, Jeff had the governor of the state recruiting him to attend the University of Oklahoma. As a publicity stunt before his freshman year, Jeff took out a full-page ad in the state's largest newspaper. "Young Businessman Chooses College." It promoted Jeff and his company. The ad mentioned that Jeff had decided to pursue a business degree at a school located out of the state. That afternoon, Jeff received a phone call from the dean of the business school at the University of Oklahoma. The dean said that the governor had seen the ad that morning, and had told the dean to do anything he could to get that boy to go to school in state. Jeff was offered a full scholarship to go to O.U.

As interesting as Jeff's background as an entrepreneur is, he doesn't dwell on the past. "I am very present-and-future focused in everything that I do." With no experience other than a paper route, Jeff gained most of his business skills from watching his father, who had an insurance company. His father now works for Jeff, running the day-to-day operations.

Jeff believes that one of the keys to his success is a willingness to do whatever it takes. "Being successful in sales means more than working 8 to 5. I put in all kinds of hours. I don't have the leisure time others do, but it doesn't seem like a sacrifice to me. If something begins to feel like a sacrifice, you may want to look for something else to do. Above all, love what you do."

Jeff feels that being a good listener has contributed to his success. "I listen carefully to what someone is saying. You can learn whether or not a customer really wants what you are selling, or whether it's just a price issue. There is a lot that can be read between the lines."

As you might have guessed, Jeff is a big fan of entrepreneurship. His advice for someone starting out is to be an optimist and believe in yourself. Jeff says, "Take chances early and give yourself a shot at something. If it doesn't work out, you can always go work for a large company, plus you will have the experience you gained by starting your own business."

▪9▪

Organizing Your Job Search

One of the most difficult things about a job search is keeping track of everything you have going on. There are résumés to update and mail out. Cover letters must be written to each individual. Remembering what, when, and to whom you mailed information is truly a challenge. Calling contacts, staying current and maintaining your research information, and generally not letting anything slip through the cracks as you juggle the remainder of your life and activities is key.

The last thing you need to say during your job search is, "I don't have time," or "Where did I put it." Organizing your time and information is a crucial skill that will determine the success or failure of your job search. Sure, it sounds like a daunting task, but it doesn't have to be if you use your time and information wisely.

Your Job Is to Find a Job

The main key to remember about managing yourself is to treat your job search as if it were a real job. Think of yourself as the president or CEO of your own company. You are running the day-to-day operations. Treat your affairs and your job search professionally and you convey that to potential employers. If you ran a company, you wouldn't work when you felt like it. You wouldn't lose or forget to write letters. You wouldn't show up for work late, or fail to keep track of what you send out. Why should your job search be any different?

Devote time to your search every day. It doesn't have to be the whole day. Maybe a couple of hours, when you can be completely focused on your job search. Treat it as if you were at the office. Allot specific amounts of time and try to make it consistent. From 2:00 to 4:00 each day, you will make your follow-up calls, review your research and write cover letters. Get into a habit and don't change it.

If you are working full-time, devote a period at night to your research or letters. If you have to make phone calls, try to take a late lunch or take a day off.

Tasks

Start by organizing your tasks. The best way to manage tasks and things to do is through lists. To make a great "to do" list, you might break things in half, such as Business/Job Search on one side and Personal on the other. Another way is to divide your list into quadrants on a piece of paper. For example, categorize things by To Do, Mail, Call, and Miscellaneous.

Keeping lists in this way helps you to avoid duplication and allows you to keep everything in one place, rather than having information on slips of paper that always find their way into your pocket or onto the floor of your car.

Just as you do with written goals, make sure to mark or check off your completed tasks. These are like smaller, super–short-term goals. Marking completed tasks lets you clearly see what you have left to do.

Another method is to get a Franklin Planner or the very similar DayTimer. These are fantastic ways for you to keep all of your information in one place and visually represented in front of you.

Information

Keep a Rolodex or address book and a backup. Keep your information or contact lists handy in a form that can be made portable and taken with you. A lot of good it does to need a phone number on the way to an interview to tell them you are running late, and that number is back at your apartment.

If you are into high-tech gadgets, you can get an electronic Rolodex for around twenty dollars (I want my endorsement check from Rolodex). It's the size of a credit card and about a quarter inch thick. You can store from 250 to 500 names and addresses in one.

Make sure to keep your information in one place and make a backup every few weeks. Keep the backup in a safe place or at a different location. If your information is ruined, you will be able to salvage it.

Keep information together or in one place by using the cover letter. You will send cover letters to everyone. Mail the originals and make copies for yourself. On the front of your cover letter, you have all of the pertinent information, such as name, address, etc. You might write the phone and fax numbers in the top right corner. On the back of the letter, keep a running log of what has transpired. Write the date and anything that went on with that contact, including: when you wrote them; when you called them; whether you left a message; when they said they would call back; their secretary's name; and the day you mailed the letter or thank-you note. Include anything that you might need to know. The following is an example:

4/14/95 Mailed cover letter & résumé.

4/17/95 Follow-up call. Left message for Ms. Brooks.

4/19/95 Follow-up call: Ms. Brooks said that she would love to meet with me about a position in a new division. Set meeting for 4/24/95.

4/24/95 Met with Ms. Brooks. (You would give details of meeting.)

4/25/95 Mailed thank-you letter—attached. (Always keep any additional letters and such stapled to the original piece.)

This way you have a running log of your conversations and correspondence with that person. You don't let anything slip through the cracks.

Keep your research information broken up or segmented by industry, individual company, or geographic location. You will be sending and receiving voluminous amounts of mail and gathering research information. To keep track of it all, assign specific folders for different tasks and the status of each piece of information. Make a "Current" or "Hot" file for things that need to be taken care of that day. Have a "To Do" file and a "To Read" or "Research" file.

You might have "To Be Mailed," "Mailed," or "Rejection" folders. Switch your correspondence accordingly. Labeling your information this way will also let you transport it and prevent anything from slipping through the cracks.

Prioritize

Do you wait until the last minute to do things? If there is something that really needs to get done, do you avoid doing it because it's not any fun? I am a piddler by nature. If there is something that needs to be done, I'm going to wait. It's like I'm going to avoid the pain of doing it if I just wait. It might go away. I know what has to be done; just don't want to do it. Consequently I rush around at the end and completely stress.

The best way to tackle a "To Do" list is to do the most difficult or least favorite things first. It's a huge mental game, but if you tackle what you don't want to mess with first thing, when you have the energy, you can crank it out in no time. Then you will be left with only the easy things to do.

You might think, "Oh, I will get the little things done quickly so I can spend more time on the big project I'm avoiding." Wrong. You will always find more little things to do to keep you from it or you will be so tired by the time you reach the major task that you blow it off.

Messages

People other than your friends are going to be calling you now. The last thing you need is for your roommate from hell to tell you, "Oh. I forgot to tell you, Jim Smith with some company called last week. I didn't write down the number, though." You might not be able to get a job after you are paroled for killing this bonehead.

Have a system with your roommates. Make sure that there is a central area for messages to be displayed. It should be clear to everyone you live with that you will be expecting some calls from companies and that you expect to be given those messages promptly and thoroughly. Be specific about what information you want conveyed. Generally, you need to know the person's name, company, phone number, time of call, and message, if there was one. Also instruct your roommates to try to act professional and not be rude to anyone who calls for you.

The days of creative phone messages are over. What do you think goes through the mind of an executive calling your machine when they hear, "Hey, dude, I'm not here. I'm out partying. Leave a message. Later." . . . Beep. Just the professional first impression you want to convey, right? Don't play music, sing, tell jokes, or act cute on answering machines . . . dude. Those tricks are great for your friends, but if you are expecting professionals to call, forget it. Sound boring? Well, it is. Is it effective? Very.

▪ 1 0 ▪

Where the Jobs Are and Aren't

After five years of consistent decline in the neighborhood of 40 percent to 60 percent, recruitment on college campuses was finally up a scorching 1.1 percent in 1994. That's 1.1, *not* eleven. Negligible. I'm no statistician, but a 1.1 percent blip is no reason to break out the champagne and celebrate. However, it's the light at the end of the tunnel.

So where do I find these elusive jobs, or for that matter where do I find any job? This seems to be the $60,000 question, or more accurately the $22,000 minus taxes question.

Start by looking at your job search from a new perspective.

The Ultimate Product

Think about marketing for a second. There are a million good ideas for products out there. But successfully taking a product from concept to shelf to successful sales involves much more than a good idea or product.

When a company markets a product, they consider the following: who is their target audience; market research; product design and packaging; promotion; and placement.

Your job search is no different from a product launch or marketing effort. Except, you have something much better to market than toothpaste, potato chips, or widgets. (What the hell is a widget anyway?) This time you are going to market the ultimate product: YOU.

Think of yourself as a product that you are selling to various companies, and the employers as the buyers. How do you identify your buyers? Where do you find your target market?

YOUR RESOURCES

THERE ARE SEVERAL RESOURCES to use that will help you locate potential job prospects. Some are better than others. The key is that you can't rely on just one. It takes a multifunctional approach, using several of the following resources.

Career Planning and Placement Service

If you are in school and are not already familiar with your college or university's career planning and placement center (CP&PC), you had better become familiar with it, and soon. If you don't register for their services, you are making a huge mistake.

It doesn't matter if you are at a large or small school. If your school provides such a service or center, use it. Even if you have already graduated, many schools allow their alumni access to the career center and use of its services. Perhaps your center has a bad reputation, or you may feel, "They can't help me. They only place engineers and business majors." That doesn't matter. You can still benefit from what they have to offer.

Even if you are not going to graduate for a year or so, go in and get to know the director and staff. Familiarize yourself with the staff, the office surroundings and the services they provide. These people can be very helpful and are fantastic contacts. Placement staff are constantly being asked by recruiters and companies if they know of anyone who is exceptionally sharp. It would be in your best interest to have your name and face constantly on their minds so they may recommend you to recruiters.

It's simply Networking 101.

"What if the companies I want don't come to campus?" Hey, it happens. Some companies only go to a certain list of schools. The career center can still help. They can put you in touch with the proper contact at your dream company, or can provide you with information about it. It's a fantastic free resource.

There are more benefits to the career center than just getting interviews. It's a great resource for referrals, networking contacts, research materials, and counseling. Campus career centers can help you with the actual interview and résumé critiquing. They also offer seminars on interviewing and résumé skills. They often have a library and resources, such as contacts and company background information. Companies, large and small, often contact the placement center to send them résumés or to refer students to their companies. That is why it's so important to maintain a good relationship with the staff.

"I go to a small school." Sometimes, smaller schools may not have the resources of a large university, or the companies that recruit at smaller schools may not be as recognizable. Yet, even smaller schools have staff devoted to getting you a job after graduation.

A trend you are finding more and more is that as the large Fortune 500 companies have scaled back their campus recruiting, the small to midsize employers have picked up their recruiting efforts. Small to midsized companies are going to be where most job growth will be found from now on.

One of the pitfalls of relying solely on the career center for your job search is that there is tremendous competition. At Texas A&M University (a school with 41,000 students), there are approximately 7,000 students who are registered with career planning each year. Not even the entire school. Yet only several hundred employers actually recruit there each year. Those employers often interview at several schools.

The competition for those few spots is incredible, when you think about the numbers vying for a coveted position. Some campuses allow companies to select only those they want to see. Others have elaborate points and bidding systems which you can use to choose the companies you want to interview with. You have a limited number of points to spend and when you are through, sorry, *no más!*

A company may be interviewing at several campuses across the country. It may be that the company you want to work for is not even interviewing at your school. Sometimes companies interview on campus even when they do not have a position available. Large companies do this, for two reasons. One is that they may be experiencing layoffs or a hiring freeze, yet want to maintain a corporate presence and keep their name in front of you. After all, you may be a future client or customer.

The other reason is that some companies are allotted an interviewing slot on a campus and they will have to forfeit their recruiting spot if they do not come to interview. So, in order to maintain their spot in the future, they interview people for nonexistent positions today.

All in all, career centers are great and must be an integral part of your career search. But don't rely on them completely. You will limit yourself and your exposure to employers.

There are too many people who use only the career planning center at their school and don't find a job. They then wonder why and claim that there aren't any jobs available. Don't put all of your eggs in one basket.

Newspaper Ads

You are looking for work. The Sunday paper comes, and after the comics, the first section you go to is the want ads. The employment sections, guidebook to your future. You scan the want ads and finally locate the job that is just for you. It has your name written all over it. You would be perfect. In your excitement you call your parents, or yell downstairs, telling them that you have a lead on a job. Of course, they are overcome with joy and relief.

Meanwhile, don't cash your first paycheck yet. The dream job listed in the paper, the one exclusively tailor-made for you, has been seen by several thousand other people that day.

Take a major metropolitan newspaper, for example. The Sunday *Boston Globe* has a circulation of over half a million in metro Boston. Guess that, say, 25 percent read the want ads, and realize that over 125,000 people have potentially been exposed to your ad. Also realize that people in New York or Washington or Kansas City who want to relocate to Boston are looking at the Sunday want ads too, and you are looking at some pretty stiff competition. It no longer seems that you have the exclusive inside track on this job lead.

Rarely does anyone obtain a career out of a newspaper. Eighty percent of all jobs are not advertised. They are obtained through other means. So if you are limiting yourself to just the newspaper want ads, you are competing with thousands of others for only 20 percent of available positions.

Many want ads can be deceiving, vague, and secretive. They might not have positions available, although they claim it. Often companies are merely collecting résumés to keep on file, or they are testing out different types of ads so they can see what the response is. You also don't know what the competition is. Some companies advertise to obtain salary statistics for a particular position.

Eric, in New York City, graduated from Bowdoin College with fantastic grades. He waited a couple of months after returning home to NYC to begin his job search (Mistake number one). Eric's job search consisted of looking at the Sunday New York Times want ads. His Sunday ritual was to get up, make coffee, and, with pen in hand, begin his job search. In it, he would find one or two lukewarm ads. He would wait until Tuesday or Wednesday to give them a call or mail his résumé in. Some weeks he would look in the paper and not find anything at all that he liked. Those weeks his job search was effectively "on hold." Meanwhile, he was sponging at his mom's apartment. This went on for a year. He finally went to law school because "there were just no jobs." C'mon.

Sure, there are success stories. However, finding a promising career out of the newspaper is like finding a needle in a haystack. It can be done, but don't bet on it.

Headhunters and Personnel Agencies

In a nutshell, if you are fresh out of school or starting your career, headhunters, search firms, and recruiters want nothing to do with you. And those that do, watch out for. Most headhunters are interested in placing established professionals in positions with a company that is paying the headhunter a fee or percentage to do so. They aren't interested in those just starting out. They are very helpful if you are looking to change careers, but I will talk about that in a second.

The number one rule is: If someone wants you to pay them to find you a job or put you in touch with someone, *forget it*. Why pay someone to do something that you can do for yourself? *Never* pay anyone an up-front fee. You don't need it.

Personnel agencies are traditionally thought of as providing tem-

Vickie, a Trinity College grad, signed up with a service like this and got burned. Prior to contacting the personnel service, Vickie had sent résumés on her own and had landed an interview with a company. The service she contracted with unknowingly arranged an interview for Vickie to meet with an executive in a different division of the same company. She was later offered a position by the first executive she met, the one she had arranged on her own. The search firm told her that since they had arranged for her to get into the company, even though it was a different division, they would take their cut, roughly 10 percent of her salary for the first year. If she accepted the first position, the personnel firm claimed she would owe them, and if she didn't pay they would sue. Vickie, inexperienced in such matters, failed to consult someone knowledgeable, or an attorney, and turned down the position for fear that it would cost her. The bottom line is: Don't pay someone for something you can do on your own.

porary work. They fill a short-term need. You don't know what you might be doing from one day to the next. You are thought of and treated as a temp by the companies you are working for. The up side is that if you do make inroads and impress people, it can often be a step toward a full-time or permanent position.

If you're established in your career and want to make a change, headhunters, search firms, and recruiters can be useful, up to a point. First of all, there are two types: contingency and retainer.

Contingency search firms or recruiters work to place an individual with a company that is their client. Their fee is contingent upon whether the firm hires you and you accept the position.

Recruiters who are on retainer are contracted by a company and paid a set fee for them to find a suitable candidate. The recruiter gets paid, regardless of whether the company hires the person recommended by the recruiter.

In either case, you are not out any money. The expense is covered by the company that is hiring you. The contingency headhunters are a little more high-pressure because they get paid only if the company likes you and if you say yes. Remember, they are employees of their client, not you.

It isn't their business to care about what you need. You are a product to them. They get paid if they place you. The biggest mistake people make is to think "I have a headhunter looking out for me." Wrong. The headhunter is trying to place people and if you don't fill a need right then, it's on to bigger things.

So much in dealing with recruiters involves timing. Contacting them or having your name introduced to them at the right time, when they have a need and a match, is what it's all about.

Realize that it's a mutually beneficial relationship. It's not "Hey, I'm looking to change jobs, what can you do for me?" They are appalled if approached with a "What can you do for me?" attitude. Approach it with the attitude, "We can help each other. I'm a valuable package that you can place with an employer (and collect your fee) and you have access to the employers. Let's work together."

Always contact more than one. They'd like to think that they are the only ones you are talking to, but it's in your best interest to have your information and name in the hands of as many people as possible. Chances are slim that you will be put up for the same position by two separate recruiters. Oh—they hate to be called headhunters. Recruiter or search firm is the politically correct term.

They don't know who you are, unless you are CEO of Ford. They aren't really going to find out about you. Write letters and send résumés. Follow up on the phone so they can find out more about you. If you are ever approached by a recruiter, be nice, even if you aren't interested. Maintain a good relationship with recruiters before you need them. Offer referrals to them. If you don't want the position, tell them of someone sharp who you know.

Bill, a Tulane graduate, was in a high-tech career and looking to make a change. He was approached by a recruiter who had an opportunity for him. (They always say opportunity instead of job or position.) Bill was interviewed by the client company's executives and offered a position. He was excited about the company and the people, but there was only one drawback. Bill had gotten married the month before. This new position required him to be out of town four out of five days every week. He was concerned about the time away from his new wife. Bill did not want to start his marriage by seeing his wife only on weekends. The company said it would be for only a year. Still, it was a major concern to him and he expressed it to the company, who understood. Meanwhile, the recruiter who had arranged everything began to call Bill and pressure him into accepting the offer. Bill told him of his doubts, but the recruiter kept on. The last straw came when the recruiter told Bill, "What's the big deal about time away? You have to make sacrifices. I travel all over the country for my job, and I'm married and have a two-year-old at home. I never get to see them, but I make a damn good penny." Bill was fed up and told the recruiter, "That's great but my priorities are apparently a little different from yours. Thanks, but no thanks." Bill could see that the recruiter was trying to push him into a position that wasn't right for him, just to collect his fee.

Databases and Computer Services

Putting résumés into large databases is a rising trend. Services such as Connexion and others offer automated bulletin boards or screening services that allow companies to pull résumés and screen for certain qualifications. Sounds neat, but think of the odds of your résumé being pulled from the thousands of others that are being electronically scanned. Also, you are totally relying on how you look on paper. There are so many other intangibles involved, such as your creativity, personality, enthusiasm, and how you get in the door. It reduces you to a pure statistic on a piece of paper—I mean screen.

If someone offers to sell you names from a database, tell them to take a hike. C'mon, you can do much of this research on your own. They are good services that do provide a service. I just rank them lower on the scale of choices. Use them as part of your toolbox.

Networking

I said it earlier, but it's worth repeating. Eighty percent of all positions are filled through networking and connections. Enough said. Go back to Part I and read about how and why you network. This and personal research are the most effective ways to discover employers.

WENDY KOPP
Founder and President,
Teach for America
Age: 27

MANY PEOPLE HAVE GOOD INTENTIONS. Those who are truly unique act on those good intentions to change people's

---

lives. Wendy Kopp is such a person. During her junior year at Princeton, she first came up with the idea for Teach for America. "I was uninspired about what I wanted to do, and thought there had to be a way I could make a difference. I was very close to the issue of education reform. It was then I thought, Young people are being aggressively recruited to become investment bankers. There was high status on Wall Street. There needed to be something to increase the status of teaching. Why not have a national corps of teachers to aggressively recruit people to teach, just as people were being recruited to become investment bankers?"

Today, Teach for America is a program that asks bright college students who majored in something other than education to commit two years to teaching in an under-resourced school in urban or rural areas. Last year Kopp and TFA placed over 400 corps members around the United States.

"It became my thesis topic." She was a Public Policy major in the Woodrow Wilson School at Princeton. "I had researched other programs such as the Peace Corps and Vista, and I began to put a plan together for how to start it. As I worked on the project, I became completely obsessed by it. I thought, Why not try to start this as a real program?"

Wendy decided to see if it could really fly. "I created a proposal and wrote to 30 random CEOs of major corporations. Ultimately, I was hoping to get a seed grant to fund the project, but I was just trying to get in the door at first." Wendy found champions for her idea very quickly. "Almost immediately I met with Mobil, who loved the idea and gave me a $26,000 seed grant. Union Carbide offered to let me use their office space in Manhattan. So, the day after I graduated in 1989, I was ready to go."

Wendy spent that first summer meeting as many people as possible, raising money, and getting people together for the first fall. "It was chaotic, absolutely crazy. The only experience I had prior to this was my involvement in a student-run organization.

But, it taught me so much about people management and fund raising."

You might wonder what it was like at 22 years old, dealing with major corporations and responsible for so many people and activities. Wendy says, "I just had an extraordinary amount of confidence. Confidence was key to everything. I just assumed that it would work. It never occurred to me that it wouldn't." She said that it helped to be a little naive and not have experience doing anything like this. "I didn't have the fears or doubts that someone older or with experience would have had. If someone were to tell me they were to start this now, I would say good luck, because I know what is involved. That naivete helped me to go forward and never doubt."

One of the things that helps Wendy in her position is stressed to the corps members, as well. "Goal setting, planning, and taking time to reflect are so important."

The past five years since graduation have been a whirlwind for Wendy. She and Teach for America have been highlighted many times on television, in addition to *USA Today*, the *Wall Street Journal*, the *New York Times*, *Time*, and *US News & World Report*. She is, in effect, the CEO of a company. Her time is very much in demand. Is it a sacrifice? "Not at all. I love what I'm doing. I have fun and love the people I'm around. I really believe in what I'm doing. I've never thought of myself as having a job, which is not to say I'm not completely overwhelmed, but if you can have fun all day long and love what you do . . . do it."

Wendy Kopp has already achieved a great deal and made an impact on education in America. Where does she want to go from here? "I'm committed to working on this and to improving education long-term. I want to be more of a force in this area in the future." She will.

.11.

Your Own Market Research: How to Find and Manage Information about Companies

He who controls the information wins.
—Quote from the movie *Sneakers*

In business, regardless of the industry, professionals require information and research about their field. Possessing information is a contributing factor to success or failure in business.

It doesn't matter what type of information it is. It could be about clients, competitors, suppliers, industry peers, trends, or the economy. Successful executives always seem to be in the know, whether it's about their own business or the business of others that might involve them in any way.

If a company is a sportswear manufacturer, you can bet that they follow the sportswear industry and are interested in some fields other than their own. They might follow the textile industry to see how their suppliers are doing and if they need to make changes. They definitely would follow the retail industry, to keep tabs on the main buyers of their products. They may even follow the transportation industry, because if there is a problem with their distributor, it can affect their product being shipped.

Do What the Pros Do

Professionals do copious research, immersing themselves in information in an attempt to head off any potential problem or surprise, and to capitalize on any coming opportunity. Before a company launches a new product, they conduct market research. If you want to enter a certain field, you had better conduct your own market research for your target industry or company.

As a future professional in your chosen industry, you need to begin treating information as if you were already in that industry today. Search it as a professional in that field would.

How? Where do you look and what are you searching for? It's pretty easy to find out what you need to know. The key ways to find information are by asking, reading, and using computers. It's a mix of reading newspapers, trade magazines, and major business publications, as well as using directories, and databases and contacting people in the industry and specific industry organizations and associations.

Begin by simply asking someone already in that field what they do to keep up on things in the industry. Is there a certain publication that they read? Do they look for specific things in the newspaper or magazines? Are there any special trade publications or industry groups that you should know about? Find out what they do to keep abreast of the industry. Take their lead and go from there.

RELEARN HOW TO READ

YES, I REALIZE THAT YOU are intelligent and fully literate. I'm not talking about some Dexter Manley type of story. (Dexter Manley, by the way, was an illiterate football star who played for the Washington Redskins.) I mean, learn to read differently. Learn to read as a professional in your chosen industry reads.

Reading is the most integral part of being a professional. It's something that everyone will have to do, regardless of profession or industry, and reading for business is very different from the reading you have done in school and for pleasure. It differs, not only in the content, but in how you read and what you get out of it.

The first step is to become a well-rounded reader. To become a well-rounded, and well-read professional, you need the proper mix of business and industry publications, current events, and culture. It comes from trade journals, newsletters, magazines, and newspapers.

What to Read: Newspapers and Journals

If you aren't doing so already, get into the habit of reading the newspaper (not the horoscopes, comics, and sports) every day. Many executives begin their day by reading up to three newspapers. What papers do they read? The *Wall Street Journal* is required reading every day. *USA Today* is recommended because it gives you a brief synopsis and general overview of events outside of business. Finally, you should read your local newspaper or the local paper of the place you want to move to.

The Wall Street Journal. The most important thing you should read religiously is the *Wall Street Journal*. Every business person in America (almost) reads the *Journal*. It's the most comprehensive source for a quick general overview of business. It's also easy to read.

The *Journal* comes in three sections and even breaks things down further by specialty or industry. The first section is the general business overview, which lists the headlines for what is inside. In it there are columns that give a one-paragraph synopsis of each item in the remainder of the paper. Save time by seeing what stories interest you and go right to them. The second section is the marketplace section. Here you will find issues related to technology, law, marketing, advertising, and executive changes, as well as an index for all of the companies mentioned in that edition. Do you have an interview with Bristol Myers that morning? Look in the *Journal* index to see if they are mentioned.

The third part is the finance and money section. Anything that deals with the world of finance and banking, as well as stock quotes, is included.

If you read the news first thing, or at least skim the *Wall Street Journal* every day, you will be prepared and won't have any embarrassing surprises. At the beginning of my career I was making a sales call to

Chiat-Day Advertising in New York. I had failed to read the *Journal* that morning. As I arrived for my ten o'clock meeting, my contact came out, looking rather despondent. She informed me that she would not be able to meet with me that day—something at the agency had suddenly come up. I left feeling as if I had crashed a funeral. Well, in a way I did. Upon leaving, I picked up that morning's *Journal* and discovered that Chiat-Day had laid off 40 people the day before. Yes, I was an uninformed schmuck. If you don't read anything else all day, read the *Wall Street Journal*. (Now, where is my endorsement check from Dow Jones?)

USA Today. I recommend *USA Today* absolutely. Dubbed "McPaper" by many for its lack of depth on any story, it offers a snapshot of everything that you want. It's like *Cliff Notes* for the news. It takes hardly any time at all to breeze through this paper but it gives you a wonderful overview of the rest of life that you need to know. Quick sports and entertainment sections give you the good BS for meetings and water cooler talk. Besides, all work and no play makes Jack a dull boy.

Your Local Paper. The last newspaper you should read is your local paper, or the paper of the place you would like to move to. The local paper lets you see what is going on in your community. If you are on the East Coast and want to move to L.A., get the Sunday *Los Angeles Times*. The Sunday paper generally will give you a good feel for a city, as well as tons of useful information.

Newspapers are also valuable for looking at trends. Here's how. Take the want ads. Not to look for a job for yourself, but to notice what companies are placing ads. If you see that a company has many ads placed or that they are placed consistently, it may mean that they are experiencing growth and expansion. Even though they might not have a position listed that fits your needs, it means that there is growth and you should try to make inroads on your own. Remember, 80 percent of all jobs are not advertised.

The local newspaper can also be helpful if you are relocating. If you want to move to another city, make sure that you read its Sunday newspaper. Check out the business section to learn about potential companies and the business climate. But also look at the metropolitan and entertainment sections. They will give you a feel for the local goings on of the city and tell you if you are moving into a cultural void.

Regional Business Publications. Besides reading newspapers, executives supplement their personal market research with regional business publications. Almost every major metropolitan area has a business publication. It's generally a weekly tabloid or newspaper geared to the local and regional business of the area. They cover business stories that the major daily paper won't. They also go more in depth than the dailies can. They are fantastic for finding leads on companies, because they cover the small to midsized employers, the start-ups and the big guys, all under one roof. They may go by such names as *Crain's New York Business*, the *Dallas Business Journal*, the *Cincinnati Business Journal*, or the *Journal Record* (Oklahoma City). A listing of several of these publications from around the country can be found in the appendix. If you can't get your hands on one, call them and subscribe. It's the best money you can spend. Particularly if you want to relocate. They will give you a good handle on the local business climate.

These publications usually have sections devoted to promotions, executive changes, up and comers, business notes, or even special sections focusing on a certain industry. Some of the sections have really stupid names. The dumbest one I've ever heard has to be the marketing and media column in the *Dallas Business Journal*. It's called "Hard Sell & Soft Soap." . . . Whatever.

When looking at newspapers or regional business publications, look for articles about trends, future developments, executive changes or promotions, new products, or expansion. This is where you gain company names and contacts, and collect practical information about company developments. This information helps you to speak intelligently when you go into an interview or client meeting.

Major Business Publications and Industry Journals. The same is true for major national business publications like *Fortune*, *Forbes*, and *Business Week*. Another great place to research potential companies and information is *Inc.* magazine. As mentioned before, most job growth will come from small to midsized companies. *Inc.* is a publication geared specifically for these smaller and medium-sized companies.

If you already know what field or industry you are interested in or will be joining, you can't start too early to read the journals and publications for that field. You want to get your hands on that type of material as soon as possible so you can be familiar with and speak intelligently about the industry and its goings-on, current events, deals, major players, new products, and executive changes.

Almost every industry has a specific publication for people in that field. In MIS and information services, it's *Information Week*. In the travel industry, it's *Tour & Travel News*. If you work at Nike, Reebok, or Timberland, you read *Footwear News*. If you are in the fashion industry, you may read *Women's Wear Daily*.

If you want to go into advertising, you should start reading *Ad Age* and *Adweek* every week. The people who are already where you want to be read them. If you had an interview with BBDO Advertising, wouldn't it help to read about them and know some of their accounts, such as Pepsi, *before* you went in?

Most industry publications are weekly or monthly. If you don't know what they are, or can't find them, call someone in your intended field and ask them what materials they read to keep up in the industry. If the pros read it, you should read it.

How to Read Faster

Newspapers often get a bad rap for being dry, boring, and taking too long to read. It doesn't have to be that way. It should only take you ten to fifteen minutes to read the *Journal*—or any newspaper, for that matter.

The trap people fall into is that they feel obligated to read something all the way through. No, it's not necessary at all. You can skim. Learn to look for what interests you. Articles are written so that they grab the reader and tell the bulk of the story in the first four paragraphs. If you see a headline that you like, read the first few paragraphs. If the first four paragraphs don't grab you, forget it. You are not obligated to read the whole thing. Reading does not have to be time-consuming at all. We are taught in school to read everything. Therefore, we feel we must read everything for fear of missing something. You can read faster and retain more if you read for understanding, rather than try to pick up the detail in each and every word. Don't feel that you are committed to finishing something if it's not important to you.

What You Should Look For

For magazines, look at the table of contents to see if there is anything of particular interest. You can save time this way by eliminating the need to read through what you are not interested in.

Exactly what do you look for in these publications? The main thing is to look for company names and contacts. This is very important because these names will be useful when you begin your job search. Look for executive changes, or when a company executive is quoted. This is key, because the person's name and title are often given.

If you want to work in a specific area or department, look for titles that name the heads of those areas, such as vice president of marketing. If you don't know what company names to look for, find something that discusses the industry in general. You are also looking for industry trends, changes, and new product developments. You are not just looking for information about companies in your industry, but the business of your clients, as well. Stay up on what is happening with them so you can better serve them and take advantage of opportunities. Researching news and periodicals is absolutely the best source of leads for customers and potential employers.

You want to mark anything that is important to you. When you are reading, always have a pen and a highlighter with you. This will let you take notes in the margins or highlight names and stories. You may also dog-ear pages, or use Post-it notes to mark pages. Many professionals keep a clip file of important stories. You should think about doing the same.

When you see a potential contact or company that you might be interested in working for, highlight it, cut it out, save it, and place it in your clip or "Hot" file to review before your meeting. You might also want to make another folder that is a "To Read Later" file. If you don't have time right then, make a copy of the article and stick it in your folder. This makes for a great way to kill time on an airplane or when things are slow.

Stay Informed

Exceptional people are informed and knowledgeable about their industry and the business of others. They get this way by reading everything in sight quickly and efficiently.

Next time you feel like watching TV, pick up a book or newspaper. Remember when your parents said that too much TV would rot your brain? Whether it's true or not, a study showed that the amount of television a person watches is directly proportional to his income. For example, a blue-collar factory worker watches approximately 20 hours a week. A midlevel manager watches approximately 12 hours per week. A vice president watches 6 to 10 hours per week, while a CEO or president of a company watches between 3 to 5 hours of TV per week. Generally, executives watch news shows.

Prioritize. I'm not saying not to watch *Beavis & Butthead* or *Melrose Place* (my two faves), just don't become hypnotized and watch crap just for the sake of sitting there.

OTHER RESEARCH TOOLS

Asking the Right Questions

Asking people in the industry about a specific company or the field itself is one great way to hear it straight from the horse's mouth. You might ask about their customers, what products or services they provide, or how they are perceived in the marketplace. If you have the opportunity to find out who one of their clients is, try to talk to the client. Tell them you are considering working for this company and would like their opinion of the organization. They can usually give you a good feel for the company. Are they cutting back; are they growing? Are they profitable or do they bleed red ink? Are they a leader in the field or a copycat? These are things you want to know. If you are having difficulty locating people to talk to, check your alumni records.

More great free information can be found from the company itself. Call the company and ask for a brochure or annual report. Pretend you are potential customer or investor. FYI, you will only be able to get an annual report if it's a publicly traded company. If so, ask for the investor relations department. Both of these sources should give you much of what you need. But remember, just like press releases, it has the company's particular slant and bias.

Databases

Technology allows you to be a super sleuth when it comes to researching companies and contacts today. Going online through a service like America Online, CompuServe, Prodigy, or even by accessing the Internet, can give you valuable information cheaply. Press releases can also be a valuable resource for information. Press releases are statements produced by a company that make an announcement promoting something or someone. They are sent to the media under the guise of being "hot news." Yet rarely are they newsworthy. They are written solely from the company's point of view and are completely biased. However, they are often written in a way that gives you valuable information about the company, such as an executive's name and title. There is also a contact and phone number at the bottom of the press release. You could learn a lot from a well-placed phone call to a press contact. They might be able to help you locate the person you should contact in the organization. Press releases are often found on the various online services, like America Online or CompuServe.

These services are geared for consumers and are relatively inexpensive. However, they still provide some great information. Other services, such as Dow Jones News Retrieval, Nexis, Dialog, and Dun & Bradstreet, are much more in-depth and are used by many businesses. These services are much more comprehensive than the consumer services, but they are also much more expensive. Most libraries, public and academic, have them and can do a search for you. Again, free info. Get it where you can.

Many companies have whole departments devoted to gathering information and research on their industry and competitors. They also pay a fortune to get this information. If you are still in school, you have your own "corporate intelligence" available for free. It's THE LIBRARY. Even if you are not in school you can still benefit from the scads of free information found there. Most of the publications I've mentioned can be found there. More importantly, most college libraries have a computer lab and access to databases that companies pay tens of thousands for.

Your public, school, or career center library is the best free resource of information you have. If you don't use it, don't sit around and bitch later about not knowing of any companies.

Directories and Lists

Directories and lists are another top place for locating companies and prospects. Directories can be purchased or found in the library. These may include the *Dun's Million Dollar Directory*, the *Advertising Red Book*, and the *Corporate Yellow Book* (real names, I promise).

The *Yellow Book* series (Monitor Publishing, New York), for example, comes in several volumes. There is the *Corporate Yellow Book*, which lists the top thousand public companies, and the NASDAQ 1000, which lists the top thousand companies traded over the counter (OTC) on the NASDAQ exchange. They provide similar books for the media, associations, law firms, and the government.

They are fantastic because they give a full-page description of the company, including name, address, phone, fax, a listing of major officers, their department and direct phone line, as well as product and industry descriptions. Everything you would want. Some even have names of executives' assistants or secretaries listed. A catalog of various directories and their official titles and topics is found in Appendix B.

Other lists can be obtained for *free* through certain publications. For example, you've heard of the Fortune 500? Sure you have. It's the annual listing of the 500 largest industrial companies in America. But did you know that several weeks after that, *Fortune* releases a listing of the Fortune 500 Service Companies? This covers any company that is not a manufacturer. This would include banking, finance, media, and retailing. *Fortune* also comes out with a Global Fortune 500.

In all of these lists you will find not only the name and pertinent financial data, but data broken up by state or region, and the address, phone, and main executive for each company are given. From there you can do the research on your own to get the proper contact and get in the door.

Other annual lists are the *Business Week* 1000, the *Business Week* 100 Fastest Growing Companies, *Inc.* 500 (this is their listing of the top five hundred fastest-growing smaller to midsized companies), and the *Forbes* 500.

These are all published annually, and if you miss the issue on your newsstands, call the magazine and order a back issue. The names and addresses are in . . . (you guessed it) Appendix B.

Earlier, I mentioned the regional business publications. Each of these publications prints an annual "Book of Lists." These are directories that list everything from the top 100 companies in a city, to the top advertising firms, top high-tech companies, the top accounting firms, etc. They cost anywhere from ten to twenty dollars and can be ordered directly from the publication. I recommend this above *anything* else if you are looking to relocate to another city.

These directories provide the basics: the company's name, what they do, address, financial figures, and a contact name. If you want to move to Atlanta (or any other city) and need the name of almost every major company in the area, call the *Atlanta Business Journal* and order their book of lists, for under $20. Out of anything that you do, spend the money on this. It's worth it. It will save you so much time and give you a feel for what businesses are located in that city.

Organizations and Associations

While we are on the topic of relocation, the Chamber of Commerce is a valuable resource for information on companies, housing, quality of life, and employers. Call the local Chamber where you want to move. Tell them that you are considering a career change or will be relocating to their city, and would like some information, including a list of employers in the area. They will generally send you what you need, for free. They are also great places to call if you have questions regarding a certain company.

Just as every industry has a specific publication, almost every field has an organization or association devoted to members of that profession. If you are in public relations, you would belong to the PRSA, or Public Relations Society of America. If you are in retailing, you would belong to the National Retail Federation. If you are involved in strategic planning for your company, you would belong to the Planning Forum. Whatever your chosen field, find out what the professional organization is.

Many groups have student rates. This will get you on their mailing lists and allow you to get their membership directory, which is what you are really after. Then you have leads and contacts specifically geared for what you need. Professional groups are also great for putting you in contact with people and steering you in the right direction to locate industry information. In fact, the associations themselves produce much of the available information, including the trade publications.

Know Your Stuff

Do your homework. Some interviewers want to see how savvy and informed you are.

During college I needed a summer job. At the time, I thought I wanted to be in real estate development. I read articles that mentioned different developers in Oklahoma City and drove around looking at their signs and projects. I called several developers and weaseled my way into some doors.

There was one firm in particular whose signs I remember seeing all over town. My first thought was that they must be hugely successful. Definitely a player. But beyond their name,

> Terry, an LSU grad, tells of an interview at First Boston, when the interviewer asked him if he read the Wall Street Journal. Terry said yes. The interviewer then asked Terry to tell him about a specific article that appeared on the front page the week before.

address, and snappy signs that seemed so prevalent, I didn't know shit from Shinola about them.

I was able to meet with the two principals. The first question they asked me was, "So, why do you want to work for us?" I told them that I had seen their work around town and was impressed by their reputation as one of the biggest firms in town. They began laughing out loud. Turned out that the whole company consisted of the two of them, a secretary, and a student lackey. It turned out I was applying for the assistant lackey's job.

I had never felt so stupid in my whole life. These guys weren't big and successful at all. They just had a lot of nice signs, but they weren't moving any property. The signs were there because they couldn't find tenants. They were anything but successful. I slumped out of there after a humiliating thirty minutes. Nothing ever happened . . . what a shocker.

The bottom line is, you don't want to be caught with your pants down in an interview because you didn't do your homework. Know who you are dealing with beforehand.

∎ 1 2 ∎

The Personal Press Kit:

Résumés and Cover Letters

Remember the marketing analogy from a few chapters ago, where you are the product and employers are the customers? Another key to marketing a product is the packaging. Every product must be packaged properly to be both appealing and informative to the customer.

An employer who has never met you knows nothing about you, other than what is in your résumé and cover letter. It's usually the first thing that reaches them. Your résumé and cover letter are your packaging, so it's important to make a great impression.

How to write a résumé is a worn-out topic. Go to any bookstore and you will soon realize that there are "How to Write a Résumé" books ad nauseam. There are a million and one titles devoted solely to writing a résumé. *Winning Résumés, Résumés That Get Jobs, Résumés That Work, Just Résumés, Your First Résumé, The Perfect Résumé.* As if that is not enough, there are also semester-long classes and workshops geared toward perfecting résumés. There is definitely no shortage of help on how to prepare a résumé.

What is funny is that people act as if the perfect adjective or that special font will make the difference between getting hired and eating out of a garbage can. They will deliberate for hours over whether to say "responsible for" or "in charge of" in a job description, or if a word should be in bold or underlined. Too many people place undue importance on résumés and the minutiae that goes into them.

It Takes More than a Résumé

Simply sending out a résumé, no matter how perfect it is, does not mean that you will be instantly hired. You may have heard a friend say, "I sent out 500 résumés, and I didn't hear from anyone." Well, what did this person expect? Expecting to land a position by sending out hundreds of résumés in a random, shotgun effect is like expecting to win the lottery. *A résumé is only one important part of the whole package.*

Listen up. A résumé alone will not get you hired. Think of a résumé as an invitation. It's meant to pique an employer's interest so they will want to meet with you. A résumé should tell an employer enough about you to make them interested, and to get you in the door, so you can sell yourself.

It Isn't a Work of Art

Remember the hours of work you put into creating your résumé, changing the fonts and size of the letters so they would look just right?

That is good. Your résumé needs to be error-free and attractive. However, your masterpiece will be given a perfunctory 15 to 30 second glance . . . then it's gone. In the beginning, employers are looking for certain things that catch their eyes, or that will eliminate a candidate immediately. Generally, it's not until after the first cut that your résumé is critically studied. What are some ways to turn your résumé into an informative and attractive package that will stand out from the mountain of cream and gray paper?

Stress Results

The business world revolves around results. What have you done for me lately? What can you do for me now? Why should I hire you? Employers want tangible results and a track record. Whether your experience is through activities, organizations, internships, or actual work, tell an employer more than the basic facts. Stress how well you did your job, what you gained from it, and what you can bring to an employer because of that experience.

If you were in a sales position, and increased sales by a certain percentage or dollar amount, write it down. If you were responsible for several accounts or clients, tell how many accounts, and if they were considered major accounts. What were the accounts worth in a dollar amount? Did you manage a staff or have people report to you? If so, how many? Did you have a budget? How large was the budget? Numbers speak volumes to people in business. Tangible results are the language that employers speak.

Do you have practical work experience that you can show or demonstrate? Even if you think your activities or experiences are insignificant, make your achievements tangible and measurable. This shows employers that you understand what the measuring stick is for the real world . . . results.

Fluff Is for Pillows, Not Résumés

Anybody can list BS fluff and filler activities on a résumé. People who do this get busted very easily. Employers read through fake or filler material like yesterday's news. If your résumé is short on experience or activities, don't list something just for the sake of taking up space. We all have met people who put bogus stuff on their résumés to make them look better. These are the people who went to one meeting of the Marketing Club in their whole college career, and list on their résumé not only that they were a member of the club, but that they were on committees and even held an office. My favorite example of résumé fluff is a person who listed under activities and organizations, Member, National Geographic Society. (FYI, anyone who subscribes to the magazine automatically becomes a member of the National Geographic Society.)

> *Every year, Mike's fraternity would give a donation to the Viet Nam Veterans Association around the time of their big '60s party. This was usually a one-hour photo opportunity for the guys in the fraternity to feel as though they were doing something good, before they would get bombed at their '60s party that weekend. On Mike's résumé was proudly listed Volunteer, Viet Nam Veterans Association. C'mon, one hour a year really doesn't make you a Nobel candidate. Don't risk someone asking you, "tell me more about . . ."*

Keep It Simple, Stupid

Keep your résumé clean and simple. Some traditional résumé examples recommend that you list the dumbest stuff. As a rule of thumb, if it's not selling you or helping your cause, don't include it.

Health. Some résumés list "Health: Excellent." I know, some résumé experts recommend it, but, c'mon, have you ever seen a résumé that says "Health: Sickly"? Initially, the only thing important for an employer to know about your health is that you are breathing air and pumping blood.

Nonsmoker. It's none of their business whether you smoke or not. It does not reflect your skills or abilities to perform. Does it? Then leave it off.

Marital status. Single? Married? Looking for love? Again, absolutely none of their business. It's also a touchy legal issue, especially for women or for positions that require a lot of travel. Don't put it down.

Objectives. Let's face it. Your objective is to get hired. Plain and simple. So don't mess around with flowery bullshit objectives on your résumé, such as, "I am seeking a challenging and rewarding position that allows me to use my degree and experience while making my employer profitable. PS. I like working with people." Get out of here!

Do *not* put an objective unless you have a *specific* goal and position you are applying for. By putting an objective on a résumé, you run the risk of your objective not being what the employer is looking for. Unless it's a perfect match, you have just eliminated yourself with the first sentence of your résumé.

General objectives make you appear unfocused. Most objectives talk only about what the potential employee wants to gain, instead of what he or she is capable of doing for the employer. Remember, the employer is looking at you as an investment. They are thinking, What is in it for me and my company? Any good interviewer knows that your main objective is to find a job that requires more than saying "paper or plastic," so skip the soliloquy.

References available upon request. If an employer wants your references, he or she will ask you, whether or not it's stated on your résumé.

Don't tell me, show me. Speaking of blinding flash of the obvious, don't list skills that are obvious or can be demonstrated. For example, "Excellent Communicator," or "Great Interpersonal Skills." As an employer, I can tell if you are an excellent communicator by the way you write your cover letter, how you speak to me on the phone, and how you present yourself during our interview. If you have great interpersonal skills, an employer can tell by how you treat everyone, especially the support staff, the secretary, and the receptionist. Do you make small talk, or do you sit there looking out the window? Don't tell an employer you have these skills . . . Show them.

Instant Killers

The small problems that can instantly kill a résumé are mostly cosmetic. You could be a Pulitzer prize winner, Rhodes scholar, and moonlight as a brain surgeon, but if you have any of the following mistakes you will quickly find your résumé in the "round file," a.k.a. the trash can.

Misspelled words. There is really no excuse for this, other than laziness. If you create your résumés and letters on a computer, you have access to spell-check. Use it. Proofread your résumé and documents several times, and then have at least two other people read it. They will be able to pick up mistakes that your eyes overlooked.

Stains and wrinkled paper. You want to become a professional? Professionals don't send wrinkled letters with pizza grease stains, coffee rings, and pencil or pen marks on them. Neither should you.

Inconsistent type. Remember that, initially, your résumé is going to be viewed for maybe 15 to 30 seconds, so make your résumé easy on the eye. You don't want the reader to get frustrated or confused trying to find information.

Have pride in what you send. Neatness counts above almost everything else, at least in the beginning. Remember, your résumé and cover letter will often be the first impression an employer has of you.

COVER LETTERS

A RÉSUMÉ ALONE doesn't do it. Many employers automatically throw away résumés that do not include a cover letter. A cover letter must always be included with a résumé. It adds more depth to your "package."

I said earlier that a résumé is an invitation, something to generate interest and to get you in the door. A cover letter is more than a prelude to the résumé. It elaborates on the résumé, and expresses your ultimate agenda. A résumé is looked at briefly and only has a limited amount of space to say what you want. The cover letter is the meat that lets you go in-depth to support what you mentioned in the résumé. For example, if on your résumé you mentioned that you increased sales 23 percent during your tenure at The Gap, in your cover letter you can describe what you did to accomplish that growth.

Oddly enough, unsolicited résumés can be threatening to an employer, or can catch them off guard. Many people see a résumé and instantly think that you want something from them, namely a job. Most of the time they are right. A secretary or executive may see a résumé and automatically send it to personnel or human resources. (You want it to be with the decision-maker.) A targeted cover letter can diffuse this anxiety and prevent you from being derailed. A targeted cover letter will show that you have done your research about the company, and allow your personality to show through.

Rules for Cover Letters

Don't ask for an interview. The first rule about a cover letter is never to say that you are looking for a job with them, or that you want an interview. At least not in the beginning. I know there is someone reading this saying, "Hey, I really do want an interview, why don't I say it?" Because if the first thing a person reads is that you want an interview, she is instantly put on the defensive and you have placed her in a situation with only two options, yes or no. Nobody likes to be approached blindly with, "You don't know me, but what can you do for me?"

Have an agenda. Your agenda is to establish a contact and try to meet with this person face to face so you can sell yourself. If you immediately ask for an interview or say that you want a job or to work for that company, the person can respond positively: "Sure, c'mon by. We were just needing someone like you. Why didn't you call sooner?"; or negatively: "We are not hiring right now." Do not give someone limited options.

Have a specific target. Begin by targeting a specific person and tell her something interesting about yourself that either backs up your résumé or is not included on it. Never, I mean never, send a cover letter blindly to Dear Sir or Madam, To Whom it May Concern, or

Dear Sirs. It might as well say, Dear Trash Can. Do a little sleuthing and target a cover letter to a specific person. Even if he ends up not being your final contact, it shows focus, research, and direction. Besides, the recipient will always pass it on to the proper person.

What to Say

What should you say in a letter like this? Don't begin the letter with "I'm a recent graduate," or "I'm a senior at Blank University." This will send off alarms that "This person wants a job." Executive assistants are trained to send these letters directly to personnel, do not pass go, do not collect $200.

How you got their name. People always want to know, "Where did you get my name?" In your letter mention that through your research you had run across his or her name, or that of the company. If someone gives you the contact's name, make sure that you include who referred you.

You are seeking advice. Next, explain in your letter that you are looking to enter this field, and let her know that you are interested in meeting with her briefly, to seek her advice on the industry, and to establish contacts. You are networking. Everybody likes to network and meet others. People aren't as threatened when you ask for advice or want to make a contact as they are when hit up for a job. Remember, the great thing about networking and advice is that people who are established remember what it was like when they started out and are often willing to help others. If you are already involved in the industry or have been working for a while, you want to position yourself as someone who has something to offer. You have skills to bring to the table. In your letter, explain that from your research you believe there may be some common interests and that you want to explore these interests further.

Explain that you included your résumé so that he may become familiar with your background. Perhaps he can help steer you in the right direction. Flatter the person. I'm not talking about being cheesy or disingenuous, but play to a person's desire to feel powerful or intelligent. It can be an ego rush to be in a position to help another person. Stating why you included your résumé also may prevent it from being shuttled to the round file as just another job hunter.

Offer several options for meeting. Give the contact several specific options for when you would like to meet. If you are job hunting out of town, plan a trip and make sure that you tell the contact which days you will be visiting the city. "I will be in San Jose during the week of October 26th." Even if you are in the same town, give the person several meeting options, "I will be able to meet at your convenience during the week of March 24th or the week of April 5th. Make sure that you set specific dates. If you leave it open, it's much easier to push it back. Set a date and work around it. It's not uncommon for many executives to plan their schedules weeks in advance. Don't be upset if that person can't meet on your recommended days—suggest an alternative.

When you will follow up. Close your cover letter by stating specifically when you will be making your follow-up call. This way either the contact or the assistant will be expecting your call. "I will be in touch next Wednesday."

THE PACKAGE ITSELF

IF YOU ARE BUYING A PRODUCT, most of the time you want to have all of the information you possibly can in front of you. You don't want to be handed a letter or one sheet telling you about the product. You want a brochure. Same thing if you are selling a product or service. You don't walk into a potential client without having some information or a brochure. Now think about the stacks of paper that are sitting on an employer's desk, or maybe the stack of gray and tan résumé paper four inches high at your school's Career Planning Office. What will make your cover letter and résumé stand out from the hundreds, if not thousands, that employers receive each year?

If you are the product, you need more than a one-page sheet like everyone else to help sell you. You want something to set your product

(YOU) apart from the rest. You need a brochure, your own personal press kit. Your information needs to be professional, exciting, and able to make it past the mail room and secretary barriers with ease to grab the attention of an executive decision-maker.

There are several things you can do to make your information look as if it came from a large corporation instead of a dorm room or kitchen table.

Start with a basic package that includes a résumé and a targeted cover letter. Double check that your phone number and address are displayed on the résumé and cover letter. Most people send information in a regular letter-sized envelope. Don't do what most people do. Using a regular envelope means that you have to fold your letters several times. When it arrives and is unfolded, it remains wrinkled, bent, and messy. It also is the same size as every other letter that comes in to the company. It runs the risk of being opened by the mail room or receptionist. Always type your envelopes. Never, ever, handwrite the address. The key is to make it look as if it came from a business instead of an individual, or worse, a student.

Go to Office Depot, Staples, Office Max, or any supply store and spring for a box of 9½-by-12½-inch envelopes and large laser labels. FYI, you will need to bite the bullet and realize that you are going to have to spend money on your job search. Envelopes, paper, printing copies, and postage alone can run a small fortune. Plan ahead and save your money for this. Don't be surprised when you have to spend money to look for a job. Long distance and travel are also expenses that you may incur during your job search. However, all is not lost. Make sure that you save any receipts involved with your search. The expenses are tax deductible.

Now that you have the necessary supplies, go to your school's computer lab or use your own Macintosh or PC to print mailing labels. Create a return label. Maybe even make up a logo. Make it look professional. If it appears to be from a company, it's more likely to be read. Direct your mailing label specifically to your contact and write ATTN: (Contact Name) at the bottom. You don't want snoops opening it beforehand.

Be sure that you call ahead to get the proper address, contact name, title, and spelling if you do not already have them. Don't be shy about calling. Act as if you are with a company. Make up one if you get nervous. If they persist in making it difficult for you to get the information you need, say you are mailing something to Ms. Smith (or your contact's name) and need to verify the information.

On the return address try not to list your apartment number. It may be a good move for you to get a post office box to use as an address. It looks more professional and you can have everything go to one place. You also don't have to worry about roommates misplacing things or forwarding your mail when you move.

Should You Include Anything Else?

What else can you do to spice up your information? How about visuals? Maybe a picture. WHOA! Hold on for a minute. I have to make the following disclaimer about this next tip.

It's illegal for you to be judged based upon your race, ethnic background, or looks. For this reason, many employers immediately throw away pictures if they are included. Also, some professions, primarily those which are more traditional or conservative, frown upon any unique display of excessive individuality, such as including a picture of yourself. I am not uniformly recommending that you do, or do not, include a picture along with your résumé. I am merely offering this suggestion as an alternative way to stand apart from the crowd if you happen to be in an industry whose attitudes and atmosphere would support this type of activity, and if you are personally comfortable with showing off a little bit.

On the other hand, if you are in a creative field and you feel comfortable with it, absolutely include it. The reason it can be effective is because not many people do it. The other reason is, even though you can argue the legality and ethics of it all you want, it really does matter if you have a nice appearance. Especially in sales and high-profile fields. Yes, it's unspoken and it's wrong, but nonetheless, it happens in the real world.

If you are blessed with being nice looking, it's an asset, so use it for all it's worth. I'm not talking about a "glamour shot," with you spread out on a bearskin rug, looking coquettishly over your shoulder, or a picture of you at your parent's Fourth of July barbecue, with corn on the cob stuck in your teeth. I mean a small wallet-size, black-and-white head shot. Much like a nice passport photo, except you dress nicely and don't look like a terrorist. Dress properly for your picture. You can have them done very cheaply at a local quick photo. Keep your receipts for taxes.

During my first job search out of college, I had not thought about putting my picture in at all. Then I had a phone interview with a gentleman at a marketing consulting firm. Everything was going well until he asked me if I could send him a picture of me. I was very self-righteous at that time and was incensed that this man would care about how I looked. I mean, I don't repulse people, at least I don't think so. But this had no bearing on my abilities. I confronted him on it and said I wasn't comfortable doing it. Why did he need a picture? He told me outright that there is a lot of client contact and press contact and he wanted someone who was nice looking. Was this unethical as hell? Yes. Illegal? Maybe. I blew the position off, but it taught me some important lessons. First of all, if someone was going to eliminate me immediately because of my looks, I surely didn't need them. Second, there are people out there all the time who judge you based on your looks. Most of it happens to be subtle and unspoken. So I decided that, since it happens anyway, I might as well use it to my advantage. It has worked on occasion in the past because hardly anyone else does it, it adds more to your résumé and cover letter, it's nice to put a face with a name, and an employer can see that I have a professional appearance and my face doesn't scare small children.

Mailing

While the good old U.S. Postal Service is the traditional method of delivery, there are several creative alternatives for making sure your information gets into the hands of the decision-maker.

Overnight delivery. If you are willing to part with the cash, FedEx or UPS Overnight is a surefire way to make sure that he or she sees it. Overnight delivery implies importance and urgency. People are more likely to open a package immediately to see what it is, even if they don't know who it's from. If you are really adventurous, you can send it to a person's home if you are having trouble reaching them at the office. Risky, but potentially effective.

Faxes. Don't fax your résumé unless the person asks you to. If you are told to send it via fax, do it ASAP. Faxing a résumé blindly is very risky, because the intended recipient may never get it, it could be mixed with someone else's paper, or the person whose job you would take may see it and eliminate the competition by throwing your résumé away. There are too many chances for it to be thrown out. Besides, faxes can be smudgy and look like crap.

Snail mail. This brings us back to the good old mail. Once you have your basic "Personal Press Kit," including your résumé, a targeted cover letter, and maybe a picture, addressed and in a large envelope, postage should run around 52 cents or more for heavier envelopes. It can add up if you have a large volume of mail-outs, but it's an unavoidable expense. When mailing your packet, ask how long it takes to arrive at the destination zip code. You will want to know this so you can follow up properly. Strike while the iron is hot.

Creative Strategies

For some of you who are extremely creative, unique, and daring, the sky is the limit for how you want to express yourself to potential employers and gain their attention. Take a look at the particular industry and field you are going into. Is there anything that is unique to it that you could do to stand out? How about the company itself? Is there anything special about the company, or maybe a product that you can use to sell yourself?

Being creative and off the wall takes guts and a special personality, but often that may be exactly what is needed to push you over the top, and ahead of the competition. For example, there is a story of a young

William, a DePaul University graduate, says, "During one of my interviews, I asked the interviewer, "what qualities are you looking for in an employee?" The woman running the meeting said, "someone with an S on his chest." Meaning that they wanted Superman. In my follow-up letter, I told her that I had what it takes, right to the letter. I had found a small Superman logo and dropped it in the envelope. It worked. I got an offer."

■　■　■

Stacey, from Temple University, applied for a position against competition which was slightly more experienced. She knew the interviewers were concerned because she was a recent graduate. After her interview, Stacey sent a box to the interviewer, containing a stuffed Kermit the frog doll with a note attached, "I'm green, but I'm good." OK, I know this story is so corny you might want to puke, but it worked for Stacey.

■　■　■

Christine, a Kent State graduate, walked into a business seminar and trade show in Cleveland. There she handed out several hundred copies of her résumé. The keynote speaker was so impressed that he read the résumé out loud during his address. Christine received five offers.

woman who wanted a marketing position with a vineyard. In order to stand out from the rest of the pack, she created her résumé on a wine label and placed it on a bottle. It was very elegant, informative, and one of a kind.

Two years ago, around Christmas time, I came back to the office from lunch. Waiting for me was a beautifully wrapped package from a local upscale department store. I'm thinking, "Great, I scored. My girlfriend must have surprised me." As I tore into the package, expecting a sweater or shirt, I found a picture, résumé, cover letter, and candy. It belonged to a recent graduate who wanted to interview at our company. He had worked in the marketing department of a department store while he was in school. It got my attention, and we asked him to meet with us for an interview.

Be creative in ways that reflect your personality. If it's forced or canned, it won't work at all. Be original. Some gimmicks are so worn out that one executive reports that she now has a collection of forks and spoons from applicants who have sent the silverware with notes saying, "I'm hungry for this job," or "I want this job so badly I can taste it." Many people are now creating baseball cards of themselves, with a picture on the front and their résumé and statistics on the back. There are many great ideas. Just make sure that it's *your* great idea. If you do something that has been done before, it will totally backfire on you.

Take chances and use unconventional resources to get your name in front of employers.

Online services and bulletin boards are becoming a more common way to learn about opportunities or even gain exposure for yourself. Check out what is available through America Online, CompuServe, and Prodigy.

Make sure that what you do is appropriate for the particular company and industry. While there have been accountants who have their résumés look like a balance sheet, the Big Six may frown on this. The package, brochure, or personal press kit, no matter what you call it or how creative it is, is only intended to get an interview and pique interest in what you have to offer an employer. Once you are in, you have to show some substance.

Paul lives in Los Angeles and is a graphic artist. He placed (or uploaded) a demo and portfolio of his work on America Online for others to download and look at. Including his information and background, Paul posted his work in the multimedia forum, knowing that professionals go in there all the time to read news and articles and to view other people's samples. A multimedia developer in another state saw Paul's work and called him. This person's company was in need of an artist and was impressed with Paul's work. Paul had never even considered opportunities in the Midwest, but this opportunity just fell into his lap because he used high-tech means to gain exposure.

▪ 13 ▪

Getting in the Door

All right. You have put in the work. You have determined what field you want to work in. You have targeted tons of companies who need *you* if they want to survive next quarter. You have read and researched more than you ever did in school. And you have finally perfected your résumé and "Personal Press Kit." You are ready for action. Now what?

Go Straight to the Top

Before you send anything or make a phone call, determine who the absolute decision-maker is in that organization. Go right to the person who has the power to hire you. In many organizations, there are several key decision-makers. Most of the time it's a high-ranking officer of the company, or an executive such as the president, CEO, or a vice president in charge of a division or department. These are the people who shape the direction of a company. They seem to have their finger on the pulse of the organization and to know in which direction it's headed, generally, because they are navigating and steering the ship.

These "top dogs" know what the needs of the organization are and have the power to hire you. Even if there is not a position open right then, they can create a position for you, if necessary.

Let's say that you meet with a vice president, and tell her about your background and ideas. She may be thinking about expanding the division or creating a special project, but has not told anyone yet, especially the personnel or human resources department. Maybe the vice president has a dormant idea and you impress her so much that you trigger her to go forward with the plan. All that was needed was the right person for the project, and you are that person.

Top-Down Persuasion

Go to the highest-ranking person that you *realistically* can reach. Then expect that person to pass you down to the right contact. Even if you contact a person in the organization who is powerful but unable to help you directly, he or she can funnel or refer you to the proper decision-maker, often with his or her blessing. This is called top-down persuasion.

If a high-ranking person in the company recommends that you contact someone who is under him, it can give you a small amount of credibility and entree. It lends you temporary credibility. Not enough to get you the job automatically, but just enough to get you an audience or have your calls returned.

If you write or call a president of a company, and she says, "I can't help you, but why don't you talk with my VP of Sales, Joe Blow." Great. The president or her assistant may leave it at that and let you call the VP yourself, or she may offer to pass your information along to Joe Blow himself. Whether you speak with the person directly or with an assistant, try to find out who the person is you need to be speaking with. Keep in mind that it may take calling two or three people in order to find out who the right person is. Don't get discouraged or impatient if the first try isn't a home run. It takes a lot of phone calls, follow-up, and name-dropping.

This is where top-down persuasion comes in. After the president of the company recommends that you contact Joe Blow, what better entree than to say to Mr. Blow or his assistant, "Ms. Smith (or Ms. Smith's office) recommended that I get in touch with you."

Joe Blow and his assistant don't know who you are. You could be a family friend, or a business contact. They don't know what your relationship is to the president, Ms. Smith. As a result, you are treated much better than if you were some geek off the street, cold-calling to ask for a job. You stand a much better chance of being listened to, simply because you were referred by his boss. You have gained instant credibility. Now, this credibility is just for the short term. It works best for getting you past the assistant, who acts as a gatekeeper and screens calls. Sound a little cheesy? Sure it is, but do you want to mow yards the rest of your life?

The Round File

A lot of people buy into the idea of going through the personnel department, office manager, or human resources. In the beginning, avoid being routed to these departments at all costs, and never, never send your information directly to HR or personnel before attempting to reach the decision-maker. The phrase you never want to hear regarding your résumé is, "We have sent your résumé to personnel." Personnel, the birthplace of mass-produced rejection letters, informing you that your résumé will die a slow death on file.

> Dear Loser: We thank you for your interest in our company. Your credentials are impressive. However, at this time there are no positions for which you are suitable. Your résumé will be KEPT ON FILE. Thank you and good luck.

This is where résumés go to die. A cemetery for poor shmucks who had the misfortune of being routed here instead of reaching the real decision-makers who could have hired them. Having your résumé "kept on file" is often worse than a rejection letter because you still hang on, waiting for the company to call, thinking there may be a chance.

Why You Go to the Decision-Maker

Why do you want to avoid these departments? Because they aren't the real decision-makers. They don't know exactly what is in the production pipeline. Don't get me wrong. Personnel and human resource professionals do a fantastic job. They fill a very specific need and function within an organization, and many companies could not function without them. They handle many other activities beyond the hiring of new employees, including administering employee benefits. In no way am I discrediting human resource professionals. They can help your career in the future. However, initially they are not your best target. Their job is to fill an immediate staffing need, not to help you create an opportunity. Personnel or HR is told from above, from the real decision-makers, "next quarter we will be expanding our marketing efforts and will need to fill three new positions." Then HR goes to work finding people to meet those requirements. You are trying to create an opportunity. You are selling yourself to decision-makers so they can either create an opening for you, or find a place to put you based on current or future needs.

It's the future needs that human resources or personnel departments may not be aware of. This is to your advantage. If a company is planning to develop a new product or considering a new project, the first group to learn about it is not the HR department. Perhaps the vice president of marketing has only discussed a project with one or two people. Maybe the vice president has only thought about expanding or adding a new staff member, but has not told anyone. The idea has been dormant. All that was needed was for you to approach the decision-maker to trigger him or her to take action. This happens quite frequently.

Getting a job is as much a function of timing as it is of qualifications. With a little hustle and hard work, you can put yourself in the right place at the right time, and create a position for yourself. Meanwhile, the HR department would have no clue that the company was ready to expand, was considering launching a new product, or entering a new type of business. They would merely tell you, "Sorry, we aren't hiring at the present time."

Timing Is Everything

Getting in the door with your target, and making the most of your "Personal Press Kit," brochure, or résumé, involves near-perfect timing. Good timing begins with your mailing. Your goal should be to synchronize when your résumé will be on the desk of your targeted decision-maker with when you make your follow-up call.

Here is how you do it. Determine how long it takes for the mail to arrive at your intended location. If it takes two days, for example, mail it on a Monday and plan to follow up on a Thursday. Try to avoid mailing around holidays and three-day weekends. Also, avoid having your information arrive on a Saturday. Saturday's mail usually gets grouped with Monday's mail, resulting in a heavy mail day. Your package may get lost in the clutter. Some experts say that Tuesday, Wednesday, and Thursday are the best days for your package to arrive, because it will get the most attention.

After you determine when your target will receive your package, plan to make your follow-up call on that day, or within two or three days of its arrival. Your follow-up call should trigger the person's memory. Your name should be fresh in her mind because your information has just crossed her desk. She has just seen your information the day before, or better yet, it's on her desk when you call. Timing is crucial. Follow up on time. Don't putz around. Call while your information is in sight, before there is time to send it to the "round file" or the contact forgets who you are.

The Best Times to Follow Up

When is the best time to call? There are certain times of the day when you are almost guaranteed not to be able to reach the person you want to contact. You stand the best chance either early in the morning or late in the afternoon.

These are slow times and there is a chance that the assistant is gone. Many execs pick up their own phones before the assistant arrives at 8:30 a.m., and after he goes home at 5:00 p.m. This eliminates the possibility that your call will be screened. You will rarely reach anyone at 10:00 a.m. or 2:00 p.m. These are the busy parts of the day. Oddly enough, lunch is another good time to call. Many executives work through lunch and will pick up their own phones while the assistant is away. You are more likely to have his attention during these periods than if you were to call in the middle of the day, while he is in a meeting, has another call on hold, and a project due in an hour.

It might seem that every time you call, you hear, "I'm sorry, Ms. Big Shot is in a meeting." Depending on when you call, either she really is in a meeting and doesn't have time for distractions, or you are getting screened. Generally, the worst days and times to make a follow-up call are Monday morning and Friday afternoon. Monday is bad because it's the beginning of the week and there is so much going on. Friday isn't great because people are ready for the weekend. Everyone wants to be somewhere besides the office, and you might not get their full attention. Plan around the holidays. Not just major Hallmark variety holidays, but also legal holidays, like Independence Day, Columbus Day, Veteran's Day, religious holidays, and other three-day weekends, like Presidents' Day and Memorial Day.

If you are still having problems getting through to the person, you might ask the assistant when would be a good time to call, or try calling at an unconventional time. You might even leave a message on her voice mail at night.

Leaving Messages on Voice Mail

If you are sent to voice mail, great. Voice mail is great because you have a captive audience. Sometimes you may be routed to voice mail and be caught off guard. Don't panic and hang up. Always leave a message. However, if you aren't ready or are surprised, you don't have to leave a message right then. Think it out carefully, and call back when you know what you want to say. Voice mail is actually better than leaving a message with a secretary or an assistant, because you can say exactly what you want, and know that your message will be received uncensored. Some basic rules for leaving voice mail messages are to always say who you are, when you called, why you are calling (refer to the packet you sent and that you would like to meet or speak with him to ask his advice about the industry) and always leave your phone number or where you can be reached.

While some people are annoyed by messages left on voice mail, it can help your cause if used wisely. Leaving messages with a secretary or an assistant is a whole other ball game.

The Gatekeepers . . . Secretaries and Assistants

Who is the most important person in the office? The president? The chairman? Nope. Secretaries, or assistants (the new politically correct term), have all of the real power in an organization. As far as you are concerned, they are initially more important than the person you are trying to see. Why? Because these people are the "gatekeepers." Their whole function in life is to keep people like you from annoying their bosses. Sales people are also on this list of those to screen out.

Don't ever underestimate the power of an assistant. As far as your job search and getting in the door is concerned, they control your world. Assistants have the power to grant access to the man or woman who is the decision-maker.

It's important to remember this throughout your career. Assistants and secretaries can quickly become allies if treated correctly, or they can shut you down if you treat them like hired help. It doesn't matter if you are in the middle of your job search or established in your career. Learn how to treat the administrative and support staff well. This applies to your own staff and the staffs of other companies, too.

Assistants have more swing and influence than you might think. Imagine you just had a fantastic meeting with Mr. Jim Bob Big Shot. Everything went well, or at least you think it did. You had all the right answers, you had a great rapport, and it was a good hair day. What could go possibly go wrong? All it takes is for Cindy, Mr. Big Shot's assistant, to say that you treated her rudely while you were waiting for Mr. Big Shot to arrive, and your chances for a job or to make a sale are as good as gone.

There is a saying in Texas, where I grew up, "You catch more flies with honey than with vinegar." Support staff can make your life a whole lot easier if you acknowledge their power, real or perceived. Think about it. Assistants, receptionists, and secretaries are all behind-the-scenes players. Secretaries and assistants don't often get enough credit. They don't have much decision-making power in the organization, and may even take a lot of crap from irate bosses. Yet the job they perform is crucial. If you treat support staff like professionals, you are much more likely to get what you want. This applies to anything, not just getting in the door.

Obstacles You May Encounter. Remember, it's the secretary's job to screen you out. This can prove to be a formidable barrier. Typically you call and ask to speak with Ms. Big Shot. Common responses to expect are:

■ *"No. I'm sorry. Ms. Big Shot is not available. May I take a message?"* Sure, leave your name and number.

■ *"May I tell her who is calling?"* You would think that your name alone would do it, and sometimes it does, but not often. Say your name and expect the next question.

■ *"What company are you with?"* Ouch! If you are currently employed, this is no problem. You have an answer. If you are a student, you are out of luck. However, you can do one of the following. You can say the name of your school. Yes, I'm with the University of Oklahoma. OK, it's a little cheesy and administrators aren't crazy about it, but it can get you past the secretarial gauntlet. He or she doesn't have to know that you are a student. For all they know, you could be a fund raiser, a professor, a faculty member. Only after you reach the decision-maker do you need to make it known that you attend the school and aren't an employee. If you aren't employed, or are out of school, you can create your own little company. It seems that everyone who is unemployed now is a consultant. Now they may consult on how to be a sloth and sit on the couch all day, but still they consider themselves consultants. Anyway. You could use your initials or a company name that represents you. If you used a logo or professional-looking labels on your mail-out, this is a wonderful tie-in. The key is to appear as professional as possible and not to appear as a student calling from a dorm room or apartment, dressed only in his underwear. Again, all of this is strictly to help you get past the first screen of the mail room and the secretary. Whatever you do, don't fumble around and say, "Uh, I'm not." Do this and you will surely be asked the next question.

■ *"May I tell her what this is regarding?"* (This one is a stumper. A sign of a very good assistant.) "I was calling to follow up regarding a package I sent to Ms. Big Shot earlier this week."

■ *"Ms. Big Shot will have to get back with you."* Fine. Leave a simple message, name, and number. If pressed about why you called, say that you were following up something you sent earlier in the week.

■ *"We forwarded your résumé to Personnel. We are not hiring right now."* (This means your information was received and you have been busted.) "Well, I'm very disappointed, because I had not intended that information to go to Personnel. I sent it directly to Ms. Big Shot because, as I said in my letter, I was seeking her advice and included my résumé so she could be familiar with my background when I called. I was not applying for a position. If there is any way you can retrieve my information and make sure that Ms. Big Shot gets it, or if I could speak to her, I would certainly appreciate it."

Get personal. If you are stalled and can't seem to get through to your contact, level with the assistant. Make it personal. "Andrew," (always get the assistant's name) "I realize that Ms. Big Shot is incredibly busy, but I would like to talk to her for just five minutes, to get her advice. If there is anything that you can personally do to help me speak with Ms. Big Shot, I would appreciate it so much." Surprisingly, this refreshingly honest plea will get you a lot of places. Don't think that because he is just an assistant, that he isn't important or can't help you. All he has to do is buzz you through to your contact, or have her return your call. If you lie or try to talk down to the assistant, your message goes into the trash can. At this point in your career search, the assistant is the most powerful person in your world.

Remember to be flexible and appreciative and to offer solutions. Ask when a convenient time would be for you to call back. If an assistant helps you out, or gives you access to someone, write a personal letter thanking him.

The Phone Call

The follow-up phone call is your brief opportunity to get your foot all the way in the door. Your packet should have piqued the contact's interest and made her familiar with your background. You mentioned in your letter that you would be calling, so she may be expecting your call. *Do not wait for the company or contact to call you.* It won't happen. If you get a phone call, fantastic, but never send out a résumé and wait for the phone to ring. This is what morons do who say, "I sent out 500 résumés and haven't heard a thing." Unless you have a unique background, or there is an immediate need or interest, it's rare that you will be called first.

Practice What You Want to Say. Before you make your call, rehearse. Don't think that you can wing the phone call. Know what you want to accomplish and how you are going to say it. However, you want to avoid sounding like a robot or as if you are reading from a script. Remember, you only have a few seconds to impress this person and make him interested enough to let you meet with him. Be prepared.

Is This a Good Time? When you call, if he or she appears startled or busy, don't push it. Be aware that it may not be a good time for them to talk to you. You can harm your chances if you barrel on through, or make your pitch, when your contact is in the middle of something else. You want to have that person's full attention.

You can actually score points if you ask if it's a good time, or if it would be more convenient for you to call back later. The last thing you want is for your contact to be distracted or in a hurry to get you off the phone. Anything you can do to respect that person's time will score points.

When you finally reach the decision-maker on the phone, mention who you are and the reason you are calling. Refer to the package you sent. "Ah hah," now the light bulb goes on. Your contact now re-members, "Sure, I remember seeing it this morning." Next, briefly tell the person something interesting about yourself and your back-ground.

Never Ask for an Interview. Fight every impulse you have to ask for an interview, or if there is a position open. This means instant death. "Round file, here I come." When you immediately ask for an in-terview, or if there is a position open, you instantly appear needy. You bring nothing to the table. The contact feels like you are using them to get something . . . namely, a job. You might as well say, "Hey buddy, what can you do for me?"

Earlier, I mentioned how people like to have their egos stroked. Once someone has reached a position of influence or power, real or perceived, it's common to want to give back and share what you know. It's human nature. Most successful people like to help others who are starting out. It reminds them of when they were in that position and someone took time to help them out, or share insight, a connection or advice that helped them get where they are today.

Appeal to people's ego and sense of power. In your letter, you stated that you are seeking advice and want to establish a contact in the industry. Believe it or not, this is networking. Although you don't know this person from a hole in the ground, it goes a lot further than "I'm looking for a job. Can you help me?"

How It Might Sound. This is a sample of how your schpiel should sound once you reach your contact. You can tailor this to fit your own personality. But remember, you don't have very long to make your point. Your goal is to get that person to let you meet with them, and then get off the phone.

YOUR SCHPIEL: *"I'm Bradley Richardson (Use Your Own Name). I recently sent you some information regarding my background."*

WHAT YOUR CONTACT WILL SAY:

■ **"Sure, I remember reading it yesterday. How can I help you?"** Proceed immediately to the rest of your schpiel.

■ **"I've forwarded it to the proper person/department."** "Thank you. Who might that be? What are his/her duties? Do you have that direct phone line?"

■ **"I've forwarded it to Personnel."** "You jerk!" (No, don't say that.) Say, "I'm sorry about that. That is not where I intended for it to go. I was writing to you specifically in hopes that I could learn more about your industry, not to ask for a job. I gave you my résumé and background information only so you could be more familiar and informed when I called." This may piss some people off, but chances are they didn't even read your package. It was immediately sent to Personnel simply because it had a ré-sumé in it. This response is intended to guilt them into talking to you. Try to get a referral, a contact name, or to worm your way in to a meeting.

THE REST OF YOUR SCHPIEL: *"As you read in my letter, I'm interested in this field, and through my research I came across your name. I was hoping to meet with you briefly for about twenty minutes, to seek your advice about the industry and how I might get started. I also thought it would be beneficial to establish industry contacts. I will be in your area during the week of the 25th. Is Tuesday good for you?"*

WHAT YOUR CONTACT WILL SAY:

- **"Sure, that would be fine. When would you like to meet?"** Jackpot! Set up a time to get together. Make sure that you get the location and directions, and confirm the time. Also make sure that you give a phone number where you can be reached in case there is a need to reschedule.

- **"Why don't you talk with Susan Davidson? I think she is the person you need to speak with."** Fine. You have just been funneled. Find out specifically what Susan does and call her. Use the name of the person who referred you.

- **"We don't have any openings."** Say, "I understand, but the reason I contacted you was really to learn more about the industry before I decided to make it my career. I also wanted to establish some contacts if I were to choose this profession." This is another guilt response, but it works sometimes. Try to get a referral or contact name.

- **"I don't know how I might be able to help you."** You want to learn more about what it's like to work in that field. Try to learn as much as possible and get a referral or another contact.

- **"Tell me more about yourself."** Go for it. A meeting over the phone will work also. It might lead to having you come in for a face-to-face meeting, or may help the contact steer you in the right direction.

- **"What would you like to know?"** Same thing. Go for it. Tell them that you want to learn more about the business and have the following questions. (Make sure to have questions prepared just in case.) Still try to meet face-to-face.

What the Reaction Might Be. These people are savvy enough to know what you are up to. C'mon, you sent them your résumé. It's obvious that you are either graduating or looking to change careers. No one is that obtuse. With this approach, several things can happen.

Either an opportunity is available at the company and you are asked to come on in, or maybe he or she is in a position to help you by referring you to someone, and will meet with you to see what you are

> *Jill, a Boston College graduate, was trying with little success to get in with various advertising agencies. However, she asked everyone she met with if they had any contacts or knew of any opportunities for which she would be qualified. One gentleman, who had nothing available at his agency, told Jill that Texaco's marketing department was looking for an entry-level person to assist with the in-house advertising. He gave Jill the name and number and offered himself as a referral. She took advantage of this and ended up getting in for an interview.*

like. Some people are willing to meet with you and tell you about a particular field. People are generally up front. If nothing is available at his organization, he still might be able to help you. He might say, "Look, we don't have anything currently, but maybe you should talk to Linda at Northern Telecom. Here is her number. You can use my name."

This company did not have a position for you, but was this a loss? No way. You still scored. You made an influential contact within the industry. You gained another lead and contact with an entree already established. Even if the phone call goes down in flames, always ask for a referral. "You have seen my information. Is there any opportunity you know of where my background and credentials might be useful?" During my own career searches, I asked this question every time someone told me no. And for almost every call where nothing developed, I picked up at least one or two leads and contacts. With each phone call, I kept expanding my network and source of leads and contacts.

This is the true benefit in asking someone for advice, Networking 101. You want to either: A) Get in the door to sell yourself in person; B) Pick your contact's brain about the industry; or C) Make another contact.

The Twenty Minute Rule. It's a cliche but, "time really is money" and until you show someone how you can make or save her money, you are a low priority item. Time is at a premium, and you will find it difficult to meet with someone for a long period of time. When you ask to meet her, ask for a very specific, brief, and unique amount of time. For example, instead of saying "I would like to meet with you," say "I would like to meet with you for twenty minutes."

Why only twenty minutes? By offering to take only a *specific, short* amount of time, it shows that you appreciate how valuable it is. Second, it shows that you are focused and can accomplish what you need in a short period. Third, I guarantee that if you get in the door, you will be in there longer than twenty minutes. Salespeople do this all the time. It's much easier to prevent someone from coming into your office than it is to ask them to leave. Hardly anyone would agree to meet with you for one hour. For some people, even thirty minutes is a stretch. If you don't ask for a specific amount of time, forget it. You may be thinking about a nice leisurely meeting that takes about an hour, while your intended contact has ten minutes to spare, so get to the point. Twenty minutes is a manageable amount of time that is not obtrusive and people can agree to easily.

Believe me, your twenty-minute meeting will change course and become an interview for all practical purposes. An interview does not have to be a formal interrogation, where you sit in a room answering scripted questions. Many, if not most, interviews are casual conversations, where both parties are getting to know each other. As you are finding out more about the company and industry, the subject of the conversation will eventually turn to you. "So, you are a senior at O.U. Tell me more about yourself. What would you like to do?" or "Why are you looking to change careers or enter this field?" Hello! What are you waiting for? Do you want an engraved invitation? This is your chance to sell yourself.

The Best Lunch You Will Ever Buy

Until you begin working, you might not be able to fathom how incredibly busy people are. Some have their schedules planned to the minute, weeks in advance. Even squeezing you in for twenty minutes can appear a monumental task. If you want an audience, you need to be flexible and even a little creative. If it's tough to schedule a time, you might try meeting at a location other than the office.

Offer to meet for a meal or coffee. The breakfast meeting is fast replacing the "power lunch." Breakfast is early enough so it won't conflict with many things at the office and it allows many executives to get an early start on the day, while killing two birds with one stone. Besides, breakfast is probably the briefest meal of the day, so your twenty minute rule is not far off. You can be in and out in thirty minutes.

Above all, you have to be flexible and offer solutions. You are the one who needs to make things happen. It's not the contact's responsibility to accommodate your schedule, or come up with alternative meeting arrangements. Meeting a contact or mentor at breakfast lets you take the initiative. Unless you are a complete pig at the table, it gives you an opportunity to shine and to pick your contact's brain.

Be a Nag

It's all a numbers game. The more hooks you have in the water, the more likely it is that you will get a bite. Use this method with many companies, not just your top choices. This way you have more irons in the fire, make more contacts, and expand your network.

Be a nag. Think like a mule and be stubborn. You will have to be persistent in order to be heard and to get a job. If something falls through the cracks, it will most likely be you. Don't take it personally if no one returns your calls. Keep trying. However, don't leave more than one message a day—it's obnoxious to call on the hour, every hour. You might try every other day. Be persistent. It takes a lot of time and hard work, and doesn't happen overnight. The Bureau of Labor Statistics states that 8 out of 10 graduates take at least six months to find a job.

Things to Remember

■ Go to the top person in your area of interest who you can realistically reach (i.e., vice president of marketing, sales manager, president).

■ Expect to be "funneled" to the right person.

■ Determine what day your résumé or PPK (Personal Press Kit) will arrive.

■ Make your follow-up call no later than three days after your PPK arrives.

■ Respect the gatekeeper (secretary/assistant).

■ Don't ask for an interview. It sounds like, "What can you do for me?"

- Seek an informational meeting to gain advice or contacts. Everyone has an ego, play to it.
- Ask for a brief, specific amount of time when setting a meeting.
- Always leave with something: a meeting, referral, name, advice, etc.
- Be persistent.

ADAM WEST
Stock Trader
Age: 29

FOR MANY OF US, a secure, comfortable position in corporate America is what we dream about. It's nice to know where your paycheck will be coming from every week. Let someone else worry about all of the little problems. Working for a big company offers security. On the other hand, there are those who want to control their own destiny. Adam West is one of those people. It takes guts to be able to walk away from the security of a big company and rely totally on your own abilities.

After graduating with a finance degree in 1986, Adam worked for a small company as a financial analyst. In 1989, he wanted to make the next move and work for a growing company in a leading industry. He laid out his criteria. "I wanted to work for a progressive company that offered growth opportunities, a team-style environment, and good benefits (in that order)." He went about finding companies that met those criteria and called the controller or decision-maker directly. "I completely avoided dealing with Human Resources." Adam sold himself and was able to land a position with technology giant EDS.

Adam's part-time hobby was investing. "I have always had an interest in the financial markets. I began playing Monday morning quarterback, like many others, and noticing that if I had only acted on my hunch or what I had thought would happen, I would have done well." Adam was a phenomenal saver. He took a small stake of his own money and began to invest and play the market. "I would study the market late at night and make my trades by phone during the day."

Adam did well and continued to save more and more money. He was doing this while he was still working full-time at EDS. "Much of what I was doing for other companies and at EDS was studying their financials and the competition. We focused on how to become a premier contender in the industry. I applied this knowledge to study potential companies in which to invest.

"After a year of doing this as a hobby, I took a look at my expenses and decided that this is what I really wanted to do. If I was ever to try it, now would be the time. I am single, no children, and if it fails I can always return to corporate life. But the last thing I want to do is be 35 years old and look back wishing I had tried this."

He mapped out a plan that would sustain him for two years. He had goals and points that he needed to reach each month to be able to sustain his lifestyle and expenses. After three years of trading on his own and working full-time at EDS, Adam took the leap, quit EDS and became a full-time stock trader. He was now playing for keeps.

"I work from my home, which is a mixed blessing. I like the freedom and autonomy it provides me. Working in shorts and a T-shirt is nice. But by the same token, I miss the interaction with others. It helps to bounce ideas off someone. I live according to my own wits." Adam is truly in control of his future. "If I succeed, it is my own, and if I make a mistake, it is mine, as well. The key is to learn from those mistakes, recognize them and move on. Wisdom from a mistake now can save your business later.

"I also like the freedom that my work and working for myself allow. All I need is a telephone and laptop computer. I can go to the lake for a week and still not miss a beat. In the future, I am looking forward to moving somewhere out in the country and working from there. You are beginning to see the trend of many private investors who either manage their own accounts or those of others and live in places like Jackson Hole or Colorado."

Another key to Adam's success is that he has identified several role models and mentors to pattern himself after. These are prominent traders and individual investors. He has established contact with many of them and now travels the U.S. discussing trading strategies and learning from them. "Even though I work for myself, networking is a big part of what I do. I had the opportunity to finally meet one of my role models recently. A gentleman who is one of the top traders in the world. I told him that I have identified him as a mentor. His help and advice are invaluable." Always pick people who are successful at what you want to do, and try to pattern yourself after them.

The two-year deadline that Adam imposed on himself has passed, and it doesn't look like he is going back to corporate life anytime soon. It looks as if Adam is going to make it. "Of course, there are months when I have my doubts, but the better I do the more confident I grow. I wouldn't have it any other way.

"The best advice I could give anyone starting their career right now would be to choose opportunity over salary. What you learn now will make money in the future." Adam also says, "Identify your purpose in life, and make sure that what you are doing contributes to that purpose."

▪ 14 ▪

Tryouts: Interviews and What Happens Once You Are in the Door

Now that you are in the door, how do you make the most of it? After résumés, interviewing is the second most worn-out topic in career searching. Just like résumés, there are countless books on interviewing. There are also classes and seminars that will help you prepare for your interviews. However, there are always things you can do on your own to practice and improve your presentation skills.

Don't Panic

You may already have an idea of what an interview is like. Some people break out in a cold sweat thinking about it. The truth is, interviews are not that scary. An interview is not intended to be a one-sided interrogation, when the interviewer is waiting for you to make a mistake and discard you in the pile of other hopefuls who answered the third question incorrectly, or had the wrong body language.

Sure, some are like that. But, some interviews are bad for no other reason than because there are jerks in the world. It all has a human element to it. An interview is nothing more than a meeting between two people who are exploring a possible working relationship. After all, sitting across the desk from you is not a company, it's a person.

It's easy to get intimidated in interview situations and let your mind spin out of control. "If I screw up this interview I will never find a job, I will have to move back with my parents. What if I say something stupid?"

The professional world is about relationships and human interaction. This begins with interviews. I don't even like to call them interviews. I call them meetings. An interview implies that a conversation is being controlled by one party. Mr. Employer asks the questions and you will answer and perform. It forces the interviewees to see themselves in a powerless situation. It shouldn't be this way at all. You aren't powerless in an interview, and you aren't there to simply jump through hoops for a potential employer. It's your future and career at stake.

Interview for Experience

Interviewing is like anything else, the more you do it, the better you become. This is why it's important to put yourself in real interview situations as much as possible. It's best not to interview with your top prospects before you have a little experience under your belt. You want to be sharpest for those.

Start slow and build up to your dream prospect. How do you get this type of experience? Line up as many interviews as possible. Talk to anyone who will see you. If you are in school, your career planning department is a great resource to practice interviews. Sign up for everything you can, even if you aren't thrilled about the company or the position. Actually, these offer the best practice of all, because you have nothing to lose. The only way to gain valuable experience is by being in the hot seat.

Practice Under Pressure

Think about an athlete or an actor. You can be the best practice player in the world, or give a brilliant performance in rehearsal, but you only find out if you have what it takes by playing in the game, or when the curtain goes up.

It's the same with interviewing. You may sound fantastic in front of your mirror at home or talking to your dog, but when a crusty-faced, steely-eyed recruiter is asking you why he should hire you, it's easy to crack under the pressure. Not all recruiters are crusty-faced, by the way.

Place yourself in real-life situations where you will be grilled, so you are able to feel the pressure of being asked questions in a live interview setting. If you are exposed to a variety of questions, you will know how to respond when you hear them again.

Being in a real interview situation is also the only way you can learn to take control of the situation and "sell" yourself. You will become smoother and more natural when you give your "pitch" or statement about yourself. Work on making it fresh each time. When the big day comes to interview for your dream job, you won't have any butterflies in your stomach, because you are prepared and know that you can take the heat.

There are certain statements and situations that you will encounter in every interview setting. Know what you will say and how you will respond in the following common situations. You should practice in your mind or out loud.

Practice Greetings and Small Talk. In every interview there will be small talk that goes on when you initially meet someone. This is basic, but you need to practice how you will respond and make a powerful first impression. Introduce yourself with authority and confidence. Have a story handy so you can make small talk and show the person that you are at ease. The worst thing that can happen is to meet someone and for there to be dead silence. Talk about the weather, the building, the traffic, sports, ask if the person has been busy lately, or any type of mindless chitchat to get the conversation going.

Practice Talking About Yourself. You will always be given the opportunity to talk about yourself. "So, tell me about yourself." Or, "Tell me what you are looking to do?" This is your chance to shine. Open-ended questions are the best kind, because you have free reign to tell about your accomplishments. Let the interviewer know what you feel are your best qualities and strengths.

Be prepared to take advantage of this opportunity. Practice what you will say about yourself. Ask yourself, "What do I want the interviewer to know about me?" This can be a concise statement highlighting your background, accomplishments, and best attributes.

Have certain points that you want to make and a logical progression to get to that point: a beginning, middle, and end. But again don't be scripted or robotic. The person you're meeting with will usually take something that he or she finds interesting and ask you to elaborate. Be flexible and go with the flow. After you have made the point, or answered the question, go back and continue where you left off.

Practice Generic Interview Questions. The same type of preparation should go into other standard questions you can expect. You might be asked, "What do you want to do?" "Where do you want to be in five years?" "Why should I hire you?" "What can you do for me or the company?" "What motivates you?" "What has been your biggest challenge?" These are some of the most common questions. Think of the best way to answer these and practice your answers.

Rehearse

Once you have mapped out in your mind what you will say, pretend you are an actor and rehearse. Get in front of a mirror, preferably by yourself, to avoid embarrassing yourself in front of others, and practice what you would say in an interview. This may feel really stupid and awkward at first. However, it's great practice because you get to: A) hear how you sound, and make corrections on wording or inflection; and B) see how you look when you say these things. Have fun with it. Better to look stupid by yourself and learn something, than to blow it in your big meeting. After doing this for a while, you will become polished. When the big moment arrives, your answers will flow.

That's Not How I Sound . . . Is It?

Another trick is to have a friend take you through a mock interview. After you get over feeling self-conscious and stupid in front of each other, it's great way to practice. If at all possible, videotape yourself. This lets you see exactly how you look when you are saying things. Each of us has little nervous habits of which we are oblivious. It could be rocking back and forth in your chair, slouching, or something really obnoxious like playing with your hair or putting your hand in front of your mouth when you speak. By seeing yourself on videotape, you can identify and correct these habits before your big day.

Same thing goes for audiotape. If you can record a practice session, or better yet, a real interview, you can identify where you need to improve the content or delivery of your presentation. It doesn't have to be elaborate. You can use a small microrecorder that you can pick up for thirty bucks at Wal-Mart or Target.

You would be surprised how many people stutter or add "um," "like," and "you know" when they are under pressure. To be blunt, this sounds unprofessional and inarticulate and makes you appear . . . "like," unintelligent, "you know." It can be easily corrected, but only if you know that you do it.

Your Appearance Matters . . . A Lot

For the vast majority of positions, it's understood that a coat and tie, for men, or a suit, for women, is appropriate interview attire. The general rule of thumb is dress conservatively, at least in the beginning. Better safe than sorry. Regardless of your chosen field, it's helpful to be well groomed. It should go without saying but, above all else, look clean. Men, make sure that you shave, comb your hair, and if you are wearing a suit or dress shirt, wear a T-shirt or undershirt. Nothing is worse than "pit rings" when it's hot. Ladies, if you are to dress up, wear hose and stay away from clunky jewelry, tight or revealing clothing, and too much makeup.

Even if you are in a creative field, it's best to dress up. You don't have to wear a suit or a dress, but clean up. To be creative, you must create something. It comes from your mind, not your closet.

Show that you have taken the time to look nice, and take the interview seriously, even if the organization is very casual. First impressions count more than you think.

Craig, a graphic designer, couldn't understand why he didn't get the corporate business he was after. He would show up to pitch clients in jeans, tennis shoes, and a print T-shirt, with his hair in an unkempt ponytail. Craig's reason was, "Hey, people expect the creative to look creative."

"That is a crock" says Kathleen, who owns a Seattle design shop. "What does it mean to look creative? If you are creative, you create something. Your work shows how creative you are, not your hair or your dress."

■ ■ ■

Bruce applied for a job as a film editor. Not only did he show up late and sweaty, but he was wearing a concert T-shirt and smelled like the Marlboro man. On the other hand, Scott interviewed for the same position wearing jeans, a button-down shirt and a sport coat. He even had a ponytail and earring, but at least he looked like someone you would show to a client . . . or your mother.

Be a Chameleon: Adapt to Your Setting

Just as chameleons change color to match their surroundings, salespeople (who are considered lizards by some) are also masters at adapting to their surroundings. You can learn a lot from both the chameleon and the salesperson. Throughout this book, I have talked about being able to identify with the person you are meeting with. If you adapt to your particular interview setting and identify with whom you are meeting, it will improve your rapport and put both you and the interviewer at ease.

Shadow the person you are meeting with. If you walk into a meeting and the interviewer casually says, "Bradley, have a seat on the couch, can I get you something to drink?" (yes, it really happens) don't vapor lock, or act like an excited puppy that peed on the rug. Go with it. The key is to be flexible and follow the verbal and nonverbal cues that people give you. If someone is speaking quickly and is very intense or fast-paced, try to pick up your tempo to match theirs. If he is slow and folksy, don't be so aggressive that you intimidate or annoy him.

This applies for anything, not just interviews. If you are meeting with someone who is obviously very conservative, don't go off the deep end to show her what a liberal free thinker you are. Meet in the middle. Don't confuse this with being a butt smoocher or selling out. All I'm saying is, regardless of your situation, attempt to find some common ground, whether it's interests, mannerisms, or personality.

Interview the Interviewer

Ask questions, and then ask more. Make your interview meetings an interactive experience. Something that impresses interviewers and employers the most is when you ask questions. It shows that you have put thought into the meeting and the company. It says "I'm concerned about my career, where I will be, and the job that I do." After all, it's a learning experience, not an interrogation where you volunteer every bit of information about yourself and get nothing in return. It's an opportunity for you to learn more about the organization, and to see if it meets your needs.

Always go into a meeting with about four or five questions already mapped out. Think carefully about what to ask. The types of questions you ask can offer insight about your abilities. It's your show, too. Ask what the organization's needs are and what the biggest challenges they are experiencing in the marketplace are. Whether you are selling yourself, a product, or an idea, you need to establish what the needs are and adapt your answers to how you can help solve them. Discuss the company's needs, not yours. Do this, and you will learn more about the company than you ever wanted to, and will appear insightful. Then adapt your answers and pitch to meet those needs. Remember, you are a problem solver.

I don't care if you know everything there is to know about this company, you still ask questions. Even if you already know the answer, it can still be a good question. It may confirm what you already know, or give you a different perspective.

An interview is not a stock show or an auction, where you are a piece of meat, to be paraded around and inspected for employers. It's give and take. Interview the interviewer. Use this opportunity to ask questions and see if the company fits your requirements and needs.

Talk to Other Employees

The interviewer or recruiter is trying to sell you on what a great place it is to work. Forget the hard sell; you want the straight scoop. The warts-and-all version of what it's like to be an employee of this organization. How do you find out this information before you start? Ask the people who will be your peers.

Ask the interviewer if he could arrange for you to talk to some current employees. Ask if you can talk to someone who is a rookie or fairly new and a veteran or someone who has been with the company for a while. You want this cross section to get both sides of the story.

The rookie is probably still excited about being there and the newness hasn't worn off. She can tell you what your first few months will be like and what you will be doing at the start. Keep in mind that she may still be "blinded by the light" or learning the ropes herself, and be unable to give you a true reading of how things work around there.

The veteran will be in a better position to tell you the straight scoop. He has seen the good, the bad, and the ugly, and can give you a more balanced viewpoint of what you can expect in your future. However, some veterans may be jaded or bitter. Perhaps he has been passed over for promotions or harbors resentment toward management. Not everyone is that way. But keep it in mind. If you are aware that this attitude exists, you can more easily identify it and make your own informed decision.

When you talk with these people, ask the interviewer if you could speak with them alone or if you could call them later. You don't want their answers to be biased because a manager is sitting next to you.

What You Might Want to Know

What should you know before you accept a position? If you are given the chance to talk with current or former employees, have questions ready. The following are some things that you might consider asking that aren't the typical things you will find in the brochure or that a recruiter is likely to tell you.

Ask what it's really like to work there. Is it a stressful or high-pressure environment? What are the normal hours? Is it expected or required to work weekends or overtime? Is that time compensated for? Is there a specific career path established and how quickly can someone advance on that path? What type of advancement is it? Are you rewarded through title, responsibility, cash, or benefits? Does the company set goals, targets, and quotas for you? How are they established? Do you have a say in setting them or are they set from above? How much paperwork is involved? Is it a political environment? Are you given freedom and autonomy or is management hands-on, keeping an eye on what you do? Are you given the resources you need to do your job properly, or do you have to beg and plead for necessary tools? What is the amount of travel, and how do you live on the road? Do you stay in Motel 6 or Marriott? Will you have client contact? If so, what kind of responsibility do you have? If not, how long before you are dealing with clients? What responsibilities and duties can you expect during your first few months on the job? What is the training program like? How does the company handle vacation or sick leave? What is the chain of command? Is it a bureaucratic organization or is it flat and loose, meaning that you can approach any executive if you have a problem or an idea? Do you work out of your house? Do you share a cube? Is the company supportive of its employees? What is the dress code? Does everyone go out for lunch or do they bring their lunches? Do people rise quickly in the organization? What is the average age of the employees? What are the day-to-day duties? What are the best and worst parts of the job and the company?

> Matt, an American University graduate, learned the hard way. "I love my job. The people are very nice, but they are all my parents' age. The person closest to my age is 39. I have nothing in common with any of them outside of work and, even then, some of them treat me like their son."

You must do a little digging and find things out on your own. Some of these things may sound trivial but they can make your life easy or a living hell.

It Never Looks Like the Picture

Don't buy into the "Oh, we are the best and it's such a wonderful place to work" routine. It may be true, but no company will ever tell you in an interview: "We have a high turnover rate." "We are under investigation by the SEC." "Our new product was not approved by the FDA." "We are losing market share." "Management doesn't support employee contributions." "Our product has a reputation for poor quality." Or, that "you will be away from your family three weeks a month." Just like you aren't going to volunteer that you were on academic probation twice and tend to procrastinate on projects. It's sad to say, but not everyone is completely forthcoming. In your questioning, don't focus only on the rosy side of work. Find out what the downside is, too.

Carrie, a University of Nebraska graduate, helped recruit and interview candidates for her company. Because of the time constraints, a decision had to be made after only one interview. The person who was offered the job had interviewed very well. He was professional, poised, and courteous, and he had the right answers. Carrie says, "A week after we hired him, I regretted it. He was the most obnoxious, childish person I had ever met. In the interview he had acted like a professional, but it was just that, an act. I couldn't tell what he would be like in the short time we had."

■　■　■

Pam, in New York, tells about a friend who asked her to speak with a young man just starting his career, in hopes that Pam could provide a little direction. This guy walks into the office, cocky as hell. He sits down and says, "So, what can you do for me?" This guy expected people to open the palace gates for him and find him a job. No wonder this guy had not found a position. Pam told him that he needed a new attitude and to hit the road. Nobody owes you anything. You don't have to be a wallflower, but have some humility and know that the world is give and take.

Nobody Owes You Anything

Anytime you go into a meeting or interview, know what you want to accomplish and have an agenda or plan. Don't just sit there waiting to be asked questions. You can follow the interviewer's lead, but know what you want to accomplish and convey. Don't expect someone to do anything for you without your bringing something to the table. This applies to interviews, meetings, networking, and business deals.

Be Yourself

It's not that hard. The majority of employers want a real person, not a robot who has memorized the answer to every generic interview question ever printed. Imagine how many times a recruiter or employer has heard an applicant say, "I'm good with people," or "I'm a self-starter." "Blah, Blah, Blah." . . . ZZZ. Hey, wake up! Be original. Don't just give lip service and say what you think an interviewer wants to hear.

You don't have to struggle to give the perfect answer. Often there is not a perfect answer. Do you think everything you say or do is really analyzed in detail? Not at all. Many times your answer doesn't matter, the interviewer just wants to see if you can think on your feet and communicate in a pinch.

Don't be someone else. The best advice is to always be you. If you are fake in an interview and are hired, you either have to really act that way at work and be miserable, or shock your employer when you are nothing like the person he or she interviewed. As you see, it goes both ways. Above all else, make sure that you know who you are getting involved with. This is where you will be spending most of your waking hours; make sure that you will be happy. Ask around. I'm not saying be a skeptic or cynic. But be cautious and make sure that you have done your homework.

Life doesn't always offer generic questions. There are plenty of interview books available that list generic questions and offer appropriate answers. I recommend that you read one. However, there are those employers who may throw you a curve, for no other reason than to see how you handle it.

During my first series of interviews my senior year, I had been exposed to a number of situations and questions. I had practiced my standard pitch statement, and could handle all the common questions. The more I interviewed, the better I became at answering them.

Yet, there was one meeting where I was completely turned upside down.

It was for a sales position. The interviewer and I got along very well. We were talking about the company, sports, school, my background, the standard stuff. Then he asks me, "If you could be any animal, what would you be?" My first thought was, "What the hell does this have to do with my abilities and a job with your company?" But I was in such an analytical, interviewing mode that I began to look for the hidden meaning in this question. I wondered what would be the symbolic meaning in the animal I chose. Should I choose an eagle, to show that I'm a leader? Maybe a tiger, to show that I'm aggressive. This is all happening in a split second, then I realized, the type of animal I chose really didn't matter (unless it was a snake or a weasel). It was how I answered the question and handled myself that was important.

I paused for about ten seconds before saying, "I would be a racehorse." (I had been to the horse races the weekend before and it was the first thing I thought of.) I thought, "Pretty cool, I'm off the hook," when he asked me, "Why?" "Duh." I quickly said something stupid like, "You get to run, you are fed and brushed, everyone pays attention to you, takes your picture, then puts you out to pasture." Not the best response.

In the professional world, you will be thrown curveballs by your boss, clients, and peers. Employers are looking for people who can handle themselves well and think quickly. Life is not like a generic, "Where do you want to be in three years?" interview question.

How Much Will I Make?

Do you talk about money in an interview? Most experts would say no, don't bring it up. Definitely not first thing or even in a first interview. When the time comes to discuss money and compensation, generally you will be given an offer, or asked what salary range you are currently in, or hope to be in.

If possible, avoid being the first to mention a dollar amount. Try to have them toss out a number first. If you are asked what you would expect to make, you might put the ball back in their court by asking, "How much is budgeted for this position?" Let them make the first move. You might have settled for $30,000, when they were going to offer $37,000.

If you are asked to name a figure, shoot high, but not so outrageous that you price yourself out of it. If you say a ridiculous figure, you will eliminate yourself immediately. Do your homework and find out what is the normal range for your industry in a similar position.

Don't name a specific amount either. "I would be happy with $26,500." Talk in generalities and don't sell yourself short. If your target salary is $30,000, say that you are looking to make in the mid to high 30's. Any experienced negotiator knows that you are going to inflate your number, and will most likely offer you something a little lower.

Interviews From Hell and Other Ways People Get Hired

Almost every organization recruits and interviews differently. Some are very hard-nosed and formal, while others are loose, casual, and away from the office. It's tough to know what to expect. The best advice is to be flexible and expect the unexpected. Don't worry about the perfect answer or response, just be natural and you will do the best you can. When you think too hard about what is going on, you make mistakes.

Don't be intimidated. You may be reamed about your grades, degree, school, hometown, or activities. Don't let it get to you. Some intentionally try to intimidate and rattle

> *Some industries and companies have reputations for having a grueling interview process. Among the toughest are investment banks and Wall Street firms. One story from the "interview from hell Hall of Fame" comes from a 4.0 engineering grad. He was interviewing in New York with a very prestigious investment bank. He says, "During the course of my three-hour visit, I met with several different people, each one cockier than the last. I received several condescending remarks about where I graduated from, mostly because it was a large public school. One individual was talking to me regularly and then in the middle of a sentence he would ask me random financial and math questions. "Do you like to ski? My wife and I went skiing in . . . What is the yield on a 30-year bond? Do you like the Knicks? That's great . . . What is 1 percent of a million?" The last guy said that he had an engineering degree, like I did. This jerk then drew a diagram of an elaborate sieve and asked me to explain it to him."*

you to see if you can take the pressure. It's a mind game. Others are just buttheads, pure and simple. Don't let anyone intimidate you. Nobody can make you feel inferior without your permission. That person was once in the same spot you were.

Testing. More and more companies are asking candidates to perform simple quizzes to demonstrate aptitude or skills. This is more common in technical and artistic fields, where proficiency can't always be determined by an interview. Employers often question how much of the work was done by the candidate and what was shared by others in a collaborative project.

To many organizations, how you will fit into its culture is as important as how well you perform your job. More companies are using behavioral testing to determine how you will perform on the job, based on your past performances, while others put you in a realistic situation to find out how you would react or perform. Jim, the presi-

Other interview settings are more open and fun, yet just as challenging. For example, at Microsoft, candidates are placed in an informal setting and asked to solve several practical problems that demonstrate how they think and analyze situations.

Yossi, a Brandeis University grad, tells of his experience at Microsoft. "I was sitting in a large lobby and a woman casually walks up. She has on jeans and introduces herself. We began casually talking about everything except business. She tells me that she recently moved to Washington. She lives far from work, and has quite a commute. It got her to thinking about gas stations. She wondered how many gas stations there were in the United States. She then asks me how I would go about finding that information. I realized that this was just another part of my interview.

"Later I am in a room and another person walks in and we casually begin to talk. He tells me that he has a new puppy. He wants to build a doghouse that would keep the dog warm and dry during the Washington winter. He asks me what my ideas are for building his doghouse, and pulls out markers for me to draw it on the board. The whole process and environment were very unassuming, but incredibly challenging."

■　■　■

Michael was a whiz kid and very talented at what he did, but he was surly, a loner, and he kept his own hours. The small company he worked for let him go because no one could get along with him. Because of this, the president of the company decided that others should be involved in the interview process from then on. This way, those people who might be working with a new person can get a gut feel for the potential employee, and see if it's someone they will be able to work with. It heads off any potential conflicts before they arise.

dent of a Palo Alto high-tech firm, says it's effective because, "People can fake their way through an interview, but they can't fake this."

Making the Most of a Bad Situation: Always Salvage Something

Some interviews inexplicably go down the toilet. There will be interviews when nothing seems to be going properly. When the interviewer is trying to cut the meeting short, or thanks you for coming, shortly after you arrive. Telltale signs that you are going down in flames are phrases such as: "We don't have anything that would match your skills"; "You wouldn't be happy in our environment," or "Thank you for your time." In the event things are going down the toilet, what do you have to lose from trying to learn or gain something from it?

Always try to come out with something positive. There is nothing wrong with asking an interviewer candidly, "You have seen my résumé and you have met with me. Is there anything that you feel I could improve?" Ask what areas they feel you were weakest in. Is it something that you can possibly improve, like your presentation, or is it just a personality issue? It happens. Ask what you did well and what he or she feels are your strengths. You might also ask for a referral or what the interviewer feels you are suited for.

The same applies for when you receive a rejection. If it's a phone call, ask how you can improve, or why you were eliminated. If you receive a rejection letter, it may be worth your while to call the interviewer to ask why you were not chosen, or what you could do better. It might have nothing to do with anything you did. Perhaps another candidate was a better fit or was simply outstanding. Don't let any situation go by, good or bad, without having learned something from it that you can take to the next opportunity. Otherwise, it will have been a total waste.

Follow Up, Follow Up, Follow Up

What sets you apart from the competition and other candidates more than anything else? What one thing makes your name and appearance stick in the minds of people? Oddly enough, it may not be what you do while you are in the interview, it's what you do after the meeting that makes the most difference in whether or not you get the job.

Follow-up begins before you even leave the interview or meeting. You need to take charge and ask when you can expect to hear a response. "We will be in touch" or "You will hear from us" doesn't cut it. You need to take the initiative to set a time frame for getting a response.

If you haven't already been given a time for when you would hear a response, it's not out of line to ask, "When can I expect to hear from you?" If you are given a generic time such as, "We will talk to you soon," take the initiative and offer a specific time. You might counter with, "Can I hear from you next week?" Always get a specific time frame. Take charge and ask if it's all right for you to call in two weeks. You might be subtle by suggesting that a time frame exists. "I will talk to you next week." You want to know when you can expect to hear something, so you aren't left at home, waiting by the phone for an offer that might not come. If the length of time you recommend is too soon or not acceptable, he or she will tell you. Don't settle for a vague answer. Asking for a definite time frame shows employers that you are serious.

If you don't have a response by the time you had discussed with the company, give them a call. Always take it upon yourself to follow up, not just once or twice. Be persistent. You must be proactive and in charge of your career.

Thank-You Letters

Always, write a follow-up letter after an interview or meeting. Regardless, if it was the most successful meeting ever or if it was a complete bust and you would sooner die than work for that company, still follow up with a thank-you letter. You should write a brief note or letter immediately after your meeting. The faster the response, the better.

It doesn't have to be a long drawn-out novel. It can be a short three or four sentence letter which thanks them for their time, emphasizes your interest in working for them, and reminds them of your discussion or a specific topic addressed and when you expect the next contact to be. Here is a sample:

Dear Mr. Gordon:

I would like to thank you for taking time to meet with me today. I enjoyed talking with you and learning more about your company. I am excited by your decision to enter this new market, and feel my experience with bovine growth hormones can be a great asset to you. I look forward to hearing from you next week.

Regards,
Bradley G. Richardson

(I don't really know anything about cows or growth hormones, but I'm willing to learn.)

Do it ASAP. The follow-up letter needs to be done quickly. No later than twenty-four hours after your meeting. Your name needs to come across the interviewer's desk while you are still fresh in his mind. Some people even fax thank-you letters the same day as their meeting. It can be a formal letter or a simple note. Just make sure that it's soon. You want to be remembered.

Prompt follow-up can make all the difference. Recently I met with some gentlemen from the U.K. about a position. I knew that they had scheduled interviews all day long. My meeting was the first of the day, at 8:00 a.m. It went very well, and it was determined that the British gentlemen would contact me later in the week. Knowing that they would be meeting with many other people that day, I had to do something to make them remember me. The interview had taken place in a hotel, so I immediately went to the front desk and left a message with the concierge. In my note, I thanked

Sometimes, follow-through is the difference between whether you get the job or not. Donna is a Hamilton College graduate whose follow-up set her apart from the rest of the crowd. Donna's boss says that she interviewed many bright people—"kids with Ivy League degrees." These kids who had great educations forgot one simple thing. They forgot to follow up professionally. Donna wrote a thank-you letter and indicated how much she wanted to work there. She was prompt and professional. The professionalism and effort in Donna's follow-up showed her boss that she would be equally professional with clients.

the gentlemen for meeting with me and mentioned how much I wanted to be a part of their team. Short, concise, and no more than three sentences. I left my message with the concierge. So, when they came out of their meetings later in the day, my message was waiting. It instantly reminded them of me, and of our meeting that morning. It also showed that I was serious, and if I took my meeting that seriously, I would treat their clients as seriously. They called the next morning. By that afternoon I had a job offer. (I politely turned the offer down after a week of negotiating, due to the extensive travel it required.)

Other Important Tips to Remember

■ Always be on time. Being late to an interview or meeting makes for a lousy first impression. If it's foreseeable and unavoidable, at least call ahead and apologize profusely.

■ Don't make yourself at home in someone's office until you have been invited. This means, don't sit down until he does, don't lean on the furniture or even think about putting your feet on a desk, and don't play with items on the desk.

■ Make sure that you are up on current events—you may be asked about something.

■ Have the title of the latest book you are reading handy (besides a textbook). "What book are you currently reading?" is a good throwaway question interviewers like to ask. It wouldn't kill you to actually be reading one, either.

■ Have an answer to the questions: "What challenges you?" "What is your greatest achievement?" "Give an example of something you have failed at." "Give an example of an obstacle you have overcome." "Why should I hire you?" And "What do you want to do?"

■ Know at least two jokes that you could tell your mother (no OJ jokes; no ethnic, gross, sexual, or religious jokes). I had one moron of an interviewer ask me "Do you have a sense of humor?" To which I said, "I like to think so, but doesn't everyone?" Moron man then says, "Show me you have a sense of humor." Like, I have a Vegas comedy act I'm ready to launch into during my interview, just to prove to this guy I have a sense of humor. Be prepared.

- Have a positive attitude . . . or at least fake it. Employers are attracted to confident people.

- Some interviews are in a formal conference room, while others may take place over casual drinks in a bar or over a meal in a restaurant.

- Don't appear desperate. Make yourself appear in demand and selective.

- Don't give one-word, yes-or-no answers. Elaborate on any answer that you give.

- Have a focus. Act like you know what you want to do with your life, even if you don't have a clue.

- Close by saying how you can benefit the organization and that you want to work there.

- If a company or organization is pressed for time and must fill an immediate need, there may be only one meeting before a decision is made. However, most take several rounds of meetings or phone calls before a decision is made.

■ 15 ■

Selling Your Grades and

Education . . . or Lack Thereof

WANTED: Jeopardy Contestants Only!

NEWS FLASH!!! YOU CAN GET HIRED WITHOUT A 4.0 GPA. I'll repeat that for you. It's possible for you to find a job (other than working at Circle K) and be successful without fantastic grades. You will survive if you do not have a 4.0 GPA, or even a 3.5 or 2.8. I will even go so far as to say, that with certain exceptions, your choice of major is not that important to your career success, either. While that may go against everything that you have heard before and make your parents and professors shriek with horror, it's true. Good grades and the "right" major are always helpful, but not crucial.

Now, before educators and parents begin cursing my name, and thousands of you see this statement as a green light to blow off your studies or forego the accounting degree to write poetry and work in an espresso bar, let me explain something.

I am in *no way* advocating mediocrity or devaluing education and grades. Nor am I saying that your choice of major is irrelevant. If you worked hard and have achieved a top GPA, congratulations. You are lucky enough to have an additional tool in your belt and have one less hurdle to clear.

I feel that your education is vitally important, and crucial to your future success. Note, however, that I said your education, not grades, is what is crucial to your success. There are many bright people who may have less than stellar grades.

Too many people become discouraged by what they hear in the press about what major is in demand, or by talk of needing a certain GPA to be in a specific field. Consequently, they become so intimidated that they fail to even try getting in the door.

Learn How to Learn

When you look back on your college career, what do you think will be the most important thing you should have learned? Sure, knowing South American history and how to tell a stamen from a pistil can be valuable and make for great cocktail conversation, but of all the things you learned, there is one skill more important than anything else: "How to Learn." How to process knowledge, ideas, and concepts. How to make observations or take information, and act upon it to get results. If you are able to do this, you will be in demand, regardless of whether you went to an Ivy League school or Nowhere Junior College.

Harvey MacKay, author of *Swim With the Sharks, Without Being Eaten Alive*, says, "It's not the subjects we study in school that have direct application to our jobs. But much of the learning we do in school is learning to work a system, learning self-discipline, learning what you like to do, learning what you don't like to do, learning what you do well and what you don't do well."

Even Einstein Did Not Make Straight A's

Since we were little kids, our society has attached a numerical value to our learning. Our parents have rewarded us for good grades since day one. We are led to believe that high grades are an indicator of future success and reflect our intelligence. In the majority of cases, this is true; good grades are an accurate reflection of ability and mastery of a subject.

However, at one time or another you, or someone you know, "played the game." Playing the game consists of cramming for a test, memorizing what you have to know, and then regurgitating it back on the exam . . . only to forget it two weeks later. You have the grade in the bag, but you didn't learn anything. People build successful college careers on this method.

Cecil Lytle, provost of the University of California at San Diego, says about playing the game, "At its worst, this false achievement can render standardized tests and grade point averages almost useless in trying to measure intangibles such as the desire and capacity to learn beyond brute memorization."

So, do good grades always indicate how bright a person is, or how she will function on the job? Not always. In the real world, it's the whole package that counts. You could be a top student but have the social skills of a doorknob, or lack common sense.

Great grades are not enough. If you have them, fantastic, they are an additional tool

> *When Ben entered Arizona State University, his father made a bet with him that if he could graduate with a 4.0 GPA, his father would buy him the new car of Ben's choice. Over the next four years, Ben worked hard and devoted all his time to his studies. Ben sacrificed his free time and involvement in other activities in pursuit of this goal. When Ben graduated, he picked up the keys to a new Maxima. What he did not pick up, though, was a job offer. Although Ben had fantastic grades, he neglected the rest of the package. He had no work experience or activities to balance his outstanding academic record. He had not developed other skills that would make him a desirable commodity in addition to his grades. Six months after he graduated, he still had not found a position and has since moved back in with his parents.*

in your repertoire to show to an employer. But don't let it rest with that. Make an effort to become as well-rounded as possible.

This emphasis on numerical success in school has many young adults shell-shocked into believing that they must have top grades and the right major for employers to even look at them. This myth—that companies only want *Jeopardy* contestants—has many grads feeling that they have to settle for something other than what they want. Many are intimidated by what they read in the press or by a company's grade requirements. They fail to even try for a position because they have average grades, or their major is "not in demand." Your major doesn't matter. For example Yossi, from Brandeis, is a history major, yet has worked for both computer-maker NEC and software giant Microsoft.

Good grades, or the reputation of your school, might get you in the door, but beyond that companies are concerned more with how you think than what you learned out of a book.

What if your academic career was less than stellar? There might be a reason why your grades are average (no, partying is not acceptable). Perhaps you worked to put yourself through school and it cut into your study time. You may have been involved in numerous campus and civic activities. If you worked while in school and it cut into your study time, how did you benefit from the trade-off? There can be any number of reasons why people don't have high marks. Don't make excuses. Turn it into a positive. In whatever you do ask yourself, "What did I learn from this activity or experience and how can that knowledge be applied to a job?" Don't let a poor academic record prevent you from entering a particular field or applying for a certain position. Lew Shumaker, manager of college relations for Du Pont, says, "There seems to be little correlation between grades and job performance."

If you can't rely on your academic record, convey your work ethic, your creativity, and your intelligence. Street smarts, hustle, people skills, and common sense are often more valuable than being able to recite textbook material verbatim.

You would be surprised at the number of successful and famous individuals who have endured academic setbacks or failures, and gone on to achieve great things. Peter Jennings, anchor of the *ABC Evening News*, who many say is the most intelligent man in television, did not go to college. Nor did Wayne Huizinga, chairman of the hugely successful Blockbuster Entertainment chain and owner of the Miami Dolphins, baseball's Florida Marlins, and the Florida Panthers of the National Hockey League. Even Bill Gates, chairman and founder of Microsoft, whose software runs on over 90 percent of the world's personal computers, dropped out of Harvard in his sophomore year; he is the richest man in America today. Remember, even physicist and hair styling pioneer Albert Einstein was once rumored to have flunked a math course, and he managed to find steady work. Don't get discouraged. A manager for AT&T says, "Give us someone with cognitive skills and we'll train them to do the rest."

A Clean Slate

The fact is, you start out as a clean sheet of paper and will learn what you need to know on the job. With certain exceptions, such as accounting, engineering, or finance, the specifics of your degree will matter little. You are starting from scratch and are on the same playing field as the competition. This is where that most important skill, the ability to learn, comes in handy.

If a pharmaceutical company was to hire two people at the same time to serve as sales reps, and one person had a 3.2 finance degree and the other was a 2.7 English major, do they start at different pay levels, or does one have more responsibility than the other? Not at all. They start out equally and will be taught what they need to know regarding the industry.

I began my career in the high-tech field of information services, yet my degree was in speech and communication. Every day I dealt with computers, baud rates, lease lines, direct feeds, alliance developers, log-on sequences, royalty rates, and information units. Before I accepted my first position, I didn't know a database from a hole in the head. I had never operated a personal computer in my life, other than typing term papers. But once I started, the company taught me everything I needed to know about the industry and technology. What I didn't learn in a formal training environment, I learned "on the job," and dealing with clients. It wasn't anything specific from my communications degree that helped me adjust quickly to my job. It was the general knowledge and skills that I accumulated in obtaining my degree that helped me to adapt and succeed.

The bottom line regarding the grade myth is: Don't be discouraged from trying for a position or a certain career because of what your grades or major might be. You may have other skills to bring to the position. Remember that employers want someone who is bright, who can take information, observations, and ideas and act on them to get results.

Scott graduated from the University of North Carolina with a degree in advertising. He now works for a medical supply company, selling equipment such as scopes used for knee surgery. He often sits in during surgery and has become very knowledgeable about anatomy, the equipment, and the industry in which he deals. Do you think he learned this in his advertising classes?

■   ■   ■

Look at Liz, who graduated with a political science degree from UCLA. Liz had always had an interest in drawing and painting, and knew that she didn't want to go to law school or pursue a career related to her degree. She decided to take some classes at Parson's School of Design to improve her art technique. She then began to design and hand paint linens. This took off and eventually mushroomed into her own business. Now Liz's company is a multimillion-dollar organization, which designs and sells hand-painted linens to stores such as Neiman Marcus. Her business is a far cry from her political science studies. She was not limited by what her major or degree was.

Should You Go Back to School?

Grad schools are reporting record numbers of applicants. The Bureau of Labor Statistics says that in 1993, 19.5 percent of people ages 22 to 24 were enrolled in graduate school, up from 16.2 percent in 1989.

Has grad school become a shelter from the job market? For some it has. If you are considering postponing your entry into the job market, or leaving a current position to go back to school, you should take a long look at what you hope to gain. More education is always a good

thing. There is absolutely nothing negative about learning, but will an additional degree make you more marketable? Maybe not.

You are too expensive. You may very well price yourself out of the market. Employers are reluctant to pay for more skill than they need. According to *Fortune*, three years ago 80 percent of Citibank's U.S. campus hires were MBAs. This year it was 60 percent. Hoyle Jones, Citibank's director of campus recruiting says, "We have to pay $75,000 or so for an MBA with first-year salary, bonus, and moving expenses. A BA costs half as much." Employers may not be willing to pay the difference when they can get another candidate for less money.

For those who may have seen the *Business Week* article saying that some MBAs are commanding six-figure starting salaries, stop salivating. This is true for only a few hundred lucky people in the country who are the top students, from the top schools, and who generally have several years' practical work experience.

Opportunity costs. After your opportunity costs, you could be in a worse spot than before you went to school. You will be out of the workplace, and without income for at least two or three years. Add to that your living expenses and tuition. To offset these costs and lost income, you are going to have to make far more money than you would have before the degree. Plus, you haven't really escaped the competition or put yourself in a better position to take advantage of the market. You may have changed your skill set, and made yourself more valuable, but you are also much more expensive. Most people who go back to school don't expect to get a graduate degree and be paid the same as an entry-level worker with only an undergraduate degree. You are going to be less willing to start at a lower position to work your way up, because you can't afford it.

Go for a reason. Know why you are going back to school. Go for the education, and how you will benefit from the knowledge in the long term. Don't do it to hide from the job market, or to bump your salary considerably.

JONATHAN ZAGER
News Booker,
the Maury Povich Show
Age: 24

IMAGINE THAT YOU are a Phi Beta Kappa, magna cum laude graduate of Brown University who was honored in business economics. What would this qualify you for? Investment banker or bond trader might come to mind. Instead, Jonathan Zager, who meets the qualifications listed above, coordinates guests for the *Maury Povich Show*.

At Brown, Jonathan was involved with the student television station. "It was very avant garde for a college station. It had its own news and soap opera. I worked my way up through the ranks, from producing to program director and eventually to station manager. I was able to get practical experience in all areas." He also created a news magazine for the U Network, a satellite network that linked various colleges. "I also did a summer internship at ABC, and worked in the summer for my dad, who is in the music and entertainment industry."

Jon was very focused early on. He always knew that, eventually, he wanted to go into television and the media. When it came time for Jon to graduate, he decided to see what companies would approach him because of his economics degree. "I still wanted to be in television, but the networks don't recruit on campus, so I decided to see what is out there."

Because he was an economics major, Jon was courted by the major investment banks. The interview process with the investment banks was grueling. "I had two interviews on campus and then a third in New York for six hours. I received an offer from one of the most prestigious investment banks. It was for a lot of money, but I turned them down. The bad thing about the banks is that they start with 7,000 applicants and when they decide they want someone, they will never leave you alone." Jon did not like the atmosphere of the banking community. "My interviewers were condescending. I felt that it would be like a big fraternity and that I would have to fit into their mold. I just didn't think that it was the environment I wanted to be in."

At the same time, a family friend had contacted Jonathan and asked if he would consider working at BBDO Advertising in New York. This appealed to Jonathan, because he could use his business background and be close to the media, which he loved. "The job offered half the salary that the investment banking job offered, but the status of working for BBDO, which handles such major accounts as Pepsi, Visa, and Federal Express, was worth it.

"I decided that, at this point in my life, I would take the risk and do something that I was really interested in." Jonathan accepted a job as an account executive and was assigned to work on the Diet Pepsi account.

"When I told the banks that I was going to work in advertising, they told me I was throwing my education away. The banks laid it on heavy, trying to get you with the money and the fact that you were picked from 7,000 applicants." Jonathan was focused on his long-term goal and was able to walk away from the money.

At BBDO, Jon gained incredible experience in marketing and brand marketing. "I loved what I did there and I liked advertising." However, after Jon had been at BBDO several months, he received a phone call out of the blue from Diane Rappaport, whom Jonathan had worked for during his summer internship at ABC. She was now at the *Maury Povich Show*, and wanted to see if Jonathan was interested in coming on board. "I went in to meet with Diane and some of the producers. They were telling me about what it was like to work there, and the more they told me, I got a rush. I remembered what it was like in college at the TV station.

"Although advertising is creative, my area was very corporate. I liked mixing business with the creative. However, advertising is a longer, more drawn-out process to see if your work was effective or not. Working in television is great if you have a short attention span. You get immediate gratification and see your results when it's on the air. I like the idea that what I do, day in and day out, can be seen by everyone in the country.

"It was a difficult decision to leave advertising and a future at BBDO, but I told myself, If I have to take a risk I must take it now. It is what I have always wanted to do.

"I never wanted to look back at any opportunities that came my way and say I wish I would have done that. I wonder what would have happened if I had tried. If it didn't work out, I can always go back.

"I didn't burn any bridges. The day I resigned, my boss called me into her office to tell me that I was going to get more responsibility on a new account. She said, We love you here, please stay." Jonathan told her, "I have an opportunity to work on a show, and I have to see if this is what I am meant to do. I agonized about the decision. They understood and told me if I ever wanted to come back, there would be a place.

Jonathan put his suits away in the closet and moved to the *Maury Povich Show*. "My first day there, I was told, You are a self-starter, find something to do. It gave me the opportunity to create a job for myself.

"I started as a news researcher. They had never had a research department before, so it gave me latitude to do what I wanted. I checked the wires and the databases, looking at news stories and helping the producers research guests and show topics."

Along the way, Jonathan learned who would be able to teach him the most about the television business. "I identified certain producers who would help show me how to do things. I had people show me the tricks of the trade about how to produce the show. I recommend that everyone have mentors within the organization to help show you how to do your job.

"I spent that first year researching and learning to book guests. Today I am a news booker. I contact guests and try to book people on the show. I am at a point where my future is wide open. I can go to another show, move to a prime time or morning program, or I can go to business school."

While you may think television is glamorous, the hours certainly aren't. "I work 12-to-14-hour days, but it doesn't seem like it at all. I love it. I never wanted a job or a grind. I always wanted to do something that I loved, and if I got paid at it, great."

His past experience helped him to realize that television is what he loves. "I think the experience is critical. I like working in television more than I did working in advertising, but I never would have known that if I had not worked in advertising. I would not have had the confidence in my decision to go into television had I not been in advertising first."

Jonathan learned that once you leave college you have to really adapt your people skills and how you communicate. "One of the biggest shocks for me was that you are working with people with all different backgrounds. They have a much broader range of experience, so your conversations are very different from in college. You have to deal with so many people who are not like you."

Jonathan Zager passed up easy opportunities to reach for what he really wanted. He was willing to take the risks involved and now is doing something satisfying to him. "I think the biggest mistake young people make is that they are afraid of taking risks. They want to take the straight and narrow path. They settle too easily and don't look at what else is out there for them.

"Be willing to make the sacrifice to do something that you really want to do. Too many people go into a company for all of the wrong reasons, not because it's really what they want to do. They take a job because it's the right thing to do, or it's because it's what their parents are telling them, but they are not going after what they want. If you are going to make a mistake, make it while you are young, before you have many obligations. Don't wake up at 30 and think that you are trapped in a box."

Does Jonathan have any regrets about not taking the money and becoming an investment banker? "I'm much more satisfied.

Besides, I go to a cocktail party and nobody wants to talk to the bankers. They all want to talk about the phone-sex operators I booked on the *Maury Povich Show*."

▪ 16 ▪

Choosing a Company and Environment That Are Right for You

When you determine what company or organization you want to work for, what factors do you consider? If you were to ask most people, money would probably be at the top of the list.

There is much more that makes up your professional life than just a paycheck. You have to be happy and enjoy the environment you work in. Think about it. There are twenty-four hours in a day, at least eight of which are spent sleeping. At the very minimum you will spend another eight hours at your job. This means that, five days a week, at least half of your waking day is spent at work or performing your job. With work taking up so much of your time, you had better like what you do and the people you are around. If you hate getting up in the morning and dragging yourself to work, no amount of money is worth it.

Marriage of Needs

A company has certain needs and expectations from its employees, just as you have certain needs and expectations from a career and a work environment. Many people don't consider their own needs when in an interview or discussing opportunities with an employer. They become intimidated or think that their needs are secondary to the organization's. "I hope I'm what they need." This is the wrong attitude. What do *you* need from a work environment?

A relationship with an employer should be a win-win situation. A marriage of needs, yours and the employers. The company has a need for an ambitious, intelligent worker, and you have the need to eat on a regular basis.

What to Consider

Environment. First of all, what is the environment like? Does it match your personality? Every organization has a distinct personality and character. This is called the corporate culture. This is the pace, style, atmosphere, and attitude of the work environment.

Is it a fast-paced, high-pressure atmosphere with deadlines and many short projects, or is it a slow and calm environment where you may have one project at a time that you are responsible for?

Is it a loose and unstructured environment, where you are given complete responsibility and power to make decisions, or is it a more structured organization providing stability and security?

> Randy, a University of Washington graduate, called his friends from school shortly after beginning his new job as a food broker. "I'm so miserable. I dread getting up in the morning and facing these people at work. I hate them." Randy's business was ultracompetitive. Even within his company, competition was stiff. His coworkers were ten to fifteen years older than him, and many had not gone to college. They saw Randy as the hotshot college kid who thought he knew everything. This wasn't the case at all, but it made Randy's life miserable.

Is it a large company with a household name, or is it a small company where you know everyone and the president knows who you are?

Coworkers. Are your coworkers and peers similar to you? Are they people you wouldn't mind spending eight hours a day with? Do you have anything in common with them?

Can you live with yourself? Do you like and believe in what you will be doing? Is it consistent with your value system? For example,

some people enjoy selling insurance because they feel they are helping people or providing a valuable service.

Is the company or industry reputable or does it have a shady image? Are you comfortable with the people you will be dealing with?

Experience Is Number One

Experience is more important than cash. Early in your career the most important thing you can get from a company or employer is experience. Experience and skills are commodities that you

> *Debra, a Ball State University graduate, is a diabetic. She has experienced first-hand how people in the health care field help others. When Debra was looking for a position, helping others was something important to her. Today, she works for a medical supply company. She is happy because she is helping other people indirectly through the products she sells.*

can take with you, and use through out your entire career.

A nice starting salary is great, no doubt about it. But what are you learning? It may seem like a lot of money now, but will it be in three or four years? If you are paid $30,000 in your first job (good luck) where will you be in three years, both in salary and responsibility? Does your salary start high and then reach a ceiling? Are you paid well, but required to spend two years as an assistant before you are given hands-on experience?

> *Chip, a Clemson graduate, was offered a position with a video game company. The job was to sell video arcade games to malls, Putt-Putt courses, and bars. The job paid well, but the idea of traveling to malls and dealing with arcade owners, or having a professional meeting in a Putt-Putt or a bar, was not the environment that Chip wanted to be in.*
>
> ■ ■ ■
>
> *Sherrie, a University of Virginia graduate, works for a small company. "I get to do everything. I do whatever needs to be done. I was hired for a marketing position, but so far I've been exposed to purchasing, hiring, and product development. I also get to work directly with the president. I don't get paid as much as some of my friends, but I'm not anyone's assistant either."*

A friend who starts out making $18,000 might be at your salary level in two years, but may also have been able to get hands-on experience and responsibility in that time. Meanwhile, you are in the same position, waiting for your chance to get the ball.

Where can you learn the most? The best way to learn is by doing. How much responsibility will you be given? What will you be doing on a day-to-day basis? Will you have one focus or have many responsibilities? Will you be directly responsible for projects or get to participate, or is there a certain time period before you are allowed or qualified to do so?

Choose an organization where you can learn the most. Look for an environment where you can obtain a broad base of skills. Many people are starting their careers with small or medium-sized companies for this reason. In a small or midsized company you may be given more responsibility and exposed to more sides of the business than you would be in a larger organization.

Where do you want to be in the future? Do you have a certain career path with your employer, or is the position a way station that provides you with certain skills that you can transfer to another organization?

Some large companies are fantastic breeding grounds for new professionals, and are known for the phenomenal training they provide. Xerox, Procter & Gamble, and Andersen Consulting are three that come to mind. An organization such as one of these may be a great solution for you. People have the option of making a career with those companies or can use the experience they have gained to move to another company. It's easy for them because the training they have received is highly valued by other companies.

When choosing a company or a place to work, determine what you are going to learn. Weigh your options. Try to determine what environment you will be able to work best in. View it as investing. You might not get a large return today, but it will pay big dividends later in your career. This may be a good opportunity to refer to the lists of likes and dislikes we made earlier.

▪ 17 ▪

Riding the Roller Coaster:

Patience and Persistence

During the Job Search

If you are told no, or someone doesn't return your calls, don't worry about it. It's rarely personal. Keep calling and make sure that your name is in front of the decision-maker, even if it's only by leaving a message. It may be that your contact is genuinely busy and you have been moved to the back burner. That doesn't mean that you are out of the running. On the other hand, he may be seeing if you really want the job.

Be Assertive

Don't take "no" for an answer, or allow yourself to be blown off easily. Some interviewers want to see if you can handle rejection and how tough you are. Don't be belligerent or take it to extremes, but don't let someone bully you either. Some employers have been known to intentionally not return a call because they want to see how badly the person wants the job. Will you call again and again or do you give up easily? The key is to be persistent and tough.

Surround Yourself with Supportive People

Stephanie, a University of Nebraska graduate, was in an interview when, shortly after the interview began, the interviewer said, "I'm sorry, I don't think you have what we are looking for. Thank you for your time." The interviewer stood up to show Stephanie the door, but she wouldn't go. She said "Excuse me, but I think I am exactly what you need. Here is why." She proceeded to tell about her qualifications and why she would be the best person for the job. She wouldn't allow herself to be blown off and shown the door before she was given a chance. She was eventually hired, and later learned that the interviewer was merely seeing if she could be pushed around or discouraged easily. The job called for someone who was assertive, and that little test was a way to weed people out.

Talk to your parents and family about your job search. They can be great for offering encouragement and support, but they won't understand exactly what you are going through.

Surround yourself with a network of people who are going through the same thing that you are. Find a group of friends who are all conducting a job search or changing careers. This offers someone who can empathize with you, give you someone to bitch to, celebrate with, and who can understand the full range of emotions you are experiencing.

It's okay to gripe about things. It can be fun to tell your war stories from interview hell, but don't bitch too much or harp only on the negative. Make yours a supportive group that encourages each other and gives you someone to identify with.

.18.

This Wasn't in the Brochure

> *Tim, a graduate of the University of Kansas, had only one company that he wanted to work for. His "dream" job was to be a sales rep for Procter & Gamble. To Tim, P&G offered everything he wanted. It was a prestigious and respected Fortune 500 firm that paid new recruits very well. To be hired by P&G was to have made it big in your first job. Tim had such tunnel vision that he would not even look at other companies. He would make fun of people who did not want to work for—or worse, couldn't get hired by—a Fortune 500 company.*
>
> *During the interview process, Tim played his cards right. He was a sharp guy and had done his homework. Tim was confident, even cocky, feeling that he would surely get an offer from P&G. So it was no surprise to him when he was offered a position as an account manager in the "paper products" division and his choice of ten cities to be stationed in. Tim had achieved what he set out to do and bragged to his friends about it.*
>
> *Tim believed that being with a prestigious company and having an important title were signs of success. He was well on his way in corporate America. He couldn't wait to begin dealing with important executives and making decisions in a Fortune 500 company.*
>
> *It was only after Tim began his new job that he realized what this prestigious-sounding position meant. The main product that Tim was to sell was toilet paper.*

Some jobs and companies just aren't what they seem. It's easy to be seduced by a fancy title or a prestigious company name. Some people are so in love with the idea of working for a certain company, due to its prestige, that nothing else matters. It's like the guy who shovels elephant poop at the circus. Someone asked him, "Why don't you quit this horrible job?" To which the poop shoveler replied, "And give up show business?" Don't be blinded by appearances.

Everything Has a Price

At placement departments all over the country, the most coveted positions are those with the big-name companies. The Fortune 500, the Big Six, the major technology or engineering firms. People are drawn to them like steel to magnets.

Don't be sucked in by company names or big bucks. Some jobs pay really well for a reason. Sometimes the reason is that the job just sucks. A company might realize that there are some sacrifices an employee will have to make and therefore compensates them extremely well in exchange. Your job may require that you travel extensively. It's not uncommon in some positions to be on the road over 75 percent of the time. Your position may require that you put in incredible hours, or that you move to a horrible location. Look at what price you will have to pay in exchange for an impressive starting salary.

Some large companies are notorious for being sweatshops that churn and burn new recruits. Consulting or accounting firms typically pay very well, but they also require phenomenal time commitments. Many new recruits spend weeks at a time at a client's location for an audit or a project. And during tax season, a new accountant is lucky to see daylight. Even associate attorneys fall victim to this. They are celebrated for being paid upwards of $75,000, but may work 100 hours a week. That doesn't leave a lot of free time to enjoy your money.

> *James, a graduate of the University of Oklahoma, was the first person among his friends to receive a job offer. At the time, being a drug rep was one of the most coveted jobs, because it paid well. James received an offer that was very lucrative. His starting salary was $35,000 a year. His friends were jealous as hell. Later, James learned where the company was moving him to Lawton, Oklahoma. His friends weren't jealous any longer.*
>
> *You may not be familiar with the thriving metropolis of Lawton, a town where the Dairy Queen is one of the nicer restaurants and movies reach town about a month late. This is not the "happening" environment you want to be in if you are 22 years old and single. James made a lot of money that year. He was also bored out of his mind and he quit his job after 14 months, to move to a larger city.*

These companies realize that there are people lining up to work for them who are cheap, eager, and able to work incredible hours because they don't have responsibilities, such as a family. They work new recruits to death, burn them out and send them on their way. This is not always a bad thing, if you are compensated for it and are gaining valuable experience that can be transferred to another company. This is why people line up to work for these companies. Ask yourself if you are willing to pay the dues, and if you really know what to expect.

Unwritten rules. There are also little unwritten rules or things required or expected that aren't exactly advertised to new recruits.

It's not all glamour. Some professions or assignments may not be as glamorous as you might think. People look at the television industry or advertising and think glamour and excitement. Well, both are exciting, but people only see the finished product and don't realize

> *Two weeks after graduating from Arizona State University, Kristie went to work for a major accounting firm. She knew that her job would be demanding, especially during an audit. After only one month on the job she found herself traveling to Ohio, spending fourteen-hour days, including weekends, at a client's location, performing an audit with her boss. She was gone for three weeks at a time, having only her boss, a man in his fifties who constantly patronized her, to talk to. Sadly enough, not until after she had accepted her position did she realize that she was required to travel for these extended periods and work in such isolated conditions. "I didn't ask the right questions before I started. I had no idea it would be like this."*
>
> ■ ■ ■
>
> *Michael, a University of Georgia graduate, started his career with a Big Six accounting firm. In addition to the normal living expenses that one incurs, Michael spent $3,000 per year simply on expenses related to going to work. This firm was very image conscious and new employees were "strongly urged" (i.e., required) to "give face." This meant being visible and portraying the right image. It also meant that employees were prohibited from bringing their lunch or taking public transportation. The additional cost to Michael was over $3,000 per year for lunches and parking, simply to go to work.*

the hours and the work that goes into it. As Jonathan Zager of the *Maury Povich Show* points out, "I think the biggest misconception regarding the television industry is that it's glamorous. It's not very glamorous at all. It's hard work. There are days when I am working 14 hours straight."

On the other hand, something that seems undesirable may prove to have the most opportunity. In my first position, I was assigned to travel to Cleveland, Ohio, not the most glamorous place in the world. It's ugly, it snows, and they have a really bad baseball team. You might think that having a market like Los Angeles would be better. But where my company was concerned, Los Angeles was a poor market. L.A. had a lot of competition and was not a very profitable market, despite its size. My counterparts in L.A. had great tans, but hardly ever hit their targets or received bonuses. Meanwhile, Cleveland, dumpy as it is, was a new market with no competition. I made a ton of money and advanced my career much faster than the people in L.A. So what if I didn't have a tan. Sometimes what seems undesirable or unexciting can hold the most opportunity.

Don't Be Seduced by Titles

Calling someone a "Sanitation Engineer" or a "Horticultural Maintenance Technician" doesn't change the fact that they are still a garbage collector and a lawn mower operator.

Check your ego at the door and don't fall for a meaningless title. Associate, Customer Service Specialist, Account Manager, Account

DON'T BE A SUCKER FOR FANCY TITLES...

SENIOR ASSISTANT MANAGING JUNIOR ACCOUNT EXECUTIVE

FIVE YEARS IN ONE JOB AND *STILL* NO RAISE IN PAY —WHAT A *LOSER!*

MAINTENANCE STAFF

Executive, Vice President—What do they mean? Some companies have twenty-five vice presidents. Just because you have an impressive title doesn't mean that you have an impressive job. In my first job, my title was Account Executive, which is Latin for "sales person." Eventually I became a Senior Account Executive, which is Latin for "sales person who does the same job for the same pay." Titles are bogus.

Titles as pacifiers. Some companies give titles to appease people when a true promotion and additional responsibility are not possible, or instead of a raise. Sometimes a title is nothing more than an empty gesture that means nothing outside that company or your mind. I think, given a choice, money and responsibility are better than a title, at least early in your career. You can't tell the phone company,

"I'm sorry I can't pay my bill this month. I didn't get the raise I wanted, but I got a swell title instead."

The Home Office

A recent trend for many organizations is to have their staffs work out of their homes. With recent advances in technology, primarily faxes, modems, and voice and E-mail, some people rarely go into the main office anymore. Compaq Computer recently had its sales force begin working from home. They go on sales calls as usual and communicate with headquarters through fax, E-mail, or phones. They only come into the office when there is a pressing issue or a meeting.

Pros. Working out of your apartment or home is a mixed blessing. On one hand it's great because you are free to do as you please. There is no commute. You can work in shorts and a T-shirt and there is no one looking over your shoulder. Working out of your home or apartment also allows you to write off a small portion of the expense on your taxes. You are usually compensated by your employer for incidental expenses. It's a great solution for many people who are married or have children at home.

Cons. On the other hand, being your own island can have a host of negatives. It takes a phenomenal amount of self-discipline when you know you don't have to be at the office by 8:00 a.m. You are the only person around. There is no outside motivation or peer pressure to get busy. You must be entirely self-motivated. There is no camaraderie other than with your dog, who keeps lying on your papers. You can never escape the office and go home, because you are already there. It can be messy and take up a whole spare room. You miss out on the buzz, gossip, and face time that goes on back at the main office. The boss can't see that you are working hard or putting in extra hours, so you are judged more on your numbers than work ethic and intangible factors. There is no one to go to lunch with. There is also the danger of putting in too many hours or overworking. I know that sounds strange—you might think it would be easy to eat Doritos and play Sega all day, and while there is that temptation, the opposite is true. About

11:00 p.m. when you have a panic attack about work, it's all too easy to go into the room and work until 1:00 a.m.

Tips for working at home. Working out of your home can be a great solution. I have done both and think it takes a special discipline and person to work at home. You need to ask yourself if it fits in with what you want and how you are most effective.

If you do work out of your home it's important to remember:

- Maintain a presence at the home office. Report in often and let your boss know that you are alive and productive.
- Treat it like an office. Close the door at 6:00 p.m. and don't open it until the next morning.
- Get dressed as you would for work and be consistent with your hours. Treat it like you are at the office, not at home.

Where is my office?

Depending on your chosen profession, chances are pretty high that you won't get an office. At least a real office with walls, a door, and a window. If you do, count your blessings.

Most likely you will be given a cubicle or a desk in an open area. Many companies who have staff that travel a great deal, are out in the field, or rotate schedules are moving toward a trend called the "virtual office." This means virtually no office. Employees share a cubicle and a phone when they are at the main HQ. This must be reserved or checked out like a hotel room. You are given a locker to keep your personal belongings or files in. It's relatively new and the jury is still out on it.

Do Your Homework

Potluck and surprises are great for roommates, dinners, and birthdays, but not where your career is concerned. Before you jump into a new position, take the time to do your homework and know what you are in for, beyond the hard sell recruiters and employers can give you.

.19.

Dealing with Rejection and Failure

*I have not failed 10,000 times, I have successfully found
10,000 ways that will not work.*
—Thomas A. Edison

During your job search process, and even after you have become a
fully functioning professional, you will take some knocks. There will
be times when your ego will be battered and bruised, you will feel that
nobody loves you, or that you're the dumbest person on the planet. You
may hear the word "NO" so often that you begin to think it's your middle name. Now, with that little ray of sunshine, realize this . . . it happens to everyone. Everyone has screwed up, fallen on their butts,
dropped the ball, and been fired, rejected, or told "no" at some point in
their lives.

It's like a rite of passage. You can't really get on with your life unless you have experienced a setback and learned to overcome it. The
way to succeed is through failure, because through failure you gain experience.

It Happens to Everybody

Your job search may be the first time many of you have experienced rejection or major obstacles. There is nothing wrong or unusual about it.
Not everyone can hit a home run at his or her first time at bat. You
aren't alone. Look at the following success stories of people who had a
tough time getting off the ground or who experienced failure in their
lifetimes.

■ Fred Smith, the founder of FedEx, first thought of the idea for
his company while in a college class. He created a business plan for

what would become his overnight-delivery service and turned it in as a term paper for his business class. The professor told him it would never work, and gave his paper a C. Luckily for Fred Smith, and anyone who absolutely has to have a package delivered overnight, he wasn't discouraged by this short-sighted professor.

■ Everyone gets fired, even Lee Iacocca, the former head of Chrysler, who is regarded as one of the most successful and savvy business leaders of our time. Early in his career, Iacocca was canned from Ford, after he had been a driving force in creating the Mustang.

■ Abraham Lincoln was one of the greatest political losers in history before he became president. Until he was voted into the highest office, he had never won an election.

■ Probably the greatest baseball player of all time was also the greatest failure. Babe Ruth was for decades the all-time home run leader, with 714 home runs. Yet, he was also the all-time strikeout leader, with 1,330.

What if the individuals mentioned above had let themselves stay down or had been overcome by their failures?

I love Babe Ruth's example, because it shows that you have to risk failing or striking out to hit the home run. Anything worth having or accomplishing involves risk. Most people can succeed to the extent that they are willing to risk failure.

Don't Be Afraid to Fail

When faced with a difficult task, most people look at all the reasons why it won't work or why it would be difficult, rather than why it can be accomplished. They psych themselves out before they even start.

Last year I heard speaker and author Bryan Tracy talk about why people are afraid to fail. In his speech, he offered one sentence that completely changed the way I approach any challenge. Ask yourself his question, "What one great thing could you achieve if you knew that you could not fail?"

What is the worst thing that can happen? Many people are scared to even try something, for fear of failing or looking stupid.

They don't want to risk rejection or having a door slammed in their faces. If failure or rejection were to happen, what is the absolute worst-case scenario? What is the worst possible thing that could happen if you fail? It can be anything from picking up the phone to call a potential employer, to being aggressive in an interview and asking for what you want. The worst thing that can happen to you is that you will be told "No," or "Get the hell out of my office."

Big deal! You are no worse off than when you walked in the door or picked up the phone. You are back where you started. If you fail, or someone won't talk to you, will you be thrown in jail? Will you be destitute, living on a park bench, talking to pigeons, and drinking a 40-ounce beer from a paper bag? NO! You might get your feelings hurt and your ego bruised, but nothing that is irreparable.

Similarly, don't fear success, either. Some people fail to try, not because they are scared of failing, but because they are afraid that if they succeed there will be more responsibility and pressure to maintain that success. This is a major cop-out. Don't worry about something that hasn't happened yet.

Don't Take It Personally

Sometimes rejection has nothing to do with you. You might be turned down or treated rudely for no other reason than that person woke up on the wrong side of the bed or she hadn't had any coffee yet. You might not get a person's full attention because he had a fight with his spouse and is taking it out on you.

There are so many things that affect an interview or how a candidate is perceived, many of which are completely unrelated to you. I once met with a woman who treated me like dirt because she had a bad Chinese meal for lunch and had an MSG headache. She couldn't remember my name or a damn thing I said. Was it my fault or was it because of anything I had done or could control? No, she was simply in a foul mood. I could have had a license to print money and it wouldn't have mattered. So, don't be overly critical of yourself.

LEARN TO DEAL WITH REJECTION~ *THE EASY WAY TO A THICKER SKIN!*

SLAM SLAM SLAM

GET A HEAD START AT HOME!

How to Get Back on the Horse
(Recovering from Failure)

■ First, you need to try again. Make another attempt or effort as soon as possible. Winners try again and don't stay down.

■ Don't dwell on your failure or setback. Don't have a pity party or feel sorry for yourself. Designate a short time to get over it—like a day—then forget it and move on. Author Tony Campolo says, "As important as your past is, it's not as important as the way you see your future."

■ Don't be embarrassed. Most CEOs and entrepreneurs have failed or been fired at one time or another.

■ Don't panic or blow things out of proportion. What seems like a big deal today, you won't even remember in five years.

Increase Your Odds

It's a numbers game. You will discover in your job search, like in many other things in life, that the more you try, the greater will be your chances for success. It doesn't matter how many times you are told no, you only need to have one employer say yes. You may be rejected thirty times before you get one person to agree to meet with you, and even more before you finally get an offer.

Your chances for success are proportional to the number of attempts you make. Look at sales, for example. You don't make a sale every time you talk to someone. In most organizations, around 30 percent is considered a good closing rate. Which means only one in three people will buy from you.

You can expect even lower numbers in a job search. For a mail-out with follow-up, expect about a 10 percent response rate. This means if you mail résumés to 500 people, you can expect to talk to only 50. Out of that expect a 10 percent jerk factor, meaning right off the top count on at least 10 percent of the people you contact to either hang up or act like jerks. Of the remaining contacts, anywhere from 10 percent to 20 percent may be solid contacts who could lead to something. As you can see, the key is to increase the number of contacts you make. The more chances you give yourself to hear "no," the closer you are to the one "yes" you are looking for.

Failure Is a Learning Process

Look at adversity as a challenge. Try to gain something from every failure or rejection. Use it as a learning process. Analyze why something did not work. Learn what was successful and what was not, and don't repeat what was unsuccessful. If you learn or gain something positive from the experience, it's not a total failure.

Opportunity can come from failure, if we only look for it. Alexander Graham Bell said, "When one door closes, another opens; but we often look so long and so regretfully upon the closed door, that we do not see the ones which open for us." Keep your head up.

AMY FELDMAN
Staff Writer,
Forbes *Magazine*
Age: 29

IF YOU ARE A JOURNALIST, one of the most exciting things has to be when you get your first real byline. People all over the country struggle, sometimes for their whole careers, covering all kinds of random stories, in hopes that one day they can write for a major national magazine. As one of the youngest staff writers at *Forbes* magazine, Amy Feldman, at 29, has reached what would be the high point for many journalists' careers.

While earning her degree in journalism from Northwestern University, Amy knew what she wanted to do and worked to gain experience through several internships with various magazines and newspapers. It was during one of Amy's summer internships that she learned that you don't start at the top in journalism. "Northwestern was known for having a very prestigious internship program that sent students to work on a newspaper over the summers. I thought that I would spend the summer working for the *New York Times* or the *Chicago Tribune*. Instead they sent me to work on the paper in Macon, Georgia. Here I was, this New Yorker in the Deep South. It wasn't where I thought I would begin, but I certainly learned a lot that summer."

After she graduated, Amy worked for a startup magazine called *Inside Chicago*. "A magazine with a staff of two and no budget." From there she moved to another magazine that covered health maintenance organizations. "The magazine went under after a couple of years, so I went back to graduate school to get my degree in international affairs. I thought hard about switching jobs."

Even though she was out of school and had a degree in journalism, she did two more internships. One with Reuters in Jerusalem and another at *Crain's New York Business*. All this time, Amy was gaining more experience and making contacts.

"Networking is important . . . extremely important in journalism. About five years ago I underestimated it, but it's crucial in terms of getting stories in and getting the job. It's truly like six degrees of separation. You call someone, and one person leads to another, that leads to another."

It was through a connection that Amy learned about an opening at *Forbes*. "In magazines, there are more job openings than they originally tell you about or are advertised in the paper. I did not have a business reporting background, mine was more general reporting. I would not have thought about applying to *Forbes*, but a friend of a friend from graduate school was working at *Forbes*."

Amy interviewed, but nothing came of it immediately. Amy recommends "staying in contact with people who are not hiring, because they are usually doing interviews for things that will be coming up six months down the road. Keep your name in front of people and pester them until something comes up. They won't think about it unless you call them." Amy's advice for someone starting their career is to be persistent. "If someone doesn't call you back, call them. It may not mean a thing that they did not call you. They may have lost your résumé and been embarrassed about it. It doesn't mean all of the terrible things that you have in your head when you are doing your first job search."

It was several months before *Forbes* contacted Amy for a second interview and she was offered a job as a reporter. As if she hadn't already been paying her dues in other positions, she now had to pay her dues at *Forbes*. "As a reporter, you double as slave duty and fact checker. You get to spend one week writing under your own name in a national magazine, and one week doing everyone else's work." She did this for three years. Last year Amy was promoted from reporter to staff writer. As a staff writer she writes under her own name all the time.

What is it like being a writer for one of the leading business publications in the world? "There is no typical day. When I'm in the office, I am mostly on the phone, doing interviews, trying to come up with the next story I'm working on. Sometimes I travel. I might do a one-, two-, or three-day interview. I like to talk to everyone in the whole operation, when I am talking with a company."

Amy says that in her business, "It's not how well you interview or your résumé that counts as much as the quality of your work and your practical experience. Everyone asks if you have three to ten clips that they can read."

When Amy finally was out of school, one of the biggest misconceptions she had was how much money you make. "I was a freelancer for a while, and it was much tougher than I thought it would be. I realized that you have to bring in more money to cover expenses, such as health benefits and self-employment tax, than you thought. You think that if I can live off of $14,000 at work, I can live on $14,000 as a freelancer, and it's not true. You need to make about $4,000 more than that to make it even out." (Yes, she really said $14,000.) "Another problem with being a freelancer was that you work alone and are left to your own ideas. At *Forbes* there are plenty of people and energy to feed off of."

According to Amy, journalism is not as glamorous and exciting as you may think. "People don't realize the amount of dues-paying that goes on in this industry. Fact checking is the grunt work and entry-level dues-paying." A major part of Amy's job is to do research for a story. She does this by reading and interviewing on the phone. "My office looks like a fire hazard, with papers and research all over the place."

Another misconception that Amy had: "You don't realize where you are going to move to get a job. My classmates and I thought we would start out as journalists in large cities. I did four different things before making it to *Forbes*." Even so, Amy is still one of the younger staff members at *Forbes*.

When asked if people treat her differently because of her age, she said, "CEOs don't understand how much you really know. They end up telling you more than they need to because they don't feel you understand. This works to my advantage."

Looking back at the road she took to reach her current position, Amy says to remember that you have to make mistakes. "In retrospect, the mistakes I've made don't look as major as I thought they did at the time." Amy tells of a survey of successful CEOs of small companies that found that almost all of them had failed previously. Instead of dropping out because they had screwed up, they took a step back and said, "What can I learn from this?" They used it to start their next company and were successful on their second or third try. Amy says, "It is not the failure that counts, it's how you bounce back from it."

■20■

Job Offers: Picking a Team

Jackpot. You have done everything right and you finally have what you have been waiting for . . . a job offer. No bread lines or soup kitchens for you. No working at Circle K. Forget Mom and Dad's couch. I'm on my own. Hey, the hard part is over, right? Well almost. You still have some things to consider before you sign on the dotted line.

Don't Jump at the First Offer

When you finally do get an offer, it's hard to resist hugging and kissing the person making the offer and screaming, "Thank you. I'm not worthy. I'm not worthy." Once you get the first offer, it's a giant relief because now you know your skills are in demand. The first one is the scariest. Now the key is to show a little patience and carefully evaluate the offer. The ball is in your court and you can call your own shots. While it's exciting, don't be so enthusiastic that you jump at the first offer that comes your way.

Ask for some time. When you receive an offer, ask any question you may have, then ask if you can have some time to think about it. Even if you know it's a slam dunk and the job you want, take a night to sleep on it. Thank the person for the offer and say that you are interested, but you would like a few days to give it proper consideration. Most employers understand and give you the time.

Make your decision in a reasonable amount of time. Generally, several days to a week is an acceptable period. You can't leave an employer waiting for a long time. It isn't fair to the employer. If you don't want the job, the employer is wasting time that could be used talking to someone who might want the job. Be fair and don't hold them up if you aren't truly interested.

Call your board of directors. During the few days you have bought yourself, weigh your options. I know it's exciting, but try to be rational rather than emotional about your decision. Call one of your mentors and ask for her advice. This is helpful because your mentor can look objectively at the position, the company, and the offer and advise you on what to do.

Sometimes you have to say no. You don't want to make the wrong choice or take something just because it's in front of you, when the right one might be around the corner. The scariest thing in the world is to turn down a secure job offer when you don't have another one in hand. I was faced with this shortly before I graduated. The first job offer I received was to sell Russell Stover chocolates. It meant that I would move to Denver, where I didn't know a soul, and work out of my apartment. I was offered a car (a generic four-door) and—here's the clincher—I would make only $17,000 a year, with no commission.

Well, I like to eat chocolates, but the last thing I wanted was to be in a sales job with no commission in a strange town, selling chocolates to little blue-haired ladies in a Hallmark store. I knew that I didn't want the job, but at the time I did not have any other offers. I was scared to death, "What if I don't get anything else? What if the phone doesn't ring? Am I destined to be chocolate boy?"

I finally realized that if I was talented enough to get one offer, I could get others. I just had to wait for the right one. When I called the candy man to tell him that I would not be accepting his offer, I felt as if I had just cut the umbilical cord. I had just passed up a secure paycheck and a car. But an hour later I realized that I would have been miserable. I would have sold out and quit within a year.

Think like a batter waiting for the right pitch. If you swing at anything that comes your way, you will strike out or miss the opportunity to hit the ball. The same thing applies to choosing a career: Don't necessarily swing at the first pitch.

It's the Whole Package

The first thing you want to know when you receive an offer is how much? In reality, it's the only thing you remember sometimes. But remember, there is a whole lot more to a job package than salary. There are many things you need to ask and weigh before accepting a job offer. Sure, salary is important, but so is the insurance package, the expense account, the moving allowances, the travel you will be doing, the opportunity for advancement, the types of clients you will be dealing with, the corporate culture you will be surrounded by, your coworkers. Who your superiors will be. Is the company stable? Will you be bored out of your mind in six months? Do they offer a 401K or matching investments? You need to have all these questions answered before you make the commitment.

Compensation Packages

Beyond the culture and what your activities and responsibilities will be, the compensation package is an area you need to be very clear about. You need to know exactly what is being put on the table as part of your compensation package, besides your salary. The other main areas that comprise a benefits package are insurance, and retirement or investment plans, such as a 401K.

Insurance Benefits. Insurance coverage is a benefit that you don't want to go without. Make sure, before you accept any offer, that health insurance is part of the compensation package. No ifs, ands, or buts. If the position does not offer health insurance benefits, find out how much it will cost to get health insurance and deduct it from the salary before making a decision.

Health insurance packages vary from one organization to another. The coverage and the cost is determined by your company and the package they were able to purchase or sign on with. Typically, larger companies have better plans to choose from and can negotiate cheaper rates for their employees than a smaller company can.

If you are just beginning your career you might not realize how important having insurance benefits is. It's a giant savings. If you get sick and spend one night in the hospital, you could be looking at thousands of dollars in bills. Health insurance is very difficult to obtain on your own. And you'll pay the highest possible premiums, if you can afford it at all—up to several hundred dollars a month. If you have an insurance plan through your employer, the company generally pays most of the premiums for you. Sometimes the company picks up everything and you have coverage at no monthly expense to you. Otherwise, you will only pay part of your premiums, which would be far less than anything you could do on your own. The company has more buying power and clout than you do, so it's able to get a better price. A few employers simply provide you with the opportunity to purchase an insurance package at a group rate they've negotiated, but at your own expense, with no contribution from the company.

While you may not see insurance coverage in dollar terms on your paycheck, it's a valuable benefit, nonetheless.

Retirement Plans. If you work for a medium to large company, you may have an option to participate in a retirement or investment program through the company. Again, you may not see the immediate benefit in your weekly check, but it offers you an investment vehicle that you may not otherwise have. If you have a matching 401K fund (more about them in the money section in Part III), it means that for every dollar you invest, the company matches those funds, either equally or maybe at fifty cents on the dollar. It's like free money and can really add up.

Salary and Bonuses. Salary is pretty self-explanatory. Initially, when you are given an offer, you will be told the straight salary amount before any potential bonuses.

Next, you want to know if there are bonuses tied to exceptional performance. It may not be applicable for your position, but if it is, find out what the criteria are. If possible, set out some guidelines for yourself then. "If I achieve X and Y, I get so much." If you are in sales or a similar position, make sure that you understand the commission structure. Find out how the targets and quotas are structured. This will make a large difference in your pay. It doesn't matter that you have a lucrative commission package if the quotas are unrealistic. Find out how many of the employees actually reach their quotas and whether they just reach or whether they exceed the targets. Is the compensation structured with a ceiling? (Meaning that if you hit or surpass your targets you get a certain amount.) Or is there no cap or ceiling? This means that if you surpass your goals you are paid according to how much you surpass them—performance-based pay.

Company Car. Depending on your position, you may be given a company car or a car allowance. While you don't see a company car in terms of dollars in your paycheck, it can be nice not to have car and insurance payments. A company car can save you about $200 to $400 a month. Remember, though, it's not like you will have a Mustang or a Lexus. They don't call company cars the "company box" for nothing. You may be styling in a generic four-door or a minivan, but hey, you are saving money. It's another valuable component of a compensation package.

These things are crucial for you to know and consider when you receive an offer.

Leave Nothing to Chance

Don't leave anything to chance. Once you accept an offer, it's too late to renegotiate or jockey for additions. Find out all the details before you start. After an offer is made, it's up to you to find out the specifics regarding the insurance package and how much and how often you get paid. Is it every week, biweekly, once a month? How much vacation and sick time do you have? How long before you can take it? In most companies you have to work at least six months to a year before you can take your vacation. When do they want you to start? Who will you report to? Find out everything you might possibly want to know before you make a commitment.

Once you have an offer, you have a little leeway on what you can ask. No one will rescind an offer because you ask probing questions about things that affect your career. Once an offer is made, the company has made an investment. The roles change and you are no longer the seller. The company is trying to sell you on working for them. Nobody has a gun to your head, forcing you to answer. Ask questions until you are satisfied that you are making the right decision.

> *Amy, a University of Tennessee graduate, received an offer and immediately accepted. Two days later she called the employer, expressing doubts. "I think I made a mistake. I don't think I asked for enough money." Sorry, Charley! You should have thought of that beforehand. The time to negotiate or express concerns, doubts, and needs is before you accept. Amy did not get more money, and although she did take the job, her credibility was destroyed before her first day at work.*

Get It in Writing

When you receive an offer and agree on terms, you should always ask for a formal offer letter, if one is not already provided. It's your responsibility to get it in writing.

An offer letter should: A) formally offer you the position; B) state or outline what the position is; C) list the compensation, start date, and any other benefits or arrangements that you negotiated.

You shouldn't feel funny about asking for this. I don't care how nice or honest the person seems, always get it in writing. This is not an unusual request and any employer should gladly provide you with one. It completely covers you in the event that something is not as you were told, or if you show up the first day and there is no position for you. Whatever you do, don't make a move, like tell your old boss to kiss off, or quit your current job, until you have this letter in hand.

There are horror stories of people who, upon receiving a verbal offer, quit their current positions the same day, only to have the verbal offer rescinded or its existence denied. Don't breathe a word to anyone at your current position or stop your career search until you get the formal offer letter in your hot little hands.

Weighing Several Offers

This is a problem you shouldn't mind having. Hopefully, you will have more than one offer on the table. If you are lucky enough to have multiple offers, you have some tough choices ahead of you.

What really counts? Look at what is important to you. Don't think about the cash, for a moment. Out of the two or three offers you have, where do you think you will have the brightest future and opportunity? Where do you want to be three or five years down the road, and which position is most likely to put you there?

Put it to the paper test. Make another list and write down side by side the pros and cons of each position. Putting it on paper may help you make a decision. If they are equally matched and you still don't know which to choose, go with your gut feeling or your first instinct.

Use it to your advantage. Having two options can also give you a small advantage with one of the parties. Anything in demand is always worth more. You might subtly let it be known that you are weighing other options and have another offer on the table. One party may sweeten the pot if they really want you. Be careful, though. You never want to appear arrogant about having another offer. Be very humble and act as if it's a very difficult choice for you to make. Hopefully, one company will raise the stakes and make your choice less difficult.

Negotiating

If you are a brand-new hire, fresh out of school, there is not a great deal that is negotiable for you. It isn't as if you are negotiating a big salary agreement, and perks such as stock options.

In an entry-level position, your salary has been pretty well predetermined and doesn't allow for much swing one way or another. There may be a company policy that dictates what every new hire gets in salary and benefits. In some situations you can possibly negotiate smaller convenience perks.

What you might ask for. If you are relocating to another part of the country, you may be able to get a moving allowance to help you with deposits and moving costs. You can negotiate a car allowance if your job requires you to travel in your own vehicle. You definitely can negotiate time off if you have a wedding or major event that was scheduled before you accepted the offer. If you have these things scheduled or will need time, don't wait until after you start to spring it on an employer. It must be discussed before you start. You can also negotiate time off to move or when your start date will be. You have nothing to lose by asking.

For career changers. If you are changing jobs, you have a little more negotiating clout. To begin with, you can really negotiate salary. Salary is easier to negotiate once you have an established track record and salary history.

Take your time and start high. The biggest lesson about negotiating anything is that your first offer is not the final offer. Don't accept a first offer right off the bat. With salary you start high and end up where you want to be. For example, let's say that you want to make $45,000. The interviewer or company asks what you will take or how much you want to make. You respond by saying $50,000. The company

Jenny, a San Diego State graduate, turned down a lucrative job with an oil company so she could work for a consumer-goods company. She had maintained a good relationship with the recruiter for the oil company and there were no hard feelings about Jenny's decision. Two months after Jenny began, her employer restructured and laid off staff. As happens most of the time with layoffs, the most recent hires were the first to go. Jenny was on the street with two months' severance. She contacted the oil company recruiter and let her know of the situation. Because they had parted on good terms, the oil firm was still interested in Jenny and offered her the original position.

■   ■   ■

Brian, a University of Minnesota graduate, passed up five offers because he didn't think they were exactly what he wanted to do. "They were all entry-level jobs, where you work out in the boonies for a couple of years and then move up," he said. Brian was a job snob. Consequently, a year after he graduated, he is selling skis in a sports store, the same job he had in school. Don't wait for the perfect dream job to bite you on the leg. Get your foot in the door and do whatever it takes, because you will move up.

is willing to pay $45,000, but will offer $40,000. You will counter back and forth, and probably end up splitting the difference at $45,000. Everybody is happy.

Be fair, but always ask. Whether you're negotiating moving expenses for your first position or salary for a career change, don't be greedy or make ultimatums, unless you are willing to walk away. Be reasonable and fair, but always try to better your position. The worst thing that can happen is that they say no. You never know unless you ask.

Declining an Offer

If, after deliberating, you decide that you don't want the position, write a formal letter, thanking the company for the opportunity and declining the position. There is no reason to go into the gory details about why you chose not to take it.

You should also make a phone call to the person you interviewed with, thanking her for the offer. It's more personal and leaves a good impression. If you are declining because you have chosen to work for another organization, it's perfectly acceptable and courteous to say so.

It's tough to swallow your pride, but if at all possible, don't make enemies. It's all expanding your network. Let companies that you interviewed with or were offered positions by know how you are doing and give them progress reports. You never know when you might need them.

Accepting an Offer

You are ready to commit. You have all of your questions answered, you feel good about your decision and you are ready to seal the deal. I mentioned it earlier but it's important to remember, get it in writing before you quit, move, or start buying anything. Once you have the offer letter and are ready, accept both in writing and on the phone.

Call the interviewer or your contact at the company and let her know that you are formally accepting the position, looking forward to working together, and starting on the day you agreed upon. That same day, you should write a formal acceptance letter stating the same thing, and keep a copy for your records.

Be Selective, But Don't Be a Job Snob

Just as you don't want to jump at the first opportunity that comes your way, you don't want to be so selective that you are waiting for the absolute dream job. Unless Ed McMahon pulls up in the van with a check . . . it ain't happening. No one starts out at the top in their dream job. Wait to pick the right opportunity, but remember it's better to get your foot in the door and work your way up, than to do nothing at all.

Should you take anything just to get by? Sure, you have to pay the bills, but have a plan that works toward where you want to be. Victor Lindquist, formerly placement director at Northwestern University, says, "If you are going to take a low-end job to get your feet wet, have a plan. Use it to move yourself up. Have an agenda, do not use it merely as a stopgap measure."

You Aren't Stuck for Life

"Oh my God. What if I make the wrong choice?" If you do, so what? Your first job is not what you will be doing for the rest of your life. Today's college graduates can expect to change careers up to five times and hold 12 to 13 different jobs, according to a research panel sponsored by the U.S. Chamber of Commerce.

You aren't committed for life to the first company you work for. The idea of the organization man or lifetime employment is over, even in Japan. Don't freak out about making the wrong choice. It happens. It's not the end of the world. Make sure that you learn or salvage something from every situation.

■ PART III ■

RUNNING THE RACE:

SUCCEEDING ON THE JOB

▪ 2 1 ▪

Time to Set New Goals

Just because you have reached your goal of finding a job doesn't mean that your days of setting goals are over. Now that you are a fully functioning professional, it's time to set new ones.

Set Your Own Career Path

Begin by looking at where you want to be in your career. Map out a course for your professional development and establish goals that relate to your career. You need to look at your career path.

Ask yourself, "What do I want to accomplish in this position? What do I want to learn from it? Where do I want to be a year from now and three years from now?" If there is not a clear career path established at your company, create one for yourself. Decide where you want to be and what you have to do to get there.

New Short- and Long-term Goals

All of the same goal-setting rules apply. You will still have short- and long-term goals, as well as your minor fires to put out every day. Set quarterly goals for yourself. A quarter, or three months, is not a long time. It's the standard increment of most businesses, also. By breaking up your professional year in this fashion, time will seem to go much faster and you can organize tasks more efficiently.

Establish quarterly goals that relate to advancing your career. This may include meeting certain individuals in the company or industry, adding a certain number of clients or contacts, learning a particular skill, becoming involved in certain groups or committees. Establish tangible goals that will help you acquire the skills necessary to progress on your career path. Each year, evaluate your progress and revise your professional goals accordingly. Always have something to shoot for, whether it's knowledge, a project, a raise, responsibility, or a promotion.

■ 2 2 ■

Getting Up to Speed:

Learning the Ropes

Some people make things happen. Some people watch things happen, and some people say what happened.
—Casey Stengel

In business, as in life, there are people who jump into a new position, take the reins of their careers, and start performing. They make things happen. But for every self-starter, there are those who wait for someone to tell them what to do next. Getting started in a new position is like learning to swim: sometimes you just have to jump into the pool and start flapping your arms to stay afloat.

Every organization has a personality of its own and individual things you must learn: a corporate culture, rules, norms, procedures for how things are done. You will need to learn everything, from how people communicate to where you show up in the morning. Every group is different. To thrive, you have to understand the organization and understand it quickly.

Forget the Red-Carpet Treatment

Many people look forward to their first day at work. It's easy to view it like your first day at school. There are new people to meet, a new desk, new things to do. Everyone will be happy to see you. You are going to do something new and exciting. Everyone will be nice to you and make an effort to meet and welcome you to the new company.

While this fresh-faced enthusiasm is exciting, don't let it burst your bubble when there is not a marching band, cake, and a banner that says "WELCOME." Nope. Not happening. You will be treated nicely and might be taken to lunch by the boss during your first week, but as far as major fanfare, you can forget it.

Some people will make a big deal out of your arrival. There are good people in every organization. They will go out of their way to meet and greet you and make your life easy. Remember these folks when you need someone to help you learn the ropes.

Then there are those who couldn't care less if you were dead or alive.

There are those who might like you better dead, because you are the enemy. They may see you as competition. "Another young punk out to take my job." "Another body to climb over on the way to the top." People who act like this are generally worried about their jobs because they are lazy or not any good. Consequently, they are more concerned with you than themselves.

To others, it's just another day and you are just another face in the hall. They are in their own little world. They don't mean to be rude to you. Actually, they are pleasant people once you get to know them. And you will meet them eventually. However, today they have other things to do which have a higher priority than meeting the new kid. Don't take it personally. While your first day at a new job is a big deal to you, to most everyone else it's just another work day.

The Learning Curve

You won't find everything you need to know in the company handbook (assuming there even is one). There may be a training class or learning period, but these won't give you many real tips on how the organization works. Important details, such as who calls the shots, what the unwritten rules are, and how the corporate politics are played. Who are the people who have the real power and influence in the company? What tips and shortcuts do you really need to do your job effectively? This is information that you must find out on your own.

Whatever your age or position, there is a learning curve anytime you step into a new job. Corporate cultures and norms can change from one group or division to the next. This is a common challenge for anyone throughout his or her career. Anytime you change companies, you will encounter a small learning curve or period when you will become acclimated to the new work environment and the way things are done.

On-the-Job Training

Just when you thought you were ready to stop learning and start doing, guess what. Rarely does anyone go straight from classroom to career without any training. Everybody starts out in the same boat, learning the business.

When you are hired for a new position, you will be given appropriate training so you can perform your specific duties. You will learn about the industry, the company, your clients, and the procedures that are the norm for that organization. Even in specialized fields such as accounting or engineering, where your degree and experience will come into play early, you will still be learning. However, there is an underlying expectation that you are already a fully functional professional who is ready to contribute to the organization.

Companies used to be willing to invest up to a year for an employee to get up to speed. Today, it costs too much. Employers want a return on their investment much sooner and are willing to cut their losses (i.e., cut deadweight employees who don't get it) much earlier than in the past.

In the professional world, unlike in school, chances are nil that you are going to be assigned a counselor or a professor to guide you. It's up to you to learn the ropes.

The great thing about the real world is that you really call your own shots. It's entirely up to you to make your mark on an organization. Unlike in school, you are not given a syllabus and told what to do and what the requirements are to succeed in this job. You are the master of your own destiny.

Rarely does someone hit the ground running. Everyone is taught something. It's like when you were a freshman or the new kid in town. You felt your way around for a little bit and learned where things were, how things really got done.

Training Programs

Every organization handles its training of new employees differently, so it's difficult to know what to expect. Some may have formal training programs, which range from several weeks up to a year. Others are a loose hodgepodge of material that you learn on the fly or whenever the need comes up. There is no standard.

Some more formal training programs try to give you a crash course of general material, an overview. You may fly to headquarters for two weeks of training, like Arthur Andersen's recruits. One new employee, who works for a large insurance company in California, spent two weeks in Boston and New York training at his company's headquarters.

Some companies formalize their training into programs that can last from several weeks up to two years. Companies like Electronic Data Systems (EDS) incorporate formal classroom training and partnering with executives and staff members, with practical hands-on experience with a real client.

EDS offers a two-year training program that has the new employee spend the first six months learning the organization and becoming familiar with a client. The next phase is a ten-week formal classroom experience, to be followed by more hands-on experience serving an actual customer.

Others, small companies in particular, may have a training class on site, which is taught by a facilitator or staff members. This classroom experience may be combined with in-the-field or on-the-job training, with a staff member to aid you.

Use the programs for everything that they have to offer. Get the most out of them. Remember that whatever training method your organization uses or even if there is not an organized training program, you should always augment your learning with your own research and development.

We Aren't Expecting Much in the Beginning

Yeah, right. Speed is the key. You need to learn the corporate culture as quickly as you possibly can. You will be given some slack for being the new kid on the block, but it's a short warm-up period. If management says, "We aren't expecting any real results for six months," don't believe it. You had better be in gear and kicking butt after month four. Make your time frame shorter than what you are told. With bosses and clients, always deliver the goods earlier than they expect.

Hitch Your Wagon to a Star

The best way to learn is by doing. The next best thing is to watch those who have mastered it or who excel. Find a mentor. Ask who is the sharpest person in the organization. Whom can you learn the most from? Who is the most respected? Who is good at what they do? Ask management and peers who they feel you could learn the most from being around. Find this person and hitch your wagon to a star! Shadow someone who is a top performer and going places. There are two reasons for doing this. One is that you want to learn from the best. If your role model is doing well and is respected by peers and management, he or she must be doing something right. The other reason is that you want to align yourself with this person. You want to be near winners and people who are successful and doing well, because it rubs off on you. You become grouped in that category by association. If that person's career takes off, you might go along for the ride.

You Are Known by the Company You Keep

Watch who you are seen with and associate with. You have heard the phrase "birds of a feather flock together." Management often buys this. Don't hang out with "bad seeds" or you will be identified as one, whatever your behavior. You gain the reputation of those you are surrounded by. It may sound harsh, but try to have nothing to do with them, even if they are the most fun people in the world.

How to find out who the stars are. Watch for who is actually listened to and whose opinions are valued at meetings. Who do people ignore? Who do management and peers speak well of? Who is full of hot air and who is telling the truth? You can find the answers to many of these questions by watching people at meetings and observing how management treats them. Are they truly listened to? Are they cut off or not taken seriously by managers? An employee's treatment by her manager often sets the tone for her treatment by her peers. If a boss constantly interrupts or contradicts a certain person, yet listens patiently and attentively to someone else, you can easily spot who ranks where on the totem pole.

Notice when everyone is trying to talk at once during a meeting. They might be screaming, or showing off somehow, trying desperately to make their point and be noticed. There is usually one person who has remained very quiet, listening and observing what has been going on while every-

Geena was close to a coworker who was an up-and-comer. This person had helped Geena learn the ropes early. When the coworker was promoted to head a new division, she asked Geena to join her in the new area.

■ ■ ■

Mark, a new recruit, was very eager and likable. He became friends with David, who was the worst-performing employee in the company. David had a reputation for being crude and lazy and the only reason he had not been fired yet was because he had been a college roommate of the vice president's. Everyone liked David, but no one respected him. Mark began spending more time with David around the office. They would also socialize outside the office on occasion. Although Mark began as a good employee and had done nothing to prove otherwise, he was looked down on for his judgment in who he chose to be around and was thought to share David's attitudes. Mark was branded a lazy "partyer" and his career hit a dead end with that company.

one else is posing for the boss. When this person finally does speak, everyone else shuts up, leans forward, and listens. This person has some obvious swing and knows what he or she is talking about. The person who is respected is listened to not because they are loud and boisterous. Instead, this person is respected and listened to by virtue of what he or she says. These are the people you want to learn from. Remember, the best leaders and managers are fantastic listeners.

Little Victories

You have to walk before you can run, so try to find projects that you can succeed at quickly. Choose projects that are fairly easy and visible. Look for little victories at first. Sure, you are eager to get in there and show management what you've got, but make sure that the first thing your employer sees is a success. Establish a successful track record early. Work your way up to a big project. This system will give you a winning image with management and give you the self-confidence you need to handle the bigger tasks.

Ask Questions

Make "why" and "how" the most common words in your vocabulary. Be inquisitive and curious. Try to learn everything you can about all sides of the business. Develop an understanding of how the whole organization works, not just your department. Ask people all over the company what they do. By understanding all sides of the business you know what the other hand is doing, and know exactly how the pieces of the organization fit together.

Why. Don't just learn how to do something, learn why you do something! Ask why a task is done a certain way, or why the company has a particular policy. It's not enough to know how you do something. To improve, you must know why it's important. It gives you a complete understanding. If someone says, "because" or "we have always done it this way," these are not acceptable answers. Ask someone else.

Be teachable. There is no shame in saying, "I don't know, but I can find out," or "I will learn it." If someone acts perturbed, don't worry about it. Avoid having someone do something for you when you can take the extra five minutes to learn how to do it yourself. You may have heard the phrase "Give a man a fish, he eats for a day. Teach him to fish and he eats for a lifetime."

You aren't expected to know everything at first. You are the rookie. People know that you will have questions, and they should be willing to help you at first. However, when someone tells you something, make sure you get it. Don't go back to the same person repeatedly for answers. He is trying to get some work done.

Don't be afraid or too proud to ask for help. How dumb will you look when you had the resources all around you, but dropped the ball because you were too afraid of looking stupid?

There are no stupid questions. Find out from a veteran, or someone who knows, the right way to do something. It will save you time, embarrassment, and extra work.

Learn by osmosis. Learning a corporate culture and norms is like learning a language. To really understand it, you must be around it all the time. Become a human sponge and observe the goings-on of the office and absorb all the information you can. Things you want to watch out for or learn about include the following topics.

CORPORATE CULTURE

LOOK AT HOW the company views certain things like money and equipment. Is it a frugal company that squeezes a buck so tight that George Washington's eyes pop, or do they throw caution to the wind and spare no expense for travel or equipment? Is it a conservative company that does not like a lot of risk or sticks with what it knows, or is it

Adrienne had recently been promoted to financial planner in her company. She was nervous because she didn't know that much about financial planning, yet her management felt she was up to the challenge. In her first few days, she ran across a financial term that was new to her, but obvious to her supervisors, who were well versed in the terminology. Risking embarrassment and possibly looking incompetent in front of her new coworkers and management, she boldly asked what the term meant. Sure, some people had to pick up their jaws off the floor. But they quickly realized that it was in their best interests to take the time to bring Adrienne up to speed and to show patience. Because they helped her understand rather than humiliating her, Adrienne was able to pick up the unfamiliar material quickly and perform her duties. She did not hold it in or pretend that she understood what the term meant. Imagine her embarrassment if she screwed up the project by pretending that she understood just because she didn't want to look stupid.

an organization that is aggressive and looking to expand and take chances?

How Decisions Are Made and How People Communicate

Does the organization communicate with formal meetings or are most things accomplished by water-cooler meetings or hallway gatherings? Look at old memos, proposals, letters, and contracts. Learn how the company communicates and what is considered normal. Ask veterans if you can sit in with them while they make phone calls or attend a meeting. Watch them often during the day and see what they do, and how they spend their time. Listen to them on the phone and see how they treat customers. Learn what the normal procedure is for requisitioning materials or placing orders. Ask to see a contract or order and learn how it's produced. Do you have authority to make decisions on your own, or must you check with a supervisor and seek approval?

What is the Image Around the Office?

How do people dress around the office? Is the attire very dressy? Do you wear a suit every day? Can you grunge most days and dress up when clients come in? Are you secretly judged and viewed by your coworkers as a clotheshorse, or does it not matter if they see the same tie or blouse once each week?

Gary was in a new position, with normal working hours of 8:00 a.m. to 5:00 p.m. He was expected to put in a normal eight-hour working day, yet he was more accustomed to vampire hours. He had previously worked at night, in an environment that allowed for people to come and go when they pleased. As long as they got the job done, it didn't matter. Gary arrived between 9:00 a.m. and 10:00 a.m., depending on how many cups of coffee he had had. He might bail out of the office around 4:00 p.m. after three or four smoke breaks during the day. His erratic work habits became a morale problem for other employees. They felt that if Gary was coming in when he wanted, why couldn't they? He was repeatedly warned until, finally, the boss determined that Gary simply was a night owl who had better look elsewhere for a job.

How is Time Valued?

Time really is money and organizations spend it in different ways. Some expect you to account for every moment. Advertising agencies, law firms, and some other types of businesses bill clients at an hourly rate for your time. Others may allow you to come and go as you please, as long as the job gets done. Results are what matter, not the clock. Look around the company and follow other people's leads. Do people work weekends? It may not be required, but is it expected? Does everyone clear out around 5:30, or do they leave when the boss leaves at 6:45? Do people take a late or early lunch? Do they come in early and leave early? Find out what the patterns are and what is expected. Some companies have an unspoken rule that no one leaves until 6:15 p.m. Regardless, always be the first person in the office, and don't be the first to leave. Everyone always notices when you come in late and when you leave early.

On the other hand there is the person who wears his or her hours like a badge of honor. If you are spending that much time at the office, ask yourself, "Am I really accomplishing something?" Are there ways that you can be more efficient?

> *Pat would arrive at 8:00 a.m. and not leave the office until 8:00 p.m. every night, long after everyone else went home at 5:30 p.m. Was Pat a devoted employee, a super worker? Not quite.*
>
> *Pat wasted so much time during the day socializing with everybody around the office and talking to friends on the phone that she had to stay late just to catch up on her normal work.*

It's What You Do with Your Time That Counts

Being a valued employee is not about how much time you put in. It's about results and the bottom line. Quality not quantity. During his prime, tennis champion Jimmy Connors was notorious for only practicing for an hour and a half at a time. His rivals would spend four to six hours on the practice court. Yet in that 90 minutes Connors gave it his undivided 110 percent attention. He put everything he had into a concentrated amount of time. He didn't need to spend four hours on court, because he was focused and got the job done in a short, intense period.

Separate the Wheat From the Chaff

Learn what is really important. You will have a lot of fluff sent your way. Determine what is critical and what is not. Einstein could not remember his own phone number. His feeling was, why waste time filling his brain with something he could look up in a book? I recommend knowing your phone number, but the point is: Don't waste time and effort on what is not important. Working hard is one thing. Working smart is another.

During your training, management will try to teach you everything imaginable. Some of it's useless BS that is taught to every recruiting class. You might not use that information for a long time, if ever. Ask a veteran what you really need to know versus what is just policy fluff. Realize that you will not retain everything, so don't get discouraged or overwhelmed. Find out what the most important things you need to know to get up to speed are.

Make Yourself Valuable

You know what your skills are. Seek and create opportunities that let you use them. Discover what your employer's biggest problems are, and make yourself part of the solution. Don't just identify a problem. Come up with a solution and do something about it. Never bitch about a situation if you are unwilling to do something about it. Make yourself valuable by using your skills to solve specific problems and fill existing needs

Expect the Unexpected

The business world is filled with ambiguity. Things aren't as black and white as when you were in school. You need to roll with the punches and expect change. Clients and bosses are fickle creatures. They can change their minds in an instant. Plans and instructions can change like the wind, so be prepared and learn to adapt quickly to new situations. The more flexible you are, the better. You need to be able to deal with change and ambiguous situations or directions.

You Are Expected to Be the Rookie

While you want to make your mark as a professional and show that you can do anything, step back for minute and allow your coworkers to get used to you. Acting like you know everything (even if you do), or showing someone up, is a great way to alienate peers in the first few weeks.

Office Politics

Love it or hate it, politics happen. You can't escape it so you might as well deal with it. There is no organization on the planet where politics are not played. If there are two or more people in an organization, politics will occur. What do I mean by politics?

Politics has a nasty reputation. The mention of the word conjures up images of a snakelike coworker plotting your demise, or an eager-to-please suck-up. Sure it happens, but politics don't have to be negative.

It's simple persuasion. Politics is using persuasion as a way of getting things resolved. Management guru (What does it take to reach guru status?) Tom Peters says that the best leaders spend day and night massaging relationships and egos (read politics). No matter how you view it—good, bad, or indifferent—politics is a necessary part of business and life.

It's all about relationships and getting along with other people. Whether in networking or dealing with a client, peer, or boss, how you treat other people will determine how far you go in your career. Politics involves everyone, not just your peers and your boss, but the people below you, and the support staff as well.

Don was a little too eager in his first position. Two weeks into his training as a sales rep, he was assigned a territory away from where his training was taking place. One morning, he skipped training and did not show up at the office until after lunch. When asked where he was, he replied, "I was on sales calls by myself." He had decided himself that he needed a little more practice, so he went out to make sales calls in someone else's territory while he was still being trained. Don thought he was taking charge and showing initiative, but instead he upset the person whose territory he was moving in on. Management was mad at him for going on unauthorized client meetings after only two weeks training and for misrepresenting the company with his limited knowledge. Not good. Don had already made one enemy, and was on thin ice with management. Our golden boy Don just didn't understand that there was a certain way of doing things at this company. A few weeks later Don took a phone call for a coworker who was out of the office. It was a potential client who had been negotiating with Don's coworker for a long time. Wanting to get back into good graces, Don thought that he would show everyone what a fantastic sales person he was, and decided to close the sale for

(continued from previous page)

his coworker. Consequently, he quoted the prospect a price of $1,000. The client instantly said "yes," and asked Don to put the paperwork through immediately. When Don's coworker returned, he discovered not only that Don had taken his client and tried to show him up, but that Don had sold for $1,000 a product that was worth close to $50,000. After the shafted coworker was restrained and his hands were removed from Don's throat, Don was promptly shown the door and given directions to the nearest unemployment office.

■ ■ ■

Lisa tells about the CEO of her company, a very high-profile and prominent businessman, who had a reputation for being very demanding and abrasive. After learning that the CEO had a degree in poetry, which happened to be her major, she struck up a conversation with him in the hall one day. To her surprise, the CEO was delightful and actually recited a piece of poetry in the hallway. From that moment on, Lisa had a connection with the CEO that no one else shared. She used it to her advantage, by maintaining constant contact and a high profile with the CEO. The bottom line is: treat people like people.

It's not a "butt-kissing" contest. Successful office politics does not mean telling people what they want to hear. It's not being ingratiating or disingenuous (a.k.a. FAKE). Successful politics is telling the truth and instilling trust. Former British Prime Minister Margaret Thatcher said, "All power is trust." Why do people participate in office politics? To gain power. To persuade someone or to gain favor from them. To get power and respect, tell the truth.

Don't say something for the sake of saying it. "Oh boss, great tie. I love the outfit. Have you lost weight? Are you working out? You look great. I think that is a swell idea." Sharp people read this like yesterday's news. Being a butt kisser gets you nowhere in the long term. Remember the kid in school who was a tattletale? Sure, he got you in trouble and was so smug, thinking that the teacher loved him. Yet, the teacher was really thinking, "What a little snitch," and he was still soundly beaten up after school. The same thing happens in the professional world. People can tell when they need boots to wade through insincere BS.

Find something in common. Winning the game of office politics means finding something in common with another person. Something you can identify with. It's about learning which buttons to push on people. That does not mean being manipulative. Some people go overboard and they usually sound false or insincere. The key is to identify with someone. If they like movies, talk movies. If they love sports and you don't know a thing about it, read the sports section and learn about their favorite team. Look on their walls for clues: books, pictures, knickknacks, trophies, or awards.

How to Recognize a Few
Select Political Maneuvers

■ Watch out for the "Good Buddy" or fair-weather friend. This weasel will be your best friend to your face and then trash you when you aren't around.

■ The fence-sitter doesn't have a solid opinion of his own. This weasel will side with whoever is good for him at that moment.

■ Watch out for anyone who criticizes you in front of superiors, or humiliates you in public.

■ Some people play harmless political games like saying anything to be noticed. They will raise their hand and wait to just say "I agree."

■ Some peers will try to climb their way to the top by stepping on others. This is stupid, but it happens.

People will always try to further their own causes, and you would be foolish not to do the same. However, don't step on others to do it.

Don't worry about professional politicians. When you see someone who is obviously "playing the game" and succeeding, it's easy to want to do the same thing or retaliate. Seeing a person advance or make short-term gains can upset you. You may even consider becoming a worm, too. However, don't step on anyone, even if it happens to you. The people you see on the way up are the same ones you see on the way down, and believe me they will remember every little thing that you ever did. Don't burn any bridges. Be firm when you have to be, but don't think that you have to become a cheesy dirt bag to get ahead.

You won't like everyone you work with, and not everyone will like you. Guaranteed. If you can't be everybody's friend, don't worry about it. Learn to deal with many different types of people, and fake it with those you can't stand.

While politics plays an important role in business and can contribute to your success, don't be consumed by it. Don't become more involved with office politics and climbing the ladder than your work. Tom Peters says, "While there is no more important activity than building relationships, there is no more useless activity than worrying over office politics." The people who try to make a career out of politics and playing games are usually found out at some point. They run out of gas and are left to deal with their lack of talent. In the end, they get what is coming to them.

Grapevines and the Rumor Mill

Remember that every organization has a grapevine. The grapevine has value, but don't rely on it. Much of it is inaccurate. Rumors are a way of life. It's up to you to either stop them or make sure that they are accurate, especially if the rumors are about you. It's up to you to set the record straight ASAP.

Find out who controls the grapevine or who is a major information outlet. Know who to get the scoop from and how accurate the information is.

Remember the game where one person begins a message to be repeated by everyone down the line? "Would you like fries with that?" ends up sounding like "My brother's dog is named Matt." Don't mistake rumors for fact. Rumors are sometimes accurate, but they can also be third cousins from the truth.

Some people will add to the rumor mill by spreading truly malicious stuff, or may go so far as to sabotage a project or prevent you from getting information you need.

Obviously, rumors can wreak havoc on your career and damage your professional reputation. Take all steps to protect yourself.

Whoa. Don't get discouraged or think that the world is full of backstabbers. Not everyone is like this. I am merely pointing out how to identify dirty politics so you won't be a victim.

How Peers Will Judge Your Success

Peers will judge you differently if you are successful. Especially if you are successful early in your career. Some will be looking to take you down or discredit your accomplishments. Blow it off. It's caused by jealousy. Would you rather be popular with losers who are more concerned with your career than their own, or keep kicking butt and showing your supervisors you have what it takes? Expect a little rejection from some of your peers if you are good. It's a lot like the idiots in school who would give you a hard time for studying when they were getting smashed and spending their time at the pub. Who was laughing when they were taking Principles of Archery because they needed to boost their GPA? Blow these losers off.

At this point, it's up to you to maintain a level of success by working harder, and making an effort not to alienate your coworkers.

Watch Out for Labels

It's common for people to be labeled: He is a snake; she is a loud-mouth; he is a baby and a whiner—the list goes on. Some labels are good, some are bad. Whatever the case, find out what your label is or how you are perceived around the office. Ask someone you trust. Find out how you are viewed by your peers and by management. If you don't like how you are viewed, or if that perception is not advantageous to your career, work to change it.

SCOTT CHESNEY
Manager for Corporate Outreach, the Buoniconti Fund to Cure Paralysis

Age: 24

ASK SCOTT CHESNEY what a typical day is like for him, and he'll tell you he deals with board members and corporations to help raise money for his organization. He says this very casually, as if it's no big deal, but not only is Scott doing something

---

that affects many people's lives—raising money to find a cure for paralysis—he gets the chance to deal with some of the most powerful and influential men and women in the country. When I spoke with Scott, he was preparing to fly to Oregon to meet with Phil Knight, CEO of Nike, at Nike's world headquarters. He deals with people like Mr. Knight on a regular basis, as well as other board members, such as Blockbuster Entertainment CEO Wayne Huizinga, entertainer Gloria Estefan, NFL Commissioner Paul Tagliabue, and tennis superstar Chris Evert.

Dealing with such powerful and influential characters is not unusual for Scott. At 24, he is one of the most poised and genuine people you would ever want to meet. This is probably one of his greatest assets.

Scott graduated from Seton Hall University in New Jersey in 1992, with a degree in Communication. While at Seton Hall, Scott was involved with the student-run radio station, broadcasting basketball games and news shows. His communications and people skills were honed through this experience. It also provided Scott with exposure to numerous university officials and distinguished alumni. It was through these activities that Scott met his mentor, Mr. Chambers, a very successful businessman and alumnus.

Scott thought he might want to go into public relations to improve his writing skills. Upon graduation, he met with his mentor, who told Scott that he should speak with a friend of the mentor's in Manhattan. That friend happened to be Robert Dilenschneider, the former CEO of Hill and Knowlton, the largest public relations firm in the world, and now the president of his own communications and crisis management firm, called the Dilenschneider Group.

Scott's mentor arranged for an introduction to Mr. Dilenschneider. "I met him with the intention of merely making a contact, and hoping for a little career advice. I was not looking for a job from him. I thought that maybe he could steer me in the right direction, and tell me a little more about public relations," Scott said. The meeting was not supposed to last very long, yet Scott and Mr. Dilenschneider seemed to really connect. "The whole tone of the meeting changed after about an hour. It became an interview. Mr. Dilenschneider said that he was considering creating a new position, and would I be interested if it came about?"

After negotiating back and forth for about two months, Scott received an offer. "I was fortunate enough to have a choice. I had two offers on the table. One near my home in New Jersey, which paid a lot more money, and the Dilenschneider offer for less money, and which required that I commute to New York." Again, Scott consulted his mentor, who told him that, despite the travel and lower pay, he could learn the most and advance his career the fastest by working for Mr. Dilenschneider. "I was starting with the very best."

Scott began as director of research for the firm. He created a whole new department from the ground up. "It was my job to use databases, news clips, and wire services to inform the executives about any news or developments with any of our clients. I was always in the know. Speed was critical. If I was late in letting an executive know about a breaking development, even by a few minutes, that executive couldn't respond to reporters or advise his clients properly." He also helped with publicity and booking clients to appear on television shows. "Two of the most exciting people I met were Lou Holtz of Notre Dame and Magic Johnson."

"My degree was not in public relations and I had never studied it in school. My degree did not matter at all. It was entirely OJT, on the job training. I learned more in eight months at the Dilenschneider Group than I did in four years of college."

Through osmosis and being in the environment, Scott learned about cause-related marketing and the value of information. Scott enjoyed his job. "I was happy and it was challenging, but I asked myself how can I recommend a strategy to a top executive or company if I have never been in that situation? There was not much growth for me in the future. I didn't feel that I was making the difference I could make." After two years at the Dilenschneider Group, Scott found his calling with the Buoniconti Fund to Cure Paralysis.

Marc Buoniconti is the son of former Miami Dolphins football star Nick Buoniconti, and was a college football player. Several years ago, during a game, Marc was injured, leaving him paralyzed from the neck down. Today, there is a program called the Miami Project, which fights to find a cure for paralysis. The Buoniconti Fund is the fund-raising arm for the Miami Project.

Scott Chesney has a special relationship with the Miami Project. In 1985, Scott became paralyzed from the waist down. He has been in a wheelchair since. He now has the opportunity to make a real difference with his work. Helping major corporations was fine, but in the big scheme of things, Scott wanted to make a difference. Not only in his life, but in the lives of others.

Today, Scott is Manager of Corporate Outreach for the Buoniconti Fund, and is responsible for a $30 million capital campaign to build a new facility for the Miami Project. He is using his connections and his experience in cause-related marketing, positioning, and public relations that he gained while at the Dilenschneider Group to raise money for the Miami Project. Scott doesn't get intimidated when talking with board members and representatives of major corporations. "It is just dealing with another person. We are doing this for a good cause. Everyone has a charitable side. That is the side I get to see most often. I just treat them like people."

One of the things Scott has learned along the way is to follow through. "Be focused on what you are doing and stick with a project until it is completed. It is easy to let your mind wander to what is next."

Also, Scott says, "Be happy with what you do. Don't be in a rush to chase the money. Success is not about money, but feeling that you are making a difference and getting noticed. If you work hard, you will be recognized and the money will follow."

The amazing thing about Scott Chesney is his selflessness. He truly believes in what he does, not just because of his own disability, but because he is making a difference in other people's lives. "My goal is to one day see Marc Buoniconti be able to raise a spoon to his own lips and feed himself. Then I will know what I have done has made a difference." This selflessness and commitment is something we all should strive for.

▪23▪

Relationships: Getting Along
in the Real World

There are certain relationships that are unique to the professional world. These relationships are very different from anything you may have experienced before. Dealing with superiors, bosses, coworkers, clients, and subordinates or being a member of a team can pose special challenges that require new skills.

No One Is an Island

In talking with professionals around the country, I've found that in every industry or field success is determined by the level of your people skills. You will be working with people in anything you do. Even if you are in what is thought of as a fairly technical field, or a position that doesn't require much client contact, you will still need people skills to advance.

Competence and special knowledge are necessary, but they can only get you so far. You will have to deal with another person to discuss something with a client, convince the boss of your idea, or give instructions to a staff member. In almost any company, industry, or position, you will deal with people. Even if you think you don't have much interaction with people, you will still have a reporting relationship with a boss. You might have staff members who work for you. If you want to sell a product or service, or convince a client, coworker, or boss of something, you will be interacting with them. Even if you are an entrepreneur working out of your home, you will interact with other people at some time. It all comes back to working with others. Failure to learn how to deal with people in certain situations and roles can lead to conflict, miscommunication, brawls, and missed opportunities and can bring your career to a screeching halt.

HOW TO HANDLE YOUR BOSS

Your Boss Is a Client

View your boss as a customer. Treat your boss as you would a client who is paying for your services. You may not be *directly* in sales or customer service. You might be in television, software, or banking, but you are in sales *indirectly*.

You want a promotion, right? To get your promotion, you are constantly selling yourself to your boss and higher-ups. Do what it takes to make them satisfied customers and in the long run you will benefit.

Respect Your Boss's Time

Managers are often master jugglers. It's not uncommon for them to have many projects at once. They have their own tasks to attend to, in addition to keeping track of you and other staff members. Their work load may prevent them from giving you the attention you need sometimes. When relating something to your boss, spare her the gory details, initially. If it's something where minutia is not important, spare her and get to the point. Don't try to weave a colorful tale when explaining a situation. Get to the point.

If you were to read a business plan, notice that they often come with an executive summary. An executive summary is a brief synopsis of what is in the report. A quick and dirty overview that gives the executive a brief snapshot of the proposal and general understanding of the project. If more details are required, they can be found in the remainder of the plan.

Give your boss the Cliffs Notes version, or an executive summary of a situation. Provide enough detail so she fully understands what you are saying. No need to get bogged down. If she wants more details, she will ask.

Get Your Boss's Attention

Sometimes it's hard to have your boss's undivided attention. Phone calls and interruptions come just as you are going to ask something. Your boss can get distracted easily.

If you have a hard time keeping your boss's attention or he becomes sidetracked easily, get to the point quickly. If you really need to talk to your boss or manager without interruptions, schedule an appointment or recommend a specific time that can be planned. You might also try to meet away from the office, away from distractions. Ask your boss to lunch or save important topics for when you are riding together on an airplane or to a meeting. That way your boss's attention will be focused on you.

Don't Be a Whiner

Inevitably, you will have a bone to pick with your boss. It might be something that your boss or a coworker has done. Perhaps it's a policy or procedure that you think is stupid and should be changed. Whatever it is, you will eventually find something to bitch about.

If you are going to complain or take a problem to your boss, always have a solution in mind. You may have a legitimate beef about something, but simply complaining doesn't help solve it. You might say, "How will my boss know there is a problem if I don't complain?" Fair enough. It's all right to approach your boss with complaints, bitches, moans, etc., but remember that you are paid for solutions.

> Renee, an Emory graduate, had a boss who would always pose a question to someone who came to her with a complaint or concern. "What do you recommend?" "How would you correct it?" She put it back in their court. By asking these questions, Renee's boss could tell if the person had really thought about the issue, or if they were just venting their spleen. If you took a problem to her without thinking it through, she sent you packing.

Don't take a complaint to your boss unless you are prepared to offer a potential solution. Seek the boss's advice but never dump on him without an idea about how to make it better. If you simply complain, you become known as someone who is never content. Become known as a problem solver, not as a whiner.

Certain Types of Bosses

Managers have different types of personalities. Here are a descriptions of a few that you might encounter.

The Bully. This person is on a power trip. He thinks the way to get results is to yell and scream. These types are manipulative and tend to humiliate or intimidate people. They are always right. Get the bully to think that something is his own idea. Don't take his tantrums personally.

The Egomaniac or Ladder Climber. This person has her own agenda. You are only a tool to help her reach that goal. Working for a person like this can be frustrating because she may take credit for your achievements. Play to her ego to get your own way, and document everything that you do.

The Old-School Boss. This person is interested in security. He is often timid and doesn't like change or for anyone to rock the boat. If you are aggressive and ambitious you may be seen as a threat. Treat this person delicately and don't try to confront him. Realize that if you want something done, you have to do it yourself, because he won't go to bat for you or champion your cause.

New Boss. Like you, she is learning the ropes, although she may be a veteran with the company. Be flexible and understanding and adapt if she decides to change something or make her own mark on the division. Let the new boss know what your expectations and goals are, and that you are someone she can depend on. Communication is the key with a new boss.

Be Open to Advice

The job of a manager is to, well, . . . manage. That can mean many things but one of them is to correct your mistakes and help steer you in the right direction. Don't get defensive when you are criticized or someone gives you advice. A self-righteous attitude and fragile ego do not play well with bosses and managers. Instead of flying off the handle when you receive criticism or advice, ask your boss how he would handle a situation. A good manager will tell you this anyway, but if a situation is heated or you feel that you are really getting dumped on, put it in his court. Find out if he has been in similar situations and how he dealt with them.

When Your Boss Is a Bozo

Don't upstage your boss or make her look stupid in public. It diminishes her power and control. If you disagree, pull your boss aside and do it in private. Allow your boss to save face or she will bring you down.

Don't go over your boss's head unless absolutely necessary. You might think that your boss is dumb as dirt and couldn't manage his way out of a wet paper bag. But there is one important detail that you shouldn't forget. Your boss is still ahead of you.

If you absolutely can't get results any other way, or if your boss has completely shut you down, go to someone above him. But be prepared to pay the price. By doing so, you usurp your boss's power and he will retaliate. You may win the battle but you will lose the war. You may get your way on that one decision, but your boss doesn't trust you anymore. You have essentially slapped him in the face. Don't be surprised when you get crappy assignments, are given extra duties, or are looked over or stymied at every turn . . . and that is if things turn out your way.

If you make an end run around your boss and fail, you have severely screwed up. If you go above your boss and that person is not receptive to your idea, or is upset that you have broken the chain of command, you may be thought of as a troublemaker. If you take this chance, make sure that it's something that is worth winning.

Don't point the blame at anyone else, or make excuses. The buck stops with you. Even if it's something that you were not responsible for or if it's out of your area, take care of it. Of course, if it's truly unfair criticism, you do not have to take the blame for something you had nothing to do with.

Your Priorities Aren't the Same

If you have a concern, get it off your chest. Don't let it fester and build up. When you keep something inside, it has a way of becoming blown out of proportion in your mind. Realize that what is a major concern in your work life may be trivial to your boss. Many people feel that the boss is concerned with every minute detail of their careers. Nothing could be further from the truth.

You think that you need new equipment. While it's the most important thing in your professional life at the moment, it's way down on the list of your boss's concerns.

It might have nothing to do with you. Just because the boss has been in a bad mood or has been ignoring you this week does not mean that he is plotting your demise. Your boss could have had a fight with his spouse or a wreck on the way to work. Bosses are human and are entitled to be in a bad mood. You aren't always the cause. Don't flatter yourself. If your boss forgets to say "good morning" to you, don't get your résumé together. If your manager has been spending time in his office with the door closed, it does not always mean that you need to start clearing out your desk. As Freud said, "Sometimes a cigar is a cigar." Don't read too much into things. If you want the straight scoop, ask.

Make Your Boss Look Good

Your job is to make the boss look good and shield her from surprises. Head problems off at the pass. If you know that sales numbers are going to look bad or something will not work, don't wait for it to happen and watch the boss freak out. Soften the blow and prepare her. Keep your boss apprised of what is going on. If you take information to your boss and provide small progress reports, you will prevent her from having to come to you to ask what is going on or to put you on the spot.

When selling a new idea or project to the boss, tell her how it will benefit the company. How it will make the company look good or how it will make the company money. If you take an idea to the boss (unless she is at the top), she is going to take it to her managers. Give your boss any information necessary to sell the idea to people higher in the organization.

It Takes More than Hard Work

The American work ethic—work hard and opportunity will come—is still valuable, but there needs to be an addition. Work hard and use your people skills, and opportunity will come. Just working hard, putting your nose to the grindstone and hoping the boss will notice, doesn't cut it anymore.

In a letter to the editor in *Fortune* magazine, industrial psychologist Michael Mercer commented on how it takes much more than re-

> *Jordan went to work for a software firm. He was a really hard worker. Jordan put in long hours and produced good results. While others were standing around his cubicle visiting or talking about last night's game, Jordan would keep his head down and concentrate on getting his project finished. He didn't socialize around the office or go out of his way to talk to any of the other staff members or managers while he was at work. He thought that the boss would see what a hard worker he was compared to everyone else and he would advance. Jordan got passed up several times for peers who may not have been as talented and definitely weren't as devoted as he was. He couldn't understand why. When this happened, he simply put his nose back to the grindstone and worked harder. Jordan didn't understand that he had to come up for air and deal with other people.*

> ■ ■ ■

> *Caroline was on the partner track in a law firm. She was a great attorney, and a fantastic researcher, but constantly had her nose in a book. Twice she was passed over for partner. The reason . . . she didn't play the game. Caroline didn't display the people skills necessary to bring in new business.*

sults and effort to make it today. "Being highly competent plus fifty cents will only get you a cup of coffee. Being highly competent plus making a superb impression on the people who make or break your career can eventually get you $100,000 annually."

They Have a Career Too

Remember that your boss has a career plan and path just as you do. Your boss is trying to promote himself, just as you are. So don't kid yourself into thinking that he always has your best interest at heart. Most times he does, but remember that he is trying to advance his own career, and has an agenda. Your boss can promote you, recommend you, teach you, look out for you, and generally help catapult your career. But remember that he is trying to advance, just as you are. Don't put all of your career efforts into one person. Spread yourself around the organization and become known. Do things for other people and become known to managers and heads of other departments.

Maintain a healthy bit of skepticism where big promises are concerned. Use the divisor theory. If you are given any grandiose promises, take what is said, divide it, and believe only half.

Being Friends With Your Boss

There is always the possibility of becoming friends with a boss or manager. You will be sharing a great deal of time and it's quite natural for this to happen. You will learn a lot about each other as you work late or travel together. You may even do things socially out of the office. There is nothing wrong with this as long as you remember that he is still your boss and that he has a lot of control over your career. Therefore, don't tell personal secrets or compromising information to your boss. It will undermine your credibility and effectiveness.

Remember this for when you have people under you as well. You can be friends with your subordinates, but it's difficult to yell at a friend if he drops the ball. There are people whom I knew professionally and thought were very competent; yet, after knowing them socially and seeing how they handled something outside the office, I questioned their professional abilities. It's tough to forget those things.

Don't Be a Doormat

> *Jana, a Pepperdine grad, trusted her career to her boss. She was very close to her boss and knew that as her boss rose in the organization, so would she. She bet her whole career on this person, often alienating others and not cultivating relationships in other areas. When her boss received an offer she couldn't refuse from another company, she was out of there. Jana was left with no one to champion her cause. Jana had not done anything on her own to promote or make herself known to management.*
>
> ■ ■ ■
>
> *Nikki, a University of San Diego graduate, worked for a company that was in financial trouble. Her boss said that she would make sure that Nikki would be spared or warned in advance if it looked like she was going to be part of the layoffs. On the day the company announced layoffs, all bets were off. The boss covered her own butt, and Nikki was left to hang out to dry. She never knew anything was coming.*

Earlier we talked about politics. Remember that politics does not mean sucking up to the boss. You will find "yes people" in every organization. They remind me of the little dogs with the bobbing head that you find stuck on the dash of a taxi or low rider.

The world is full of suck-ups who tell people exactly what they want to hear. Some managers love to be surrounded by people who tell them they are right, even if they aren't. A famous movie studio chief once said, "I want everyone to tell me the truth even if it costs you your job." Don't agree just to be agreeable, or because she is the boss. This does you, your boss, and your company a great disservice. If you truly have a better way to do something, or a different opinion, present it. Be frank and direct with people. Don't allow yourself to be walked on.

Tell Your Boss Where You Want to Be

To have a good relationship with a manager or boss, you must communicate what you need and want. I'm not talking about saying what tasks you will and will not do. Tell your boss what you feel is the best way for you to get along and work effectively together. A boss can help your career development, but only if he knows where you want to go. Tell the boss about your career plans, what you would like to accomplish, and what you need to reach those goals. If you need his assistance or help, tell him. Your boss is a resource and is there to help you. It's not an adversarial relationship. You work in tandem. The better you do, the better he looks. It's in his best interest to see that you do well.

Think Like Your Boss

Try to identify with your boss and follow a pattern similar to hers. There is a saying, "If you want to be the CEO, you act like the CEO." This goes for attitude, dress, hours, and work ethic. Don't be a clone, but don't work counter to her either. If the boss arrives at the office at 8:00 a.m. and leaves at 6:00 p.m., you shouldn't show up at 8:30 and leave at 5:30. You'll score points if you always arrive earlier and stay later than your boss. Even if it's just ten minutes, get there before she does.

If your boss is a very people-oriented person and outgoing, don't sit back and be reserved. Use the language and buzzwords that she uses. This way, when you are talking, she can identify more with what you are saying. Find out what buttons to push in her, and what qualities she admires in people. Learn what she values in employees. To find out, ask around or ask your boss directly. She will respect the fact that you are taking an interest in learning what her expectations are. You will also know how you will be judged and you can get on the right track. It's best to ask these types of questions early in your tenure with a new manager or boss. To play the game, you have to first know the rules.

HOW TO HANDLE CLIENTS

You Work for the Client

The key to dealing successfully with clients and customers is quite simple and straightforward, yet takes considerable effort. Whatever your position, you are serving customers. Everyone has customers and clients. If you are in publishing, your client is the author or reader. If you are an accountant, your client is the company you are performing an audit for. If you are an engineer, your client may be the committee you are trying to convince to accept your new design. Both inside and outside the organization, everyone has clients. You think that the boss pays your salary, but it's really the client. Without the clients and customers, everyone would close up shop and go home.

Be a Straight Shooter

The most important rule about having successful client relationships is to tell the truth and treat the client fairly.

Always be up-front with clients. If you have their respect and trust, you more than likely will have their business. If you don't know the answer to something, don't BS your way through it or give false or inaccurate information, only to come back later to correct it. If you don't know right then, say so. "I'm sorry, I don't know, but I will find out the correct answer for you."

Be a straight shooter. Say what you mean and mean what you say. Don't soften the blow. Don't say challenge when you mean problem. You don't fool anybody. The client may not like what you have to say or may even disagree with you, but she will definitely respect you.

Don't be known as someone who rides the fence. Have a position and stick to it.

Do what you say you will. Clients become wary of the "over-promise." Oh, sure, we can do that. It slices, dices, juliennes, and will get the paper for you if you like, We can get that in pink, yes ma'am. Americans are the most marketing-savvy consumers on the planet. We know when we are being sold to and have become wary of big promises. Motivational and sales guru (there is that guru word again) Zig Zigler (his real name) says to "under-promise, and over-deliver."

Be fair with clients. A relationship with a client or customer is not an adversarial one. You are there to help each other, so strive for a win-win deal, one that both parties are happy with. If you screw someone around or treat them badly once, you get their business that once. But they will remember and you will never do anything with them again. Treat clients as though they are going to be with you for a long time.

Treat clients as people, not as accounts. Don't act as if you are only interested in their money or service. You are dealing with other human beings.

There is no easier sale in the world than repeat business and referrals from happy clients. Your reputation extends far beyond your immediate clients. People are more likely to tell someone about bad service and products than good.

Respect Your Clients' Time

Treat your clients' time as if they are paying for it. Often, they are. Time really is money in some organizations that bill out hourly for their services, such as law firms, advertising agencies, and some accountants or consultants.

Be on time for appointments. If you are going to be late, call ahead. Don't keep a client waiting and thinking you are going to come. Allow them to be productive during the time that you were supposed to be taking. Cater to their schedule.

Be flexible with your schedule. Try to accommodate the clients' schedule if possible. Offer to meet at times or locations that are convenient for them. If you need to meet at their office, go. Offer times such as early breakfast meetings or lunch that can save their time but still give you the opportunity to meet with them and be productive.

Face-to-face meetings are best, when possible, because it's good to see whom you are dealing with. But if something can be handled using technology, fax, phone, FedEx, or any other tool, use it and save their time and yours.

Acknowledge that you respect their time and find it valuable. This will be obvious by your actions, but tell them as well, "I know that you are busy; I'll be brief." Thank clients for their time and let them know that you appreciate it. It's obvious, but people like to be told.

Call people back promptly. No one likes to be left hanging. If you are unable to get back with them, apologize, but don't make excuses. Simply say, "I'm sorry for not being able to get back with you." There is no need to go into details: I was on vacation, my car died, or I got another call. Clients don't need to know it, and you don't want to run the risk of making them feel that something else was more important. It's bad enough that you were late or missed an appointment.

Clients Buy from Those They Like and Trust

It's not always the company that has the best product or price that gets the business. People do business with someone they like and trust.

Don't take anyone's business for granted. Large or small, the customer pays your salary. Without them, you can turn out the lights and go home, because the business, any business, will go under.

Brett, a marketing executive in San Diego, says that he used to deal with a particular supplier who had a good product at a decent price, but the person who had his account was a jerk. "He was undependable and made excuses when shipments were late," said Brett. "He had the attitude that he was the only game in town. We dumped them for another company whose products are more expensive, but they value our business and are a pleasure to deal with."

Clients as Friends

In the course of your professional life, you will have some clients who become your friends. That is a wonderful thing about business. Some people whom I claim today as good friends began as clients or business contacts. This is great. But remember that, as long as they are clients, you still have a professional obligation to them first. They or their company are paying you for a service or product. Because you are friendly with your contact does not mean that they deserve service that is less professional than a client you have met for the first time. This client should receive exceptional service, because if he or she is let down it could affect the friendship. The opposite is also true. If the friendship sours, the business arrangement could be affected.

> *Jeff had a major advertising agency as a client. He became a good friend of his contact, Stacey. Jeff set Stacey up on a date with one of his friends. Stacey and Jeff's friend dated for several months. Their relationship fell apart and ended badly. Stacey felt awkward around Jeff and, as stupid as it was, she held Jeff responsible, since he had introduced the two of them. It greatly affected their professional relationship.*

Similarly, don't date clients. Bad move. What happens when you break up with them? What if you ask a client out and are turned down? Imagine the embarrassment if you had been intimate with them and it didn't work out. How could you face this person professionally, with them knowing that you snore or drool in your sleep?

Follow the Client's Lead

I've mentioned it several times already, but it's worth repeating: Identify with your clients. Look around their offices for pictures and clues. Ask about their hobbies and interests. Also, follow their lead on how to act or pace yourself when meeting with them. If they are fast-paced and want to talk business, cut to the chase. Don't try to chitchat about the weather or the lovely picture of their dog. Conversely, if someone is taking his time and leaning back in his seat, do the same.

I made the mistake of not reading the other person when I met with an executive at the headquarters of Major League Baseball. The walls are lined with the most fantastic photographs of players throughout history. When I entered my contact's office, he, too, had incredible pictures and sports memorabilia, the most unique being a team photo from the national champion UCLA Bruins basketball team from the 1960s coached by the legendary John Wooden. Apparently, my contact had played on that team. The gentleman seemed very brusque and did not smile much. I could tell walking back to his office that he was all business. Nonetheless, I commented on how I loved the photographs, especially the UCLA photo. He looked at me and said "That is a basketball picture. Did you know you are in the baseball office?" I quickly concluded that it was best to forget the small talk and get down to business.

Focus on the Client's Needs . . . Not Yours

Don't tell the customer about your problems or remind them of the effort you are making. Good service should be expected and given freely.

Don't Make Excuses

If you have an irate customer, acknowledge that there is a problem. Apologize, don't make excuses or tell the customer about why you can't do something. Clients have problems and concerns of their own; don't burden them with yours. Offer solutions. Kill

Sam, a 24-year-old computer salesperson, sold over $100,000 worth of computers in one sale, the biggest order of his life. The client wanted delivery on a Friday. Sam had already scheduled that day off so he could play golf, but arranged to postpone his game until later that afternoon.

On the delivery day, he showed up at the client's office in his golf gear, ready to beat a path to the course afterwards. Sam made a big production out of telling the client that this was normally his day off, but that he had come in just to do this. The client thought, "I just gave you over $100,000, from which you received a nice commission, and you are making me feel guilty because you have to deliver the equipment." Sam should never have opened his mouth. The client did not need to know that he had come in on his day off.

A week later, the client decided to return one item so she could get an upgraded model. Sam wanted to charge a $50 restock fee. The fee was nothing compared to what the client had spent and would have spent in the future. However, Sam told the client that he could not forget that charge because it would come right out of his own pocket. On a $100,000 order, the boss would have blown it off to keep a customer happy, and Sam would not have been out any money. Instead, Sam lost all future business with this client because of his actions. He should never have told the client that it affected him personally. Don't nickel and dime people. You want them to come back.

them with kindness, but don't patronize or trivialize their concerns. Don't ever tell a client to calm down. Even if he is acting like a child, don't treat him like one.

Don't pass the buck or make excuses. Ritz Carlton Hotels has a philosophy regarding customers that we all can learn from. At Ritz Carlton, when you receive a customer complaint you "own" it. You solve the problem and don't pass it off.

Never say, "It's not my job." Everything is your job, whether it's in your job description or not. Winners do whatever it takes to get the job done. That willingness to do whatever it takes is noticeable to clients and managers.

Nothing enrages a client more than, "Our policy is." Believe me, you will score more points by making a customer happy than by reciting corporate policy. Any competent manager will realize this.

Provide solutions and opportunities for your clients. Instead of making excuses, ask, "What would you like me to do? How can I correct this situation? What would make you happy?" Don't ever use the phrase "to be honest" with a client. They might believe that you haven't been honest before now.

Dealing with an Upset Client

Always show clients (or anyone) respect. The client *is* always right. However, you don't have to put up with disrespect or being berated. There comes a time to stand up for yourself.

Some clients like to throw their weight around and challenge people. Some weirdos and insecure power freaks see it as a game. You get this attitude frequently from people who don't have a lot of power in their office, or who are constantly being told what to do. When this person becomes a client or is in an environment where she can make some decisions, she can become demanding and try to make up for how she is treated by others in the office. She feels she has the upper hand and wants to use it. Recognize this attitude and be wary of it.

The best way to handle this type of person is to make her feel important and respect her power, real or perceived.

Sometimes a person who is on a power trip will challenge you just to see if you can take it. Actually this type of person can be fairly common. This person is like the school bully. As soon as you stand up to her and show her that you are not going to back down, she will treat you with respect.

I had a sales meeting at Goodyear Tire in Akron, Ohio. The morning of my meeting my rental car had a flat tire in the hotel parking lot. I called my contact to apologize and to reschedule the meeting later in the day. When I arrived that afternoon, the person I met with intentionally ignored me, then trashed me and my company any chance she got. At first, I thought she was simply giving me a hard time, but it went far beyond that. After an hour, she said flat out that my product wasn't any good and that she was not interested. I thanked her for her time and said that I needed to be going to my next appointment. "Ms. Thing" told me to sit down. She said she didn't care about my other clients. It was my fault I was late this morning and my other clients could wait because she had waited. She demanded to see more, even though she wasn't interested in what I was selling. I had enough. This person had no interest in our product and I didn't have to take this abuse. I snapped back, "I'm sorry about this morning. As I told you, I had a flat tire this morning. I think Goodyear tires were on my rental car." She looked at me stunned. After a few seconds, she broke a smile and then cracked up laughing. She then politely asked me to stay longer. She had been having a bad day and did not mean to take it out on me. Her whole attitude changed and she became a client that day. Some people respect you more if you stand up to them.

Watch What You Say and Do

Don't ever tell off-color jokes or curse in front of clients. Even if he is the most foul-mouthed person on earth, and most of his words begin with the letter F, don't do it. I don't care how comfortable you may feel around him, you don't want to be viewed that way.

Don't drink at lunch. The three-martini lunch is a thing of the past. How can you perform when you go back to the office if you have been boozing at noon? At dinner, there is nothing wrong with having a drink. But remember that your professional reputation extends past 5:30. You don't ever want to be stumbling drunk with a client. You can lose much of your credibility.

You may see some older professionals drink and tell the best jokes in the world, but perception and image are very important. An older person might be able to pull it off because people have seen them behave that way for years. She might have a reputation for it. And while that behavior might be tolerated, she still looks like a foul-mouthed drunk. A young person has no reputation or big image as the life of the party or a rough-and-tumble boozer to live up to, and that behavior coming from a young person is not tolerated by many people.

Don't badmouth your competition, clients, or your company in front of a client. If you want to complain, do it to someone else. Bad-mouthing or speaking ill of a client cheapens you. It appears that you have nothing else to support you, so you have to talk badly about someone else. There are ways to be seen in a favorable light over a competitor other than talking trash about them. Speak well of them. "Yes, we are in a business similar to XYZ Company. They do a good job; however, they might not have as much experience in this area as we do."

Don't Be Too Flashy

Don't tell clients of your extravagances or upstage them. "I just bought a new boat." "See my new car." Never let on that you are making a fortune from a client. Sure, they know that you make money from their business, but if you tell them about your new car, boat, or vacation or suddenly dress like Diamond Jim or Jane, they begin to wonder if you are charging too much. Remember, for all practical purposes, the

THE INTERVIEW~ PERSONAL STYLE PUZZLER ✕ 101: "WHAT'S WRONG WITH THESE PEOPLE?"

SO, YOU WANT TO BE A JUNIOR ACCOUNT EXECUTIVE?

SO, YOU WANT TO BE A FOOD SERVICE PROFESSIONAL?

SO, YOU WANT TO BE AN ENVIRONMENTAL ACTIVIST?

client is paying your salary. If you look like you are doing *too* well, clients begin to wonder if it's at their expense.

If you're lucky enough to have a Rolex watch, or an Armani or Chanel outfit, don't wear it to client meetings. Look good, but don't dress better than your clients. If you are dealing with a forty-year-old person who makes $40,000 a year and has two kids at home, don't show up in your new Armani and Ferragamo shoes. You may be well dressed, but you will look like a well-dressed idiot. There is nothing at all wrong with having nice things—just don't flaunt them. You want to be known for your professional merits not your style points. Besides, how many twentysomethings wear a Rolex or a $1,200 suit that wasn't a gift? You will look spoiled.

> *Eddie used to deal with newspaper reporters. If you have ever been to a newsroom, you know that they aren't very formal. The latest style for men is circa 1960s geek, with short-sleeved shirts and wide ties. Not a lot of effort goes into dress. So that the news hounds would relate to him more, Eddie would intentionally "dress down." Because he wanted to be on the same level as the reporter he was dealing with, Eddie would save the expensive suits for later.*

HOW TO HANDLE PEERS AND COWORKERS

YOU WON'T WORK IN A CAVE. In most positions, you will interact with other people on the job, if not every day, at least occasionally. It's not just getting along with your boss that can help advance your career anymore. You must get along with the people you work with. Your peers and coworkers can be valuable in making you look good and achieving your goals. Your skills or deficiencies in dealing with other people in your office can either stifle you or make things go smoothly.

How you work with your peers is becoming increasingly important in the workplace. Your success in dealing with coworkers demonstrates your leadership abilities. Leadership skills are not just for managers. Being a leader means providing an example your peers can respect.

Remember the Little Things

It really is the little things that count with people. Be polite and say "please" and "thank you." People like to be appreciated. If you see a coworker who has done a good job, tell her. If a coworker has helped you out of a pinch or done a favor for you, tell him that you appreciate it. Take that person to lunch.

Develop Strategic Relationships

Build relationships outside your department and area of expertise. They can be valuable when you need things. Get to know the people in accounting. They can process your checks faster. Buddy up with your support staff, secretaries, security guards, etc. And definitely become good friends with the technical or computer staff. They can help you out in a pinch. Don't alienate people. Help them to accomplish what they need and they will help you. If you scratch my back, I'll scratch yours.

Don't Brag

Don't be a bigmouth or brag in front of your peers. Acknowledge your successes but don't stick them in anyone's face or get the big head. You are only setting yourself up. People will look for you to fail and love it when you fall. Instead, be humble in front of your peers. You can never rest on your laurels. You must keep proving yourself every day.

What Goes Around . . .

Go out of your way to help someone. Author Bryan Tracy calls it the "law of reciprocity." In a nutshell, what goes around comes around. If you help a peer out with a project or lend a hand for no reason, these things have a way of being repaid when you need it. Also, if peers tell you something, don't break their trust. Don't become known as a gossip; don't talk about others. If you are told something in confidence, don't run to your boss with it. By the same token, don't tell a coworker anything that you don't want told. Don't expect secrets to be kept.

> *There is a tale of a famous Fort Worth oil man who began his career as a land man (he negotiated leases). This was in the days of telephone switchboards when an operator in the building had to place the call for you. The other land men in his company would wait in a long line to place their calls. It could take forever to get a call through. The switchboard operator was a very large woman. She was given only a small, backless stool to sit on during the long day. She obviously was uncomfortable. The soon-to-be-famous oil man took it upon himself to buy the operator a large, comfortable leather chair. She was so appreciative that whenever he needed to place a call and there was a long line in front of him at the switchboard, she would say, "Oh, you have an urgent call coming in. I'll put it through." With a wink, she would place his call for him, ahead of all of the others. All it takes is a little kindness and treating others like human beings.*

Respect Is Better than Popularity

It's often better to be respected than popular. How do you gain respect among your peers? Action. You become respected by your peers by setting an example. What does it take to be a leader? The easiest way to lead is to stand out in your performance, your attitude, your integrity, and your willingness to help people.

Sometimes the people who are respected are not always the most popular. Being respected among your peers may mean bucking the trend.

> *Everyone loved Dan at his office. He was fun and outgoing, always had something to say, and was always the first one to organize an event, such as a softball game, after work. Yet Dan would sometimes pull one over on the company by saying he was on a business trip when he wasn't. Several times, Dan went to Los Angeles for business trips, but would have one meeting scheduled and then play for the other two days he was there. He would also fudge small amounts on his expense report, or skip work to play golf when the boss was out of town. Sure, everyone thought Dan was fun and likable, but, because of his lack of character, not many people in the office respected him.*

HOW TO WORK IN TEAMS

OFTEN IN YOUR CAREER you will either work with a partner, on a committee, or as a member of a group or division. Groups have special dynamics that require certain skills to accomplish tasks.

Being a team player does not mean sacrificing yourself. It means being a contributor, participating, and sharing. When assigned to work in a group, make sure the group has goals or an agenda. A common problem for many groups or teams is a lack of direction and focus. As a team member you need to make sure that the team has a goal. Is it to brainstorm ideas? To increase sales? To devise a new pricing policy? To design a project?

Leadership

Another common problem in teams and groups is leadership. There can be conflict if several dominant personalities try to run the show, or the group may flounder if no one takes the reins. When groups form, there may be an assigned leader, or one may arise from the team members. Some groups can even manage themselves. Regardless, clear-cut responsibilities must be determined and delegated. Will leadership be shared? Will one person be a facilitator?

Clarify how leadership and decisions will be handled. Your responsibility as a group member is to make sure those issues are addressed, so the group can focus on goals. Establish ground rules for the group.

Leaders, not dictators. Some people go on ego trips when they are in groups. They think it's their personal group, and become territorial or try to psych out other members. Don't be intimidated. Hold your ground if you believe in your idea. Make people substantiate and support their claims or ideas. If you see someone getting run over or being apprehensive about participating, try to make him comfortable.

Communication is Critical

Most of all, working in teams takes patience, empathy, and communication. It's important to share your ideas and establish a clear channel or pattern of communication with the other team members. Teams, like the individuals who make them up, have different personalities. It can be difficult when team members don't know each other. Try to establish a system of communication so everyone can be clear on what is going on and where they stand. You may have a different style of communicating or doing business. Respect the other person and, even if you disagree, try not to restrict their ideas early on. Encourage everyone to participate.

Participate. If you don't voice an opinion, you have no right to complain when you don't like the decision. Don't sit back and criticize everyone else's decisions or ideas. Participate and produce ideas and opinions. When the group does reach a decision, support that decision. No one likes a negative person or doomsayer.

HOW TO HANDLE CONFLICT

IT HAPPENS. There will be conflicts with others. It may be a disagreement or a full-fledged, knock-down drag-out. No matter whom the conflict is with, there are some common rules for dealing with it successfully without damaging the relationship.

Use the passive voice. It's so easy to start blaming someone in an argument. You did this. You did that. You don't get it. You are stupid.

You are wrong. When conflict arises, don't use the word "You." People hear "You" in a heated situation, and feel they are being attacked. They instantly shut down and don't hear what else you are saying.

Attack issues and address situations instead of attacking a person directly. Rather than saying, "You didn't do it right," or "You are wrong," phrase it passively. "This wasn't done correctly." People will respond much better to something phrased passively. You are saying the same thing, but you aren't attacking them. Don't get me wrong. You can ream someone pretty well if you want to, and still phrase it passively. If you know you must talk to someone and it will probably turn into a conflict or tense situation, don't begin the conversation with something negative.

Do it on your own terms. You can't please everyone all the time, and definitely not everyone will please you. When you are upset, think before you fly off the handle. Don't just react. Use your head. Settle down and count to ten. You don't have to react immediately. The best way to handle conflict is to approach the person when you are ready. Confront the person on your own terms and be direct. Get it off your chest and then forget it. Don't brood.

Let people save face. Keep conflict or disagreement with clients or bosses nonconfrontational. Don't try to get the best of clients or they won't come back. Don't hammer your boss into letting you have your own way or you won't ever get it again. Being a good, tough negotiator doesn't mean that you win and they lose. Try to make all of your relationships a win-win for everyone.

HOW TO ENTERTAIN CLIENTS

IN THE PROFESSIONAL WORLD, you will be called on to entertain clients. Yes, it's true. If you're entertaining clients, you are viewed as the host.

This can be an intimidating experience if you have never done it before. Rule one. Clients don't do fast food. You can rule out any place with a drive-through and a playground. Seriously, locating a restaurant is important. Select the location according to what you are trying to accomplish. Is it truly to entertain? Then it could be a louder, more boisterous atmosphere. Are you there to conduct business? If so, you may want to find an establishment that offers privacy and a quiet atmosphere for conducting your business.

Make reservations ahead of time. Make your reservations well in advance. Prepare for this as you would a meeting. If it's a restaurant you are familiar with, stop in ahead of time or tell the maitre d' that you have an important meeting and ask if they will arrange it for you. This is necessary in some large cities, or very popular or busy restaurants. If it's somewhere you take clients frequently, tip the maitre d' or manager to keep him from seating you in the smoking section next to the kitchen. It doesn't hurt to have about three restaurants that you can choose from when you need to take a client out.

Find out if your guests have a preference or special concerns and needs. In New York, a coworker and I were to entertain a large client at dinner. We took it for granted that he liked steak, so we made reservations at a popular steak house. C'mon, who doesn't like steak? A vegetarian, that's who. To make matters worse he was a vegetarian who was a strong animal-rights activist. We walked into the steak place not knowing this. As we opened the door and our guest saw the sides of aged beef in the window, I knew we had a problem. That night we had Chinese food.

Let the maitre d' know you are entertaining clients. If you arrive before your guest, be seated and tell the maitre d' that you are meeting someone. Tell them your guest's name and what he looks like. When your guest or guests arrive, stand to meet them.

You really aren't there for the food. Don't start eating until your guest does, and if he hesitates, tell him to please go ahead. Don't be a pig and don't order foods that are difficult to eat, like ribs and spaghetti. Avoid foods that will give you death breath, like heavy garlic or onions. You may also want to keep mints or a toothbrush back at the office so you don't kill anyone with the green cloud billowing from your mouth after these meals. Try not to eat big, heavy lunches if you have meetings in the afternoon. They will put you to sleep.

When the check comes, be quick to pick it up. If you've asked someone to dinner, lunch, etc., it's expected that you will pick up the tab. Don't give your guest the opportunity to pick up the tab or split the check. Tell the waiter to be sure to give you the check. When the check arrives at your table, simply pull it close to you or in front of you. Don't tab out until you both are ready to leave.

Always get a receipt. Until the President does away with writing off entertainment on your taxes, always get a receipt. A helpful hint is to write the name of the person you met with on the back of the receipt. You can keep this for your expense report or taxes.

▪24▪

Organizing Your Life

Guard well your spare moments. They are like uncut diamonds. Discard them and their value will never be known. Improve them and they will become the brightest gems in a useful life.
—Ralph Waldo Emerson

"I don't have time." "Where did I put it?" "My hard drive is full." These are three common complaints from young professionals. Managing time and information is a pain. You can become overwhelmed very quickly. Before, you thought, how can I possibly find enough things to do in eight hours? Now, you find yourself working 10- to 12-hour days and still not being caught up. Having a system and really organizing your life will help buy you some time and freedom, and prevent some headaches.

If you thought that juggling school and a social life were difficult, just wait until you try to harness your professional life, information, social life, finances, etc.

Organizing time and information in the professional world is much different from keeping up with schoolwork or even a career search. You have a lot of balls to juggle. To keep them all in the air you need a system.

TIME MANAGEMENT

Set Priorities

How do you fit 28 hours' worth of work into 24? The first lesson is: Don't procrastinate. Don't put anything off. List your daily activities and prioritize them.

In the course of a day, there are many little problems that come up. You can get lost taking care of the details and busywork that need to be done. Meanwhile, the important tasks fall by the wayside or must be done in a panic at the last minute. Set priorities. One professor explained time management with the following analogy. Think of your time as either stepping on ants or shooting elephants. (I know it's not a very PC example, but too bad.) Do you want to step on a bunch of ants and mess with small tasks that aren't very important, or do you want to bag an elephant and spend your time accomplishing something major and productive? Don't get caught up in busy work.

Learn to Delegate

A problem that I and many other twentysomethings I spoke with have is learning to delegate. The small antlike projects are often things that can be passed on to someone else. That does not mean pawning off work to other people or shirking your duties. It does mean that if you have an assistant, receptionist, secretary, intern, partner, etc., and they can ease your burden, let them do it. It's uncomfortable, at first, to ask a secretary or someone your mom or dad's age to do something trivial. But unless you can learn to detach yourself from those thoughts and realize that it's their job, you are going to be swamped with work and putting out many little fires.

Often, time is wasted because people don't, won't, or can't delegate. It's much more than shoving something in front of someone and saying "here, do this." Unless proper directions are given, it can take longer to redo something than if you had done it yourself.

Delegating takes trust and communication. You must trust the other person to do a good job and leave them alone with it. Sure, you may feel that the only way to do something right is to do it yourself, but you will then be late with the few things you are actually able to accomplish. Let go of the control and trust the other person.

However, to do a job properly, as you would do it, you must communicate what you want done. You can't bitch someone out for doing it wrong when you didn't take the time to show them how it was supposed to be done in the first place. Take the time to give proper detailed instructions and be willing to answer questions, which are bound to pop up. Computer programmers have a saying for writing code, GIGO (garbage in, garbage out.) The same holds for giving directions. The product is only as good as the directions you give.

Know How Long Something Will Take You

Have a good idea of how long something should take you. If you have a project ahead of you, figure how long each piece will take. It's easier to judge how long something will take when you look at it in terms of smaller parts that make up the whole. Make a time line. A common mistake is to be too optimistic about how long something will take you, or to not think about it at all. This only leads to finding yourself spending two or three times as long on a project as you thought you would.

Be Flexible

Don't get too ambitious about time management. You will make a list and plan your day down to the minute, but at the end of the day you only have half your list done. Plan for distractions. Interruptions happen. Plan for them and don't let them upset you. Leave an hour open throughout the day for any unexpected tasks or emergencies. If you are too rigid with your schedule, the minute you fall behind or something else pops up, you will be bent out of shape. The unexpected meeting that your boss called. The phone call that was supposed to be 10 minutes took 45. Your friend called for 20 minutes. You went to the bathroom. Have a plan but learn to adapt and handle what needs to be done.

Other things can and do waste your time. Prepare for them. Decide what is important and what is not. Don't be afraid to tell someone that you are busy, or that you can't do anything, or can't talk to them now. If someone walks by your cubicle or office and wants to talk or asks you something, hold your ground and tell them you will talk with them later.

Be Selfish with Your Time

Set a specific time to meet with people, or to take care of certain activities. That way you can plan around the meeting or activity. If someone says, "we will get together later," nail them down to a specific time, so you don't get involved with projects or phone calls just when he drops by your office to meet with you.

The same applies for deadlines and projects. Don't just say, "I need it later," or "the project is due next week." Be very specific and clear when requesting and giving times. "I need the report by Tuesday morning." Avoid confusion and surprises. Be selfish with your time and use it wisely.

Using the Phone

Picture yourself on the phone. You have three other things to do. You check your voice mail and there are four other messages. What do you do? Immediately assess the situation. What are your priorities? If the phone calls aren't urgent, return them all at once at the end of the day. Take from 4:00 p.m. on to call back. I don't care how busy you are, always return phone calls, preferably within 24 and no later than 48 hours. Even if they are unimportant, call them back and make an effort. It helps build a good reputation for you. If you respond to people quickly, when you need something, they will remember and will help you out quickly in return.

Returning phone calls. If you have a message from someone you don't want to talk to, you should still call them back. However, you don't have to talk to them. Here is how. Call after work or early in the morning and leave a message with their voice mail saying that you are returning the call. You have returned the phone call and cleared yourself, but still avoided talking with that person. You have also bought yourself some time. If he or she doesn't have voice mail, call at a time when they are likely to be away from the office and leave a message with the receptionist or whoever might answer. Lunch time, 8:00 a.m., or 5:30 p.m. are good times when people might not be around.

Reward Yourself for Small Goals

Reward yourself. Have a prioritized list of things that need to be done and set up a small reward system for when you accomplish them. Tell yourself that you won't get up from your desk until you make twenty phone calls. When you do, go downstairs for a Coke or snack. I hate being cooped up in the office all day, so one thing I do is tell myself if I accomplish this and that, I will go outside for a walk. My office is near a park, so if I work hard and accomplish what I have set out to do, I will leave for thirty minutes. Make it a game for yourself. If I get these three things done today, I will go out tonight, go shopping, play basketball, whatever it may be. But stick to it. If you don't get it done, you don't treat yourself. You work late or stay home until it's done.

Unexpected Meetings

If you are working feverishly to get something done before five and need to meet with someone, go to their office or cubicle ("veal feeding pen," as Douglas Coupland refers to them). Try not to have meetings in your office when you are in a hurry or the person is a big talker. If you are in someone else's office you can leave when you want. It's much easier for you to stand up and say, "Thanks for the answer," and cruise, than it is to ask someone to leave your office. You control the tempo and length of the meeting. You can stay longer or leave whenever you want.

Write Everything in Your Calendar

When you attend a meeting, always take your calendar or DayTimer. This way if other meetings are necessary, you have all that you need right there to plan accordingly. You can look way in advance and take care of things then instead of saying, "Well, let me check and I will get back with you."

Have one calendar. A common trap that people get into is to have several calendars. They have one at the office, a DayTimer, a wall calendar, one at home, one for business, and one for personal use. Consequently, they write something down on one and then forget to look at it. None of them are consistent. Have only one calendar that you write everything down in. Use it for both business and personal. By doing this, you don't have to reconcile any other calendars, there won't be any conflicts, and you won't let things slip through the cracks because you will have it all at your fingertips.

I just mentioned DayTimers. DayTimers are a great investment. Filofax, Day Runner, or Franklin Planner are among the best of the other brands. These are books that allow you to manage your time and keep your schedule and any pertinent information in one place. You will have all of the data you need in one place. You can keep phone numbers, addresses, notes, and so forth and can schedule everything right there. Make the investment.

Use Your "Down Time" Wisely

Plan for "down time" and use it wisely. Down times are moments such as when you are commuting on the train or bus. You are stuck in traffic. You are riding in an airplane or taxi. You are waiting to have your car repaired or in the doctor's office. It's fifteen minutes until five and you can't start another project, but you can't leave until your boss heads out at five. The dead periods where you would otherwise be twiddling your thumbs or picking your nose. Make this time work for you.

Have an ongoing project that you are working on, or something to read. I always keep a notepad and a pen on me so I can write ideas or map my strategy for the next day. A client keeps newspapers and magazines handy so he can get his reading done on the train commute. One recently married professional keeps several notecards on her so she can write her thank-you letters when she is riding in a taxi. It can be anything. Listen to books on tape in your car. There are a million and one distractions and things that demand our time. Don't let them control you. The more wisely you use your time, the more time you will have for the fun things you want to do. Think about it. Time is more precious than money to some people. Some companies allow their employees to purchase extra vacation days and free time. This is, of course, one option, but the other is for you to control your time and not let it control you.

Causes of Poor Time Management

- Working without a plan or list.
- Killing ants instead of elephants. Small-priority items over high priority.
- Trying to do everything. Not delegating.

- Perfectionism. Trying to do everything perfectly instead of just getting it done.
- Failure to plan and control interruptions.
- Can't say No.
- Not thinking ahead.

MANAGING INFORMATION

HOPEFULLY, YOU ARE already accustomed to juggling many balls at a time. College prepares you pretty well. But when you are in the professional world, the stakes are higher and you have more to deal with. You know when you see the professional jugglers. They start doing two balls, then three or four. Then when they really get warmed up, they start juggling knives, axes, and flaming torches. The professional world is like an advanced juggling act. Information will be coming at you from all sides at once. You have to have a system for managing it somehow, or you will find yourself chin high in a mountain of paper and unable to find anything.

Don't Be a Pack Rat

The first rule about managing mountains of paper is to practice what I call "waste basketry." Have you ever noticed how some people are pack rats? They keep everything from old wrappers to ticket stubs. My favorites are the people who keep the Cool Whip containers because you don't know when you might need one. You have pack rats in business, too. They are the ones whose desks you can't see, or they have stacks several feet high laying on the floor. You have to move the empty Pepsi cans and week-old Snickers to find a place to sit. There is no place for this in business.

Get rid of what is not necessary. Remove the potential for clutter by making an immediate decision whether something is worth keeping. If you are hesitant, have a special file for it to go into. Otherwise, throw it away. Worthless memos, junk mail, duplicates, old scratch notes, whatever. If it can't be used or it has outlived its usefulness, toss it in the trash. If you don't do it immediately, at least do it once a week. Otherwise, the piles will grow and become completely unmanageable.

Read It Only Once

A good deal of time is wasted reading the same thing two and three times simply because it's on your desk. If you've read it once and haven't thrown it away, take a pen and mark the corner with a check or your initial to show that you have already looked at it. Hopefully, you will file it immediately or place it in the stack for it to be filed. If not, at least when it escapes from the junkyard known as your desk and crosses your eyes, you will know that you have seen it before and that you do not have to spend time on it again.

Managing E-Mail and Computer Files

Many offices are attempting to become paperless. This means that the paper mountain of garbage is becoming an electronic mountain that eats up memory. Many offices use E-mail and computer files. The proliferation of E-mail has made communicating more efficient, but it has also opened the door for some people to be even lazier.

E-mail. You might chat back and forth with a friend of yours, or someone will put a joke or general notice on the E-mail. Great. Use it, then trash it when you are done. There are two reasons for this. One, the amount of memory you use could make it difficult to get what you need from the system. Your old E-mail files slow the system down and use memory. The other reason is that if the boss or someone else important were to check your E-mail files, he or she won't find incriminating evidence of your lack of productivity: Jokes about the boss's wife, your latest OJ jokes, or your coworker's sordid details of last weekend's activities. Erase anything that is not important.

Computer files. The same is true for computer files. Having excess material and files on your hard drive or network will make it more difficult for you to keep track of everything. I recommend making special folders for certain projects, letters, memos, reports, etc. Think of your computer files just as you would a regular filing cabinet. Place all documents of a certain type in the folders and you will know exactly where to go when you need it.

No cute file names. Don't use cute names for files. At least with Macintosh you can have long file names, but if you are using Windows or a DOS machine you are stuck with eight-character file names. This can make things very tough. Try not to be too cute or complex when naming a file. You will never be able to find it again, or two months later you won't remember what it is. Make it something that is descriptive and can be remembered.

If you have revisions of a file or document, number them sequentially like report1, report2, etc. Another idea is to remove or delete the old versions so you will not be confused about which to use. If you don't want to delete them totally, you can create a folder called "old files," or save them to a floppy disk. The bottom line is to have a place for old material to go so you can get at it in case of an emergency. It leaves your current working area clear.

Always back up your work. There is nothing like the sheer panic that occurs when it's two hours before your presentation and your hard drive crashes or the file containing your report is nowhere to be found. It's always then that some smug coworker walks by and says "Did you back it up?" NO, you butthead! Would I be freaking out like this if I had? <u>ALWAYS BACK UP YOUR WORK</u>. Make an additional copy that can be kept in another folder on your hard drive and also make a copy on a floppy disk that you can store elsewhere. The same goes for hard copies of documents. Make sure that you make copies and duplicates of anything that is very important or can't be replaced. Keep these duplicates in a safe place at another location or away from the originals.

Back up your work while you are working on it. Computers have been known to freeze, crash or fall victim to power out-

> *Cindy thought that she was safe because she backed up her files to another folder on the hard drive. A lot of good that did when her office was broken into and her computer was stolen.*

ages, which generally happen just as you are about to finish the report that you have worked on for two hours. Save your work every fifteen to thirty minutes. This way if you lose some work it won't be the entire thing. Many programs have auto-save features. If available, use them. It can save you a lot of frustration.

Keeping track of files. An easy way to view your files is to have them sorted by date or name. Windows and Macintosh allow you to sort your files by Name, Date, Size, Type. Name is simply an alphabetical listing and Date helps you determine which are the most recent files.

Be careful with your password. With more organizations being networked and allowing sharing of files, a simple safety tip is to not share your password. Don't make your password something incredibly obvious like your name, initials, or birthday. Those are the first things people try when attempting to crack passwords.

Always Carry a Pen

You never know when a good idea will come up, when you might meet an important contact, need to take notes, or write a phone number or name. For these reasons, carry a pen and something to write on with you always. It could be a small notepad or 3x5 index cards. Slender reporter's notebooks also work well because they fit in the pocket of a jacket. Keep it on you, in your jacket, shirt, purse, wherever. Just make sure that it can be reached easily. Get a decent pen and keep it with you.

Make Things Easy to Find

There are things that you will use more frequently than others. Certain phone numbers and addresses need to be kept on a sheet that is in front of you or can be found easily. Keep a list of the ten numbers or addresses you use the most on one sheet of paper, and have it posted in front of you in plain view.

Important names and numbers, such as bank account information, records, and credit cards need to be kept in a place where you can get to them easily. It helps to put this information on one page or record and to keep it in a safe place. In case you are ever ripped off, you can have all of this information already recorded.

Piles and Files

If you subscribe to the stack theory (keeping everything in organized piles around your desk or office), at least designate each pile to mean something specific. This pile is to be filed. This pile is stuff that I have to read. This pile needs to be handled immediately.

Have a system. When it comes to filing, do whatever works for you. If you can find it, good for you. That is the key. Make sure that your system is easy to understand and enables you to find things quickly. Some ideas include color coding labels or folders, with each color representing different tasks, departments, and types of documents.

Make paper and computer files match each other. Another tip for managing files is to coordinate your paper filing system and your computer files. Use the same heading names and labels. You may also want to consider duplicating or following how your boss keeps his or her files. Do whatever works for you, but if you are the only person on the planet who knows how to find anything, you are going to be up a creek without a paddle if someone else needs to find something and you are nowhere around.

Use the system you choose. People can come up with a million great ways to organize time and information but they don't do any good unless

> Bonnie has duties and documents that are spread over four departments. It's very important that she can find things and not get them mixed up. She uses color coding to keep track of things. Each department is represented by a different color. Anything that is generic or miscellaneous has its own color too. Within the departments, or colors, files are kept alphabetically by topic. If something has more than one sheet of paper, she gives it its own folder. If it's something that is only one sheet, she puts it in a general folder which is alphabetized A-Z. She goes through those generic folders once a month and trashes anything that is not useful.

you use them. That is often the hardest part. Get into a habit of doing these things. Develop a pattern for putting things away. It's as simple as setting a certain time each week or once a month to file things and reduce the stacks. Just don't let it get out of hand or say "I'll get to it."

Cool Gadgets to Help You Organize

The computing power found in a simple calculator is more than could be found in a 1960's computer which was the size of a room. Technology has produced some incredible things. Most of all, it has produced some great gadgets that help you to organize your life. All these are fairly inexpensive and can be huge time savers.

Pick up a microrecorder. They can cost from $20 to well over $100. Once you get over the fact that everyone sounds like a chipmunk on tape, you will find that it can be really useful. You can take notes, ideas, memos, or draft letters. There are too many things that happen during the day or things that cross your mind that you forget from one moment to the next, so why not be prepared. Make the most of your time and don't miss a thing with a recorder. They can also be used to CYA (cover your ass). More on that later.

Buy an electronic Rolodex. There will be times when you have to have a phone number or an address and you can't bring your DayTimer with you or reach into your briefcase or tote. These little gizmos are the size of a credit card and about a quarter of an inch thick. They have a little keypad where you can enter names, phone numbers, and addresses. Most devices also have a calculator feature. They run around $20 to $30 and can be found at a discount store like Target, Best Buy, or Wal-Mart. Depending on which model you get, they will store between 150 and 500 names. These are great to keep in your pocket or purse, and when you need something immediately, it's right there. Incredibly convenient.

Contact software. If you have a PC or a Macintosh, I highly recommend getting a contact manager software package. These programs combine the best of all worlds, such as a database, scheduler, DayTimer, and word processor. You can keep a database with names, addresses, phone numbers and any critical information you want about a person. Many people keep their client lists or prospects on these systems. They are also great for personal use. They can be customized to store birthdays, titles, spouse's names, shoe size, whatever. The databases are easy to use and can be searched and segmented any way you want. You only want a list of people who are in a certain zip code? Done.

Another great feature is that it keeps your schedule for you. If you need to call Fred to talk about a report that is due, you can schedule it and an alarm will go off at four. The screen will pop up and let you know what you have to do. Some popular programs are ACT and Maximizer. They generally run from $100 to $250 but they can organize your whole life. If you spend most of your day on a computer or are very comfortable with one, this can save you so much time. They are very easy to use.

Money manager software. If you are the type of person who finds money in the cushions of your couch or stuffs it in your pockets or purse in little balls, chances are you aren't the best money manager in the world. High-tech solutions to managing your money and finances are the common software programs like Quicken and CA Simply Money. There are several other programs of this sort, but I feel these two are the best. They are under $100, and give you a graphic representation of a checkbook, so you can write checks on screen and it keeps the records for you.

You can have different accounts, such as savings, checking, IRA etc., and it allows you to track where your money goes. So if you want to find out how much money you have given to Texaco this year, you can pull it up. As with most of these packages, the toughest part is remembering to do it. The only way these things will save you time is if you use them.

▪25▪

Communication Skills

The skill most critical to career success is communication. People skills are paramount. No matter what you do, at some point in your career you will interact with people. You will write. You will listen. You may even be asked to speak in front of a group. It's not always your technical superiority that makes you effective. You could be the most intelligent woman alive or have discovered the cure for cancer, but if all of that information is locked inside your head, you are useless.

You might think that a company such as Microsoft would be full of propeller heads with Ph.D.'s and their heads in the clouds. Sure, you can find that. But, surprisingly, you have people who have degrees in English, Finance, History, and other disciplines that seem totally unrelated to software. As one executive says, you can teach anyone the numbers and the technical aspects of something, but you can't always teach people how to communicate.

A manager at Boeing says, "You have to know the three R's, but you also have to work with other people. We don't need a lot of Lone Rangers." A VP at a major manufacturer says, "Most of what we do is in writing. You can't use colors and pictures for everything." It doesn't matter what is in your head if you can't tell anyone about it.

MAKING A GOOD FIRST IMPRESSION

PEOPLE ARE QUICK to make a judgment when meeting someone for the first time. You can make a lot of ground with someone by your first impression. On the other hand, it's hard to recover from a bad first impression.

Introduce Yourself

Make the first move to introduce yourself to people. If you see someone coming to talk to you, greet him as he is approaching you. Always say your name if you haven't seen him in a long time, or you are not sure if the person remembers who you are. People forget names all the time. Don't assume people know who you are. They may know your face, but can't remember your name for the life of them. It can be big-time embarrassing when someone doesn't remember your name, so help them out. "Hi Phil, I'm Bradley Richardson. Nice to see you again."

Now, What Was Your Name?

When greeting someone, especially for the first time, repeat that person's name as you meet them. Use it very soon in the conversation. As you are shaking that person's hand say, "It's very nice to meet you, _insert name here_." It adds a personal touch and it will help you to remember the name. People enjoy hearing their own names. Repeating a person's name shows that you are listening and lets you establish a recognition between a person's face and name, but don't overdo it.

What if the tables are turned and you vapor lock on remembering a person's name. The face is familiar but this person could be the Pope, for all you know. What do you do? First, reintroduce yourself, "Hi, I don't know if you remember me, but . . . ." They may respond by offering their name in return. Another trick is to bring someone else into the conversation and have that person introduce herself. By introducing the new person first, Mr. or Ms. "No Name" will most likely offer their name. Problem solved. If no one is around to bail you out, either suffer and fake it, or apologize for your forgetfulness and say, "Excuse me. I seem to have forgotten your name."

Small Talk

When you are introduced to someone, or particularly when you have a meeting at a person's office, smile and start some small talk. There is nothing more uncomfortable than the silent pause after you meet someone. Find something to BS about. Talk about anything that will put the other person at ease. If you have traveled into town, talk about the city or your trip. Comment on items in the office or on the walls. You can even ask simple throwaway questions such as "How many people do you have in this location?" Or "How long have you been with the company?" In a business setting, very few people greet you at the door, say "hello," and then jump right into business as you are walking in the hall. Be human and loosen things up. It's easier to deal with people when you treat them like people.

Greetings

When meeting someone in an office lobby or reception area, don't sit. The chairs are often too small or so cushy you look like a little kid when you try to get up. You can't help but look awkward. Having your knees at chin level or trying to crawl out of a chair does not make a very cool or powerful first impression. Stand as you are waiting for someone. That way when they arrive in the reception area, you can easily turn and greet them immediately. You look more confident and in control if you are already standing.

Don't be caught doing something else in a lobby area, unless you are reading the company's annual report or brochure. You can use the phone; however, if your contact comes out, immediately drop what you are doing. Be prepared to give that person your full attention.

Shaking Hands

Always offer your hand to someone. At least in the Western hemisphere, a handshake is a common courtesy. It's a friendship gesture and a professional courtesy. Don't be afraid to make the first move and offer your hand to anyone you meet or when you see someone again. It's an open, welcoming gesture that makes people feel more comfortable around you. You are extending an invitation for them to come closer and to get to know you.

Handshake rules apply to everyone, men and women. Don't give someone a dead fish. That is worse than not shaking hands at all. You know the kind, when you shake a person's hand and it feels limp and lifeless. What a fake, lame gesture. Grasp a person's hand firmly and squeeze. Some communications experts say that there is no specific time limit for a handshake, but let the other person be the one to break contact.

Don't hold on or fail to give a person his arm back. You don't want to be viewed as some touchy freak with a hand fetish, but hold it firmly until he or she breaks away or releases pressure. If you are shaking a person's hand, make it a firm handshake, not a dainty-half-of-your-hand shake, but don't break his hand either. Don't patronize someone by holding half her hand or giving a gentle squeeze as if she is a frail creature. Shake a woman's hand just as you would a man's.

Look Into My Eyes

When you are greeting someone, look him straight in the eye as you speak to him. Don't be shifty-eyed. Eye contact instills trust. I'm not talking about being bug-eyed and never breaking contact, or staring so intently that you burn a hole in the back of a person's brain. But people are very suspicious of someone who can't look them in the eye. It also shows that you are actively listening, even if you really aren't hearing a damn thing someone is saying.

Speaking in Public

Studies have shown that one of the greatest fears of Americans is the fear of speaking in public. Chances are high that at some time during

Jordan, a Michigan State graduate, had help helped her boss research and prepare to make a presentation for three months. The speech was to be in front of board members of a foundation, and was to include influential people in the audience. Her boss was supposed to give the presentation, but thirty minutes before it was to begin, he turned to Jordan and said, "It's your show. You are running the meeting." She, of course, freaked out, but then regained her composure. Having helped prepare the material, she was familiar with it and was able to make a great presentation. It goes to show that you never know when you are going to be in a situation where you will have to speak in front of others.

your career you may be asked to speak in public. You may have the luxury of preparing for it, or you may be thrust into a situation.

Speaking in public does not have to be a scary event. I'm sure you have heard of the old trick to overcome stage fright, which is to imagine every person in the audience naked. While it may be somewhat effective and enjoyable, there is a lot more involved to becoming confident and comfortable when speaking in public.

Identify Your Audience

The first step when speaking in public or making a presentation is to identify your audience. Find out who you will be speaking to and what type of presentation or information they would like to hear. I made a big mistake once in misreading my audience. I was asked to speak to a group of employers and corporate recruiters, most of them HR (Human Resource) professionals. I was to speak on creative ways for young people to construct a career search. I forgot that my audience made its living having job applicants go through them and their Human Resources Departments. The HR people didn't take too kindly to my views about going straight to the decision-maker and bypassing HR. After I was fed to the lions, I chalked that one up to experience.

Identify with your audience and address them in a way they can understand. Don't refer to Beavis and Butthead if you are addressing the American Association of Retired Persons. Grandma might not get it. Don't extol the virtues of liberalism if you are speaking at a local Republican fund-raiser. You get the point.

Plan Ahead

Whom will you be speaking to? What do they anticipate hearing? How many people will there be? How long do you have? What is the setup of the room? Find out the specifics of your presentation ahead of time.

Practice before you speak. Never wing a speech. You will be nervous enough being in front of an audience. Even the pros who have done it a thousand times still get butterflies. Most likely, you won't have the time or the presence of mind to make it up as you go. Prepare ahead of time what you are going to say and have an idea of how long it will be. Tempo is important. You will usually talk faster than you normally do because you are nervous, so know where to slow down and speed up. Know where you need to emphasize. Take your time

Always use notes. Never go up there without notes or an outline. People prepare speeches differently. There is no set way to do it, but one of the most effective is by having an outline, with key notes, phrases, and statistics on a 3x5 note card. Index cards do not cause a distraction and are discreet when you refer to them.

Have everything that you need at the table or podium before you get up there. Have plenty of water or a drink next to you. You may not need it, but you don't want to have a coughing spell or lose your momentum by asking someone for a glass of water. If you need to take a drink, just do it. Don't be self-conscious or act cautiously. If you act and move confidently and with purpose, you can pull off a lot in front of an audience. Things that you may feel are really noticeable, the audience really can't see or doesn't care about.

Don't Panic

In your mind, everything gets blown out of proportion. You magnify every mishap, botched word, or gesture. If you think that your knees or hands are shaking, remember that the audience probably can't see it. They don't notice nearly as much as you think they do. If you are nervous, hold on to the podium, lectern, or table. Lean against it or walk around it if you have to. Act naturally.

Remember the movie *Broadcast News*, where the guy finally gets his big break to be an anchor? He is so nervous that he starts sweating and soaks through his suit. If you are sweaty and need to wipe your face, don't avoid it. Just do it. Don't try to be subtle and act like nothing is wrong as it's dripping into your eyes. You look stupider fidgeting and hoping that no one notices the sweat dripping off your chin, than if you confidently and deliberately wipe your forehead with a handkerchief or napkin.

Have you ever been in a wedding, choir, or other event when you have to stand for a long period? One thing experts tell you will avoid fatigue is to bend your knees and shift your weight. Sounds simple, but if you forget to do it, your legs will get tired and give out, sending you straight to the floor. While audiences will overlook many things, passing out and falling on your ass is not one of them.

Things to Avoid While Speaking in Public

Don't lecture. You know what it's like to sit through a lecture, or to listen to someone reading from a book or directly off the page. BORING. No one likes to be *talked at* or *lectured to*. Never read a speech word by word. You will sound canned and your audience will lose interest. The most effective public speakers involve the audience and are personable in their delivery.

Talk to your audience and involve your audience. Use examples and anecdotes that the audience can identify with. Get them to laugh, to raise their hands, or to participate in some way. You know that you have accomplished this when you see a visible response from the group such as laughter, smiles, nodding of heads, or objects being hurled at you. Avoid lecturing. Make it a dialogue. People retain more if they are involved than if they are merely listening.

Let the audience know if you will take questions. If you are going to field questions, tell the audience that you will be happy to answer questions at the end, or when you have finished your main presentation. If you don't do this, you will have some wiseass in the front row who disagrees with you who will ask questions every five minutes. His interruptions will cause you to stop, lose momentum, or possibly go off on an undesirable tangent. If someone is persistently interrupting you, tell them that you can meet with them afterwards, or that you will address their questions at the end. It's your show. Don't let someone get you off track.

If it's the boss or CEO who is interrupting or derailing your presentations, you can go with it and answer his question, or politely let him know that you will be covering that subject in a moment.

Don't give handouts at the beginning. Try to avoid giving handout materials at the beginning of a presentation. If you do, the audience will be reading the materials while you are speaking and not concentrating on what you are saying. I used to provide a handout at the beginning of my speeches which outlined what I was talking about. As a result, the audience skipped ahead to the point they were interested in and neglected the other material. My message lost its impact and I had the same jerk mentioned earlier who would ask questions about something I wasn't talking about yet.

Presentation Tips

When speaking in public, speak so that the last person in the room can hear you. You want to be heard by everyone. Projecting your voice to the back wall guarantees that you will be heard. Don't scream. Projecting is not screaming.

Make eye contact with audience members. Find some friendly faces in the crowd, or people who have responded positively to one of your stupid jokes, or something you have said. Key in on these people, and look at them to gauge how you are doing. From time to time, scan the audience and look at everyone. This gives the impression of involving people and personalizing your presentation. If someone in the audience sees you looking at them, they see you as a person, rather than a distant speaker.

LISTENING SKILLS

WHEN YOU THINK of a good communicator, you may naturally think of someone who is a good speaker or writer. Yet many executives feel that the most important skill in becoming a good communicator is listening. While many successful executives are outspoken, they don't talk a mile a minute. They listen and observe. When they do say something, they are informed and can speak intelligently because they have listened carefully. Expressing your ideas or positions intelligently, orally or in writing, is a byproduct of listening well. Through listening comes understanding.

The key to being heard is not to talk more. It's to listen more. You should spend more than 50 percent of your time listening. The more you talk, the less you listen. The more you talk, the less others will listen.

What makes a bad listener? Have you ever been talking with someone and while he or she was saying something, you were already thinking ahead to what your next witty retort might be? If you have, you weren't listening to that person. Sure, you want to think about what you are going to say before it comes flying out of your mouth, but don't think so far ahead about what to say next that you don't hear what the other person is saying now. Without having all the necessary information, it becomes easy to jump to conclusions or make judgments

Don't be scripted. Think about what you are saying. There are some common responses that make you sound like you are reading from a script. "How are you doing?" "Fine thanks, and you?" Don't sound like a robot or give pat answers. Really think about how you are going to respond to that person. You can only respond effectively to a person by listening.

Aggressive Listening

Listening aggressively does not mean thrusting your lobes in front of a person's mouth while saying "talk to me, talk to me." Instead, aggressive listening means to actively make an effort not only to hear, but to understand the other person. A few small tips that may sound corny will actually help your retention and understanding.

Listen intently. As I said about first impressions, making eye contact with a person as he or she is speaking conveys that you are interested in what that person is saying. Make normal, comfortable eye contact. Not a deep, soul-burning gaze.

Body language. Use body language and gestures to let the other person know that you are listening. Nod your head or lean forward as you are listening. Use your voice to confirm to that person that you are listening. "Uh huh," "mmmm," and other fun guttural sounds will suffice. Verbally let the person know that you understand what he or she is saying. Use phrases such as "Yes, I agree," "I understand," or "I see." Paraphrase what the person has said to you and repeat it back. Two phrases that make this very easy are "If I understand you correctly . . . ." and "What I hear you saying is . . . ." In short order, repeat what you have just heard, or how you interpreted it. This way, if you misunderstood or did not get it right, that person can correct you right then, before there is a chance for misunderstanding.

Do you understand? Make sure that you are clear about what people are saying. Be positive that you heard and understood them. Big mistakes occur when someone thinks that he or she understood the other person but the message was misconstrued.

It's Not How Much You Say

Don't feel compelled to say something. Sometimes silence is golden. Silence provokes people to say more than they would otherwise. You can learn a lot this way. Many people are uncomfortable with silence, so they keep talking just to prevent it from being awkward. This works very well with people who you need information or a decision from. Try this the next time you are in a situation where you are expected to say something next. See how long the silence goes before another person picks up the conversation.

> *Amber tells of a colleague who in meetings would ask stupid questions, or questions that had already been answered. Sometimes the colleague would make stupid statements for no reason other than to be heard. She would raise her hand to state the obvious or be redundant. "I agree with what you are saying. I think our goal should be to make a profit." SO WHAT. Everyone knows this already. This person just wanted to hear her own voice, thinking that these pearls of insight would get her noticed. It did. Management thought Amber's coworker didn't know when to keep her mouth shut. The only attention she got was negative.*

Don't ask questions for the sake of asking questions. Ask to understand. Talking to hear yourself talk or just to be heard can be very dangerous.

Think before you speak. Often, people who talk too much are insecure. By talking, they are trying to validate that they are smart, knowledgeable, and in demand. When in reality, it's the opposite. The person who is respected for his or her opinions chooses opportunities to say something very wisely and selectively—listening, becoming informed, and gaining insight before choosing to speak.

YOUR PROFESSIONAL PRESENCE

COMMUNICATING EFFECTIVELY involves much more than what you say. It's also how you say it. Your delivery, tone, and nonverbal gestures affect how your message is received.

Move confidently and smoothly when talking with your hands or gesturing. It's OK to talk with your hands, but don't make quick, jerky motions. Speak with enthusiasm. Enthusiastic and upbeat speech does not mean acting hyper and talking so fast that no one can understand you. Nor does it mean sounding like a preacher or used-car salesman.

Keep your voice even and steady. Speaking smoothly and at a moderate pace makes people feel more comfortable and helps you to be understood. Find a happy medium. If you are so excited that you speed up and start running words together, you will make the person you are talking with nervous. If you are speaking in a flat monotone, you will have to periodically wake them up.

Change your pace, sometimes. There may be occasions when you want to alter the pace of your delivery to get a certain response. Maybe your conversation needs to be slowed or sped up, so you should act accordingly. If a person is going off on tangents or getting ahead of where you want the conversation to go, try to slow it down on purpose.

Don't slouch or lean on a table. Michael was in a meeting with a client and wanted to feel comfortable. So he slumped in his chair and then leaned forward, putting both elbows on the table and resting his head in his hands. Comfortable? Very. Professional? Not at all. Try not to look like you are at your kitchen table or at a bar. Like your mother said, "Sit up straight." Act like you want to be there. If you are slumping in your chair or fidgeting, it's obvious that you want to be somewhere else.

Make people notice you. Consultant Debra Benton, in her book *Lions Don't Need to Roar*, recommends pausing for a second upon entering a room or meeting. It sounds corny, but you make a presence. People will notice you. If you are late or are just arriving, let people see you. Don't try to slink into the room so that no one notices. You are noticed anyway. Don't act like a weasel sneaking in the back door. Remember, you can get away with a lot of things if you do them with confidence or act like you know what you are doing.

WRITING SKILLS

YOU CAN'T ESCAPE writing. Letters. Memos. Contracts. Reports. Plans. Every industry has a different way to write and correspond. During your first few days on the job ask if you can see old letters, reports, memos, or anything that you may have to write dur-

Greg was a little hyper and didn't think things through before he opened his mouth. He was so eager to make a good impression and let people know what he was talking about, that he cut people off and finished their sentences, often making himself look incredibly stupid.

Greg finally stuck his loafer in his mouth in front of a client in a big-time way. The client was talking about a particular company she worked with. The client was telling Greg, "One of our main clients is Lotus, you may be familiar with them, they make . . ." Greg interrupted, cutting the person off mid-sentence, "Yeah, yeah, sure, I know all about Lotus. They make great cars. I love the Esprit." The client looked at Greg as if he were the rudest if not the dumbest human on earth at that moment. "No, if you would let me finish, I was about to tell you Lotus, the software maker, they make Lotus 123, and Lotus Notes. Perhaps you have heard of them?" "Hot Rod Greg" was sent packing with his tail between his legs. Listen to everything a person has to say before you chime in. Unless you are a mind reader, don't interrupt or finish another person's sentences.

ing your tenure there. This will help you to learn the particular style, content and verbiage that is common for your industry and company. Writing in an engineering firm is very different from in an advertising agency. There are some general rules, however, about writing well in the professional world.

You Can Always Improve

The first thing to realize is that there is always room for improvement. There are two surefire ways to become a better writer. The first is to read. Yes, reading other people's (good) writing serves as an example of what you should do. Read as much as possible to help improve your structure and grammar. The second way to improve your writing is to . . . WRITE. Practice. Write as much as you can. If your writing skills are lacking, write short stories, letters to your family, or keep a journal.

Even professionals who are thought of as good communicators or who count on language and writing for a living are always practicing. Mike Tirico of ESPN SportsCenter is someone who makes his living talking, yet Mike says that if there is one thing that he still works to improve every day, it's his command of the English language. If you have ever seen one of Mike's broadcasts, you will know that he is a fantastic communicator, but even he is always trying to improve.

Most of us aren't even close to that level. Tony Good, Public Relations Director for EDS, says that it's a sad comment that today a person who is only a mediocre writer stands out above the crowd. Writing today is that poor. If you want to stand out above the rest of the competition, become a good writer. People do notice.

Clear and Concise

Business writing is usually an exercise in economics and efficiency. This is not school, where you have to work to stretch out a paper. The boss will not come to you and say, "I need a fifteen-page report." (Unless, of course, you are in journalism or another writing-intensive field, such as public relations, where length may matter.) Otherwise, make sure to keep it short, clear, and concise. The goal is to get your message across and understood as quickly as possible. Remember, time is money. Your time and your coworkers'. You aren't there to write the great American novel. Don't be verbose. Don't think that writing for business means that you have to be a technical writer. Write like you speak and gear it so an eighth grader can understand it. I realize that you are writing for much more than the average thirteen-year-old, but write so it's concise and can be understood through the clutter. You don't get points for how eloquent and crafted your memo is. You get points if it's understood.

Write Legibly

Write legibly. Unless you are a doctor writing a prescription or a pro athlete giving autographs, people must be able to read your signature and handwriting. Nobody cares if you have a really cool and elaborate signature.

If you have bad handwriting, (which I have), work on it or write everything on a computer and print it out. I write most of my personal correspondence on a word processor for that reason.

Make sure that you write your name on (or at least initial) and date all correspondence like memos, notes, letters, or anything that you are passing along. You want to get credit for it and if the recipient has a question, she knows to come to you for an answer.

Proofread everything that you do. Earlier I mentioned how simple mistakes such as grammar and spelling can ruin you. Use spell-check and, if necessary, have others look at it. After you complete something, read it aloud. Does it make sense and get your point across? Always double-check things.

USING THE PHONE EFFECTIVELY

DEPENDING ON YOUR chosen profession, you may do most, if not all, of your business on the telephone. Jeff, who deals in computer sales all over the world, does almost all of his business over the phone.

Many brokers and people involved in financial markets deal predominantly on the phone as well.

With our increasing global economy and the need for instant information, the phone and all of its accessories has become one of the most important communication tools available. There are several tips for using it effectively. Many of us fell into bad phone habits while in school, but they can be broken easily.

Answering the Phone

It starts with something as simple as answering the phone. How you answer the phone is vitally important. If you are at the office, don't just say "hello" like you do at home. Answer it professionally by identifying yourself. Say your name. This lets the person calling know that they have reached the right person. "This is Bradley Richardson." Even just your name will do, but never say your last name only. "Richardson here." Way too cocky. (Unless you work in trading, where time is money, and it's good to be cocky!)

Identify Yourself

When you are calling someone, always say your name and company. Tell the receptionist who you are and the company you are with. When you reach the person you are trying to contact, tell whoever answers your full name and company, as well. Even if you are familiar to them, don't assume they know your first name or can identify your voice. You will realize that during the course of a day you will have a million and one things running through your mind. If someone you met once or twice calls and says "Hey, this is Stephanie," you will draw a complete blank. So identify yourself fully. If someone does this to you, have your receptionist or secretary (if you are lucky enough to have one) screen calls by asking what company the caller is with. It may trigger something or help you remember.

Using Voice Mail to Your Advantage

Voice mail. The proliferation of voice mail is incredible. According to *Fortune*, there were almost 12 million messages left on voice mailboxes last year. It seems almost every office has it now, and people are communicating with it more and more. Some companies make it so difficult to reach a person that you wonder if everyone has left on holiday or gone home. Voice mail and answering machines are here to stay, so use them to your advantage.

When you leave a phone message, always leave your phone number and the time you called. The person you are trying to reach may have misplaced your number or may not want to look it up. Even if you think he knows the number, leave it on the machine. Make it easy for someone to return your call.

Let people know the time and day that you called. Leave a complete message if it's suitable. If something can be decided or solved over voice mail, do it. Don't keep playing phone tag. It's possible to have an ongoing conversation and resolve what needs to be handled. That is one of the wonders of this technology.

Leaving Your Own Phone Message

If you are leaving a greeting message that others will hear on your voice mail or answering machine, remember that it represents you professionally. Don't leave stupid or cute messages like when you were in school.

You don't know what the next person calling you will think of your witty message. It's best to be polite and somewhat conservative where phone messages are concerned. Avoid leaving any of the following messages or any other wonderfully witty response that shows what a smartass you are: "We're not here, so leave a message. At the beep, you know what to do." Don't have a duet with your roommate where you chime in unison "Susie and Tracy aren't in right now." Don't play music in the background, no matter how cool you think STP or the band *du jour* is. Leave a simple message, "You have reached Bradley

> *Eric learned this lesson the hard way. After interviewing for a job with a magazine, he left town for a few days. He forgot to change the message, which joked how he was going to be away a while, because he and some buddies had gone to Africa to hunt wild boar for the weekend. Sure enough, upon his return there was a message from the editor of the magazine. He went into panic, fearing that the editor must have thought he was the biggest shmuck to ever walk. "Mr. Professional Writer." Luckily, the editor thought it was funny and offered Eric the job despite his wild boar hunting experience.*

Richardson of The BGR Group. I'm not available at the moment. Please leave a message and I will return your call as soon as possible." I know it's not the most exciting thing in the world, but go with it.

Is This a Good Time?

When you call people, you don't know what is going on at the other end of the phone. They could be managing a crisis at the moment. They might have someone in their office, or be in a meeting. If they sound busy or distracted, extend the courtesy of asking, "Is this a good time?" or "Do you have time to talk?" You can make a bigger impact and have a better chance of being understood or getting what you want if you are considerate of their time. Similarly, if someone calls you while you are in a meeting, say that you will call back. The person in your office generally has priority. Don't leave someone hanging who has made the effort to physically come to your office.

Speaker Phones

Don't use a speaker phone if you can help it. It may feel cool, but you sound like you are in a tunnel. Whomever you're talking to will hate it. It makes people feel unimportant, largely because you are probably doing something else while you are talking on the speaker phone. That person does not have your undivided attention. If someone puts you on one, ask if he or she will take you off. You don't know who else is sitting there, listening to your conversation. Don't ever say anything confidential on a speaker phone. For that matter, don't say anything really important on a cellular phone or airplane phone either. You will have zero privacy.

Rules for Using a Cellular Phone

Rules for using a cellular phone are quite simple. Don't be obnoxious with it. It can be a valuable tool, but don't be the type of jerk who takes it everywhere and shows off by using it at the movies or in a restaurant. One Big Six accounting firm prohibited its associates from carrying cellular phones, to avoid looking pretentious. If something is so important that it can't wait, you shouldn't be going out to eat or to a movie anyway. Unless you are a doctor or are saving lives, don't be conspicuous with it. Use it, but be subtle and respect other people around you. No one else really wants to hear your conversation in the restaurant as you scream on this thing. It shows inflated self-importance. Cellular phones can be incredibly useful and time-saving tools if used wisely.

THE LANGUAGE OF BUSINESS

YOU CAN'T SPEAK in the professional world like you do at home or as you did in college. Don't use slang, foul language, college speak, or technobabble. Many people aren't going to understand your little lingo or slang words. Even mainstays like "dude" and "sucks" are inappropriate. These words are such a common part of everyday language today, but still are not thought of as the most professional choice of words. You are dealing across many different socioeconomic groups, racial groups, and generations. Not everybody will understand you or find it cute and amusing. They will find that you, quite simply, can't communicate. Communicate clearly. You get points for being understood, not for being cool.

Don't Curse

You may cuss like a sailor at home, but in the professional world it has no place. Sure, you find some professionals who use the f-word as a noun, verb, and adjective or as an endearing term, but remember how important your new professional reputation is. You can be understood without doing that.

Don't Be Sexist

Don't use sexist or gender-based language. No generalizations such as he, his. Never assume anything. When in doubt, find out if it's a Mr. or Ms. Speak clearly.

Know the Buzzwords

Every industry or business has its own particular language. There are buzzwords for everything. Ask someone you work with what those are if you can't pick them up from conversation, but most importantly learn them quickly. But don't fall victim to technospeak as many in high-tech and engineering fields do. No one will be impressed with your dazzling knowledge of the lingo if they don't know what you are saying. If you are with a group that understands and speaks that language, great. Otherwise, make sure that you don't lose people.

Be Understood

Don't mumble or put your hands in front of your mouth when you speak. Ditch the filler words. Your client or the person you are interviewing with *will* count the number of times you say, "you know," "uh," "like," and "really."

Look for Nonverbal Cues

You can tell if a person is listening to you or understands what you are saying by watching how he or she reacts. If someone is fidgeting, shifting, or looking away, he might be bored. If a person's eyes glaze over or his brow is furled, he or she may be confused. Pick up on this and switch your tactics.

Be Able to Talk to Everyone

Think like a chameleon able to adapt to your surroundings. Be able to talk to the person on the shop floor, the technical staff, the CEO, the sales person, the secretary, and the accountant.

Let's Agree to Disagree

It may come as a big shock, but people won't always agree with you. That's all right. You can disagree with someone and still communicate effectively and maintain the relationship. Many great ideas can come out of a disagreement, because an alternative solution or compromise must be reached. Disagreement is not a negative. The key to dealing with a disagreement is empathy. Try to see the other person's point of view and respect it, even if you disagree. Don't try to shove your position down a person's throat. Emphasize the positive when presenting your side. There is a lot of ego invested in some people's ideas. No one will listen to you if you cut down their idea or make them feel stupid. A great transition to present your views is to say, "That's a great idea, but have you considered this?" Be *for* something, instead of against it.

Be Polite

Again, it really is the little things that people notice. Courtesy and the golden rule work very well in business. You get more from people if you treat them as you would like to be treated. "Please." "Thank you." "I appreciate it." These three little phrases can do more for your career than any others. Use them often.

Acknowledge people who do things for you or pass things your way. "Hey, Jill, thanks for the article," or "thanks for doing that for me." People like to get credit and be acknowledged for things. People don't get enough of it. Whether it's a job well done, a small favor, or good news, recognizing people can take you a long way.

Ask if you can call a person by his or her first name. Don't assume you are on a first-name basis, particularly with clients or people much older than yourself. Most of the time a person will wave it off and say, "Oh please, call me Scott."

Don't just tell someone you are putting them on hold during a phone call. *Ask* if you may put them on hold. You can't treat customers and others in business in the casual way you treat your family and friends. Actually, you should treat *everyone* politely.

Communicating in Meetings

Meetings, gatherings, powwows, events, whatever you choose to call them, can be highly productive or the biggest waste of time in the world. I've been in meetings where the goal was to decide whether to have a meeting. Seriously, I would rather have watched grass grow. Here are some tips to make the most effective use of your time in meetings. These apply for both informal and formal meetings.

Is this meeting really necessary? If you are running a meeting or are just a participant, try to keep things simple. Meet with goals in mind. If you are running a meeting, make sure that everyone knows when and where it will be and what it will be about and how to prepare. Don't have a meeting unless it's absolutely necessary or if there are no other ways of getting a problem resolved. Time is too valuable to waste on BS meetings, yet they happen in every organization.

Establish rules. Have some order to your meeting so you can reach your goal. If it's a brainstorming session, you might make the rule that no one criticizes an idea immediately. This allows for a free flow of ideas. If there is a particular order to speak, fine. Whatever you and your group choose, make sure there are rules and that everyone knows them.

Some groups love to rehash problems that have already been discussed. Learn to recognize when this happens and ask the group to move on, or take the initiative to change the subject. Work for a solution or something in particular. Don't just sit and toss things around.

Sit in view of the most powerful person in the room. Just as when you were in class, where you sit in a meeting can be important. If you are in a meeting with your boss or a client, try to sit opposite or in view of the leaders. This way you will get noticed. When you aren't saying anything, you will be in plain view of the leaders, and when you speak, you will be looked at directly.

Working a Room

A different type of meeting is the cocktail party, reception, or trade show. At any organized event where there are many people you can meet and network with, place yourself near the door. This allows you to talk to many people without being stuck with them for a long time. Also, never sit at a business or cocktail party. You can get trapped with someone who is boring. Work the room and don't go straight for the food. Don't pitch a tent and camp out at the food table.

Persuasion and Influence

One of the most common functions of communicating is to influence or persuade another person. The best way to influence or persuade someone, whether it's a boss, client, peer, or anyone, is to make them think something is their own idea. Plant the seed of an idea or what you want in that person's head and let him think he thought of it. Your job is to help them believe that it's a great idea. As I mentioned earlier, people tend to make an ego investment in ideas and decisions. Someone is more likely to champion an idea if he or she believes that it's their own. This also works well with your parents, boyfriend, or girl-friend.

▪26▪

Getting Noticed: Become Your Own

Public Relations Firm

You are always selling yourself and your ideas. It's a constant effort to get noticed within an organization. The key to rising quickly and being promoted is to make your achievements and accomplishments known to the people who matter and can influence your career. Those people can only know about your abilities if you tell them and make yourself visible.

Make Yourself Visible

Be seen by as many people as possible. Make sure that you know everyone in your company or division. Volunteer for committees, teams, or tasks forces. Ask to make presentations at company meetings or functions. Look for any opportunity where you will be seen by many people in the organization and where you will have a chance to make an impact and affect policy. Better yet, find opportunities related to the bottom line and add immediate value.

Take a high-profile project. After you have a few successes under your belt and are comfortable in the new position, you can take a few chances to show what you can do. At this point you can get noticed by seeking the high-visibility, high-reward jobs. These might be the more risky assignments that others are scared of taking. If you feel that you have what it takes to succeed or at least make a good showing, go for it.

It's easy to think that a safer project with less risk of failure would be more desirable than one where your chances of failing were high. However, early in your career this isn't always the case. If you take the challenge and fail, big deal. It was high-risk anyway—everyone knew it. You at least score points for getting in the ring. However, if you succeed, you are an instant whiz kid.

You might say "Why would I do that? There is so much opportunity to fail." That is just it. The more there is to risk, the greater the possible reward. If you accept a task that is very risky, many people expect you to fail. If you don't succeed, so what. You haven't disappointed anyone. You are young and were not expected to succeed anyway. No real harm done to your career.

On the other hand, if you were to accept a challenge at which everyone thought you would fail, and succeed, you look like a hero. Positions like this offer a great opportunity. Win or lose, you can't go wrong with taking the risk. Management will look at you favorably for getting in there and giving it a shot.

Be Your Own Spokesperson

Become your own spokesperson. Let people know about any positive event or accomplishment through notes, memos, and by telling them. Think of notes and memos as your "personal internal press release." Copy them to your boss and his superior. If you send a report to your boss detailing your latest accomplishment, discovery, or observation, let people know. Sign your name prominently on everything you do. If you pass an article to someone, write your name on it, "Thought you might like this. Bradley."

Don't be a braggart, but in the course of conversation, let people know what project you are working on. Tell them how you closed a certain deal, how you achieved something difficult or unprecedented, or relate a situation where you have been dealing with a certain client. When you are facing management or your boss, tell them what you are working on or what you have recently accomplished.

Another way to do this without being so obvious, is to ask for advice. Tell your boss that you are working on certain projects and would like an opinion. This way the boss knows what you are up to and will

There is a tale of a soft drink executive who, early in his career, was given the opportunity to lead an overseas assignment. It was a product launch. He had no experience at it, but had enough guts to accept the challenge. He failed miserably. Dejected, he was prepared to be laid off or demoted. He felt his career was at an early dead end. What happened instead was that the company, seeing his promise and ability to take risks, promoted him. The company felt that it was a difficult situation in which to succeed, but that he showed ingenuity and determination. He may have failed on that project, but he displayed the qualities needed to succeed in the future.

keep an eye out to see how his advice turned out. Make people aware of things.

Tell People What You Think

The problem with some people is that they are waiting for someone to ask them their opinions. When that day comes and they are asked for their pearls of wisdom, they fold. They either don't have an opinion or won't express it. Even if it's counter to others, have an opinion and positions on certain issues. Let people know what you think.

I'm not talking about forcing your way of thinking on someone when they don't ask. However, if you feel strongly about something and take a position, people notice. They may not agree, but they will notice. Having an opinion at least shows that you have put some thought into an issue or problem.

Make Yourself a Resource

Make yourself a resource who people rely on and can go to for questions, information, special expertise, or access to information. Become an expert at something that people need. You might know a special procedure, or have technical expertise in an area. You might be very helpful and always be there to answer a question. Even keeping up with the grapevine and knowing what is going on around the office can make you a resource who people come to. Whatever it may be, make sure that you offer something special that everyone needs, or wants to come to you for. Whether it's a peer or your boss, make yourself invaluable. Become such an asset that these people must rely on you for assistance.

Meet People Outside Your Company

Join and participate on committees and in volunteer organizations. Become involved with industry associations. Making yourself known and promoting yourself can take place outside your own company also.

There may be a day when you need another job or want to leave the company you are with. Making and maintaining industry contacts is crucial. You can gain exposure within the industry by joining various trade groups and associations. Go to trade shows. You may even write an article or a letter to the editor of an industry or business publication. You never know when a new opportunity may come up from a competitor who is familiar with your accomplishments.

Use the Open Door Policy

Many companies claim to have an "open door" policy. What this means, is that your boss's door is open to you, and that he or she is willing to talk to you any time. It lets management say, "we are approachable and willing to listen to our employees." If your company or boss offers an open door policy, make sure that you use it.

The problem with open door policies is that not enough people take advantage of them. Sure, sometimes it's a disingenuous gesture, but there is only one way to find out. The benefits are limitless. Approaching your manager through an open door policy is a great way to toot your own horn, pitch an idea, voice a concern, or make your career plans known. Don't be afraid of approaching your boss or upper management. The worst thing that can happen is management will know more about you, and can now match your face with your name.

Dealing Cards

When you meet someone, always tell him your name and offer your card. Even if you are sitting in an airplane or meet someone in passing, make sure that you introduce yourself. Spread your name around with people and make sure they know it. You should always carry business cards with you and remember to give plenty of them away.

As important as giving your card to someone is to make sure you collect theirs. Always ask for someone's business card. It will help you remember his or her name, and expand your Rolodex.

Keep notes. When you meet someone, write notes on the back of her card or on a 3x5 index card. Just two lines about something special to remember her by or what you talked about. It's also a nice gesture to drop a short two-sentence note after meeting someone. It doesn't have to say anything more than, "I enjoyed meeting you last week. Stay in touch." It may seem insignificant, but the small gestures are what stick in a person's mind. Also, most people our age fail to do this, so when you do, it makes an impression. It also refreshes her memory, and reinforces your name.

Be Different

Some people follow the sheep or herd mentality, doing things the same way as everyone else. Keeping a high profile and being noticed takes constant effort. Always be on the lookout for ways to stand out and be different. Not weird different, but unique. Look for things that others don't think of, or ways to do them differently with your own style.

GLENN J. SOLOMON
Magazine Publisher, Attorney, and Commercial Real Estate Executive
Age: 28

MOST LARGE CITIES HAVE a local "city" magazine, such as *New York* magazine and the *Washingtonian*. Cities such as Atlanta, Boston, Los Angeles, and Indianapolis all have local magazines, as well. These magazines are often very high-profile. They

---

are critics of local culture and they chronicle who's who and what is hot in the city. Three years ago, Dallas lost its flagship magazine, *D* magazine. Poor management and decreasing readership forced *D* magazine to close its doors, leaving a void for the city.

Earlier this year, the talk around Dallas was about a young man from New Orleans, with no previous publishing experience, who intended to purchase the rights to *D* magazine and fire up the presses once more.

When the word broke that 28-year-old Glenn Solomon had caused this phoenix to rise again, people in the community and in the publishing world wanted to know, "Who is this kid?"

Glenn Solomon grew up the son of a very successful New Orleans businessman. "I was always surrounded by business in my family. My father could smell a good deal. There were a lot of expectations for me." Glenn did not start off with the idea of becoming a publisher, attorney, and commercial real estate executive, all of which he is today. His original goal was to become a film director or producer. Yet, after a brief stint at the USC film school, he decided that film wasn't his calling. He spent time at three other colleges around the country, before finally graduating from Louisiana State University with a degree in General Studies.

From there Glenn went straight to law school at Tulane. "I knew that I did not want to be an attorney, but the legal education was a great foundation for business, or whatever I decided to do." In addition to his legal education, he learned about becoming an entrepreneur. Glenn and a friend started a note-taking service and made a nice little profit. Even then, Glenn knew how to identify and take advantage of opportunities.

Upon graduating from law school, he took the bar exam, even though he did not want to practice as an attorney. Actually, Glenn did not know exactly what he wanted to do, but he had an idea of where he wanted to do it. "I was deciding whether to move to Atlanta or Dallas. Both cities offered a lot of opportunity." Let me say that opportunity for many recent graduates means a place where jobs are plentiful. Opportunity to Glenn was something on a different level.

Unlike the majority of us, Glenn was lucky enough to win the genetic lottery and was born into very wealthy family. Yet Glenn is very different from many twentysomethings who are fortunate enough to have been born to wealth. Glenn Solomon is a "doer."

When asked what he attributes his success to, he says, in a sincere and unassuming manner, "I'm just a guy who has some money." True, he does have some money, but he also has incredible people skills and business sense. "I'm a little bit of a showman and I can entertain," Glenn says.

His flair for promotion and people skills have served him well. Shortly after Glenn moved to Dallas, a friend approached him with the idea of purchasing two office buildings, which could be picked up very cheaply. "My friend's father was in the business and we tried to emulate his success. We believed that with a little marketing and effort the buildings could be leased and filled with tenants very easily." Glenn saw the opportunity and purchased the buildings. After networking and hosting several parties for commercial real estate brokers in the area, Glenn's showmanship resulted in having the buildings leased to near capacity. This generated a great cash flow, which would help launch the next project. ("Real estate just wasn't fulfilling to me.")

Glenn heard rumors that the rights to the name and the subscriber list for the old *D* magazine were up for sale. Glenn knew nothing about the publishing industry or what it took to run a magazine. But he looked at the old company's financials, and thought that the problems that plagued the magazine in the past were caused by poor management. If he were to run the magazine, he could cut costs considerably and run the magazine at a nice profit. He knew that he could hire people with publishing background to help with the day-to-day operations of the magazine. Some of his current employees were also magazine staffers and writers at *D*.

So, how does one go about purchasing a magazine? "I picked up the phone and called American Express Publishing, who happened to be the owners, and told them I was interested in buying it." Sounds simple enough. "We negotiated for several weeks and at one point it was sold to another party. I made that person an offer, and eventually won the bidding."

Buying buildings and magazines can be pretty heady stuff for a 28-year-old. I asked Glenn if people treated him differently or did not take him seriously at first, because of his age? "No. In the beginning, I did most of my business over the phone. I knew what I was talking about and spoke the language, so they had no idea how old I was. When people did finally meet me, it was too far into the negotiations."

Glenn now has about twenty employees, many of whom are older than he is. "When I started this, everyone tried to give me advice. People will try to give you advice. Take it. Even if it is negative advice, you can learn from it. But make sure that you learn to tell what is real constructive criticism and what is bitter criticism."

Glenn also says, "Postpone instant gratification. Don't take the money and run. If early in your career you chase the money and work for what is easy, you will pay for it later. Sacrifice as much as you can early on. Take the job that pays you less, but will give you range. Make those sacrifices now and it will pay off later."

Stick to it and make the commitment to see things through. "It takes many little steps to make the whole. I made the commitment to law school. It was hard, but it's something that I use every day, and it will benefit me in thirty years."

Glenn's advice to someone just beginning a career is to love what you do. "I love what I am doing. I snap out of bed every morning and it doesn't feel like work to me. The amount of money that you make doesn't matter. It's [whether] you enjoy what you have. You never know where things will lead you, but if you follow where your heart leads you, whether it makes money or not, you will realize that you are successful because it's what you wanted to do." According to Glenn's definition of success, he is truly successful.

▪27▪

Keeping the Edge: Staying Sharp and Moving Ahead

When you quit getting better, you stop being good.
—Anonymous

Several weeks or months into a new position you are beginning to loosen up and adjust to the real world. You start to feel comfortable. You have learned the ropes and are quickly getting up to speed. Now you need to look at what will make you more valuable. How can I move ahead? Just because you understand what is going on doesn't mean that it's all downhill and coasting from here on. You have to prove yourself every day. How do you keep the edge day in and day out, throughout your career?

Be Self-Motivated

Look for things to do and seek opportunities. No one will hand you an engraved invitation, so don't wait for someone to tell you what to do. You must make your breaks. If you see a need, fill it. Carve out your own little niche or specialty, and become an expert at something. Consultant and author Richard Moran says, "The main function of a business is to produce and sell something. Get close to those activities." Make yourself valuable by being close to the front line so you can contribute to the bottom line.

Look for ways to make things happen and then act on them. I can't remember where I first heard or read this quote so I can't take credit for its insight. I have it displayed in my office where I can look at it every time I am contemplating going forward with what I think is a good idea. It says "Action produces results. Knowledge is only potential power until it comes into the hands of someone who knows how to get herself to take effective action." Don't talk about something. Get off your butt and do it. Too many brilliant men and women die in obscurity or never reach their potential because they don't take action.

Keep your eyes open for opportunities and ways you can contribute, both in and outside your area and company. You don't know when an opportunity may present itself. Keep your résumé updated and keep a copy with you in your portfolio. Always have your eyes and ears open to new opportunities and always hear people out who want to talk to you about a position or opportunity . . . even if you are perfectly happy where you are at. You can always say "No thanks."

See the Big Picture

Try to see the big picture. It's easy to look for immediate gratification or the quick fix early in your career. What is in this for me? Where do I fit in? How does this affect me? You add more value to an organization and can spot opportunities for yourself more easily by having a macroperspective when looking at your organization and career.

Notice how one thing can affect many others. As you accept more responsibility, don't be as concerned about where it will get you in the short term. Look at what a decision or situation means down the road. What will you learn from it? How you can use it later?

Try to view things as a chess match. Chess masters aren't as concerned with the one move they are making at that moment as they are about the overall condition of the board. They are formulating a strategy, and are thinking many moves ahead. They see the board in terms of how they want it to be. The big picture.

It's very easy to criticize a company's judgment or question why something was done a certain way. Before you are quick to discount these things (some of which may be truly stupid), try to look at how they affect the general direction of the organization or what they are trying to accomplish. Where do they fit into the total scheme?

Don't Rest on Your Laurels

You always have to keep proving yourself. While a track record and past successes are valuable, in most organizations it's "What have you done *LATELY?*" Current results are the true measuring stick. Never stay satisfied. You should always be striving for more and looking for a better way to do things. Question everything. If people had been content with the horse and buggy, the automobile would never have been invented. Don't become fat and complacent.

No one is ever safe from being canned. Even big-name CEOs and executives who you would think are secure are getting axed left and right for everything from poor stock performance to the need for new blood.

Continuous Improvement

The Japanese, who have become legends in their commitment to quality, have a word called *kaizen. Kaizen* means continuous improvement. Just as manufacturers are constantly looking for new ways to improve their products, you should always be striving for continuous improvement of your personal product—your skills and abilities.

Invest in yourself. The best job security you can have is to keep your skills updated and keep trying to improve. Constantly learn and increase your knowledge. Take classes. Keep up on trends and information in and out of your industry. Learn something new. Pick up new skills. See if your boss will pay for you to go to seminars

After Mike graduated from Purdue, he began a very successful sales career. During his first two years, he was an incredible success. Mike set company sales records and made a ton of money. Management was praising him and telling him what a great future he had. He began to believe his own public relations and became lazy. "Hey I don't have to work that hard now. Look at what I have done." He was able to slide for a few months before his managers became concerned. When he was questioned about his performance, he said "Hey, look at what I have done for you in the past." His performance continued to slide. Mike thought he was bulletproof.

By the end of the year he was ranked near the bottom of the company, but was still acting as he did when he was on top. He felt that people should respect him and management should appreciate him for what he had done in the past. Sure, he was valuable in the past, but he was no longer pulling his weight. By the beginning of the next year, Mike was fired. Mike was in shock when he was let go. He did not understand how this could happen after all he had done.

Our friend Mike also teaches us another valuable lesson. During the days when he was making so much money, Mike thought the good times would never end. After he began to experience a little success, Mike bought a house. Then he bought a Porsche to go with his other car. He became "Mr. Cell Phone," impressing friends by ordering pizza from his car. The only thing he wasn't doing was cruising the high schools in his Porsche with a "Mr. Microphone." The next year, when things weren't so good, Mike was stuck having to unload his house and the Porsche. The lesson here is that the rug can be pulled out from under you any time. Get a grip and save for a rainy day.

or classes. If your company provides a tuition re-imbursement so you can further your education, take advantage of it.

There is always something else to learn. Just when you think that you know it all and have exhausted every avenue for learning, look again. If you want more juice from a lemon, you squeeze the peel the other way. Look for other ways to squeeze your company for more to learn.

Be Flexible

Things in the professional world will not always go as planned. Clients and bosses have a peculiar way of doing the opposite of what you think they might. Your ability to go with the flow and adapt to what is going on around you is crucial to keeping your edge professionally.

Deadlines may be moved forward or pushed back. Requirements or specifications on a project may change when it's halfway completed. Emergencies pop up. You may even be asked to decipher cryptic instructions that don't make any sense. My personal favorite is when your boss or a client is making a request or giving you instructions. Rather than being clear, he or she says, "You know what I mean," fully expecting you to be clairvoyant. From that point, it's a crapshoot whether it's done properly.

There will be times when you aren't given any direction, or guidance. Don't moan about it. Deal with it. This is how the world works. It can be unclear and ambiguous. You are part improvisationalist, mind reader and short-order cook. The earlier you learn to adapt to constant change and deal with ambiguous directions or situations, the more effective you will be. Rarely will things in the professional world be black and white or clear-cut. Directions, instructions, decisions, and choices all include many variables that can affect the outcome. Change occurs as quickly as the wind, so become a fast study and learn to pick things up quickly.

PROFESSIONAL APPEARANCE

YOUR PROFESSIONAL APPEARANCE matters. To some, this may be the most obvious thing in the world. But you would be surprised how many people arrive for job interviews or client meetings dressed like a bike messenger.

Certain dress is accepted in different organizations and in different parts of the country. Susan Bixler, in her book *Professional Presence*, says that there are three rules about your professional appearance that remain consistent:

- If you want the job, you have to look the part.
- If you want the promotion, you have to look promotable.
- If you want respect, you have to dress as well or better than the industry standard.

Pretty simple stuff.

You may have heard the saying that if you want to move up, dress like the person two levels ahead of you. It's true. You are going to command more respect if you dress professionally and are well groomed. If you dress like a kid or a low-level person, you will be treated that way. Even if yours is a casual office, you can dress nicely. Stay away from T-shirts or jeans, at least when you meet with clients. Who is going to trust you with their account, money, or product if you look like you bag groceries at Food King?

Dealing with Casual Day

Many offices are moving toward casual Fridays. Remember that casual generally means "nice" casual. Be comfortable, but remember you are still at work and are representing yourself and the organization. Casual day does not mean a T-shirt, Birkenstocks, and jeans shorts. Women

James, a free spirit, worked for a high-tech firm. He had acquired several tattoos in his travels and was now exploring the fun and exciting world of body piercing. Casually looking at him, it was difficult to tell that he wore any accessories, but the more you listened to him speak, you noticed that he had an odd lisp. It was so noticeable and distinct that you wondered if he seriously had a speech impediment. But if you got a closer look when his mouth was open, you realized his tongue was pierced. My first question was "how does this guy eat?"

His fondness for body piercing and his complete incomprehension of how the real world works came to light when he asked his boss if it would be all right to get his eyebrows pierced with an inch-long bar. Since James occasionally met with clients, this was vetoed. A major blow to personal freedoms, I know . . . but c'mon, you're scaring the customers. How you choose to decorate your nipples and buttocks is your choice, but at least keep offbeat accessories and tattoos limited to places only a loved one can appreciate.

shouldn't take their fashion hints from Amanda on *Melrose Place*. Her skirts are too short for anything outside of Friday Night.

Before someone in an ad agency or a systems engineer gets my home phone and harasses me for trying to act as the fashion police, I realize that appearances and norms vary among industries and around the country. Just remember, it's the work that shows how creative you are, not how you dress.

What is that Smell?

Pay attention to how you smell. Yes, smell. I'm going to assume that using deodorant is a regular part of your morning ritual, so enough said. What I am referring to is cologne and perfume. Use it in moderation. Everyone likes to smell nice, but it's not Saturday night and you aren't on the prowl.

When you use a perfume or cologne for a while, you tend to forget how strong it is. It's easy to put on too much, which results in an aromatic cloud that follows you everywhere and alerts people to your arrival five minutes before you get there. Be aware of it. Also, if, God forbid, you smoke during working hours, don't come back to the office smelling like a pack of week-old Camels, or as if you spent your afternoon in a bar. It's not very professional.

CYA . . . COVER YOUR ASS

THE WORLD IS FULL of acronyms: MP—Military Police, APV—All Purpose Vehicle, RV—Recreational Vehicle, PC—Personal Computer or Politically Correct, and of course the most important acronym for your new career, CYA—Cover Your Ass. If you don't CYA your career could be DOA.

You are on your own for making sure that your bases are covered and all responsibilities are handled. No one will remind you or prod you to check and double-check. If something slips through the cracks or isn't perfect, all fingers point to you. Make sure that you take care of what needs to be handled and prevent any surprises. Don't take anything for granted or assume that everything will be taken care of.

Document Everything

One of the most obvious ways to cover your ass is by documenting everything you do that might be important. This goes for phone calls, letters, or notes from a meeting. If you call someone on a certain date, write down what you talked about in your DayTimer. When you have a meeting, when a promise or agreement is made, or whenever something good or bad happens, write it down. People have fragile memories. Some people genuinely forget things. Others are more selective in their memory and have trouble remembering details when it might harm them.

Ask for names. If a person promises something to you or gives you information, get his name and write it down. When your boss asks if you took care of something or if you found something out, you can answer confidently. If the information was wrong, you have someone to trace the problem or faulty information back to, and save your butt.

Keep a performance file. Place duplicate copies of every important memo, idea, presentation, successful pitch, contract, or statistic in a file for your protection. Also include a record of days and times you stayed late or came in early. If you do anything special, mark it down and make a copy. This file can also double as your performance file to help you prepare for your annual review.

Keep people informed. Tell different people around the organization about what you are doing. This merely serves as protection if you need a witness or another person to validate what you have done.

Another way of doing this is to send duplicates or carbon copy (cc) important papers, letters or documents to the appropriate people, and to managers.

Use a recorder. If you are in an extremely sticky situation or what is being said must be remembered correctly, use a microrecorder to tape the conversation. If the specific conversation is critical or involves something that could easily be denied later, record it. I'm not condoning stealthy or devious behavior, but having something important on tape can protect you and clear up a "my word against yours" situation. It's legal to record a meeting or conversation you are involved in, as long as all parties involved are aware they are being taped.

Get Confirmation

Call to confirm things. If you have a meeting, or anything critical scheduled, make sure that you call to confirm and double-check. If it's a meeting, lunch, or a proposal, confirm by phone that things are on track and going to happen. Again, always get names or confirmation numbers and write them down. Have a way to track the problem if things go foul.

Follow up. Have a handle on certain situations and know the status of projects. If you are stopped in the hall and quizzed, you can answer intelligently and know what is going on.

> Charlie was assigned to a committee with two other people. They were to prepare a report to present to board members. Charlie did her part, as did another team member, but the third waited until the last minute and forced the others to pull an all-nighter the night before the presentation. The lazy team member thought that the others would help bail him out because they were in it together. Charlie couldn't let the person sink, because it was her reputation on the line as well. They were too far behind, and the presentation was a flop.

You Are on Your Own

Don't assume your teammates, coworkers or anyone else will cover you, or take care of something for you.

Don't rely on others to bail you out, do your work for you, or keep up their end. If you are in a group or team project, keep track of your teammates' progress. It's your reputation on the line.

If they need a kick in the butt, it's your job to show them your shoe or get it done yourself. It's entirely up to you to protect your career. No one else will do it for you.

CREATIVITY

Imagination is more important than knowledge.
—Albert Einstein

Generate Many Ideas

Certain professions are thought of as inherently creative, yet everyone can be creative. Your ability to be creative is proportionate to the number of ideas that you generate. Good, bad, or indifferent, come up with as many ideas or solutions as possible. The one idea that is successful for you may come only after analyzing ten others. It's a numbers game. Don't worry about the bad ones.

Tom Peters says that schools and corporations wring the creativity out of people. He is right. We are taught to come up with one correct and perfect solution, when in fact, in the real world, the cliché that there are a thousand ways to skin a cat really holds true. Seek multiple solutions.

Put on New Glasses: Gain a Different Perspective

Re-engineering is a popular buzzword in business today. Take the same approach to seeking creative ideas. Re-engineer a solution. The key to becoming a creative thinker, even if you are the most button-down person in the world, is to view things differently. Look at a situation, problem, or tasks from a perspective different from what you are used to. If you keep seeing a situation the same way, or achieving the same result, put on a new pair of glasses and look at it in a different light.

It's like when you are watching a football game on TV. You can't see the penalty or fumble, but when the camera changes angles or another camera is used, you see the play differently than before. That is the simple secret to becoming creative.

Brainstorming and Idea Farming

How do you generate creative ideas? Through brainstorming, idea farming, or free association. There are many other names that describe a process by which you come up with as many ideas as possible in an uncensored environment. Not every idea you have will be good. It's a numbers game. It may take ten average ideas to come up with the one that is just right. Don't quit after you have one good idea. When brainstorming or generating ideas, always come up with no less than three.

Don't immediately judge ideas. When you are brainstorming, don't critique or judge ideas at that moment. You are just trying to get as many on paper as possible. After you have many to choose from, go back and weed out the ones that don't sound so good after reviewing them.

The same idea applies if you are generating ideas on your own or with a group. Don't censor or evaluate an idea until it's on paper. Remember, people have egos, and those egos will get bruised and stepped on if your first reaction to a person's idea is "that is the dumbest thing I have ever heard," or "that will never work." Respect another person's ideas and she will do the same for you. Have a group rule that says there will be no comments, moans, groans, shrugs, sighs, or rolling of the eyes. Even if it's the dumbest thing you have ever heard another human say, don't critique until everyone has had a chance to give their ideas.

The good thing about brainstorming is that often your solution is not a single idea that was put forth, it's a combination of bits and pieces from all of the ideas. While one person's idea as a whole might not be workable, there may be a certain element that might be helpful, or may trigger you to think of something else. Take many ideas and combine the best elements of each to reach a good conclusion.

Map Your Ideas

Another technique for producing creative ideas is to use an "Idea Tree," "Idea Map," or an "Idea Octopus." Yes, the names are very corny, but feel free to be creative and make up your own name for them. As mentioned earlier, sometimes when you are thinking, one idea triggers another related idea. What the idea tree or octopus (you be the judge on the names) does is to provide a diagram or graphic representation of your ideas to show how your thoughts flow together.

Here is how it works. Write down your main idea. Now, add a branch or line for each extension of that main idea, using a key word or phrase that represents the new trigger topic. From there, keep adding lines and extensions as topics and related ideas come up. Make them fairly detailed. Remember in English class when you diagramed sentences? It's the same principle. You are adding extensions that represent each part of an idea. If you are the type of person who takes a piece of paper and writes everything you can think of with no rhyme or reason, only to look at it later and wonder what goes where, diagraming your ideas in this manner will be helpful.

Change Your Routine

If you are in a creative rut, change your routine. Do something different. It might be going a different way to work, or changing your morning routine. You might change the pictures in your office or house. Do something to take you out of what is familiar to you and to force you to look at something from a different perspective.

Take Time to Think

Do you ever take time out just to think? I mean purposefully sit there staring out the window daydreaming? It wouldn't surprise me if you said no. Most people are afraid of being busted by the boss, so they try to look busy. Fact is, most people probably don't devote enough time to thinking, planning, and exploring an idea. There is nothing wrong with daydreaming. Harvey MacKay, author of *Swim With the Sharks Without Being Eaten Alive*, says that there is nothing wrong with employees staring at walls. It shows that you are thinking. Just make sure you are thinking about business or something useful and not about next weekend or your next vacation. Devote time specifically for generating ideas, organizing your thoughts, and simply being creative.

Everyone Is Creative

Finally, don't put pressure on yourself or worry about being creative. It does come easier for some people, but everyone has the ability. It becomes a self-fulfilling prophecy when you say, "Oh, I'm not very creative." Say that to yourself and sure enough you won't be very creative. Being creative is not predetermined by the way you dress, the music you listen to, or even the profession you go into. Creativity can be found in design, manufacturing, engineering, sales, finance, accounting, teaching, or almost any other field. Even people who are traditionally not thought of as creative can put forth original ideas. Like with any other skill, it takes practice. The way to practice is to generate ideas. When you read the newspaper, or hear of a situation in your company or with a client, ask yourself what would be another way to tackle this.

Become curious and ask questions. Just as when you were a child, make the word "why" a common part of your vocabulary. There is almost always more than one way of doing something. Tom Peters, in his book *Liberation Management*, says that to foster creativity, be willing to ask what you think are the dumb questions. The computer mouse was a result of someone asking why all computer commands came from keyboards. Challenge the status quo. The results will amaze you.

HOW TO MAKE GOOD DECISIONS

Whatever the setting, professional or personal, you will be faced with choices and decisions that need to be made. The outcomes of those choices vary in importance. Some might be as simple as where to go for lunch, while others have major consequences. Making decisions can be difficult. However, there are several steps to help simplify the process and help you to make decisions and choices more directly:

- Learn what obstacles you will encounter and decide how you will overcome them.
  - Seek advice.
  - Think about it.
  - Make your decision.
  - Forget about it.

Decisions are usually made based on two criteria—information and gut feeling or instinct. Of course, the best choice is an informed decision that feels right. However, some situations demand more of one than the other.

Determine what your goal is or what you are trying to accomplish by reaching this decision. What is at stake? What are the criteria that you need to weigh? Are there any obstacles or warning signs that alert you?

Be Informed

Seek as much information as possible. Look at both sides, the pros and cons. One of the best tools I have found for making good decisions is to play devil's advocate. I can do it myself or have another person play the part. By looking at the other side of an issue, or a worst- and best-case scenario, I can see what the consequences might be. This allows me to weigh the outcomes and consider the pros and cons.

> *Glenn, a Tulane grad, found a supplier who had a surplus of Louisiana State University and New Orleans Saints umbrellas shaped like football helmets. Glenn thought he could easily sell these at LSU and Saints football games. Against the advice of friends and others who said there was no way it could be done, he purchased the surplus umbrellas. He arranged for the stadium to sell the umbrellas. The concessions manager agreed to let Glenn sell the umbrellas at the stadium but would not pay Glenn up front. The only way he could sell them would be on consignment. Glenn had a gut feeling that this would work so he agreed. During the first LSU home game, it rained cats and dogs. Glenn sold out of the umbrellas immediately. The stadium concessions manager had a change of heart and wanted in on Glenn's idea, offering to purchase umbrellas outright for the next games. "Sure" Glenn said, "but the price just went up." Sometimes you have to go with what you feel is right.*

Seek Advice

Include others in your decision-making process and seek their opinions. Use people as sounding boards. Talk to one of your mentors or someone who has been faced with a similar choice. Find out how someone else in a similar situation reacted and dealt with it. Use successful examples to fuel your decision.

Listen to Yourself

Go with your gut feelings and instincts. If you feel something is absolutely right, and the data support it, go with it. Sometimes you can go with it even if the information or other people say it won't work.

Don't Be Too Quick to Answer

Take time to think about it. Look at all of the issues and ramifications of your decision. Don't answer immediately or impulsively. If you are put on the spot and in your mind you have the least bit of hesitation, take the hint. Back off. Take time to think more about it before you give an answer. All you have to do is ask for time to think.

If other people are involved or will be affected by your decisions, consult with them before doing anything. That goes for your boss, teammates, or family. Especially family! You have a responsibility to other people. If your decisions will affect them, they must be consulted or considered before you react impulsively.

I was once in a crucial negotiation with my boss, which was reaching a stalemate. Both of us were frustrated and getting upset. The other person needed to buy some time. I wanted to reach a decision right then. My boss made an offer that on the surface seemed like a temporary solution. I thought about it and knew that I should wait and think this through clearly. I saw that this choice would affect people besides myself (like my wife!). I paused for almost five minutes. "Perhaps I should think this through and answer later," I kept saying to myself. Instead, I was so anxious to reach a decision and get this behind me that I said "yes" on the spot. I remember temporarily thinking that I had won. About ten minutes later, after I had left, it hit me. The other person got exactly what she wanted. She was able to buy time, because I had reacted impulsively. I had let my patience, or lack of it, get the better of me. Beyond that, my decision was not in the best interest of the other person it affected. The operative word was "Bonehead." Did I make a bad decision? YOU BET! Did I learn from it? YOU BET!

You make your bed; you lie in it. You will have some misfires and bonehead decisions. The only truly bad decisions are those that you don't learn something from. Don't dwell on it or focus on your regrets. Pick yourself up and learn from it. Don't be too hard on yourself.

There will be times when you are faced with choices that are equally matched, and you will vacillate between the two. The moment of absolute certainty never arrives. Make your decision and live with it.

·28·

How You Are Judged:
Performance Reviews

If you are going to play a game, you want to know the rules. The same holds true with your job. If your performance is going to be judged and evaluated, it would be nice to know how you are being judged, or what the criteria are. The rules can be different in every organization. Some judge you solely by the numbers. Your performance and bottom line are all that matter. Others use more subjective criteria, such as teamwork, effort, morale, and creativity. You may have scheduled performance evaluations or be told how you will be judged, but remember that *you manage your own career.* In the end, it's up to you to find out when and how often your performance reviews will be. Don't depend on anyone else to do it for you or to look out for you.

> *Jenny, an Arizona State grad, went for eighteen months without her boss or anyone evaluating her work. In that time, she did not receive a raise or a promotion. She was in limbo. No one had ever approached her to discuss whether she was doing her job well or if she needed to improve. Finally, she'd had enough. Jenny took her career into her own hands. She told her bosses that she wanted to advance in the company, and that, to improve, she needed to know where she stood. She requested a performance appraisal to evaluate her career and made sure that one was scheduled every six months from then on.*

If you are unsure of your status, or feel that there is too much time between formal reviews (more than a year is too long), ask to meet with your boss every quarter or six months for a progress report.

Plan Your Attack

Prepare and plan well in advance for your performance appraisal or review. Use your CYA (Cover Your Ass) file to document your performance. Your boss or supervisor will be prepared and will have all of the information and numbers needed to evaluate you. You are there to work with management to establish goals, to learn how to improve, and so forth; but remember that it's up to you to either defend or support your work and accomplishments.

During one annual review, I could tell that my boss was not particularly enthusiastic about being there. He was covering some basic numbers and figures, and was following a generic evaluation form. Merely going through the motions, he would nod and tell me without any enthusiasm, "this was good," or "this needs work." This review was going to determine my raise and salary for the next year. My place in the pecking order of the company would be decided by the opinion of this bozo who would rather be fishing. This was my career we were talking about. If he had somewhere else to be or if this was a token meeting, thanks, but I would like a little more attention please.

I had had a very successful year, and I had prepared a full report highlighting that year's performance, with graphs, examples, and rankings compared to my coworkers. You name it, I had it. I had stats and figures that management had never considered. My boss droned on, giving me the standard speech of "You did well, but you can do better next year. Do you have any questions or anything you would like to add?" Well yes, I do. I showed him my facts and figures and all of the information and documentation I had prepared over the past year to show what my achievements were.

Management was blown away. What I had put together displayed in dollars how much I was worth to the company that year. It could not be disputed. It was there in black and white. I received my annual raise plus a special bonus that year, only because I went to bat for myself.

During your evaluations, make it known where you want to be down the road. Tell management your goals and find out what it would take to reach them. If you want to be promoted to account executive from assistant, to manager from flunky, find out specifically what it will take and what you have to do to get there. Have a game plan and make that plan known to the people who can help you achieve it.

Raises Aren't Automatic

A raise is not a God-given right. Some companies give token raises to cover increases in the cost of living, maybe between 1 percent and 6 percent, but don't expect one to come automatically. You have to earn it. You have to sell your boss on why you are worth it. Again, this is done by documenting examples and figures that show why you are valuable. Chances are, you aren't going to double your salary from one year to the next. There may not even be a significant jump. In some companies, a 10 percent increase is really good. And don't forget to deduct taxes when you get your million-dollar raise. Remember that a raise is spread out through the year. So when you get a $2,000 raise, it only amounts to a little over $38 a week before taxes and other deductions.

It's as Good as Money . . . Sort of

It is becoming common for some organizations to offer perks, time off, or titles instead of raises. If you are offered a package instead of a raise, evaluate it carefully and make sure that it will benefit you in exposure, responsibility, or opportunity. You be the judge of your particular situation.

You may want or deserve a promotion, but there is just nowhere for you to go. Increasingly, companies are moving people sideways in the organization instead of upwards. Horizontal movement throughout a company has become quite common. It can be very advantageous. You can learn about other areas of the business, gain more experience, or take on a different challenge. As organizations become flatter and less hierarchical, lateral moves to other departments, locations, or positions will become even more common. However, if eventually the organization doesn't make it worth your while or doesn't use the skills and training it gave you, shop around. You are a free agent.

Sometimes you may get the itch for a promotion or more money, and a new venue or a quick cash fix acts only as a temporary solution . . . a Band-Aid. Ask yourself, "Is it a promotion that I really want or is it time to leave the company?"

WHEN IT'S TIME TO MOVE ON

INEVITABLY IT COMES TIME to pack up and move on to greener pastures. Everyone does it. Lifetime employment is a fantasy these days. Experts say that we can expect to have over 11 jobs spanning five careers during our working lifetime.

It can be tough leaving a job. Making the choice to leave a company is not an easy one. If that choice is made for you, it's even harder to leave. Whether you leave on your own or are asked to resign (the PC term for fired), how you handle the transition is very important.

When Do You Know You Are Ready to Leave?

There will be times in almost any position when you are bored or dissatisfied, but look hard to decide whether you made the wrong choice and that it truly is time to move on.

If you are looking to change careers, the best time to look is when you have a job, not when you need one. That way you are in demand. You are always more attractive to an employer when you have something to bring to the table, rather than when you are in dire need. When things are going well, there is no pressure to get a job quickly. You can be more choosy and call your shots, rather than feeling pressure to take the first offer dangled in front of you because you might lose your job or be fired at any moment. Never quit a job to look for another. Always have something in place before you leave. Look a few steps ahead.

The telltale signs. How do you know it's time to move on? You know that you have been there too long if you see peers begin to move up and you haven't, or if you are doing a great job and no one in the company is moving up. It's time to go when you have reached the pay ceiling for the job you are doing, or when you are so bored that it's not challenging anymore. Coming in late and leaving early, apathy, taking sick days more and more, or just not wanting to be there anymore: These are good indicators that something is wrong. If you experience any of the above, move on before you are forced to move involuntarily.

Change happens. Sometimes the company changes dramatically and is no longer structured or operated as when you began. New management or ownership can alter the culture and the direction of the company. These changes may not fit with your needs or values. Look for the writing on the wall in your company or industry. Is your firm no longer a leader in the marketplace, or no longer competitive? Is your industry in decline or at risk of becoming extinct? Author and economist Paul Zane Pilzer, in his book *Unlimited Wealth*, gives the example of the vinyl record industry. Just ten years ago, all records were on vinyl. Today music is on cassette or CD. The people whose business it was to make and supply the record industry with the vinyl are now out of business.

If you notice any of the following going on in your organization, it is generally time to reevaluate your options: loss of big contracts or clients; changes in regulations or laws, which hurt your industry; dissolution of partnerships and strategic alliances; loss of market share; cutbacks, belt tightening; restructuring; staff reevaluations (a.k.a. "getting rid of deadwood"). If your company is not surviving, neither will you. You aren't a captain, so don't go down with the ship.

Job Hopping

You aren't committed to a position for life, but you don't want to get a reputation as a job hopper, either. A job hopper is someone whose résumé lists a different position each year.

Job hopping can mean one of two things. The first is that you are so spectacular that you are offered new positions each year with different companies. While possible, it's highly unlikely to happen during the first three years of your career. The second possibility is much more plausible. Job hopping shows an employer that you are a problem, incompetent, or not committed. I know it sounds harsh, but that is how it looks to an interviewer.

Unless your job is making you suicidal, you need to stay for at least a year. Anything less than a year really sends up red flags. Two years in your first position is ideal. With a minimum of two years experience under your belt, you have shown commitment and have a basic skill set that you can transfer to another company.

Do not quit or leave a position unless you have another one already lined up. The other thing that makes employers skeptical is if you have large gaps in your résumé, or periods where you did nothing. It is always easier to find a job when you have a job. It's the old idea that something in demand is more desirable. Even if you resigned, it looks as though you were canned and causes an unexplainable gap in your résumé.

Leave on a Good Note

As badly as you want to tell your boss, "You couldn't manage your way out of a wet paper bag, you have bad breath, and you should kill yourself," hold your tongue. These people may be able to help you someday. Even if you were let go (another PC term for fired), you don't want to give anyone more reason to trash you in a recommendation. If a potential employer calls your last boss, you want the last impression your coworkers had of you to be favorable.

When You Say *Adios*

When you have finally decided to leave, have all of your affairs in order before you make an announcement or turn in your resignation letter. Always write a letter informing your manager of your resignation. It doesn't have to be the Magna Carta. Just three lines saying that you will be leaving, that you appreciate having been given the opportunity to work for the company, and when your last day will be.

Professional courtesy says two weeks notice or suitable time for a replacement to be found is enough time to let an employer know that you are leaving. Some companies want you to help the new employee make the transition. However, don't be surprised if you are asked to leave immediately, so it does not affect other employees' morale.

If you are shown the door that day, don't get mad when you are told to gather your things and leave. There will be no tearful good-byes or farewell lunches. There will be no time to go over old files or papers. You won't be allowed to pull all of the really cool things you wanted off your computer. You may have to give back your Rolodex and certain supplies. Some companies view all these materials, including names and contacts, as company property. Therefore, make sure that you clear out everything that you may need before you tell the company *adios*.

If you do stick around, don't slack off just because you are leaving. People always remember first and last impressions, and tend to forget what was in the middle. You could have worked like a mule for three years, but if during the last two weeks you were late, blew things off, and didn't care, your coworkers and managers' final thoughts will be that you were lazy.

Let People Know Where You Are

Lastly, when you change companies, let people know about it. The worst thing you can do is to fall off the face of the earth. Write letters and let your contacts know what you are doing now. Maintain those relationships. They are so hard to come by, don't waste them by letting them fall through the cracks. Make clients, suppliers, friends, any contact, aware of your recent developments.

▪ 2 9 ▪

Ethics and Integrity

Character . . . not wealth, power, or
position . . . is the supreme word.
—John D. Rockefeller

Among the qualities most admired by CEOs are integrity, ethics, and honesty. Whatever field you go into, your professional reputation is the most precious thing you have and should be guarded very carefully.

An Ohio State University study found that smart people can do at least one dumb thing without others considering them stupid. But moral people can't do *one* dishonest thing without others labeling them as immoral. You get a reputation and it sticks to you like gum on your shoe. Many industries are small and tightly knit. Word gets around quickly. If you have a reputation for being dishonest, a cheat, a liar, or a thief, people will find out and you are labeled.

The "do anything it takes to get ahead" mentality is wrong. Good guys/girls *don't* finish last. I know the press is full of stories of people who have made millions by unethical means. However, why are they in the news? Because they are CROOKS! Crooked people don't get ahead . . . they get caught.

Michael Milken and Ivan Boesky have been glamorized by the media. These are brilliant people, but they were stupid in one regard. They got caught. You will *always* get caught, no matter how smart you think you are.

The stakes don't matter. The fact that the men mentioned above were involved in multimillion-dollar scams is irrelevant. If you were to cheat on an expense report for five dollars or take office supplies, it's the same. It's the principle, not the dollar figure. The cash you make up by cheating on a five-dollar expense report or by lying to a client to get extra terms on a contract is not worth losing your job and reputation.

Your Word Is Your Bond

Say what you mean, and mean what you say. In some financial circles the phrase, "Your word is your bond," is taken very seriously. If you tell someone something it's as good as done. It means, "You can count on me."

If you tell a person something, stick to it. Don't go back and forth or deny its meaning. Don't beat around the bush or dodge issues or questions. If you want to say something, just say it. Don't allude to things or talk around a subject. People respect directness and frankness. On the other hand if someone ever tells you, "I appreciate your candor," know that you have crossed the line. Diplomatically translated, it means, "you blunt little SOB."

What I Meant Was . . .

Don't tell lies, even small ones. You can get your stories crossed up, and there is nothing worse that being caught in a lie. You will never be trusted again. You can't recover. People may not like the truth, but they will respect you for it more than if they catch you in a lie. La Rochefoucauld said, "Almost all of our faults are more pardonable than the methods we resort to hide them." With that said, I won't hide this from you: I don't know who the hell La Rochefoucauld is.

▪ 3 0 ▪

Attitude and Emotions

EGO

Check Your Ego at the Door

Hopefully, you will experience success early in your job. If you are lucky enough to do so, it can be easy to get the big head. You begin to feel that you can accomplish anything. You are fearless, bulletproof. Confidence and pride swell in your chest from a job well done. Of course, then there is the swelling of your head that comes from believing your own hype and thinking that you can do no wrong. When your head gets too big to fit through the door, remember where you came from. Don't rub it in or flaunt it in front of your coworkers and friends

Upon graduation, most people leave school on the same level, except varying degrees of debt. Shortly after you begin your career, some of your group of friends begin to pull ahead. It may be with titles, promotions and responsibility, or financially. After about three years, you begin to see a disparity among salaries. If you are lucky enough to become successful financially, don't make a big deal out of it in front of friends. If you do, you run the risk of alienating people.

Be aware that other people may not be as lucky as you. Sure, I know that you may have worked very hard to achieve that success, but that does not give you the right to forget who you are and where you came from.

Sam Walton, founder of Wal-Mart, was at one point the richest man in America. From humble beginnings in Bentonville, Arkansas, Mr. Walton's family became one of the wealthiest in the world. Yet, legend has it that as rich as old Sam was, he still drove his beat-up old pickup truck until the day he died. He never forgot who he was or let his ego get out of hand. Don't take yourself too seriously. A job is what you do, not who you are. Don't let it turn you into a jerk.

Confidence vs. Arrogance

You have nothing to be arrogant about. You haven't proven anything yet. There is a world of difference between being confident and being arrogant. Confidence is being self-assured that you will do what it takes to get the job done. Arrogance and cockiness stem from feeling that you automatically deserve something, or that you are better than anyone else. There is nothing wrong with striving to be the best. Making your accomplishments known to the people who can help your career is not arrogance, it's simply taking your career into your own hands.

Everyone Is Replaceable

Anyone can be replaced. If you are good at what you do, it's easy to see the contributions you make to the organization, and to feel that the place couldn't run without you. You may think that you are so good at what you do that the company couldn't find anyone who could take your place, or that the organization will crumble upon your departure. Management will offer you cars, vacation time, and a bonus to reconsider and stay. Forget it. Don't even kid yourself. While you are important to the organization and you do make valuable contributions, you are expendable.

Life goes on after you leave, so don't get too wrapped up in your own self-importance. You see it in sports, television, and business. Just because one player, character, or executive decides to leave doesn't mean that the organization falls. Even when superstars like Joe Montana and Michael Jordan are no longer around, the 49ers and the Bulls still suit up and play. If you want to see how much you will be missed by an organization when you are gone, stick your finger in a glass of water. Notice how much water is still left in the glass when you remove your finger? That is the same impact you have on an organization when you leave. Anyone can be replaced.

PRESSURE

You Aren't Saving Lives

At some point in your career, you will find yourself under a great deal of pressure or stress. Any number of things can cause it. Some stress is caused by external factors, such as a boss or deadline. Much stress is generated internally. Your internal desire for perfection or to do a good job can be a contributor to stress.

During the day, if you are experiencing stress or beginning to feel overwhelmed, take some time out, even if it's just for 15 minutes. Get up and walk around. Leave the office. Sit outside. Get some fresh air. Getting out of the office does wonders. Sometimes it can't be helped, but try to avoid sitting at your desk through lunch.

Earlier, I talked about change and being flexible. Realize that change happens. Being able to roll with the punches and not freak out when things don't go as planned can help alleviate a lot of stress.

If you are dreading certain tasks, get rid of them early. If there are calls, a meeting, a potential conflict or sticky situation, anything that you know will stress you out, get it out of the way early. If you wait, your day will be spent focusing on the impending confrontation or undesirable task. Getting it behind you allows the remainder of your day to be free and clear from worry and stress about the event you are avoiding. It will be over. You will be more productive and at ease.

> Amy is a copywriter for a major advertising agency. Advertising, with its tight deadlines, is a notoriously stressful industry. During one particularly stressful period when she was under a lot of pressure, Amy was losing sleep and was often sick to her stomach. Recognizing Amy's condition, her boss pulled her aside and put it in perspective. Her boss said, "Don't worry about it. You aren't saving lives. You are selling f___ing advertising." That pretty well sums it up.

If you are in a tense or emotionally charged situation, humor will often diffuse it. Crack a joke or say something incredibly off the wall. You and probably anyone else in the room could use a laugh.

Unless you are saving lives, it's probably not a big enough worry to ruin your health over. It's just a job. What is the worst thing that can happen? They can't kill you or hold you prisoner in the mail room. Yes, you could lose your job. Big deal. You are young. You can always get another. You aren't 50 years old, with kids at home. World peace is not resting on your shoulders. C'mon. Lighten up a little.

Anyone who is good at her job will think about it outside work from time to time. But if it's affecting you negatively, if there is pressure from a project, a client, a deadline, or a tyrannical, psychotic boss with a split personality, leave it at the office. The minute it begins to affect your family, friends, or health is the time to reevaluate whether it's really worth worrying about.

BURNOUT

Pace Yourself: There is No Spring Break

Unless you are a teacher or professional student, there are no more Spring Breaks. No summer vacation. No month off for the holidays. Your freewheeling days as a world traveler and vagabond have ceased. Weekends and the occasional three-day holiday weekend will become the only time when you recharge yourself. For that reason, it is critical to pace yourself. Otherwise, you will hit the wall in about six months and burn out.

It's not uncommon for someone in his first job to come out of the gates as fast as he or she can go. You are in a new job and want to make a good impression, so of course you come in early and stay late. You come in on weekends to catch up and learn as much as possible. You do anything asked of you and then volunteer for more. Then, about six to nine months into your new job, you run out of steam. What? You aren't president yet? You haven't been given a raise or a promotion? You ask yourself, "What am I doing?"

Many companies see eager recruits enter a company and achieve phenomenal results during the first six months or year. Then their performances begin to slip. The reason? Burnout. A career must be thought of as a marathon; it's not like a short, fast sprint. You might not have the finish line in sight. To run a marathon you need to pace yourself and not use all of your energy in the beginning.

Sometimes when people move up in an organization very quickly without recharging their batteries, they reach a certain level and become burned out and disenchanted.

Other factors that can lead to burnout include management or surroundings that are not supportive, lack of recognition for hard work or a job well done, or if there is no end in sight on a project or task.

Have Many Small Projects

One way to combat burnout in the early stages is to segment your year into small increments. Think of it in terms of many small projects with a beginning and an end. It makes it easier to work for something when you see an end in sight. Have targets, milestones, or a completion date to shoot for. I always try to have at least one thing to look forward to. It might be a trip, a meeting with a certain client, or a deadline. It's like setting little goals for yourself and it gives you something to look forward to, so you don't feel like a gerbil on a treadmill.

Take a Break

Take your vacation time. Initially, that won't be a problem. You will wonder where your scant two weeks went. Yet, some people who have been working longer wear their vacation time like a badge of honor. "I haven't had a vacation in four years. There just hasn't been time." I've got two words for these people . . . MAKE TIME!

Don't get wrapped up in your own self-importance. The place can function without you for a week. People who hoard their vacation time are miserable to be around. They feel that they are so important to the organization that if they were to leave, for even a week, the place would close shop and cease to exist. Actually, by taking a vacation, these souls without a life would be more productive and more valuable to the organization. Check to see what your company's vacation policy is. Does it roll over from one year to the next? This allows people who hoard their vacation to say, "I have eight months vacation when I want." Or does your company have a "use it or lose it" policy? It's the most common. If you don't take your vacation time before the end of the year, you lose it. So, as the end of the year approaches, take off between Christmas and New Year's. Go see your family. Go to Puerto Rico. Come back with a tan. Whatever you do, refresh yourself. It will do both you and your employer good.

You don't have to take all of your vacation time at once. Spread it throughout the year. Two days here, three days there. Make it a series of long weekends. Don't worry about just getting in a car or hopping on a plane and going away for a few days. You can grab some friends or even go by yourself. After completing a big annual project, go to the Caribbean to lie on a beach and veg out for three days by yourself.

Beware the Sophomore Slump

If you have achieved great success during your first year, you need to beware of the sophomore slump. It happens in school, with athletes, and on the job. If you begin your career with a bang, people will be looking at you and expecting great things. This is a positive. But it can also work against you. If you spend everything you have during your first year and burn out, your decline in year two will be very noticeable. Also, if you show everything you are capable of during year one, how do you top it? A funny thing about management is that, even if you do spectacularly, you are expected always to outdo your performance of the year before. If you set a standard, you will be held to that standard, even if it's far above your peers or the average. This is good, because it presents a constant challenge, and when you maintain it you look even more fantastic. But the downside is that if you use your bag of tricks to do everything early in your career, you have nothing left to show. If you peak too early, you will constantly have the bar raised.

"Don't show off every day, or you will stop surprising people," says Baltasar Gracian. "There must always be some novelty left over. The person who displays a little more of it each day keeps up expectations, and no one ever discovers the limits of his talents."

WANTING MORE RESPONSIBILITY

Everyone Pays Their Dues

Everyone. Repeat "everyone" has to pay their dues. So must you, even if it means being a grunt. Accept it. Everyone experiences a learning curve. Even seasoned executives don't enter a new organization at full swing. How long that learning curve is, is entirely up to you. You can shorten the curve by checking your ego at the door, being open to learn, and doing whatever it takes.

It's easy to get your ego bruised when you are new to the job. I realize that you are young and highly educated, and that you feel quite capable of running the joint if given the chance. It's frustrating when you see people with the IQs of lint ahead of you on the organizational chart. The more ego you display, the more miserable you will be, the less you will learn, the more people you will piss off, and the longer you will remain junior assistant account executive in charge of copies and coffee. So, watch the ego.

Sometimes, you'll think that you are smarter than your boss. In some (many) cases, it will be true. But no matter how big a bonehead you think he is, hold your tongue. Though you may feel your boss or management isn't qualified to shovel elephant poop at the circus, he still controls your immediate future.

If it gets so bad that you can't handle it anymore, *don't ever* make your boss look stupid or try to get her fired. You will lose that battle *every* time. You have two choices. The first is to quit. The other is to do everything in your power to make your boss look so good that she gets promoted and is moved away from you. It also makes you look good by association.

DISAPPOINTMENT

Nothing Is Perfect

At times you will be disappointed. Everyone is. No job in the world is perfect and no company in the world will live up to all your expectations. That is not being negative. It's merely being realistic. There are shortcomings to every job. Some are just bigger than others. Don't expect perfection. You will beat your head against the wall trying to find that Holy Grail.

PATIENCE

Understand It Before You Change It

Understand the organization before you try to change it. Being an ambitious eager beaver (that's something my Mom would say, "eager beaver"), you want to help the company as quickly as possible, or make that one suggestion that will turn the company around and land you the corner office in about three weeks. Restrain yourself from bringing about organizational change in the first few weeks. It's fine to ask why something is done a certain way or why not. But have your facts straight before you offer your expert opinion. It could be that your idea has been tried before and failed miserably. The reason something is done a certain way could be because it was the boss's idea, and what the boss says goes. Right or wrong, logic and reason don't always dictate corporate decisions.

In my first job, the design of the offices was very contemporary but they weren't functional. The layout was an open bullpen with asymmetrical cubicles, jagged angles for the desks, and floor-to-ceiling columns, four feet in diameter, running through the middle of many cubicles. It was artistic, but easily the worst layout for human beings to work in. Early in my tenure, I asked a coworker if the same person who designed our offices also designed mazes for lab rats. I was then informed that the rat-maze designer happened to be the company president's lovely, yet artistically-challenged wife, and that he wanted to keep her happy.

That swell idea you were about to ream belongs to the boss or the boss's spouse. You never know. The company survived long before you were around, so wait a few weeks before proving that you are the corporate savior you think you might be.

MIKE TIRICO
Cohost, ESPN SportsCenter and NFL Prime Monday
Age: 27

MIKE TIRICO IS THE youngest anchor at ESPN, the national cable all-sports network. He can be seen nightly on *SportsCenter*, or any Monday night during football season sitting next to former quarterbacks Joe Theisman and Phil Simms as the host of *NFL Prime Monday*. At 27, Mike displays poise and professionalism light-years beyond most twentysomethings.

Raised an only child in New York, he grew up listening to Marv Albert call games for the New York Knicks and Rangers. "Marv Albert is someone who I idolize. I read in his autobiography that he attended Syracuse University." As it turns out, Syracuse University has a reputation for turning out top sports broadcasters. In addition to Albert, Bob Costas and Dick Stockton graduated from Syracuse. "Although I loved sports, I knew that I wasn't going to make it as an athlete. I saw early on that journalism was the way I was going to stay close to sports, so I went to Syracuse."

While there, Mike became involved with the student-run radio station. The sports department for this radio station, WAER, was outstanding. It allowed Mike and students involved in the program to travel all over the country to do play-by-play announcing for Syracuse teams. "Unlike many people, I always knew what I wanted to do. I feel I am very lucky, because I wasted no time in my career.

"Working at the radio station and gaining hands-on experience helped me more with what I do every day as a broadcaster than anything in the classroom. The radio station and my experience as an intern for a local television station allowed me to see ahead of time what my life today would be like, and let me see what I would be doing. Internships are the greatest tool, but are underused."

Mike's big break came when he was broadcasting a basketball game between Syracuse and Georgetown. The next day, Larry King, in his column in *USA Today*, wrote that if he ever needed to hire a sports broadcaster, he would call Syracuse University and have them send the next one who is ready. Mike and his partners were excited that they were recognized. Several weeks later, when he and his friends were in Washington, D.C., he called the *Larry King Show* and asked if they could come by to watch the show. While they were at Larry King's radio show, the group was asked to come on the air for thirty minutes. This gained Mike and the others some publicity back home. "It was after this that I received a phone call from the news director at the CBS affiliate in Syracuse and was offered a spot as weekend sports anchor." After two years doing that, he was named sports director, at which he spent two more years.

How does a 24-year-old make it from covering sports in a medium-sized market like Syracuse, New York, to anchor of the hottest sports show in television? In 1990, without knowing anyone at the network or being connected in any way, Mike sent a copy of his demo tape to ESPN. "The response I got was, you are good, but a little young. Call us next year. I thought it was a polite brush-off." However, ten months later he sent in another demo tape. "This time they said, Hey, you have improved. We would like to give you an audition. I went to Connecticut to audition. I thought my audition was awful, but they loved it. Less than a month later I was offered a job with ESPN, and in June 1991, I moved to Bristol to anchor the 2:30 a.m. edition of *Sports-Center*. Mike has since moved to more desirable time slots and also hosts *NFL Prime Monday* (a pregame show for Monday night football and wrap-up of Sunday's games).

"It all happened so quickly, I was a little overwhelmed. But ESPN has a real family feel to it. The way people are on the air is really how they are. It made it easy once I realized that they are just people. It removed the 'awe' factor."

If you or I mess up on the job or make a mistake, only a few people might learn about. If Mike Tirico makes a mistake on air, millions of people know instantly. Being prepared is critical. Mike says, "You don't know what might happen, so I prepare for every eventuality. The one thing that has helped me the most in my career has been to overprepare and overread. If you use half of what you prepared, then you have probably prepared the right amount."

Having never been in a setting like ESPN, Mike followed the example of successful people whom he admired. "Pick out one or two people and try to follow what they have done to be successful. When you see something about someone else's delivery or what they do, you can see what you like, and use it to improve."

Mike is always trying to improve, because he knows that the next kid from Syracuse is waiting to take his chair. "I thought it would be easier now that I have made it, but there is always someone behind you. If I could give anyone starting their career any advice, it would be that you are replaceable. There is always someone who is smarter, more aggressive, and cheaper than you. I never forget it. That is what keeps the drive going."

You might think Mike has reached his dream, but he still has dreams to chase. "Sure, I dream someday of broadcasting a Super Bowl. I figure that I have about 30 more years to chase that. And once you have done one, why not two or three? With every job there is another challenge to chase after."

∎ 3 1 ∎

Compensation, Finances, and Making the Most of Your Money

SALARY AND COMPENSATION

How Much Will I Make?

Last spring, while speaking to a marketing class at a major university, I conducted an informal survey of the students. I asked the class, "In your first job, what do you expect your starting salary to be?" Readers play along.

These students said that they realistically expected to make between $25,000 and $50,000 per year. We are talking about people with bachelors' degrees and little or no work experience who seriously expected to make this much money in an entry-level position. If this was the salary range you answered, I've got two words for you:

WAKE UP!

Sure, there are exceptions. Some people are lucky enough to command a substantial starting salary, but they are rare. The College Placement Council, in their annual salary survey, found the average starting salary for college grads to be $24,000. For business majors, the average was $23,820 and it was $22,349 for humanities majors. The figure is higher for some industries, such as engineering and finance, and less in fields such as advertising or journalism. Overall, people just don't make a ton of money. Having a college education at least puts you ahead of the pack. According to *Newsweek*, the average salary for all males between the ages of 25 and 34 is only $26,197; for females the average is $21,510.

You Must Be Kidding?

At this point you may be saying, "Yeah right, there is no way I will work for that little." I don't want to pop your balloon, but, yes, you will. Don't worry, it's a normal reaction and your naivete is shared by thousands of others. It was also my attitude until I was so eloquently enlightened by a man in Dallas.

One of my first interviews was with a sports marketing firm. The interview was going very well, until we got to the subject of money. The gentleman asked me how much I expected to make in this position. I had not researched the industry and had no idea of what the normal starting salary was, yet I didn't give it a second thought. I knew how much money I wanted to make. The number rolled off my tongue so effortlessly and casually, "I think $30,000, would be good to start." I sat back smugly awaiting a response.

After I said this, I could see the pressure build in the man's face as he became very red. He seemed as if he were about to explode, which he did. He laughed at me and then screamed, "$30,000, huh. I'll tell you something kid. In whatever you do, you are going to make $18,000 a year and you will like it. Now get out of here and don't let the door hit you in the butt."

What a jerk, but I learned two valuable lessons from that: A) Don't shoot your mouth off until you know the normal starting salary for your industry; and B) Lower your sights. I obviously did not go to work for that jerk, but he was right about one thing. I ended up making a starting salary even less than what he mentioned, and I loved it.

When $15,000 Is Better Than $25,000

For the past few years you have been subsidized by the Bank of Mom and Dad or you have worked and managed to scrape by on a few hundred dollars a month. A night of fine dining for you consisted of Little Caesar's pizza with double cheese, purchased with coupons, of course. If you felt like splurging you might get a topping. After living on $500 per month, you are ready to cash in. But don't be seduced by a certain salary or swayed by a few thousand dollars. At this point in your life, you won't see a huge difference in your lifestyle if you are making $23,000 rather than $18,000. While several thousand dollars is a lot of money, after taxes you will not see a significant jump in your standard of living.

For this reason it is more important to look for experience over money. When it came time for me to make a selection, I had several job offers on the table. Some positions offered as much as $10,000 more than others. I asked one of my mentors what I should do. He gave me the best piece of advice I've ever received. He said, "Take the job that pays you $15,000, but teaches you how to make half a million."

Let's face it—you are the cheapest labor this side of Mexico. Companies realize this and are going to exploit it. You are educated, enthusiastic, teachable, and willing to work hard. They are trying to increase revenues yet keep costs low. You are part of the low cost equation. A company can get you for half what they would have to pay a middle-aged person, so why would they pay you a $30,000 to $40,000 salary?

You can use this to your advantage by learning as much as possible from your first job. It doesn't matter what your starting salary is. Whatever you make will seem like a lot of money compared to what you had in school. You are not going to make a fortune in your first job anyway, so why not learn the skills it takes to make a fortune?

Experience Over Cash

Go for experience and opportunity over cash. Look at your advancement opportunities, exposure to clients, responsibility you will be given, what skills you will learn, and what contacts you will make. If there is a great opportunity in one of these areas, it can offset what you may feel is a low salary. Sure, it would be nice to make $28,000 in your first job, but if you are nothing more than a well-paid, overworked grunt in a bureaucratic dead end, where does that get you? I think boomers call this "paying your dues." Sure, you are going to have to pay your dues; just make sure that you get the most out of it in return.

TAXES

Who Is Uncle Sam and This FICA Guy?
The Wide World of Net and Gross

One of the most common problems that twentysomethings encounter is financial trouble. The first major financial obstacle is realizing that you won't have as much money as you thought you would. Simply because your salary is $20,000 per year doesn't mean that you will take home that much.

In school, hopefully you learned the difference between gross and net income. I'll give you a quick refresher: Gross income is before taxes, net is after taxes. Your net income, or the amount you will actually have to spend, is the amount after taxes (Federal, State, Social Security, Medicare) and insurance costs. A good rule of thumb for figuring out your net income is to figure that one third of your gross will go to cover taxes, insurance, and other fees taken directly out of your check. That, of course, can vary.

What this means is that instead of taking home the $25,000 your base salary might be, you will take home around $16,000 to $17,000 to spend on bills, savings, and other expenses.

Who do you have to thank for that? Let me introduce you to Uncle Sam and his buddy FICA, two of the greediest bastards you will ever meet. Taxes have plagued mankind around the world for centuries. On the bright side, taxes in the United States are among the lowest in the world. Many European and Scandinavian countries have exorbitant tax rates, well over 50 percent.

Nonetheless, taxes are a way of life. All of the deductions on your check explain where everything goes. There is Federal income tax, which is responsible for the greatest chunk. Then there is Social Security, which we will be lucky to even collect. Any applicable state and city taxes are also deducted, besides any insurance premiums that your employer does not cover. Like the guy in the movie *Raising Arizona* said, "Government sure do take a bite, don't she?"

How to Get a Windfall: Deductions and What to Claim

Starting out, your taxes will be fairly simple, unless you have a trust fund or inheritance or are just making a ton-o-cash. Remember that it's better to have more money deducted from your check than not enough. Claim zero dependents, if you are single with no children. This means more money is deducted from your check. You might be saying, "What? Give the government more money?" The more money you deduct throughout the year, the greater your chances of getting some back at the end of the year. Whatever the number of dependents you claim, you end up paying the same amount of tax.

If you overpay on your taxes, you get a refund. The alternative is, of course, having to scrape up enough cash to pay your taxes in April because you had the disposable cash throughout the year but blew it on CDs and a trip. Hardly anyone on a shoestring budget is disciplined enough to save money designated specifically for taxes. Having more taken out of your check is like buying peace of mind. You don't have to worry about it when the time comes to file, and you will get it back. Getting that refund check is like a windfall. It can be vacation money, new clothes, whatever.

Unless you own a home, have your own business, or are extremely generous, chances are good that early in your career you will simply take the standard deduction. There won't be a great need for you to itemize. However, if you itemize deductions on your tax return, make sure that you keep all receipts. Keep all receipts for expenses you incurred during your job search. That would include travel, meals, supplies, postage, and moving expenses. The cost of these expenses can often be deducted. You also want to keep receipts for any donations or contributions. This can be for cash or the dollar value on clothes, furniture, or other items donated.

If you are going to use the EZ form for your taxes, it shouldn't be difficult at all. As you begin to earn more and the more complex your finances and investments become, you may want to find someone to prepare your taxes for you. You can also do them yourself and then have an expert review your return. Tax professionals can be found for a reasonable price and are more familiar with ways to help you keep more of what you earn.

INSURANCE

INSURANCE COVERAGE IS something you want to understand fully before you ever have to use it. If your employer offers several coverage options, choose the one that provides you with the maximum coverage.

It may cost a little more, but if you use it once, it will more than pay for itself. If your insurance, whether it's health or dental, includes regularly scheduled checkups or teeth cleaning, make the effort to use these benefits. You are paying for them. If you know you are going to leave a company, make sure that you get all your checkups and any medical or dental procedures you need taken care of before you leave the company or change your coverage.

The worst thing you can do is to let your insurance coverage lapse or to not be covered after you leave an employer. Generally, if you are moving from one position to another, your new employer will provide you with health coverage. However, it usually takes one to three months to activate everything so that you can use it. In that case, it is wise to carry over or extend your insurance benefits. The term for this is COBRA. If you are leaving an employer, you typically have the option to extend your coverage for up to 18 months. Of course, the catch is that you pay the entire premium amount. That means that if you were with a company and you were paying $50 per month while your employer was paying the remaining $200 per month of your premium, when you leave and extend through COBRA benefits, you will be responsible for the entire amount of the premium. In a nutshell, health insurance isn't cheap! Make sure that you understand what type of coverage you have and know who to talk to if you have a question or a problem.

DEBT

COLLEGE GRADUATES who entered the job market during the recession of 1991 carried an average debt load of $7,000. This debt consisted primarily of student loans and credit card debt. If anything, the amount of debt that people carry just starting out has skyrocketed, particularly since tuition has risen at most campuses in the United States.

Debt is like a hole that you can't climb out of. I realize that debt is a way of life and can't be avoided in many situations. I used student loans to get through school and have maxed my credit cards more than once to get by in the early stages. I think that Citibank should change the name of their building in New York to the Bradley Building. I should at least be customer of the month.

Excessive debt is like starting a race already behind. Everything that you work for will go to pay the debt. Debt can wipe you out if it's not kept in check and managed properly. Student loans are manageable. I know many people who have student debts in the tens of thousands, yet at least with student loan debt you are paying a low interest rate. The ELSC (student loan folks) makes its money because the terms cover the next millennium and beyond. By the time your loan is paid off, your grandkids are ready for school and you end up paying over $10,000 for the original $2,000 loan. This may be a small exaggeration, but it's very small.

Credit Cards

The real debt killer is credit cards. Credit cards are a catch-22. During your senior year, your mailbox is filled every day with offers for credit cards. Paige, a senior at Texas Tech, reports receiving at least three a week. She has to laugh when the letter says, "Because of your outstanding credit history you have been approved for a $2,000 credit line." Outstanding credit history? "I have never had a credit card in my life until this year," she says.

It's so easy to sign up for every card that comes your way. The problem is, some people think it's free money. "Hey, I just got my new Visa. Let me take you out and break it in."

The next thing you know your card is maxed out. (Most credit cards have a credit limit that you can't exceed. American Express does not; however, they monitor your spending patterns, so if you usually spend $200 per month and suddenly try to buy a car, red flags go up.)

There is absolutely no reason you need three MasterCards, two Visas and four gas cards. You should get an American Express card and a bank card, such as Visa or MasterCard. If you're given the choice, the Citibank AAdvantage Card is a great deal, because you can collect air miles on American Airlines for every dollar you spend. Every little bit helps. Discover is good, too, but it's not accepted in as many places as the others, and the 1 percent cash back is not a big deal. If you spend a fortune, you may get under ten bucks back.

Shop for the lowest rate. If you have a choice of cards, choose the one with the lowest interest rate. Some credit cards have interest rates as high as 21 percent. Anything less than 15 percent is decent. The interest doesn't matter if you pay your cards off every month. While this may be tough, it's the best way to stay out of debt. Think of your cards as cash. You still have to pay cash—you are just delaying it for thirty days. Unless it's a big-ticket item, try to pay cash or pay the card off in full.

American Express is great for this, because you have to pay it off in full every month. It is truly a charge card, rather than a credit card. The downside to Amex is that you can forget where you stand at the end of the month. If you put too much on it and forget, tough, you still have to pay the amount off in full. I like using it because it makes me think about whether I have enough every month to pay it off.

When you shouldn't use cards. Never, never buy groceries with your credit cards. Especially if you carry over the amount from one month to the next. You have used the groceries, but are still paying for them. You are also paying more than if you had paid cash, because interest is being charged.

This goes for buying things on sale too. If you are buying something on sale to save money, don't keep the balance on your credit cards over a month. The amount you are paying in interest is killing any savings you made by purchasing the item on sale.

Get one or two gas cards for emergencies. Otherwise, pay cash. The same goes for department store cards. Get one or two for special things. Don't sign up for every store credit card. The interest is unreal and you can put it on a bank card or pay cash if you have to.

Don't fall for paying the minimum. A good chunk of your minimum goes to pay interest on the debt. If you have a $1,000 debt on a credit card and the minimum payment is $50 per month, it will take you at least 20 months to pay it off. And that is only one card. What if you have four or five like that? Your minimum payments quickly add up to a substantial amount. The amount you are spending on credit card minimums could be a car payment or add up to a nice savings account.

Pay Your Bills on Time

Pay your cards and other bills on time. Information regarding the promptness with which you pay your bills is sent to a credit reporting agency. So, if you are consistently late or miss payments, it goes on your credit report. When you try to buy a car or a house or to get a loan, it will be on your record and could affect you negatively. The due date on your bills is the day the check should be there, not the day you are supposed to mail it.

Be responsible with your debt. You might have heard the saying, "Guns don't kill people, people kill people." It's the same type of thing with credit cards. Credit cards don't get people in trouble financially. It's people's irresponsibility with credit cards that gets them into trouble.

You will have debt in the course of your life. It is rare that anyone can purchase a car or house by paying cash. But some kinds of debt are better than others. Don't go into debt to boost your image. Live within your means. Reducing credit card debt and keeping it to a minimum should be your priority. Do this and you will start on the right foot financially.

> *Anne got her first job, with a prestigious consulting firm. She felt she needed a new car to enhance this prestigious image. So Anne, who was making $28,000 a year, bought a brand-new BMW convertible. After about three months, she realized that the payments and insurance were killing her. She was so strapped that she couldn't afford to go out or have any other luxuries. Every penny went to pay for her car. Anne really enjoyed having a cool car that sat in her driveway because she couldn't afford to go anywhere in it.*

UNEXPECTED EXPENSES

IT SEEMS THAT IT just takes more money to live when you are out of school. When I graduated from college, I was accustomed to living on

$500 per month. Out of that $500 I could pay rent, eat on a regular basis, wash my clothes, put gas in my car, and occasionally have a good time. So naturally, when I began my first job I thought, "I will have so much disposable income, it will feel as if I have won the lottery." There were more additional and unexpected expenses than I had ever dreamed of. To avoid being bled dry, make sure that you prepare for these little surprises.

Clothes

These unexpected expenses begin with your clothes. During the interviewing process, you had your "interview suit." This one nice outfit was meant to impress the potential employers and show them what a clean-cut presentable person you were. It worked. You got the job. Now you have to show what a clean-cut and presentable person you are five days a week. People might catch on after you have worn the same outfit three days in a row. Plan to buy additional work clothes. Go for quality. People can tell a cheap suit or outfit. You can tell because it will not last more than a year or two if you wear it consistently. Stay away from flash and trendy stuff. Look for sales. After Christmas is a great time to buy clothes, because stores typically have big sales during that time. Unless you absolutely have to have something that moment or can't live without something, don't shop for clothes unless there is a sale.

You will also have to buy a briefcase, satchel, tote, or portfolio. Of course, these are good things to ask for as graduation gifts.

Real Furniture

Chances are, if you have lived in a dorm or furnished house or apartment, you will have to buy a bed and other furniture. A bed is the number one thing to buy. If you can only afford the mattress and box springs, fine. Worry about a headboard later.

There are several stores that provide great furniture and housewares for a reasonable price. You might try places like Pier 1 Imports, Crate and Barrel, Storehouse, or IKEA. Some of these stores have lines specifically geared for people starting out in their first apartment or house. These places are great for inexpensive housewares, too. It really doesn't cost that much to have real glasses that match, instead of plastic cups from the pizza place.

Try to go for functionality. Get a couch and a kitchen or small dining room table. This at least gives you a place to relax and sit other than on the floor. A table is essential, because if you have to work, write something down, or even eat, it's nice to have a place other than on your couch or bed.

If you are single, don't go to an upscale furniture store and blow a lot of money. If, or when, you get married, chances are that the furniture you buy will not go with your spouse's or won't match the rest of your new house.

Laundry

Other unexpected expenses include dry cleaning and laundry. Try to use coupons and learn to iron. If you haven't learned to pick up your clothes from the floor by now, maybe at $1.50 a shirt and even more for a blouse you will hang them up so you can wear them again.

Commuting and Going to Work

Getting to work is another costly nightmare. Before, it was a matter of throwing on the Nikes or Reeboks, putting the hair up or a hat on, and walking across campus. Today, it's a logistical hell, which you pay for. In some cities, such as Los Angeles, Phoenix, or my home of Dallas, a car is a must. Public transportation is minimal and, due to the layout of the city, simply not feasible. Therefore, you must drive.

Depending on the length of your commute, it can cost a pretty penny to fill your gas tank every few days.

If you live in a city where public trans-

Kelly drives a Ford Explorer and has a forty-five-mile commute each way, every day. She spends between $200 and $300 per month on gas to go to work. What about tolls? Parking? Some companies are gracious enough to provide parking or even to pay for parking for their employees. If your company is not, you are stuck shelling out anywhere from $2 on up per day, just to go to work.

portation is adequate, you can take the subway, Metro, L, T, or a bus. Even then, you are incurring an expense. If you live in New Jersey or Connecticut and work in Manhattan, you are paying some decent coin to come to work each month.

Plan for these additional expenses so you won't be shell-shocked when they arise.

SAVINGS

SAVING MONEY IS A difficult but crucial thing to do. You can't spend all of your salary or live check to check. You need to save for a rainy day or special occasion. Savings serve as a safety net. Rule of thumb is that you should have savings of at least two months' salary. In the event you lose your job, you will still be able to pay the rent and eat.

This is easier said than done. Especially early in your career. Another general savings rule is to put away at least 10 percent of your salary. Again, it can be tough at first, but start saving anything you can, even if it's $15 a week. If you have a stash of cash, you can breathe easier when your car needs repair, you get sick, or you want to take vacation.

Make It a Habit

The easiest way to start saving money is to make it a habit. If you make a commitment to saving money each week, simply by writing yourself a check and depositing it, you will soon have a nice little stockpile. Think of it as paying a bill. Make it automatic.

Another automatic way to save money is through direct deposit. If your company offers direct deposit as an option, take it. When your money is directly transferred into your account, you can designate a certain portion to be placed in a savings account. Direct deposit allows you to save money automatically. It acts as a little mind game you can play with yourself. If you never see the amount that is being sent to a savings account, you will never miss it from your take-home pay.

401K and IRA

If your company offers a 401K plan, participate in it. It's the best investment and savings plan available. It's like free money. 401K plans are set up by the company, and allow you to designate pretax dollars (gross income) to be deposited into a fund that the company will invest and manage for you. You do not pay taxes on the money until you pull it out at age 65. Some companies, as an added benefit to their employees, will make a matching investment. This means that, for every dollar you invest in the 401K, the company will add a certain amount. It may be 50 percent of your total investment, or the company may match your investment dollar for dollar. This truly is free money. Rarely can you get a 50 percent or better return on your money. You are allowed a certain pretax amount, generally 9 percent, to contribute to a 401K.

If your company does not offer a 401K, you might consider another type of investment. An IRA, or Individual Retirement Account. You are allowed to contribute up to $2,000 pretax to an IRA, which can be invested in certain mutual funds. This type of account can be set up through a broker. If you are fairly inexperienced in such matters, I recommend that you go to a local Fidelity or Charles Schwab office. They will answer any questions and help you.

LEASES AND LIVING ARRANGEMENTS

YOU MAY HAVE already negotiated your first lease or had your first apartment.

Don't get locked into a long lease, even if the terms are really good. Your life can change very quickly. You may move, be transferred, or get married. Breaking a lease is as difficult as leaving the Mafia. Property companies are notorious for tracking you down, suing you, and pretty much ruining your credit if you mess with them. If you are going to break a lease, make sure that you have your facts straight. Moving for work-related purposes, such as a transfer, is generally acceptable for breaking a lease. But don't sign your life away on a lease.

Moving into an apartment can be very costly. Security and utility deposits can really take a bite. It's not uncommon to put up the first and last months' rent as security deposit. If you put up a $200 fee for a security deposit, be surprised only if you get it back. Apartment landlords are known for finding problems with the apartment that were there three people before you arrived and charging you for the damages.

Safety is Worth the Price

Safety is worth any amount of money. If it's a choice between saving money and living in the 'hood, or paying a few bucks more and being safe, go for the safety. It will be worth it, for the peace of mind.

If you travel for your job, or if you go out of town on the weekend, try to be discreet around your apartment complex. Don't let many people know that you will be away or that you have a steady travel pattern. Crooks look for this. While you are gone, keep the lights and the radio on to make it look like you are there. Or you might consider buying a timer to turn them on and off while you are away. Don't leave messages on your answering machine that say you are out of town, either.

For additional piece of mind, spend the extra money and purchase renter's insurance. It is fairly inexpensive (as little as $100 per year for every $10,000 of coverage). It protects you in case your apartment or rented house is broken into and you are cleaned out. It also covers you in case of fire, smoke damage, or flood. Replacing your wardrobe, stereo, TV, VCR, computer, and any other personal items that thugs like to take would cost you a fortune. A couple of hundred dollars to protect yourself is a steal. No pun intended.

If You Like to Sleep at Night . . .

When choosing an apartment, try to avoid one on the first floor. You don't want to hear your neighbors walking above you, among other noises in the middle of the night. Also, ask for an apartment away from the pool or elevator. These are both very noisy locations. It might be fun and convenient to be near the pool when you use it, but when you are trying to get some sleep the night before your big meeting, hearing the drunks down the hall throw each other into the pool makes this a less than desirable location.

▪32▪

Life on the Road: Travel

As part of your job, you may be asked to travel. It can be anything from a series of short day trips to a nearby city to travel halfway around the globe for weeks at a time. Today, you must often go to wherever the business is. It won't always be in your backyard. Since traveling may be inevitable, you might as well learn to make it as comfortable and trouble free as possible.

Milk It: Join All the Special Programs

Traveling for the company isn't all that bad if you make it work for you. Join all the special clubs for frequent flyers and frequent guests. Airlines and hotels give special mileage credit or points. The more miles you fly and the more nights you stay, the more points and freebies you get. These free programs are promotions that allow you to redeem your points for travel or free rooms or upgrades. You can get these points simply by signing up for the program.

If the company is paying for you to travel, use it to your advantage. You have to be there anyway. Consider it an extra perk. Many people, myself included, have taken vacations for nothing. My frequent flyer points covered my first-class airfare to Hawaii for my honeymoon. You are putting in the time on the road, so make it work for you.

You also want to look into getting a Citibank/American Airlines AAdvantage Visa card, or joining American Express Membership Miles. The dollars you spend are applied to the frequent flyer program you belong to. A list of several frequent flyer and hotel programs is included in the back of this book.

It has been reported in the press that some companies want to keep their employees' air and hotel miles. I think that there will be a minor revolt by employees if those rules are ever truly enforced on a large scale. You can't ask someone to be away from his or her family and not let them benefit in some way.

If you fly a lot, consider joining an airline's convenience club. These are found in most larger airports around the country. You generally have to pay for these memberships on your own. They can run around $150 to $200 a year, but the convenience of having a nice area where you can relax, clean up, make calls, or sleep, is invaluable when you are laid over for six hours, or if your flight has been canceled. If you use it twice, it pays for itself.

Car rental firms also have special clubs which have reciprocal relationships with airline frequent flyer programs. Car rental programs can allow you to get special discounts, free coupons that you can apply to personal use, early check-in, or special upgrades.

Many special programs for airlines, hotels, and car rental agencies allow you to do cool stuff like cutting to the front of the waiting line, or not having to wait in long lines at all to check out of your room or get on a plane. You can also request your choice of seat and receive special upgrades to suites, first-class seating, or luxury or sports cars. All at no extra charge.

Many of these programs and perks still fall outside the guidelines of most companies' travel policies. You might not be making a fortune, so why not make it better for yourself on the road? Take advantage of these perks.

TRAVELING BY CAR

IF YOUR JOB OFTEN requires you to travel by car, join AAA. For a minimum annual fee (well under $100) it offers peace of mind that you won't be stuck in the backwoods with some big-eared guy playing a banjo. AAA can jump your car, tow it, bring you gas, or fix a flat. AAA will also recommend a reputable dealer or mechanic or tow your car there. It doesn't cost you a thing. It's all part of the service they provide and it's covered by your dues.

If you spend a lot of time traveling in the car, get a cellular phone. It's not pretentious, it's a matter of making the most of your time and of being safe. If you are running late for an appointment, have gotten lost, or have car trouble, a car phone will definitely be worth the cost. Besides, you can never find a pay phone when you need one. See if your company has a corporate discount plan with a mobile phone company. You might also see if the company will cover part, if not all, of your cellular phone expenses.

MAKING RESERVATIONS

Make Reservations Well in Advance

Make reservations at least two weeks ahead of time. I know this is not always possible, but if you know your travel schedule and make reservations well in advance you can get a better price and you stand a better chance of getting a room. In some cities, there are particular times of the year when it's more difficult to get a reservation. There are peak periods, when there may be two or three trade shows or conventions in town, or it may be vacation or tourist season. This is often the case in such cities as New York and Boston.

When making a reservation, for flight, car, or hotel, always get a confirmation number and the name of the person you spoke with. If something goes wrong, or your reservation is lost, you have proof and have a much better chance of correcting the situation.

Discounts

Travel costs can add up quickly. It's in your and your company's best interest to get the most bang for your travel buck. To do this you must actively seek and ask for discounts.

Discounts are a weird thing in the travel industry. Who travels the most? Business people. Who pays the most? Business people. Because of the demand during the week, airline tickets and hotel rooms are more expensive for business travelers.

Many companies negotiate special discounts for airfares, hotels, and cars. Sometimes, unless you are with a major company that has considerable buying power, the discounts are not as deep as what you could probably negotiate on your own.

The key to getting a good rate is to ask for a discount. If you were to call a hotel and ask for a room, you would not automatically get the cheapest rate. You would be quoted what is called the "rack rate." The "rack rate" is the off-the-street, no-discount price that only schmucks who don't ask for discounts pay.

It's the same with airfare and car rental. Ask the person who is handling your reservation if there is a better price or a different way of booking your fare. All you have to say is, "What is the best price you can get me?" Hotels, in particular, have special rates for people who are doing business with certain companies in the area. For example, if you are going to Chicago to do business with Sears, they may have a special rate with certain local hotels applicable to any vendor or person doing business with Sears.

If you belong to a special organization, industry group, or association, you can probably get special discounts, as well. Often, AAA members can get special rates and discounts at hotels. All you have to do is ask.

HOW TO GET BETTER SERVICE

Look the Part

If you look like a kid, you will be treated like one. Once, I was coming back from New York late on a Friday afternoon. Before my flight, I had changed into casual clothes. I was in jeans, a leather jacket, and a baseball cap. As I walked into the Admirals Club to check in and showed my membership card, the attendant looked at my card and suspiciously eyeballed me. She then sarcastically asked, "Is this your father's card?" I cracked up laughing and then pulled out my membership cards showing that I flew over 50,000 miles a year with their airline and that I was returning from business. I also told her I didn't appreciate being patronized that way.

For all she knew I could have been an athlete (except that I'm smaller, have less money, and don't wear a lot of gold jewelry). Actually, as far as she was concerned, I was someone important. I was a customer. I received many upgrades out of that little faux pas. However, if I had been dressed more like I had come from a business meeting rather than a basketball game, I might have been given more respect. When traveling in airplanes or checking into hotels, dress up. It doesn't have to be a suit or anything formal. You simply get more respect and better service if you look nice and are dressed as a professional than if you are casual.

Can I See Some ID?

Renting a car can be an adventure because of your age. If you are over 25, you have nothing to worry about. If you have not yet reached that milestone, you are in for a world of fun and frustration.

Many car rental companies have raised the minimum age you must be to rent a car. In most states you have to be 21 to rent a car, except New York, where you must be 25. Because of the potential liability car rental firms are exposed to by renting a car to someone under 25, many are raising the minimum age to 25 years old. If you are not 25 you can be charged an extra fee or premium. As if the fee weren't bad enough, the age restrictions imposed can make you feel like a kid and place you in compromising situations.

My own similar experience with car rental hell happened when I was scheduled to meet with Warner Lambert, the large drug maker in New Jersey. I was staying in Manhattan and arrived that morning to pick up my rental car, only to find out that I was too young. I was 24 at the time. I had been using this company for two years, but not in New York. Not even a call from my boss to the rental company's headquarters could get me a car that day. I had to reschedule the meeting.

> *Lori tried to rent a car from a major car rental company while a client was with her. The rental company turned Lori down because she was only twenty-four. "Not only was I embarrassed because I felt that I needed a note from my Mom, my client had not realized that I was so young. They were shaken up and we almost lost the account."*

When I finally met with the people at Warner Lambert, we all got along very well. There were four people, all around my Mom's age. They asked me why I had to reschedule the meeting. Since we all got along very well, and our business together was successful, I told them about my car rental fiasco. Luckily, they were good-natured about it and gave me a hard time. They asked me if I needed a note from my mother to make it back through the Lincoln Tunnel. As they were laughing at me, I'm thinking, "yeah, real funny." Check out the rental car situation ahead of time. You don't want to be stuck.

Hey Kid . . .

Though you are a professional in the work force, some people may treat you differently because of your age. Most people will treat you with respect and as a professional, while others may treat you poorly, provide you with bad service, question your abilities, or even try to trip you up. You don't have to take that type of crap from anyone. The best way to deal with someone treating you poorly or making a big deal of your age, is to keep your composure and let the results and your work speak for itself. Know your facts and do your job well. This will dispel any doubt about your abilities because of your age and command more respect.

COMFORT IS KING

SINCE TRAVELING CAN be a laborious, exhausting experience that takes away from the comforts of your home, there are some tips to make your journey more comfortable.

When Flying

Where to sit. Sit as close to the front of the plane as possible. It's a smoother ride, for sure. Yet, the main reason for sitting toward the front of the airplane is so you aren't held prisoner in the airplane for thirty minutes after it has landed. Have you ever noticed how, the moment the door opens, every person on the airplane stands up, grabs their bags, and blocks the aisle? Even the people with window seats in the back are trying to cram in the aisle so they can get out sooner. Avoid this stampede. Sit up front and make a speedy getaway. Plus, you get where you are going sooner than the people in the back do.

If you are tall, the exit rows and bulkheads have more room between the rows, so you don't have to eat your kneecaps. Depending on what you like, the window seat is good for the view, and you can have something to lean against when you want to sleep. It's bad for when you need to go to the bathroom because your fellow passengers hate you for making them get up. The aisle seats are great because you can stretch your legs into the aisle for more room. You can also make for a speedy getaway to the bathroom. Then again, if the person in the window seat has anything to drink, you are going to get up anyway, when they go to the bathroom. You can request the seat of your choice. I recommend this or else you are at risk of sitting in the middle seat between two large, sweaty men with elbows as sharp as knives.

Some other tips include:

■ Try to get to the airport well in advance. It never fails that when you are running late to catch your flight, the security agent asks you to empty everything in your pockets, there is a long line to get your boarding pass, and nowhere to put your overhead luggage once you board.

Save yourself the aggravation and plan to arrive at least 45 minutes be-forehand.

■ Always use the curbside check-in unless you must arrange for your ticket. It's much faster than going inside, and yes, you tip these people. The rule of thumb is a buck a bag.

■ Before you go to the airport, call to see if your flight has been canceled or is late.

WHEN IN HOTELS

■ Don't stay on the first floor. The first floor has too much traffic and is too noisy. You are also safer on the higher levels, because it's harder for someone to wander in off the street. Don't stay next to the elevator, for the same reason as not staying on the first floor. Also, there is too much traffic and you will hear the elevator bell all through the night.

■ If you don't smoke, make sure that you request a nonsmoking room. Often, you can tell if a smoker has stayed in the room previously.

■ If you are going to be on the road for several days or an extended period, take something from home that will make your hotel seem more comfortable and familiar. This could be a picture, a small stuffed animal, or a book. Anything that will make it seem a little less cold. Take any personal toiletries that you really enjoy. Hotel soaps and shampoos vary. Some are great, some really suck. Always ask for more towels than you need.

■ To make sure that you don't oversleep, leave multiple wake-up calls and also use the clock alarm. Cover yourself.

WHAT TO PACK

Take What You Can Carry On

The more you bring, the more you schlep. The more you schlep, the greater the risk you will forget something. Try to take just enough so that you are easily mobile. The biggest lesson regarding packing is that you will never wear everything you take. Try to coordinate and mix and match (like Garanimals) so you won't have to take much. Try to keep it limited to one hanging bag. In the perfect world, you should only what you can carry on, but I know that sometimes doesn't happen.

Spend the money on good luggage. It's worth it. Good luggage, like Hartman, Boyt, and Tumi, is expensive, but it can withstand a nuclear explosion. You are paying for quality and durability. Don't overpack your bags. When you are having a very difficult time zipping your bag, you need to rethink what you are taking. Bulging zippers are the primary cause for blowouts. You don't need to have a baggage blowout in Boston during winter. Picking your shoes and shirts up out of the snow is not fun. I know.

Your Bags Didn't Make the Flight

Carry on anything that is important to you. *Never* check a briefcase or tote bag containing important work. You may never see it again. I'm not willing to trust my career to the good folks who handle baggage. Carry on any clothes you will need immediately. Always carry on your toiletries and the suit or clothes you will be wearing for your first meeting. That way, if your luggage is lost you don't have to cancel your meeting. I learned this the hard way.

Once, when flying to La Guardia from Dallas, I carried on my suit, but I checked the bag that contained my dress shoes. Sure enough, the bag did not make the flight. I woke up the next morning up for my nine-o'clock meeting with only a suit and the black cowboy boots that I had worn on the plane.

What could I do? It was too early to buy a new pair of shoes before my meeting. I decided to brave it. Hey, oil guys in Texas wear boots with their suits. I go to my meeting feeling that I should introduce myself as "Hi, I'm Billy Ray Doofus from Texas. I parked my horse out front. Now let's make a deal." Luckily, no one noticed, or at least they were kind enough to accept my eccentricity. Later that morning I went directly to the shoe store and bought some grown-up shoes. Remember the Boy Scout motto, "Be prepared."

EXPENSE ACCOUNTS

The Basics

If you are given an expense account, don't abuse it.
That is the number one rule where this is concerned. Don't be a martyr and sacrifice comfort or quality to save a penny or two. But treat your expense account like it's your own money and don't be frivolous.

Document everything that you do and save receipts. If you don't save receipts, don't be shocked when you aren't reimbursed for your expenses. If you don't write things down, how can you remember how much you spent and where you spent it?

Keep track of expenses daily. Make sure that you complete your expense report every day. Keep all of your receipts in one place and fill out your report when you get back to the hotel or after work. If you wait until you get back from your trip, you will have an unwieldy mountain of receipts and you will have forgotten where they are from.

Stay within your limit. Some companies give you a per diem, or a daily allowance. Stay within those guidelines. Sometimes it may not be possible. If you go over your allotted amount, explain the circumstances in your expense report or get approval. It may be to your benefit to stay as far under the per diem as possible. Some companies allow you to keep what you do not spend of your per diem. It's then in your best interest to keep costs low.

Don't put personal items on your corporate card.
Even though you will reimburse the company for them, it can be a bad habit to get into and can lead to questions about your integrity. Keep yourself above reproach and separate personal expenses from business expenses.

Don't Get Taken

There are some expenses on the road that are ridiculous. Business travelers are gouged for certain items if they aren't careful. Avoid this highway robbery and subsequently being yelled at by your boss for falling victim to the convenience items that hotels and car rental companies place before you. Three examples come to mind:

Gas at airports. Always fill the rental car with gas before you bring it back to the airport. If you wait to fill up at the airport, you will be charged an exorbitant rate per gallon.

Room service and mini-bars. Room service is always more expensive and a surcharge of 15 percent to 20 percent is added simply to bring it upstairs. Then an additional tip is tacked on. Also, keep snacks in your hotel room and avoid the $3.50 Snickers and $2 drinks in the mini-bar.

Hotel room long distance. Lastly, never dial direct long distance in a hotel. Hotels charge the highest rates for long distance and can have surcharges on top of that. Hotels make unbelievable amounts of money by marking up telephone calls. Take a phone card with you and use it.

ROAD WARRIOR BLUES

How to Battle Homesickness

If you are in a strange city where you don't know anyone, it can be boring and lonely. When you are in this situation, the worst thing you can do is to stay cooped up in your hotel and flip the channels or watch movies.

If you get cabin fever or have spare time, explore the city. Use the trip as a chance to see and learn about another city or a part of the country you aren't familiar with. Your business may take you to places that you would not otherwise think about visiting or vacationing in.

Granted, Des Moines, Iowa, or Reading, Pennsylvania, may not be on the top of my list of exciting destinations. But I can't stand to hear some grumpy old business traveler tell war stories about, "I've been to Atlanta before. Nice town, although I only saw the airport and the Hilton across the street." Well you didn't see Atlanta, you moron. Get out and explore. Learn the history. Go to a museum, take in a show or a sports event. If you are in a city for several days, there will be some downtime. Don't stay cooped up in the hotel and watch videos all night. Take advantage of being able to travel on someone else's nickel.

You can find out about local activities through the concierge. He can be a valuable ally. He can get you reservations and help with directions, and he also has great connections around the city. Remember, always tip for good service. You can tip at least $5 or $10 at the end of your trip if he has been helpful.

It's tough to do something by yourself. Especially at first, but don't be self-conscious about it. You may feel like a dork going to a movie, a museum, or sporting event by yourself and, especially, going out to eat by yourself, but who cares? You don't know anyone in town anyway.

TIPPING

ALWAYS TIP FOR GOOD service. You don't have to be Diamond Jim or Jane, but a well-greased palm can find you a cab when it's raining or snowing, get you moved to the front of a line, or get you a reservation in a restaurant that is packed.

Here are the general tipping rules. Bellhops and skycaps get a buck a bag. In restaurants 15 percent to 20 percent is expected for good service. Concierge staff should get five to ten bucks depending on the value of their service and information. Doorman, a buck in good weather, two or three in inclement weather. Cabs have tipping rules also. For a short ride, let them keep the change (e.g., for a $2.50 ride I give them $3). FYI: New York cabbies rarely give small change back anyway. They *expect* it as part of their tip. (Even if they were surly and didn't know how to get where you wanted to go.) For longer rides, give them a buck or two extra for the tip.

When in Cabs

■ In some cities, you may have to take a taxi to your destination. The key to not getting "taken for a ride" or being overcharged in taxis, is to act like you know where you are going. If you act clueless, you can be taken the long way around.

- If possible, find out ahead of time what the fare should be. Ask a cop, skycap or bellman what the fare is to the airport, downtown, or your hotel. If your cab fare is within two to four bucks of what you were told by the cop, it's usually OK. Don't be like the foreign students who were taken from Kennedy Airport in New York to Manhattan and charged $1,500 for what is normally a $40 ride.

- If you are having a tough time catching a cab, go to the nearest hotel. Cabbies are always waiting for fares at hotels.

- If you are in a hurry, tell the driver you will make it worth his while to get you there quickly. If you do this, tip him generously. In some cities, such as Washington, D.C., cabs are allowed to take more than one passenger. If you are in a hurry, ask him to take you first, or to not pick up additional passengers or share the ride with anyone. Tip well if they do this for you.

SAFETY ON THE ROAD

YOU CAN NEVER BE too safe when staying on the road. If you are traveling by yourself in a strange city, it's wise to let the front desk, the concierge, or someone know where you will be going and when to expect you back. I know this sounds like your mother, but if, God forbid, anything happens to you, like getting knocked on the head in a strange city, at least someone will have an idea of where you are.

Always use the additional chain and dead bolt locks. They protect you in case of theft or if a duplicate key is floating around by mistake.

Don't broadcast the fact that you are from out of town. Find out ahead of time where the bad parts of town are and where you need to avoid. Some parts might be fine during the day, but are dangerous later in the day or in the evening. Downtown Cleveland for example is busy during the day, but at night or on the weekends it clears out.

You want to be careful. If you ever find yourself in a situation where you feel uncomfortable or unsafe, follow that feeling. Trust your gut. You may be in a bad part of town, in a cab, or in a situation where you feel threatened. Don't think, just act and get out of there. Crooks look for people who are traveling or look out of place. There are too many weirdos out there who prey on travelers, so trust your instincts.

Resources

A partial list of airlines, car rental agencies, and hotel phone numbers and programs can be found in Appendix B.

■ 3 3 ■

The Don'ts of Business:

Things to Avoid

In the workplace, there are several things that are absolute taboos. At some point in your career, you may be exposed to sexism, racism, or nepotism. Many of you will witness it, while others sadly enough will experience it firsthand. Whatever your background or heritage, it's important to recognize these and other negative elements of the workplace, so you can prevent them from happening to you or to someone else. In addition, there are several things that can affect your career that you will want to avoid.

PREJUDICE

BUSINESS IS MORE GLOBAL, and the workplace is more diverse than ever before. It is almost guaranteed that at some point in your career that you will be working with others who are not exactly like you. To be an effective executive today, you must open your mind and be tolerant of all heritages, ethnic backgrounds, religions, and sexual orientations.

If you ever make a disparaging comment, a malicious remark, or even joke about another person or group, based on their color, ethnic or religious background, gender, or sexual orientation . . . *prepare to be fired*. It's that simple.

The workplace is too diverse today for anyone to openly display any type of prejudice, without paying the price. Making racist or sexist remarks on the job can cause you more problems than being fired. You can get also sued, and rightfully so. Today's workplace has no tolerance for no tolerance. I don't care how harmless you think it may be. Even joking or playful remarks can be hurtful to others, and hurtful to your reputation. If you make prejudicial comments or exhibit this type of behavior, in the best-case scenario, you look like a backwoods idiot. If you really cross the line and offend someone who will take action against you, not only can you be fired, but you and your company can be sued. You will also be branded and labeled for a long time to come. Bottom line is, it's a bad idea.

What If It Happens to You?

Discrimination and prejudice are not always overt. They're often very subtle, through stereotypes, generalizations, nicknames, lack of opportunity, second-guessing, or general disrespect.

You don't have to belong to a minority group to experience it or do something to stop it. Even

> *Chad had been in a difficult negotiation with a client. Afterwards, he sent an E-mail message to his coworkers telling of the negotiations. In it he described the client as "The Jew" and made disparaging comments relating to the character of the client and what a tough negotiator he was. The shit hit the fan the moment Chad sent his E-mail, which he thought would be seen in a private cocoon within his company.*
>
> *One of Chad's coworkers was meeting with a client in New York, and was reading his E-mail while the client was present (which you don't ever want to do). When he read Chad's message, the client was looking at the screen and saw the remark referring to another client negatively as "The Jew." As you might have guessed, the client who read the message was Jewish. The client was completely offended and will never do business with Chad's company again. But there is more.*
>
> *Chad thought that since nobody in his company was Jewish, what was the big deal. The big deal was that one of his coworker's wife and family is Jewish. He read the message and tore Chad apart verbally.*

if it's not directed toward you, it can still be offensive. If a coworker or your boss makes a prejudicial comment about an individual or a group, or if he is simply being a foul sexist pig, let him know that you don't appreciate nor will you tolerate those comments. You do not have to accept prejudiced behavior and remarks from anyone, even your boss. You are protected legally.

Don't accept the, "Oh, I was just kidding or didn't mean anything by it" excuse. Make that person feel two feet tall.

If you are bonehead enough to make a racist or demeaning comment, you should be careful who you make it to. Even if you think you are safe making a stupid comment, or that the person thinks like you, don't do it.

Don't be stupid enough to practice it. And don't be spineless enough to tolerate it. There is no place for it at all.

SEXISM

WOMEN MUST DEAL with varying forms of sexism. As a woman, you deal with sexist remarks, unwanted advances, and people doubting your abilities simply because you are a woman. As with racism, some forms of sexism can be very overt while others are more subtle.

Probably one of the most obvious examples of this is in little words or names that women are called. In the Southwest, you hear a lot of Honey, Darling, and Sugar. The only people who should be calling you that are your dad, your boyfriend, or your husband.

If someone is being particularly gross or suggestive at work, you don't have to put up with it. Tell the person that you don't appreciate that language or behavior. If it persists, document everything, use a recorder if necessary, and tell a supervisor. If that doesn't work, seek legal action.

> *Jill, a University of Georgia graduate says, "You have to decide how you are going to handle it. If a fifty- or sixty-year-old man calls you 'honey' in a sweet way and you can tell he meant no harm, what can you do? He has been doing it all of his life. You can tell him he is a pig until you are blue in the face. But he won't change."*
>
> *Pick your battles. Jill chooses to use it to her advantage. "I will be sweet as can be to get my business done. If I were to correct every sixty-year-old man who called me honey, I would never get anything done." However, if someone younger uses Honey, Sweetie, or any other choice degrading term, in a negative way, such as, "Look here, honey" you can tell them to take a flying leap.*

Women can also experience a subtle form of sexism by people doubting or questioning their abilities.

Whether you are directly affected by racism, sexism, or homophobia, don't stand for it in the workplace.

DON'T GOSSIP

THERE ARE THINGS THAT you will learn in business and professional settings that are confidential and should be kept that way. If your company is working on a special project or has privileged information, be careful who you tell that to. If it's supposed to remain in the company, keep it there. If a client tells you something or you have special knowledge of a client's developments, keep their trust and don't tell everyone you know.

Being "in the know" is fun. It's a feeling of power to be able to know something before it happens or understand the real scoop on something. For example, I have had the privilege of dealing with many clients who are household names. Being involved with these companies you see some dirty laundry or are exposed to special projects that they may be working on. I may be aware of a development that will be launched in six months, but no one in the public is supposed to know about it. It is my duty to respect that company's privacy and not discuss what I know.

Loose Lips Sink Ships

Be careful whom you tell things to and where you have certain discussions. Don't discuss business in the elevator after a meeting, or in the lobby. Don't tell a coworker what a schmuck your boss is in the elevator. The woman riding with you could be his wife. If you have a meeting or negotiation that goes well, don't talk about it until you are out of

Shelly, a Seton Hall grad who works for the sports division of a major television network, says that the kind of sexism she encounters is subtle. "I would have game scores and statistics for producers and instead of accepting what I was saying as fact, they would ask me if I were sure. When a male analyst brought information to them, there were no questions asked. It was almost as if because I was a woman I was not as sure of my answers." To combat this, sadly, many women and minorities have to work twice as hard and be doubly sure of their work. "If you are a minority, the margin for error is slim," says one African American woman in the retail industry.

the building. Don't call from the pay phone downstairs or talk about the points you are trying to get the other person to give in on.

Be careful where you discuss business. Don't talk about important business in bathrooms, airplanes, elevators, or restaurants. Use discretion anywhere there are large concentrations of people. You don't know if the person next to you is a competitor, will steal your idea, or knows who you are talking about.

Last year I was having lunch in New York and three gentlemen sat at the table next to me. The tables were very close together, and I was unintentionally able to hear their conversation. As it turned out, these three were my counterparts at our largest competitor. I learned this when they mentioned my company and some developments in the industry. They talked business, developments, and strategies for the next hour. I sat there riveted, with my face stuck in a newspaper. I learned more about that company simply because these guys were talking about sensitive data in public. You don't know who is around.

Don't Be Seen Wasting Time

Don't spend all of your time talking or socializing at the water cooler or break room. People notice. The people who hang out at the water cooler are most likely going to stay there.

Even if you smoke, don't hang out with the vultures who crowd doorways huddled together in their smoking gangs. They look like derelicts and smell like crap. Don't you have anything better to do than hang out in a doorway loitering during working hours?

KEEP YOUR PRIVATE LIFE PRIVATE

Don't Live Out Your Own Soap Opera at Work

Most people work in cubicles, small open areas separated by partitions. Don't go into shock when you aren't shown the corner office. There is virtually no privacy in cubicles. Be aware of it and act accordingly. Namely, watch what you say on the phone, because everyone can and will hear you. Don't have a screaming fight with your parents, landlord, boyfriend or girlfriend while you are on the phone in your cubicle. If you are making social calls, realize that everyone else, including your boss, hears you and notices how much time you spend chatting rather than working.

Another thing to remember about cubicles is the lack of security and physical privacy. Don't leave anything on your desk that you would not want others to see. This means important papers or personal items. You can keep them there, but remember that people come by all the time, and things that are lying on top of your desk for all to see have a funny way of walking off your desk. This includes bills, bank statements, letters, and checks.

Don't Share Details of Your Private Life

Don't discuss or listen to sexual escapades in the office. You don't want to be anywhere near something that could be construed as harassment, and these days you can't be too careful. Walk away, don't even risk it. Walk away. You don't know who might be offended by a comment. You don't want to be associated just because you are standing there.

Don't get drunk in front of your boss or in front of people whose respect you need. It's very different from in school. In the professional world, when you see Sam liquored up Friday, puking his guts out, and calling for his Mommy, it's really tough to take him seriously when he gives you a proposal Monday.

You can't recover from that. Have fun, but don't be a buffoon. If you want to act out of control, do it with your friends away from work.

Don't discuss personal finances with coworkers or your boss. Your personal life is no one else's business. You don't want people to make judgments about your pro-

> *Diane got drunk at a company outing. She was a little loud by nature, and the booze magnified it. Under the influence, Diane felt compelled to inform everyone that it was her "special time" of the month and that she was very emotional that evening because her jeans wouldn't fit right. She later tried to kiss every male at the function who had a pulse, married or not. Several months later, she was put in charge of a group of people at work. Those who remembered Diane's drunken behavior would not take her authority seriously. She had lost all credibility in the organization, and was branded a lush and a flirt.*

Mike was in charge of a division in a software company. He would talk openly about his personal finances, credit cards, debts and loans. Everyone in the office knew that Mike was leveraged to the hilt, made foolish investments, and mishandled his finances. The message being sent was, Mike can't manage his own finances, he has a budget and is running the division. It did not instill confidence among the troops.

■ ■ ■

Melissa and Eric began a little interoffice fling. The ill-fated romance was short lived, as most are. The relationship died and the two parties ended up hating each other. As could be expected there was major conflict with the two being in the same office, but to compound matters, the two were assigned to be partners and work together in the same territory. It became so heated that Eric asked to be transferred to another division.

Another interoffice romance ended in flames, and the two parties ended up sharing the same cubicle at work. How about a little tension? How productive can you be when the person that "did you wrong" is four feet from you every day?

fessional life based on rumors from your personal escapades.

Nothing Is Secret

If you have a secret and want it to remain a secret, don't tell anyone at the office. No one at work can keep a secret. I don't care how hard or earnestly they try. OK, it might be a bit of an exaggeration about everyone, but don't be surprised to find out that your plans to look for another job are made public, or that the whole office knows that you sleep in the nude, or have a snake tattoo on your butt.

Warning sirens should go off when you hear, "Don't tell anybody I told you," or "They didn't want me to tell anyone, but . . . " I don't care if it's your best friend at work, telling this person what you had for breakfast can be a bad move. Telling this person a secret is the equivalent of broadcasting it on CNN.

Don't Date Coworkers

Don't ever date people you work with. Unless you are going to marry the other person, it will end badly.

Just don't do it. One person will be completely miserable, and everyone in the office will be watching the two of you. This goes for one-nighters with coworkers too. It may be tempting, but don't do it. If you do, prepare for the "walk of shame" when you come in the next morning, because I guarantee, everyone in the office will know by noon.

NEPOTISM

A Can't-Win Situation

Nepotism. According to Webster, nepotism is: *favoritism shown by persons in high office to relatives or close friends especially in granting jobs.* Which leads me to say: With rare exception, never, ever work for a husband and wife where there is a direct reporting relationship. The same goes for lovers, siblings, parent/child relationships, and all family members. All these fall into the category of no-win situations. You, as an employee, will lose almost every time. Think about it. If you approach a manager and tell her that her husband or the person she is dating dropped the ball, did something stupid, or shirked his responsibility, who will the boss side with? Sure in theory it's nice to think that we are all adults and professionals, and can make decisions based on the facts at hand. "We wouldn't think about favoritism."

Even disagreeing openly can cause problems, unless it is the most unique of working couples. If one were to openly criticize their spouse in public as they would a normal employee, they know that it would be a really cold night or an ugly Thanksgiving.

Criticizing coworkers. If you approach a manager with criticism or a problem with his spouse or family member, he will get defensive. I don't care who it is, or how "professional" they are, the first natural reaction is, "You jerk, that is my wife you are talking about, so watch your mouth." Of course no one would ever say this to your face, but your stock can only go down.

Nepotism doesn't just affect your relationship with management. It has an effect on your competitiveness with your peers. The spouse, lover, or family member in the lesser position will always have the advantage of having access to knowledge and information before you do. It puts a new meaning to "having the boss's ear" (both figuratively and literally) when you can discuss things in the middle of the night. The family member will also have special influence with the boss that you won't.

Again, there are exceptions. There are some couples with fantastic working relationships who can separate the two. But the bottom line to remember is that you will always be second fiddle.

DRUGS

IF A COWORKER IS DUMB enough to offer you drugs, walk away. Even if it's your boss. I'm not going to make a moral judgment. If you do them, that is your deal. But it could come back to haunt you in a big way. Don't even risk it. Don't feel that you have to do anything to keep your job or move up the ladder. If you are ever fired, or threatened because you refuse to participate in anything like drugs or sex, there is one word you need to know: LAWSUIT.

▪34▪

Rookie Quick Tips

Everyone makes mistakes starting out. Everyone. The key is to learn from them. The following are a few quick tips and things that twentysomethings around the country have learned the hard way or wish that someone had told them before they began their careers.

- ▪ Be proactive and take charge of where you want your career to go. Don't let someone else run your career for you.
- ▪ Become a jack-of-all-trades and learn as much as possible. Be cross-functional. Don't let yourself become pigeonholed or forced into a certain area.

- Compete against yourself, not the person in the cubicle next to you or down the hall.
- Go beyond what is expected of you.
- Don't be average. Average sucks. If you are average, you are as close to the bottom as you are to the top.
- Being mature doesn't mean acting older than you are. Being mature means making responsible decisions and being accountable for your actions. It means being poised and confident in certain situations.
- Just because you are wearing a suit or a tie doesn't mean that you can't be yourself. Don't take yourself too seriously.
- Be prepared for anything.
- If you don't know the answer, know where you can find it.
- Understand everything about your health insurance before you need it.
- Once you succeed, you have to work twice as hard to maintain that success.
- Pick your fights carefully.
- Be protective of what is yours. Don't let your territory or market be cut in half because you performed well. Companies think, "If you achieved great results by yourself, think how well we would do if we put three people in your market." Your slice of the pie is cut by two-thirds, but you are expected to get the same results.
- No one told me I would actually see so little of my paycheck. Taxes suck.
- Don't mess with the IRS. They will hunt you down like a dog.
- Don't be afraid to ask questions.
- Live as cheaply as you possibly can, at first.
- Always keep your résumé updated and keep a copy with you in your portfolio. You never know when an opportunity may present itself, or when you may be told to hit the pavement.
- Work doesn't have to be work. You can love what you do.

▪ 3 5 ▪

Managing Your Life and

Finding Success

By working eight to five you will soon find out that you don't have time for many activities you took for granted during college, such as going to the cleaners, the grocery store, playing basketball, or shopping whenever you want. Chances are, you are probably working longer than from 8 a.m. to 5 p.m., so there will be hardly any time at all left over. What do you do? You still have to eat and wear clean clothes. How do you make time for yourself and what needs to be done? Your weekends will be when you get caught up on the things that you used to handle during the week.

EVERYDAY THINGS

MOST OF THE MUNDANE tasks can be handled during the week. Going to the bank, picking up and dropping off laundry, even grocery shopping can be done before or after work, or during lunchtime. Try to find services and stores with locations close to work or your home. In many urban areas, buildings are equipped with services such as cleaners on-site. Look for these convenient services and use them. See whether your bank has a branch near your office.

Climbing the Mountain of Laundry

I've known people who have bought thirty pairs of underwear and socks so they could postpone doing their laundry for a month. Try not to wait until your laundry is a pile six feet high before you do it. If you wait, you will find that you are spending all day Saturday picking lint balls out of the dryer. A better way is to do smaller loads throughout the week. If you have a washer in your house or apartment, drop a load in before you go to bed and dry it in the morning. Granted, this may not be the best way to have Downy-soft laundry like your mom's, but it sure saves time.

Paying Bills on Time

You can get so busy that things like paying your bills can slip through the cracks and you wonder why suddenly there are no lights. To keep track of important finances and make sure that you pay your bills on time, have a designated place with folders for your bills. Know when bills are due and devote a certain day each month to writing checks. You may even write them all at once and stick each check in its envelope. You don't have to mail it right then, but when it's due you can just seal it and drop it in the mail box.

Eating on a Regular Basis

When the drive-up folks at Taco Bell and McDonald's start to know you by name, or the Domino's driver has a reserved parking spot at your apartment, it's time to look into eating a little healthier.

Cooking at home is a lot better for you and a hell of a lot cheaper, but when do you fit it in? Sunday night, take an hour and prepare meals that you can heat up later in the week. Make a big bowl of pasta or rice. Maybe cook chicken that you can eat later in the week. This way when you are pressed for time during the week or when you come home tired, you don't have to mess with doing anything special. You have something good already prepared and you can slap it in the microwave.

When you put the numbers to it, eating lunch out every day can really add up. The average fast-food meal will run you between $4 and $7. If you were to count only one meal a day for five days a week you are still looking at between $80 and $140 per month. In reality, most young people eat both meals out because of convenience. Take your lunch occasionally and use the money you would spend on fast food to treat yourself to a nice restaurant instead.

You may work late and eat at 7 p.m. one night and 11 p.m. the next. If possible, try to eat at a regular time every night and don't eat just before you go to bed. I know it's tough to do. If your only choices are to eat fast food or to starve, make sure that you choose wisely and look for something that won't stop your heart on the way down. Most places now have salads, chicken, or potatoes.

Take Care of Yourself

Your new working lifestyle may cause you to spend a minimum of eight hours per day sitting in an air-conditioned office. During that time, your only physical activity might consist of going out to lunch, walking to another office or walking to your car. Oddly enough, you will be tired and drained when you get home, so getting your butt off the couch to go work out is not a high priority.

This new sedentary lifestyle, combined with fast food, will result in several additional pounds and maybe a new wardrobe. The key to not having to buy a new wardrobe each year or to show pictures of what you *used* to look like is to eat right and be active. I can tell you from experience that your fantastic metabolism comes to a screeching halt at about twenty-five. Mike tells of adding thirty pounds during his first year on the job. "I went out to lunch every day, where I had a huge meal, and then I grabbed a burger or pizza at night."

Remember, it's easier to keep weight off, than to take it off.

Try to work out, if possible; at least go for a walk during the day or take the stairs at work. It may be easier for you to work out early in the morning or right when you get home—whatever works for your schedule. Maybe buy a bike or rollerblades to use on the weekends. It takes a lot of work but it's worth it. You will feel better and release stress.

GET A LIFE . . . OUTSIDE THE OFFICE

IF YOU AREN'T CAREFUL, your life can easily resemble a gerbil on a treadmill. You wake up before the sun rises, you leave the office after it goes down, only to beat a trail back to your apartment to eat whatever doesn't move in the fridge, watch TV, and then do it all over the next day. Your work will take up the bulk of your time and attention, but that is no reason to let it dominate your life or allow yourself to fall into a social rut. Get off the couch and have fun. Get involved with things other than your career.

Sometimes that is easier said than done. Especially if you move to a new town, or only spend time with people from work. Start by making new friends; widen your circle of friends.

Have Friends Outside Work

Hang out with people other than those you work with. You will make some very good friends through work. Some will result in long-lasting relationships, but if all you do is hang out with people from work you end up talking about work. Plus, what happens when you leave or your professional relationship changes (for

> One 28-year-old attorney, who moved to Kansas City from Philadelphia, says, "All of my friends are through work. I know every attorney in town, but they are either my parents' age or I talk to them at work every day. This may sound bad, but I get really sick of talking with other attorneys."

example, you might become your friend's manager)?

Nobody Will Knock on Your Door

Making new friends is not always easy, especially if you move to a new town. It's not like when you were little and moved to a new neighborhood. People won't come to your door and ask you to come out and play. You have to make the effort. Suck it up and make an effort to meet new people. The first few times are the toughest. You may have to go some places by yourself. Don't sit at home and wonder why you don't have anything to do unless you make the effort to get out of your comfort zone. You have to make the first move.

How do you meet new people without being a groover or hanging out at a bar? You might consider volunteering in the community or a civic group. Find activities that support the arts. Become active in your church or temple. Join a sports league. If you don't know about the local sports scene, go to a local YMCA or sports club and ask how to join.

Widen Your Circle of Friends

Even if you have a group of friends from your hometown or college, it's good to broaden your horizons. Over time, some of your friends will go by the wayside. You will hang on to some of your college friends, but will grow apart from others. The lives of each of you will change. You will both develop new friends, new interests, and perhaps the friendship will fizzle out or not have the same intensity it did in college. While it may be painful, don't be discouraged when you grow apart from some of your college friends. It's very normal.

If you are asked to do something with a group of new people, don't hesitate because you don't know them or you aren't comfortable in groups. Go just to expand your base of friends. Even if it's an activity you aren't crazy about, don't be too picky. If you turn people down repeatedly, they stop asking.

"What Do You Wanna Do? Uh, I Dunno."

"There is nothing to do here. I'm so bored." If your life has become an endless series of dinners and movies, or spending your evenings watching the local Rico Suave work his magic at a bar, open your eyes.

There is plenty of entertainment in most cities, if you look for it. In addition, after you start working, you will soon realize that you can't go out every night. Not only is it expensive, your body can't rebound like it used to. You can't go out until two in the morning and expect to be at work by eight.

Do Things in Groups

Plan group activities. Big groups are fun and harmless. There is no pressure of looking like a date, and if one person is boring, you can always talk to other people. You also expand your group of friends, because new people are being asked to participate all the time. You can plan group activities, such as going to a ball game or meeting at a sports bar. Plan for your group of friends to go to a festival or take a mini–day trip to a nearby town or lake.

> *Have a dinner party or have a group of people over for dinner. Beth, a Georgetown graduate, started a dinner club with her friends. Once a month Beth and five friends have a dinner party at someone's house. Each month, a different person is designated host. Someone brings wine, another person brings dessert, and so forth. Make it nice and bring guests.*

If you can afford it, buy season tickets to the local theater or symphony. Many communities have arts groups that offer cheap packages for young professionals. Go in with a group and buy a block of tickets. This is great because every weekend for the next five months, you at least have something to do. It's prepaid entertainment. If you don't want to use the ticket or are busy one night, you can give it away. It's also great to buy two for yourself. This way you can take a date or ask a friend.

Find a Hobby

Develop a hobby or outside interest. You can't think about work 24 hours a day, or at least you shouldn't. Learn a new skill or find something that can occupy your time other than watching *Love Boat* reruns or doing your laundry.

Keep yourself multidimensional by doing things that are completely outside and unrelated to your job. The most interesting people are those who have done a little bit of everything. Experiment.

Having hobbies and outside interests will take your mind off work, so when you get back to the office you will be fresh and pay more attention to your work.

List things that you want to do. If you want to learn to play the guitar, take a cooking class, or learn to ride horses on the weekends, do it. Most cities have a local college or even a junior college or community center that offers classes. Take a class to learn something you always wanted to know. Learn to paint or take karate. Whatever you choose, do something to occupy your time and give your life a little more meaning than what you do from 8 a.m. to 5 p.m.

WHAT IS SUCCESS?

Success is not measured by how you do compared to how somebody else does. Success is measured by how you do compared to what you could have done with what God gave you.
—Anonymous

> *One of my favorite success stories is about a guy I went to college with. For a graduation gift his parents gave him a two-week trip to New Zealand. He ended up staying longer than two weeks. He called his parents and said he had met a young businessman and was going to work for him over there. A year later, he took his savings and moved to Fiji, where he opened a taco stand. (Yes, a taco stand in the South Pacific.) After selling it for a nice profit two years later, he moved to Seattle, where he is now a magician. This guy did not take the traditional or easy route. Many people, including his parents, would call him a bum. (Do you think his parents regret the trip?)*

What does it mean to have achieved success? Is it money? Financial success is the most obvious barometer in America. The amount on your W-2 and how many possessions, clothes, and toys you can acquire are the most easily identifiable characteristics of having made it. But the longer you remain in the workplace, the more you realize that each person has his or her own definition of success, and therein lies the key to becoming truly successful. Have only your own standards and don't aspire to anyone else's version of happiness.

Who is to say that someone making $25,000 a year is less successful than a person who makes $250,000? Sure, one person makes more money than the other, but there is more to life than what your paycheck says at the end of the month. To some, success means having enough free time to play golf, to spend time with family and friends, or to be there for your children when they get home from school. To others it means not having to answer to anyone but themselves, or it may mean having the security of a steady paycheck and knowing that the bills are paid.

Define your own meaning of success. If it is financial, work for that. If it means experiencing as much as possible and living abroad before you are thirty, go for it.

The only person you have to answer to is you. As you grow older and gain more responsibility, your definition of making it will change as well. Once you establish roots, such as a home, marriage, or even children, you may not feel like traveling or putting in the hours, or you may work harder because you see something to work for.

Job Enrichment

Quality of life doesn't have a price tag. It doesn't matter how much money you make if you aren't happy. An attorney recently told me of a study that found that over 80 percent of attorneys were dissatisfied with their careers or weren't pleased with their choice to practice law. Look at dentists. Generally, dentists make a decent living, yet it's rumored that among professionals they have one of the highest suicide rates. These are people who are making serious money, and they don't like what they do!

Today, many our age are looking for job enrichment instead of the home-run career. Job enrichment is being able to wake up every morning and say, "I love what I do." To look in the mirror and respect yourself. To have time to do the things that you want to and to be financially secure enough to pay your bills. To many, this is success, and it doesn't matter if you are a garbage man or the CEO of a Fortune 500 company, you can still meet all of those criteria.

Glenn Solomon said it earlier, "Success is being able to enjoy the things that you have." You can't take it with you and you will only get older. Perhaps you came from a split home. I did. Success can be a good marriage. It can be doing your job the best you can, and enjoying what you do. You get one chance at life, and you will only be this age once. So do what makes you happy and don't burn yourself out or

> *Kent, a UCLA graduate, worked in the high-pressure, fast-paced world of advertising for two years. His job as an account executive for a major agency was challenging, and he appeared to be on the fast track. To most people, Kent seemed to be a very successful young man, yet Kent didn't feel that way. He was under constant pressure. The hours were long and the demands of the job were getting to him. He didn't realize the pressure he would be under when he went into advertising. To Kent, freedom and spare time to pursue his hobbies and outdoor activities were most important. His picture of success was someone who could control his own schedule and be able to leave work behind at the end of the day. He took stock of what was important to him and decided that he would never be truly happy in advertising, no matter how "successful" he became. Upon reaching that decision, Kent moved to Anchorage, Alaska, to work for a nonprofit agency. He loves his work and the easy lifestyle and is truly happy. Kent found his own definition of success and is pursuing it.*

waste your youth chasing the bucks. The money will eventually come.

Don't Compare Yourself to Others

No matter how good you are, or at what level you are, there is always someone who runs faster, jumps higher, makes more money, has a bigger apartment, or is moving up the ladder faster than you are. You will drive yourself crazy if you try to keep up with the Joneses. There will always be someone for you to compare yourself to. Everyone does it. Using another person as a barometer or measuring stick is very common. "How much is she making? I can't believe that he just got a promotion. They just bought a new house. She drives a what?" It doesn't stop when you get older, either. I know people who are in their fifties who compare their performance and career paths with others. It's human nature to see how you are doing against the next person.

This can be depressing and frustrating if you aren't where you want to be, or if someone has passed you or achieved great success before you have. Be happy with what you have control over . . . yourself.

Keep It In Perspective

When you are lying on your deathbed, drawing your last breath, you won't look back on your life and say, "I wish I had spent more time at the office," or "I should have closed that deal."

You will think about your family, and wish that you had spent more time with your parents, your spouse, or your children. You will want back the thirty minutes that you spent worrying over a file, and wish you had been on a golf course, or listening to music, or spending time with friends. Ask any divorced, grizzled, old executive and he will tell you he wishes he had done things differently.

People make unbelievable sacrifices for what they think is important. To make it in the professional world you have to make sacrifices. That is a given. Just make sure that you sacrifice the right things. Be devoted to your work and employer, but remember a company won't love you back. Growing up, your family may have been one of the things sacrificed to a career. Looking back, you might wish that maybe your Mom or Dad had been around more, instead of spending so much time at the office. Don't be a workaholic. Have fun and spend time with your family and friends.

Be, Do, Have

The first thing someone asks at a party is often, "what do you do?" This fascination with what a person "does" forces us to categorize and make judgments based solely upon a person's occupation, not who they are. Don't confuse doing something with being something. A job or career is what you do, it's not who you are. Your worth as a human does not depend on your position or title within a certain company. If it did, would someone who sells fertilizer (cow manure) be a crappy person?

What if you get canned tomorrow or no longer work in that profession? Are you less of a person? Are you different because you don't have a certain position anymore? Don't be so one-dimensional or shallow that you are defined by what you do for a living or because you work for a certain company. Jobs and companies will come and go, but you will always remain *you*. Have pride in who you are.

Life Goes On

Be able to walk away and leave work, and the worries that come with it, at the office. Believe it or not, the safety of the free world does not rest on your shoulders. Don't get so get wrapped up in a sense of overworked responsibility and self-importance that you take it home with you and make your roommate and friends miserable. Try to balance your personal life with your professional life. The two will overlap, but don't let problems at work ruin your personal time or let yourself become so driven that you eat, sleep, and breathe for the company. No matter how important you think you are to the organization, the day after you pack up and leave, the doors will still open and people will show up for work like they always have. In the big scheme of things, it's only a job.

Keep a Journal

Early in your career you will go through many changes, professionally and personally. Keep a journal. Write down what you are feeling at certain points of your life. How do you react to situations? What activities do you do? It's a fun and helpful learning experience to look back on these and see how much you have grown from one year to the next. It's great to look at some of the stupid stuff you did and see how you have improved as a professional and a person.

When you are keeping a journal, write as if no one will ever read it. Don't censor anything. Write it as a letter to yourself (no "dear diary" stuff) and for God's sake don't leave it lying around.

Be True to Yourself

Once things are going well for you, don't forget the hard work it took you to get there. If you overcome an obstacle or experience a setback, don't forget what you learn. Next time you are faced with a difficult situation, you will be able to draw on it. Remain true to yourself and don't forget where you came from.

SHARE THE WEALTH

The influence of each human being on
others in this life is a kind of immortality.
—John Quincy Adams

Hopefully, you are well on your way to becoming a successful young professional in the field of your choice. Through hard work or the right breaks, you have accomplished your goals or are well on your way. With your prosperity and education comes responsibility to your community. With a large disparity between the "haves" and "have nots," it's important that we use our skills, education, and abilities to give back to those who aren't so fortunate.

Give Time, Not Money

Being young and just starting out, you probably can't support many activities simply by writing a check. However, give what you have plenty of . . . yourself and your time.

People our age have created programs all over that are making a difference. Whether it's Lead or Leave, Third Millennium, Boston City Year, Teach for America, or President Clinton's AmeriCorps program, volunteerism is on the rise among twentysomethings.

The best place to start is in your own backyard. There are countless programs in your own community that are always in need of volunteers. Find any causes or organizations that you feel strongly about and contact them. You might volunteer at a local food bank once a month, or help adults learn to read one night a week. Take a weekend to volunteer at the Special Olympics.

It might be Big Brothers and Big Sisters or the ASPCA, if you are an animal lover. If you are handy with tools, call Habitat for Humanity, which helps build homes for low-income families. Feed the Children distributes food and clothing to the poor in urban and rural areas. You could work with AIDS patients to help run their errands for them. You can answer phones at a teen crisis line, or serve Thanksgiving dinner at a shelter. You might consider Junior Achievement, where professionals teach one class a week to junior high or high school students to help them learn about business. Whatever your interest, find something that you feel strongly about or that is close to your heart, then give what you can.

To learn about what organizations and opportunities are available in your community, call your local Chamber of Commerce or Department of Human Services. They might be familiar with local charities and organizations, or they might even produce a directory.

Be Committed

If you volunteer, be dependable and make the commitment to stick it out. There are many well-meaning people who begin a project and fail to finish, or leave when it becomes difficult or unpleasant. This is irresponsible. It's not only an organization that is being let down, but often another person who needs and depends on the help of volunteers. If you are going to do it, be committed. It may not be easy, but it is rewarding. That which may seem unpleasant is what causes you to grow and benefit the most from your service.

Serving as a volunteer and giving back to your community gives you immeasurable benefits and a different perspective. There is no feeling in the world like giving back to your community, or seeing the appreciative face of someone whom you have helped.

Too often we look only at our own situations and get wrapped up in our own problems. "My boss is a jerk, I'm broke, I have no life. All I do is work. I need a new car. How can I get by on $24,000 a year?" When you think you have it rough, or complain about not being able to make it on $24,000 a year, helping someone who is not as lucky as you are puts it in perspective. It helps you remain grounded. You are young and have your whole life ahead you. Give a little bit of your time to make a difference in someone else's life. That is what being a success is.

COOKIE LEHMAN
Director of Promotions, NHL Hockey Team
Age: 26

IF YOU ARE A SPORTS FAN, outside of being an athlete, your ultimate dream might be to work for a professional sports team. (OK, your ultimate dream would be to collect a pro athlete's salary, but let's get real.) Cookie Lehman is actually living a sports fan's dream, as Director of Promotions for the Dallas Stars of the National Hockey League.

After graduating from the University of Texas with a degree in journalism and public relations, Cookie didn't have a clear picture of what she wanted to do, but she did have some interesting criteria for what she wanted in her first work environment. "I moved to Dallas, thinking I might like to be involved in public relations. I was also interested in working in sports, because I have been involved in sports throughout my life, but more than that, I really wanted to work in a tall building."

In addition to targeting employers and sending résumés, every day she would go to one tall building in the morning and another in the afternoon. Starting at the top she would go to every office in the building, dropping off her résumé. Cookie eventually scored by getting a job with a sports trading card company, handling their promotions and eventually their public relations . . . and yes, it was in a tall building.

In that first position, she helped with event management, she wrote trading cards, and she worked on special projects with the NHL and NFL. All the time, she was making various contacts. "Here I was fresh out of school, with no experience, getting to deal with all of these big wheels. I didn't know how to do anything. I had to feel my way through and convince people that I knew what I was talking about.

"The company I started with was small and growing. A small company is a great place to start because they will let you do everything and give you a chance." The downside is that the company might not survive. Cookie was eventually let go when the company laid off two-thirds of the staff.

Back to square one. Cookie had maintained her contacts, but it was still a rough period. "I had to swallow that pride and get in the unemployment line. It was tough at first, but then you realize, I'm 23 and here are people in their fifties who made $100,000 a year. I gave myself a weekend to feel sorry for myself, then on Monday I called everyone I knew and started networking."

One of the things Cookie did was call the International Sports Commission in Dallas and offer to work part-time as a volunteer. "I thought that it would keep me near the center of the action in the sports world and that I might make some connections. I basically sat in front of a computer and input information for three hours a day." It was about this time that the announcement was made that the North Stars of the National Hockey League were planning to move the team to Dallas. The team's owner sent one of his staff members ahead to Dallas to make preparations.

The advance man was formerly with the International Sports Commission and had stopped by the Commission for some help. "It was here that I met this person. I told him about my past experience and gave him my résumé. I kept in contact with him for the next few weeks. He had passed my résumé along to the person who is now my boss. He contacted me, and after a short, informal interview, I was offered a position with the team.

"I am in the entertainment business. If you want to be in this business, you have to be willing to work hard, long hours . . . weird hours. I work weekends and nights. You just have to do whatever it takes." When selling herself to her employers, Cookie really stressed the fact that she was young and energetic and didn't mind the work and effort it would take.

You might think that, as an employee of a professional sports team, free tickets would be a great perk. Sure, Cookie goes to the games for free, but she rarely gets to see the action. "During the games I am all over the arena. I make sure everything, other than the game itself, goes smoothly. This can be organizing volunteers at the front of the door who are handing out promotions, running the contests on the ice between periods, doing the contests in the arena, coordinating the PA announcements, taking care of VIPs, and I also order all of the give-away items." Cookie is so busy during the games that she has to wear a radio so people can locate her.

After Cookie started, one of the first things she did to learn the business was contact the people at all of the other teams who had her same position, and ask them questions and advice. "I learned a lot that way. I also learned a lot on my own by making mistakes."

Cookie tells how one mistake taught her to be prepared for anything. "We were doing a pregame ceremony, where a celebrity was to drop a puck. We also had two other events going on and, moments before the puck drop, I realized that I didn't have a puck for the celebrity to drop. We are on the ice and everyone is out there, so I grab a role of black tape which could double as the puck. It would not have been a big deal, except the camera zoomed in and got a close shot of the puck for the screens in the arena. Everyone in the arena laughed and booed. Apparently it wasn't that big a deal, because everyone at work thought it was funny, including the president. Still, I was so embarrassed. The next day at work, my coworkers had put a giant poster in my cubicle. It was a blown-up picture of the puck drop. You could see the players laughing in the background, and it said, 'Cookie

Lehman Ceremonial Puck Drop.'" Cookie always carries a spare puck with her at the games now.

She says that many people she works with in the Stars' office and around the league are young. "You have to be young to do this, because the pay is low and the hours are long. But the perks and experience are fantastic."

Cookie knows the value of connections and is constantly making contacts with people on the sponsor side of the business and with other teams. "I don't think enough young people use the contacts they make. I have learned to get a business card from everyone. Always keep networking, because you never know when it can come in handy."

APPENDICES

APPENDIX A

What Can I Do?

Industry Profiles

Some people say, "I want to be in consulting, or television, or advertising," but when asked what that really means or what they will be doing, their eyes suddenly glaze over. Many people enter a field without knowing really what it involves, or they eliminate certain fields simply because they are not aware of all the opportunities available to them.

This section offers a brief overview (a Cliffs Notes version) of what it is like to be a rookie professional in several different fields.

There are several key questions that you might want answers to before embarking on a career. These include, among other basic questions: How much can I make? (Very important.) Where will I start? What will I be doing? What skills do I need? What is the career path?

I have spoken to experts around the country, ranging from recruiting officers to company presidents to twentysomethings who are employed in these positions, to obtain a general picture. When it comes down to it, no two companies are alike, but I hope that this gives you a rough overview of what it is like to begin your career in these professions.

If your industry of choice is not covered, I apologize. Bear in mind that some fields are so diverse and there are so many career options that there is no way I could possibly cover them all in this space. However, I hope this gives you some food for thought and piques your interest in exploring career opportunities you had not yet considered.

To obtain more information on a certain profession, please refer to the relevant section of the appendix and contact the appropriate trade association, call a professional in the industry and conduct an informational interview, or write to me and I will help steer you in the right direction.

ACCOUNTING

Accounting today is much more than bookkeeping or "bean counting." Accountants have evolved to become business consultants who often help monitor and steer the financial health of an organization. Many Big Six accounting firms have full-fledged consulting practices, although they often are autonomous and separate from the accounting side.

What Will I Do?

Accountants do audits and analyze, prepare, and verify financial data or reports for managers and executives in corporations, private individuals, and government organizations.

There are several routes you can take. Public accounting is the largest area and includes accountants who work for themselves or for a firm like one of the Big Six. Management accountants work in-house for a corporation or private group and monitor that company's financial information. Others choose to work for the government or an agency. As an accountant, your duties will primarily be auditing, observing and making recommendations about a company's financial direction, or serving as a tax expert.

Auditing is examining a client's financial records and reporting whether the records are accurate and correctly prepared. Tax work involves working with an individual or corporation and advising them on the most advantageous tax strategies, and making sure that they adhere to certain government regulations, guidelines, and restrictions. Accountants also help an organization design an accounting structure and system. If you work in-house for a company, you might be assigned to work in an area such as taxation, cost, or budgeting.

Where Do I Start?

In public accounting, the typical starting position is that of associate or analyst. (Public accounting is the most popular field in accounting and hires more than any other sector of the industry. Last year, public accounting firms extended more offers to college grads than any other type of employer, according to the CPC annual survey.) After a brief training program (approximately one to six weeks) to teach you the documentation, standard format, and the way of doing things at the firm, you will be assigned to a project with an actual client. You will work as a member of a group under the supervision of a senior team member, partner, or manager. Initially, there is a fair amount of hand-holding and supervision. After you become more comfortable and experienced, you are given more responsibility.

APPENDICES

Sometimes the groups or teams have a market sector that they specialize in. Many larger firms have whole groups devoted to certain industries, such as health care, retailing, manufacturing, or technology. At first, chances are you will be exposed to several different industry groups. Eventually, you will gravitate toward a special industry sector.

According to one Big Six recruit you are a "Lotus Jockey" during your first year. You help do audits, analyze numbers, and do a lot of number crunching.

It is a very structured environment and involves extreme detail work. During your first year on the job, you will continue to learn the documentation and improve your procedures. You will also study to obtain your CPA license (a state board certification, which involves passing a very rigorous exam). Often the firm will aid you in your studies. As the year goes on, you will continue to be introduced to many industries.

Most likely you will be traveling to a client's location for an audit. This could last for weeks at a time. Scott, a Big Six recruit, says that these assignments generally last around six weeks. "Travel is probably the most difficult part of the job," says Scott.

The hours are often long and some seasons are more hectic than others. Depending on your specialty, the end of a quarter or tax season can be crazy.

How Much Can I Make?

Undergraduates who choose to go into accounting do fairly well financially; they can expect to make in the high twenties the first year. The starting salary will vary according to where you live and the size of the firm you are with. Sometimes a signing bonus, which can be anywhere from $1,000 to $5,000, is given.

In addition to your base pay, some firms pay for overtime after a certain number of hours worked. You can use the overtime as vacation or collect it as pay. Another nice perk is that firms often provide for your travel back home on the weekends, or pay for your spouse to visit when you are away from home for an extended period. Insurance, retirement, and expense accounts can be expected at most firms and companies. Additional perks include membership in professional groups and help in paying for additional training and education.

What Is the Career Path?

In a Big Six setting, you can expect your first promotion in two years and the second three or four years later. You can choose the partner track and attempt to move up through the organization. However, because of the contacts established and the exposure to many industries, most people leave public accounting and go into private industry after about two to four years.

What Skills Do I Need?

A strong accounting and business background including a degree, preferably in accounting, is the minimum. Math and computer skills are a must. Traditionally, accountants have not been thought of as people-oriented, but this is no longer true. You must be a good communicator. You will be dealing with clients and recommending proposals. Mark, another Big Six recruit, says that he must often communicate with clerks and people who are not as educated as he is. "As the outsider in the office, it is important that they trust me and understand what I am saying." You must also be flexible and able to deal with change. You will work with different people all the time. The teams and groups can change with each assignment. Extracurricular activities will set you apart from other recruits. Experience and business acumen count for a lot in this field. If you can get auditing or accounting experience through an internship or by working for a small company while in school, do it.

Who Are Some Top Companies in this Field?

The Big Six are the top public accounting firms. They are: Arthur Andersen; Ernst & Young; KPMG Peat Marwick; Deloitte & Touche; Coopers & Lybrand; and Price Waterhouse.

ADVERTISING

You can do many things in advertising besides making commercials. It's a very broad field with many different opportunities. You can work for an agency or for the client. In an agency setting, the work is split into three main areas: creative, account, and media. They differ greatly but are interdependent. The creative side is made up of artists and copywriters. The account side deals with the client or account, and acts as a liaison between the client and the creative department. They are known as the "suits" and are more businesslike than the more free-spirited creative. Media is responsible for buying media time and space, and planning where to place print and broadcast ads.

Where Do I Start?

The entry-level positions depend upon the area you want to go into. In some agencies you will start as an assistant or junior to someone. Others start out as full staff members. On the account side, you will typically start out as an account executive of some type: junior, assistant, or account service trainee. You will work directly with the client and act as a business and marketing consultant to help plan and develop strategy. You will monitor the cost and expenses of the client's project. Your main job is to work at improving the relationship between the client and the agency. After about a year you will be promoted to full account executive.

As a creative, you will begin working on actual projects by writing or designing. Depending on how good you are, you may have your work in print or on the air very shortly after you begin.

Media planners and buyers often start out as assistants and help collect and analyze statistics, map out media plans, or negotiate print or broadcast buys. In most of the positions mentioned you will begin by working under the supervision of a more senior staff member but will be handling actual projects.

How Much Can I Make?

There are conflicting reports on how much you can make, ranging from peanuts to a whole lot. It depends largely upon the agency and your position. Creatives tend to make more than anyone else, followed by account executives, and lastly, media planners and buyers. One major agency reports that first year creatives and account people start at around $25,000 a year, while media planners and buyers usually make in the high teens to low twenties. That same agency says that advancement can come rapidly and substantially. Top creatives and account people can make close to six figures within five years. On the other hand, you have those who might as well be volunteering their time. As one media buyer for a large New York agency put it, "This is a great field if your parents can subsidize you." At her firm, first-year recruits make less than $20,000.

What Is the Career Path?

It's another industry where relationships and networking are crucial to a new position and more money. It's not uncommon for people to hop from one agency to another to advance or to increase their salary.

You will start out as a junior or assistant in almost anything you do. There are varying degrees of seniority, which bring more responsibility and exposure. Your advancement is dictated more by your talent and the needs of the agency than your tenure. Experience and a successful track record are the keys to advancing in this business.

What Skills Do I Need?

Your skills will depend upon the area you go into. If you are on the account side, you need business skills, including an understanding of marketing and general business. Your presentation and communication skills must be fantastic, because you are not only dealing with the client, but you are often conveying what the client wants to the creative department. Many account executives have business degrees or MBAs.

If you are in media planning or buying, you must be very organized and comfortable with numbers and figures. Most people who enter the media side tend to have degrees in advertising.

Creatives need to be first of all . . . creative. Most artists have extensive training and degrees in the arts or have graduated from special programs. Writers come from a much more diverse background. It's your talent rather than your background that matters. There are writers who have biology or economics degrees. In either creative field, you *must* have a portfolio of your work. This can be a book that has hypothetical samples of advertising solutions or actual work for a client.

Because of the environment, you must be able to work well with others and on a team. You will have your work criticized at some point, so there is not a lot of room for ego. The hours are long and the pressure can be great when faced with deadlines and the whims of a client.

If you can get experience before you start, you will be ahead of the competition. It's an ultracompetitive business. Try to get an internship to gain experience and learn the business. Many agencies hire their own interns.

Where Can I Find Them?

There are major agencies in New York, Chicago, Dallas, Los Angeles, and most other major metropolitan areas, although New York is still the champ. Agencies can be of all sizes; however, an agency's success is not determined by how much staff it has, but based upon billings or revenue. To locate agencies around the country you might refer to the Standard Directory of Advertising Agencies (also known as the Agency Red Book).

BANKING

Banking is another field that is incredibly diverse, with many career options. To be in banking means much more than being a loan officer or a teller. Banks and financial institutions today are offering more services to their customers than they have in the past. Some banks are offering investment and portfolio management for their clients, while others perform auditing and personal or corporate finance. This has opened up many opportunities for those interested in this field.

Where Do I Start?

First you must decide which area of banking you want to go into. Among your choices are loans, credit, auditing, investments, operations or administration, corporate finance, and systems. Depending on the organization, you may begin as an auditor, analyst, or trainee.

What Will I Do?

It varies according to your department, but you will most likely be assigned to work under an experienced supervisor. Some banks have formal training programs, while others have you train on the job or in the field. Your duties will depend on the division or program you are in. If you are in operations or administration, you will be responsible for managing individuals and their work flow. You will be responsible for making sure that work is done properly and that your staff meets certain deadlines. As a corporate analyst, you will most likely do financial modeling, analyze financial conditions, prepare proposals and projections, and conduct database management.

How Much Can I Make?

Depending on the area you work in, you can expect to make between $23,000 and $30,000, including benefits such as insurance and 401K. Plus, you get those fantastic bank holidays.

What Skills Do I Need?

You need a business background. According to a college relations officer for one of the largest banks in the country, "This field is so competitive, and we have extremely qualified applicants sending us material every day, that we

can't even look at someone unless they have some type of work experience."
She goes on to say that this experience does not necessarily have to be in a
bank, but something that demonstrates your work ethic, management abilities, and exposure to the professional world.

Regardless of your major you should have an understanding of marketing,
customer service, and sales and have some course work in accounting.

It's a very structured and professional (read: conservative) environment.

What Is the Career Path?

Your career path is wide open. Many people train in one area and either
move up the ranks of that department or explore other avenues within the organization. Training programs generally last between one and two years.

Where Are They?

Many larger banks and financial institutions recruit on campus. While
some do so on a national basis, the majority of them hire on a local or regional
basis.

CONSULTING

Consulting is one of these nebulous areas that can mean many different
things depending upon the situation. Consulting firms work with a wide range
of industries and specialties. Some of the primary areas in which consulting
firms assist clients are: strategic management recommendations, implemen-
tation, and systems and technology.

Consultants collect and analyze data, make recommendations, and implement their proposals. As in accounting, some consulting firms divide their
business into sectors or teams that respond to certain vertical market specialties such as manufacturing, retail, health care, information technology, or financial services. Firms may have a special area of expertise. One may be
strong in management or re-engineering, while another may be an expert in
systems.

Where Do I Start?

The market for undergrads is somewhat limited. In most cases you must
have your MBA or another advanced degree. When you read in *Business Week*

that grads going into consulting are making six-figure starting salaries, remember that is *not* for undergrads.

Programs available for graduates with bachelor's degrees are typically analyst positions. Deloitte & Touche offers business analyst or systems analyst positions for those with bachelor's degrees. Other firms offer similar positions. These positions are generally two- or three-year assignments, after which you are expected to go back to earn your MBA. Rarely is a recruit asked to remain on board after the two-year period without going back to earn an MBA. Most firms will assist you in applying to an MBA program.

You will most likely work on a project team at a client's location. This can be for several weeks at a time. There will be much supervision and detail work. The activities will depend on the firm's specialty and the client's needs. You may be involved in financial analysis, business re-engineering, strategic planning, competitive assessment, cost management, productivity, improvement, or helping clients implement recommended strategies.

It is exciting work where you can gain broad exposure and experience. It's also a very demanding environment.

How Much Can I Make?

Depending on where you are in the country, your education, and experience, between $30,000 and $40,000. You will also have insurance, a retirement package, and a travel and expense account. Some firms offer a one-time hiring bonus of between $2,000 and $5,000.

What Is the Career Path?

As mentioned earlier, an MBA is expected and rarely can you advance without it. As with accounting, you can go the partner route or, as many do, take your experience within a certain industry to work for a client or become an entrepreneur. You may have noticed that there are many parallels between consulting firms and public accounting. Some firms, such as Andersen Consulting or Deloitte & Touche, have units devoted to both.

What Skills Do I Need?

If you want to make a career out of consulting, an MBA with top grades (generally a 3.5 or better), plus three years experience are the minimum requirements for the advanced partner track. To get noticed for an analyst program, you must be near the top academically. You must also demonstrate leadership abilities and drive. This is done through activities in the community or on campus. Recruiters want to see if you have a strong commitment to any particular project or cause. Other things that recruiters look for are communication skills, maturity, sense of humor, high energy, experience working with a team, competitiveness, and strong goals and aspirations. Experience is another key. "We don't look for skills as much as we look for talent," says the director of college relations for one major consulting firm.

Who Are Some Top Firms?

Deloitte & Touche, Andersen Consulting, Bain, McKinsey & Company, Booz Allen, EDS, Boston Consulting Group, and most of the Big Six accounting firms. If you wish to live in a certain location, you might contact the local office directly. Few firms have central recruiting.

ENGINEERING

Engineering encompasses many different specialties and sectors. Basically, engineers design and create machinery, systems, and processes. They determine how things work and how separate components integrate into a plan and work together. They evaluate a design, including cost, reliability, and safety. Whether it's an airplane, a car, a computer, or the package that orange juice comes in—you name it, there is a good chance that an engineer had a hand in making it.

Engineers can work in areas such as testing, production, design, or quality. Many engineers work on the manufacturing side. The actual design and construction is what is traditionally thought of when people mention engineering. But, increasingly, there is a whole service side to engineering. This involves consulting and advising manufacturers on their processes, quality control, and procedures. You may be hired to troubleshoot manufacturing processes, evaluate specifications, or set up a manufacturing system. Some engineers are even involved in sales. This is a promising area for many engineers. Using their technical knowledge, they can sell directly, assist a sales team, or help in the installation of a complex piece of equipment or process.

There are over 25 different types of engineers, including petroleum, electrical, chemical, industrial, aerospace, civil, and mechanical. Each type works in its own specialty but has basic training that is applicable to many different areas.

Where Do I Start?

Many engineers start out as an associate or junior engineer. Some are lucky enough to go straight in as an engineer. Your training will depend upon the organization you are with. You may go through a formal program that teaches you the proper procedures and ways to do things at that particular company or you might work under the supervision of someone more experienced.

Much of what you will do is learning on the fly. There may not be a manual for many of the problems you will encounter, so you must find out on your own. Steve, an engineer at Texas Instruments, says "You must be a quick study. If you don't know the answer to a problem or how to do something, you must learn it quickly or find someone who can show you how."

What Skills Do I Need?

Whatever area you specialize in, you must be comfortable with computers and extremely proficient in math. Communication is a skill that most engineers need. It doesn't matter what design is in your head if you can't put it on paper and tell someone how to build it. You will constantly be interfacing with clients and other engineers. You should also be creative, analytical, and detail-oriented.

A bachelor's degree in a field of engineering is the minimum requirement. Grades are important. This is a discipline where your technical proficiency is important. Starting out, the best way to demonstrate it is though your grades.

What Is the Career Path?

The career path is varied. Some have a career with one company. However, many engineers start at a large company, training, learning skills, and making valuable industry contacts. They then take that experience and move to a smaller company or specialty engineering firm.

How Much Will I Make?

Engineers are among the highest paid of any graduates. Starting salaries range between $30,000 and $40,000 depending on your background, area of expertise, and location. Generous benefits packages are usually included, as well.

Jobs are plentiful in private industry, engineering firms, and government agencies and departments. Engineers are in demand and heavily recruited on campus. Last year, graduates with technical degrees received 42.3 percent of all job offers made to people with undergraduate degrees, according to the CPC Salary Survey.

GOVERNMENT

If you have a desire to help shape the future of the free world, there are plenty of opportunities for you. The most obvious is to work for a congressman or a senator. However, there are so many organizations that are either part of, or affiliated with, government that your possibilities are almost unlimited. Some basic jobs to consider, both on and off the "Hill," are with the various committees, the Senate or House offices, Republican or Democratic National Committee, the RNC or DNC Senatorial and Congressional campaign committees, various trade associations, lobbyists, law firms, and think tanks. In addition to that, there are opportunities with the executive branch and the numerous government agencies.

Where Do I Start?

It depends on what area of government you enter, but on Capitol Hill the most common entry-level positions are legislative correspondent or legislative assistant. Assistant is a little higher up on the food chain than a correspondent. The committee version of an assistant is called a professional staff member. However, some people start out as receptionists or doing anything they can to get in the door and establish contacts. Networking and connections are critical to landing a job and moving up.

If you don't want to move to Washington, D.C., an area you may want to explore is state government. This may be an easier route to gaining experience and exposure than trying to crack the competitive "Beltway" scene in Washington. One Hill staffer says that the Federal bureaucracy is so huge it can take a while to understand how the process works. A state government is of a manageable size, so you can get a feel for how things work and take that experience to Washington, if you choose.

What Will I Do?

Each office is organized differently. As an LA or LC, you generally will respond to mail, write statements, and perform basic legislative duties, such as tracking and preparing legislation. You may also contact constituents back home. There is a lot of phone work and writing.

There may also be some grunt work. Everyone pays their dues. One Hill worker warns, "If you think you are above making copies, this place is not for you. Unless you have experience doing something else, you must be willing to work for meager pay for a while."

It's a unique environment. You will spend a lot of your time becoming acclimated and learning how things are accomplished. One seasoned Hill staffer says, "People come up here with delusions of grandeur and think that they can change the world, and it just isn't going to happen. It can be frustrating because your victories and accomplishments are often incremental. You lose much more than you win."

Some Hill workers claim that it also differs from other fields, in that you will be doing everything for yourself. "There is not as much support staff as in the private sector," says Kelly, who works for a congressman.

How Much Can I Make?

They don't call people in the government civil servants for nothing. Starting pay in government is considerably less than in the private sector. It, of course, depends on the position and area you are in, but the salary range is anywhere from $10,000 to $20,000 a year. The low end would be for a receptionist or legislative correspondent. On the Hill, salaries tend to be lower in the House than on the Senate side.

Lobbying firms and organizations off the Hill may pay better. However, this depends on the industry they represent and the purpose of the organization. As would be expected, a lobbying firm representing private industry will pay better than a nonprofit.

In addition to your salary, the government offers a benefits program with a menu of insurance choices and a retirement plan.

The perks are going to be in attending parties, meeting powerful and influential people, being near the center of power, and being informed on issues.

The downside is, of course, the low pay and the hours. One Senate aide says that your hours may be very unpredictable. "If a senator decides to filibuster, you can be there all through the night."

What Is the Career Path?

There are opportunities in all branches of the government. It varies from office to office. Some people tend to stay at one office for a long time, while others use positions as stepping stones to move around to different committees or opportunities on the outside. There is no set tenure or career path. It depends on the work you do and the training you have.

Craig, who works for a senator, says, "The hardest thing is to break through the barrier and get your first job. Once you are in, it's a lot easier to move around. It's a matter of being at the right place at the right time and being very aggressive." He recommends trying to meet as many people as you can.

What Skills Do I Need?

You will find people with all types and levels of degrees. So there is no prerequisite. However, before you invest much time and effort pursuing a career in this area, make sure that you have an interest in the political process and a basic understanding of how government works.

You must communicate and deal well with people. It also helps to be very aggressive. People who are serious about working on the Hill blanket the place with résumés and try to talk to as many people as they can. It's very competitive and there are many bright, well-educated people vying for the jobs.

What Are Some Resources?

There are several resources that people use to find job announcements. Among them are the Democratic Study Group Job Bulletin, the Senate Placement Office, and *Roll Call*, which is a weekly newspaper on the Hill. You might also pick up a copy of *The National Journal*, another weekly, which has a section that discusses job openings and who has changed positions.

MERCHANDISING

Merchandising involves getting goods to where they can be purchased by consumers. You can be involved in merchandising by working in a retail store or as a buyer or merchandise manager. Merchandising can encompass many different products, including clothing, furniture, consumer goods, and machines, for example.

What Will I Do?

Buyers purchase merchandise for resale to consumers. They work with sales and marketing managers to determine how products will be distributed, priced, marketed, and advertised. Some larger department stores or merchandisers like Target or Wal-Mart might have many buyers, with each one specializing in a certain area, such as china or ladies' leather goods. A company like Pier 1 Imports might have just a few buyers who cover a broader area of purchasing, with responsibilities such as furniture, dishes, and bath items.

Buyers must be knowledgeable about the products. They go to market or to the wholesalers to view products, negotiate prices, and buy the proper quantities for their stores. Buyers must be up on any trends or new products in their areas of expertise, so there is a lot of reading and travel. You will visit many trade shows, showrooms, and conferences.

Your communication skills must be fantastic, because you are not only dealing with the wholesaler or manufacturer, but often dealing internationally with exporters, meeting them face to face, or talking with them on the phone or faxing information at all hours of the night. There is a lot of paperwork, in which you will track sales, get information on the products to the stores, and follow products as they travel from the vendor to the store. It's a high-pressure job and very competitive.

Where Do I Start?

You may start out as a merchandising assistant or assistant buyer. Buyers usually have more experience or must first go through an extensive training program.

As an assistant buyer or merchandising assistant you act as a liaison between the buyer and the sales department, advertising, and distribution. You make sure that nothing happens along the way and that the stores have enough product and the proper shipments.

What Skills Do I Need?

While many have degrees in merchandising, the best background is experience. If you have spent any time in a retail setting, use it to your advantage to learn about how things work at headquarters. Seretha, of Pier 1 Imports, says too many people work retail and view it as a dead-end hourly job. You have to realize that there is all of this going on back at headquarters and that you can be a part of it. Many people work their way up through the ranks, from working in a store, to managing it, to moving to headquarters and becoming a buyer or department head.

In addition to understanding merchandising and retail, you should also have a solid communications background and a good understanding of business, primarily marketing, sales, and promotion.

Some companies, such as Neiman Marcus, Dillard's, or Foley's, have formal training programs for their buyers. Others plug you in as a merchandising assistant or assistant buyer and let you fend for yourself. It's up to you to learn on your own. Sink or swim.

What Is the Career Path?

After you are buyer, you can move to another department, such as advertising, visual merchandising (creating the displays), or distribution and shipping (handling logistics and moving product from the manufacturer to the store).

If you are an assistant buyer or merchandising manager you can usually expect to have a review after six months.

How Much Can I Make?

The pay is OK. You start out in the low- to mid-twenties. The perks are great, though. Insurance, 401K, stock purchase opportunities, and a merchandise discount. "The discount on merchandise is by far the best perk," says one Gap employee.

The hours can be erratic and long. Holidays and certain times of the year are more hectic than others. Some employers recruit on campus, but the majority of positions can be found through word of mouth and connections.

PERFORMING ARTS

To be involved in the performing arts is to be involved in the theater, music, or dance. You can be a performer or on the business side of the arts, such as administration, fund raising, public relations, or ticket sales. If you aren't a performer, but have an artistic need and desire to be in the arts, this may be a great outlet for you. Some arts organizations are nonprofit and seek donations and government funding, while others are private or for-profit enterprises. Most local communities have both kinds of arts groups.

While most opportunities in these fields are in New York or Los Angeles, you don't have to move to either coast to pursue this field. There are opportunities all over the country. Theater or dance companies and symphonies can be found in major metropolitan areas, such as Chicago, Boston, Cleveland, Seattle, and even Salt Lake City.

Where Do I Start?

Performing arts encompasses much more than just being an actual performer. It's split into three different areas: A) Administration: company manager, house manager, audience manager, public relations, marketing, bookkeeping, business manager, fund raising, or box office sales; B) Production: everything from the creating, moving, and designing of costumes, sets, props, lighting, or wardrobe; C) Performing: actor, director, choreographer, musician, dancer, or conductor.

Much of the hiring is done is through auditions, word of mouth, and being at the right place at the right time. Obviously, this field is incredibly competitive. You must have a thick skin and a decent savings account and be skilled at carrying many plates at a time. Because rejection is frequent and work is not, many supplement their slight income by becoming waiters and waitresses, or finding other part-time work.

What Will I Do?

Starting out, you will do everything that needs to be done. You might start as a volunteer or intern. This is how you get noticed. Depending on your particular focus, you will be a jack-of-all-trades. On the business side, you may handle publicity and fund raising, and write proposals. As a performer or on the production end, you may help with set design, clean up, block scenes, or help orchestrate rehearsals.

The hours are long and you must be willing to work very hard for rehearsals and performances. This is one of the most competitive and lowest-paying professions. Bear in mind that there are other opportunities outside of being a performer that will allow you to remain in the performing arts field.

How Much Can I Make?

Not much. Elyse, who is with a children's theater in Milwaukee, says that her first job paid $75 a week. After three months, she got a raise to $175 a week. "You aren't going to get rich in the theater." Starting out, you can expect anywhere from $0 (yes, many people work for free to get started) to $15,000 a year. This will vary according to where you live, the size of the company you are with, and how frequently you work.

If you are with a professional company, you may get insurance and benefits. "The perks are intangible," says Elyse. "It is a relaxed work environment and I love what I do. However, the low pay is the worst part of the job. Last year I had my salary frozen for a month, because we were in a deficit situation." Actors, dancers, and musicians all have unions, which guarantee certain wages and benefits if you qualify.

What Is the Career Path?

There is not exactly a career path. It's very transient work. It may require that you move between companies and cities to find work. Try to work part-time in order to decide if it's really the lifestyle you want. Advancement comes as you gain a reputation and a body of work. Many people vacillate between the performing and the production side.

What Skills Do I Need?

Many people have bachelor's degrees in either theater, music, or dance; however, talent is the main requirement. You can also formally study certain aspects outside of performing, including design and stagecraft. Regardless of the discipline, people are constantly taking classes or attempting to perfect their craft.

On the business end, a liberal arts education is great because it prepares you for everything that you might do. You must be able to adapt and think on your feet. Problem-solving skills are crucial, too. If you are in administration, your communication skills are important because you will be meeting with board members or trying to raise funds.

To learn more about opportunities in the performing arts, contact the Theater Communications Group in New York. They publish a newsletter called Artsearch, which lists job openings and internships nationwide.

PUBLIC RELATIONS AND COMMUNICATIONS

The main opportunities in public relations are with an agency, as a free-lancer, as in-house staff for a company or organization, or with a government agency. Almost any organization that deals with the public uses public relations and communications experts in some capacity. One of the main responsibilities of PR professionals is to help get a client's point or message across to the media and the public. It differs from advertising, in that you are trying to convince news and media sources that your story is newsworthy and deserves to be written about, rather than buying space or time to present your commercial or ad. Public relations experts issue press releases and handle the media during crises. Another important function is developing relationships with the media so that their clients will receive favorable press coverage. Many times you present your point of view or an announcement, then a reporter determines if it's newsworthy or if he needs to alter it.

Where Do I Start?

The best and most common route is to start in an agency. Many people gain experience and make contacts in the industry and eventually move into the private sector to work for a company. You will most likely start out as an account executive of some kind (either junior or assistant AE).

The other option is to work in-house with a company or organization. However, it's much more difficult to find entry-level positions in this area. In-house PR counsel falls under several different categories—corporate communications, community relations, investor relations, government affairs, public affairs, and crisis management are a just a few. Each group handles a different specialty, yet all fall under the public relations or corporate communications label. For example, media relations staff is responsible for responding to questions from the media. Investor relations helps to prepare annual reports and is responsible for any communication involving investors.

What Will I Do?

In an agency, you will be given fairly limited client contact. Major client contact is left to more senior and experienced staff. Beth, who has been in public relations from both the agency side and as a marketing communications specialist with Deloitte & Touche, says, "Public relations is a very labor-intensive business. Initially, you will spend a lot of time doing gofer work, preparing press kits, updating media lists, making follow-up phone calls, and compiling information." As you become more experienced you will begin to handle the press, plan events, create press kits, write speeches, organize tours and television presentations, and learn to put a good spin on your client's story.

What Skills Do I Need?

Many people have degrees in public relations; however, journalism and English majors also fare well. Primarily, you need to be a good communicator and have particularly good writing skills. You must also be energetic, a fabulous networker, and creative. An understanding of media and general business is also helpful.

Increasingly, you must be able to work as part of a team in an integrated communications effort. These teams usually include experts in marketing, public relations, and advertising.

Experience counts above all else. You can gain experience through an internship or writing for a publication. Save any clips or spots that you write or get placed. They will be valuable for a portfolio you can show to an employer.

How Much Can I Make?

The pay is low, very low. You can expect to make a starting salary in the mid- to high teens, depending on where you live and the agency or company you are with. Benefits, such as insurance, are included. Among the fringe benefits are the people you get to meet and the events that you get to attend. It's a lot like television in that it appears much more glamorous than it really is. The hours can be long and the pressure great when there is a crisis or deadline.

Who Are the Top Firms?

The top firms are in New York, Chicago, Washington, D.C. , and Los Angeles, but there are agencies large and small all over the country. Among the largest public relations agencies are Hill and Knowlton, Burson-Marsteller, Daniel J. Edelman, Fleishman Hillard, Manning Selvage and Lee, and Ruder Finn. Call the PRSA Public Relations Society in New York for more information regarding a career in public relations.

PUBLISHING

To be in publishing generally means that you work for either a magazine or a book publisher. You can be a writer, an editor, a researcher, or a fact checker. You can also be on the other side of the publishing arena and be an agent or in publicity and sales.

Where Do I Start?

If you are in book publishing, you will most likely start out as an assistant. Don't freak out or think that you are above it. Almost everyone starts here. It's not uncommon to see bright people who have master's degrees working as assistants. There is a lot of tedious dues-paying in the publishing business.

In book publishing, it is rare for people to have secretaries. Most people have assistants, so the starting position is to be someone's assistant and learn by being around them. This means that you will be answering phones, writing letters, proofreading, making copies, and generally doing anything else that is asked of you.

You may have to do this for at least a couple of years. Advancement is slow in book publishing. Use your boss or someone else to network and act as an internal champion for you. Have them teach you as much as possible. If after a while you can tell that this person will not (or can't) help you advance . . . move on.

On the editorial side, you will eventually advance to some form of editor. As an editor, you will work closely with authors and agents, review manuscripts, help with layout and design, and coordinate production of books. You usually work on several projects at once.

You will do a huge amount of reading, often at night or on weekends. You might think that editors would spend their days reading, but, oddly enough, that is not the case. Most reading is done outside of work.

If you don't want to be an editor but still have a desire to be in the publishing business, you might look into sales or publicity or try working for an agent. Even in these areas you will most likely start as an assistant.

Although sales staffs vary from publisher to publisher, their main focus is to represent the publisher and sell books to the bookstores and booksellers. Publicists work closely with the author and the media to organize tours and publicity for their authors.

As an agent's assistant, you may still do secretarial duties, such as answering the phone, but you may also get to read manuscripts and recommend them to your boss, make contacts, and observe how deals are done from the other side of the business. This can be a great way to enter the business. It depends on your particular boss and the responsibilities that she gives you.

In magazine publishing, the low man on the totem pole is often the fact checker or researcher. While it may seem like grunt work, it can be a valuable position and teach you a great deal. You will make numerous phone calls, learn how to locate people and information, and double-check facts and stories.

What Skills Do I Need?

There is no special degree required, although liberal arts and English backgrounds are advantageous. There are several special publishing programs around the country that teach you the basics of the business and also offer a placement service. These programs are through various colleges and universities and often last several weeks. One of the most popular is a six-week co-ed program at Radcliffe, in Cambridge, Massachusetts.

You must love to read, and have excellent English skills, both written and verbal. You will be communicating with authors, agents, and coworkers all the time. You also *must* know how to type.

Something that will set you apart or make your search much easier is to determine who publishes the books that you like to read. Learn something about the publisher and the types of books that they produce. This may give you an idea of the type of publisher you want to work for.

What Is the Career Path?

On the editorial food chain there are many different levels (associate editor, managing editor, senior editor). All do pretty much the same thing. The difference is in the seniority and responsibility involved.

Advancement is much slower on the editorial side than in other areas of publishing. There are very few lateral moves. If someone is in sales and then wants to move to editorial, they often start back at square one. People tend to stay in an area and rise in that department. Again, experience is the main thing. There is not often a set career path based on tenure. It's based more on how good you are and what opportunities open up.

Your connections count for a lot. As one editor says, "It really is who and what you know." Your connections will help you to learn about projects early. It's an industry of lunches and connections. Staying in contact with people inside of your own publishing house, as well as agents and authors, is incredibly important to your career. It's not uncommon for people to hop around from one organization to another.

"Some people go into publishing and after about two years realize that it isn't for them, or they don't want to wait, so they go to law school or get a graduate degree," says one young editor. "Those who stay past that two- or three-year period tend to make a career out of it."

How Much Can I Make?

You don't do this to get rich. The pay is low, overall. However, depending on whether you are in sales or editorial, the pay may vary. In book publishing, you can expect to make between $16,000 and $20,000 in your first year. This, of course, depends on the publishing house. You will receive insurance and retirement benefits. One of the unique perks is that you get free books. You are also constantly surrounded by bright people and the projects you work on can be very interesting. The hours can be long. One editor says, "It's like being in school. You always have reading and work to do. This is not a job you can leave at the office at 5 p.m." Make sure that you love books and reading before you enter this profession.

Where Are They?

If you are serious about being in book publishing, you should be willing to move to New York. The center of the publishing universe is New York. There are pockets around the country where some major magazine and regional book publishers are located, but over 90 percent of the work is on the East Coast.

People get hired in publishing through on-campus recruiting sometimes, but the vast majority learn about positions and are hired because they know someone. Use your network.

SALES

The core purpose of almost any organization is to generate revenue, or make money. The most common way to do this is through sales—sales of a product that a company produces or of a service the company provides or performs. The variety of organizations that have a sales force is almost unlimited.

Sales positions are not limited by a certain industry, degree, certification, or area of the country. If you enjoy it and are skilled at it, sales can be one of the most lucrative and wide-open fields available.

Where Do I Start?

There are many names for those in sales. Account executive, sales professional, sales representative, sales associate—they all mean roughly the same thing. Your amount of responsibility will be different from company to company.

Your training will depend on the organization. Some companies have very formal training programs that require you to learn the products or services thoroughly before you are allowed to have direct contact with a client. Some large companies, such as Xerox, Procter & Gamble, and many of the consumer goods companies have fantastic training programs. Some of these training programs are so well respected that people who have this training are highly sought after by other companies.

Other organizations give you a crash course in the product or service and send you into the field to learn on your own. You may also be assigned to a sales support position for a short time, where you will perform support activities for salespersons and learn how they perform their duties. Sometimes you will be partnered with a senior sales person for a few weeks to follow her around and learn the ropes.

What Will I Do?

Regardless of the field or product, sales people do a lot of the same things. Duties will be split among several activities. First will be prospecting, or determining who your potential clients will be. Some organizations provide you with leads, while other sales reps must do research on their own. This may involve reading or making many phone calls to learn about a company and determine the proper person to contact.

You will also spend much of your time on the phone trying to set up meetings or talking with clients to determine their needs. There may be a great deal of travel involved to make sales calls or service existing accounts. Some reps travel up to 80 percent of the time.

Customer service is another big part of your job. You must be available to take care of your client's needs, no matter how insignificant you think they are. There may be a lot of paperwork and follow-up phone work to close a sale. You must also stay current on the activities of your competitors and happenings in your industry.

Most sales people are assigned a territory or market. This is a group or area that they are responsible for. It can be a geographic territory or it can be a group of potential clients categorized by name, type of business, size of business, or other criteria. Some people are responsible for many, even several hundred, accounts, while others spend their time working with two or three major accounts that need a lot of special attention.

The hours can be long and erratic. Many reps have a flexible schedule, allowing them to work when they want, while others adhere more to a standard nine to five. You may have a nice office with an assistant, or you may share a loud and noisy cubicle or bullpen with other people and do everything for yourself. With the availability of computers, faxes, and phones, many organizations now have their sales people work from their homes.

How Much Can I Make?

Your potential income is truly unlimited. It depends on the product you are selling, the commission structure your company has, and, of course, how good you are. Sales people who make over six figures are not uncommon. However, there are others who have a tough time making it month to month.

Starting salaries can range from $15,000 up to $30,000. There is no constant. Many organizations structure their compensation with a combination of base salary plus commissions and bonuses. There is a trend to offer a base salary that isn't extravagant, but that is substantial enough to pay the bills. The bulk of your income will come from commissions—income based upon a percentage of the amount of goods sold, targets met, or quotas reached.

Many organizations give their sales forces generous expense accounts, in addition to insurance and retirement benefits. Sometimes a car or car allowance is provided.

A potentially lucrative, yet risky, endeavor is commission-only sales. This means that you do not get a salary, but are paid only commissions. Since the commissions are usually a high percentage, this is great if you are selling a lot and making commissions. But if you have a bad month, or a series of bad months, you can be eating ramen noodles. Actually, what happens is that you are allowed to take a "draw," or advance, against future commissions earned. If you are having a rough patch and keep taking draws against anything that you will make in the future, you can get way behind.

The best form of compensation is a healthy mix of both base salary and commission. This way you don't have to worry about paying the bills, and can focus on your job of selling.

In sales, sometimes your earnings can vary from one year to the next. It depends on how good a year you had. It's wise to be very disciplined with your savings. Then, if you have a bad year or a slump, you have something put away.

What Skills Do I Need?

First and foremost, you must be a good communicator. This includes being a fantastic listener. Your livelihood will depend upon your people skills and persuasiveness.

You must also be assertive. People often confuse sales with glad-handing or high-pressure tactics. While some sales people certainly are cheesy and some industries are known for it more than others, the best sales people see themselves as consultants rather than peddlers or vendors. "You must show the client how they will value and benefit from your product," says Shelly, a sales person in Los Angeles. You need to be persistent and have a thick skin, because rejection is a way of life.

Generally there are no special degree requirements; however, some organizations have preferences. Generally, grades or a certain type of degree are not as crucial as experience.

Because you are often working on your own and there may not be much direction, self-discipline and motivation are things you must also possess.

Certain sales cycles can take longer than others. Some sales people work for over a year just to close one deal. For this reason, patience is necessary.

Many people like sales because they feel more in control of their future. They would rather let their income depend on their abilities than wait for someone to notice their work and give them a raise.

What Is the Career Path?

It's wide open. Many go into sales management. However, it's not uncommon for some sales people to stay in sales and forego management, because they can make more money from commissions than being paid a straight salary in management. Some gravitate to other areas of the business, such as marketing or product development, or they become entrepreneurs.

Once you have solid sales experience and a successful track record, you are very marketable. You can take your experience to many other organizations, regardless of industry or product. You can always learn about the industry and apply your skills at closing sales and getting orders to that particular business. Experienced sales people are always in demand.

It's a competitive field. You will face competition in the marketplace from other companies vying for your customer, and competition inside your own organization, as well. Companies often have rankings and sales contests among coworkers.

TELEVISION AND RADIO

To work in radio or television, you have several choices. When people think of these fields they generally think of being in front of the camera or on the air. This is called the "talent," and is one career option. But there are many other opportunities available to you, either behind the scenes in production or on the business and administration side, which includes marketing, publicity, and advertising sales.

On-air talent includes anchor, reporter, host, and DJ. Behind-the-scenes production staff includes producers, directors, and camera and sound people.

Television and radio stations need to promote and market their stations, just as any company does any product or service. They generate revenue by selling air time to advertisers and sponsors, so there are opportunities in publicity, marketing, and sales. Advertising sales is very similar to any other sales position.

Where Do I Start?

This is a *super competitive* field, on either side of the camera or microphone. Traditionally, radio is easier to break into than TV.

If you think that having a fresh degree and a burning desire to be Dan Rather will get you a job in a major market, give it up. The major markets are the toughest to break into. Stations rarely look at anyone who is not polished or who lacks experience. Everyone pays their dues . . . big time. If you want to be on camera, your best shot is to move to Nowhere, Nebraska, and give the cattle report for a year. Start with a smaller local station or affiliate.

Your résumé doesn't matter nearly as much as your "package" or demo tape. This is a video or audio portfolio of your best work. It is what most stations and shows want to see and hear. People generally make their tapes while serving as interns.

Behind the scenes, start out doing anything you can, for free. Learn everything possible. If you have spare time, learn to run the camera and the sound, and have someone show you how to edit. You will most likely start out as a production assistant, researcher, fact checker, or grunt. You will make phone calls, go on shoots, line up guests, carry equipment, write copy, or interview subjects.

How Much Can I Make?

Salaries vary depending on your location, but generally they are low. You can expect to start out in the teens or low twenties, plus insurance benefits. Talent and production staff are sometimes initially employed on a contract basis rather than as full employees. This serves as a trial period.

Many people start out as interns or unpaid volunteers. This is important, because experience and being at the right place at the right time counts for a lot. Do whatever it takes to get in, even if you have to do it for free.

While it appears to be glamorous work, it is not. The hours are long and there are many sacrifices of your time. You might miss holidays and family events. To quote one cub reporter, "The news doesn't stop on holidays." The hours are also erratic. You may work Wednesday through Sunday from 2 until 11 p.m. On the other hand, "Having everyone in town know who you are is pretty cool, too," says one reporter.

What Is It Like?

The atmosphere is informal, sometimes even sloppy, and isn't for anyone whose feelings are easily hurt or who is easily offended by foul language. It's a high-stress, high-pressure, precision business. People are often very blunt and downright rude. It's nothing against you. It is just the pressure of the environment.

What Skills Do I Need?

You have to be creative and patient, a good writer and communicator, and know how to type. If you are on the production side, you need to have technical experience and be familiar with the equipment. If you hope to get a job as on-air talent, you can't have a strong accent. A lot also depends on your look or voice. Many people have degrees in radio or television, but your degree doesn't matter nearly as much as your talent and experience.

What Is the Career Path?

There is not a set career path. You advance by receiving more responsibility and exposure. It's a very networked industry and you must begin to work your Rolodex early. Many people job hop in order to rise and make more money. In front of the camera, you know you are advancing when you get better stories, time slots, or exposure. You may then begin to receive offers from other stations. Some people get their breaks because they are in the right place or are available when a situation or crisis arises.

Where Are They?

Most of the main television and radio shows are produced out of New York or Los Angeles. However, your best shot is with any local affiliate news department, radio station, morning show, or so forth. These positions are found mostly by word of mouth and networking and internships. Campus recruiting is rare or nonexistent.

APPENDIX B

Resources

SPECIAL ADDRESSES AND TELEPHONE NUMBERS

National Directory Assistance (How to find any phone number in the country.) 1 (Area Code) 555-1212 (The most important number you can remember.)

FEDEX
800/238-5355

UPS
800/742-5877
(Very important to remember for when you must send your boss's package overnight.)

FORTUNE MAGAZINE
Time and Life Building
Rockefeller Center
New York, NY 10020
212/522-2582 Single Copies and Reprints
800/621-8000 Subscriptions

FORBES
60 Fifth Avenue
New York, NY 10011
212/620-2220 Single Copies and Reprints
800/888-9896 Subscriptions

THE WALL STREET JOURNAL
200 Liberty Street
New York, New York 10281
800/778-0840

INC.
38 Commercial Wharf
Boston, MA 02110
617/248-8426 Single Copies and Reprints
800/234-0999 Subscriptions

BUSINESS WEEK
McGraw-Hill Inc.
1221 Avenue of the Americas
New York, NY 10020
212/512-2000
800/635-1200 Subscriptions

LOCAL BUSINESS JOURNALS AND BOOKS OF LISTS

ATLANTA BUSINESS CHRONICLE
AUSTIN BUSINESS JOURNAL
BALTIMORE BUSINESS JOURNAL
BOSTON BUSINESS JOURNAL
BUSINESS FIRST OF BUFFALO
THE CHARLOTTE BUSINESS JOURNAL
CRAIN'S CHICAGO BUSINESS
CINCINNATI BUSINESS COURIER
CRAIN'S CLEVELAND BUSINESS
BUSINESS FIRST COLUMBUS
DALLAS BUSINESS JOURNAL
THE DENVER BUSINESS JOURNAL
CRAIN'S DETROIT BUSINESS
FRESNO BUSINESS JOURNAL
GRAND RAPIDS BUSINESS JOURNAL
HOUSTON BUSINESS JOURNAL
JACKSONVILLE BUSINESS JOURNAL
JOURNAL RECORD (Oklahoma City)
KANSAS CITY BUSINESS JOURNAL
LOS ANGELES BUSINESS JOURNAL

LAS VEGAS BUSINESS PRESS
BUSINESS FIRST OF LOUISVILLE
MINNEAPOLIS-ST. PAUL CITY BUSINESS
NEW MEXICO BUSINESS JOURNAL
NEW ORLEANS CITY BUSINESS
CRAIN'S NEW YORK BUSINESS
ORANGE COUNTY BUSINESS JOURNAL (Orange County, CA)
ORLANDO BUSINESS JOURNAL
PACIFIC BUSINESS NEWS (Honolulu)
THE PHOENIX BUSINESS JOURNAL
PHILADELPHIA BUSINESS JOURNAL
PITTSBURGH BUSINESS TIMES and JOURNAL
THE PORTLAND BUSINESS JOURNAL
PUGET SOUND BUSINESS NEWS (Seattle/Tacoma)
TRIANGLE BUSINESS JOURNAL (Raleigh/Durham)
ST. LOUIS BUSINESS JOURNAL
SAN ANTONIO BUSINESS JOURNAL
SAN FRANCISCO BUSINESS TIMES
SAN JOSE BUSINESS JOURNAL
TAMPA BAY BUSINESS JOURNAL
WASHINGTON BUSINESS JOURNAL (Washington, D.C.)
WICHITA BUSINESS JOURNAL

The business journals listed above also provide annual books of lists for each city. The directories generally cost between $15 and $30. Subscriptions, back issues, and the book of lists can be purchased by calling the publication directly. The directories may be available on computer disks as well.

TRAVEL PROGRAMS

Airlines

AMERICAN AIRLINES
800/882-8880 *Reservations*
AADVANTAGE PROGRAM
affiliated with
   Rental Car: *Alamo, Avis, Hertz*
   Hotels: *Hilton, Holiday Inn, Intercontinental, Marriott, Sheraton, Ritz Carlton, Wyndham*

DELTA AIRLINES

800/221-1212 *Reservations*

FREQUENT FLYER PROGRAM

affiliated with

Rental Car: *Hertz, Alamo, Avis*

Hotels: *Hilton, Holiday Inn, Hyatt, Marriott, Radisson, Sheraton*

UNITED AIRLINES

800/241-6522 *Reservations*

MILAGE PLUS

affiliated with

Rental Car: *Hertz, Alamo, Avis*

Hotels: *Hilton, Holiday Inn, Hyatt, Sheraton, Westin*

CONTINENTAL AIRLINES

800/525-0280 *Reservations*

ONE PASS

affiliated with

Rental Car: *Avis, Dollar*

Hotels: *Doubletree, Marriott, Radisson, Sheraton*

NORTHWEST

800/225-2525 *Reservations*

WORLD PERKS

affiliated with

Rental Car: *Hertz, National, Alamo*

Hotels: *Holiday Inn, Hyatt, Marriott, Radisson*

SOUTHWEST AIRLINES

800/435-9792 *Reservations*

COMPANY CLUB 800/445-5764

Not affiliated with any car rental companies or hotels

USAIR

800/428-4322 *Reservations*

FREQUENT TRAVELER PROGRAM

affiliated with

Rental Car: *Hertz, National, Alamo*

Hotels: *Hilton, Omni, Radisson, Hyatt, Marriott*

Hotels

RESIDENCE INN
800/331-3131 *Reservations*
affiliated with
   (Owned by Marriott, but Residence Inn does not have a frequent-
   guest program)

HOLIDAY INN
800/465-4329 *Reservations*
PRIORITY CLUB
affiliated with
   Airlines: *Delta, Northwest, United, American*
   Rental Cars: *Hertz*

SHERATON
800/325-3535 *Reservations*
CLUB INTERNATIONAL
affiliated with
   Airlines: *American, United, Delta, Continental*
   Rental Cars: *Hertz*

HILTON
800/HILTONS (445-8667) *Reservations*
HILTON HONORS
affiliated with
   Airlines: *America West, American, Delta, United, USAir*
   Rental Cars: *National, Alamo, Avis, Thrifty*

MARRIOTT
800/228-9290 *Reservations*
MARRIOTT HONORED GUEST CLUB
affiliated with
   Airlines: *American, Delta, TWA, USAir, Northwest, Continental*
   Rental Cars: *Hertz*

HYATT
800/233-1234 *Reservations*
GOLD PASSPORT
affiliated with
   Airlines: *Delta, Northwest, United, USAir*
   Rental Cars: *Avis, Budget*

WESTIN
800/228-3000 Reservations
WESTIN PREMIERE
affiliated with
    Airlines: *United, USAir, Northwest*
    Rental Cars: *No Car Rental*

INTERCONTINENTAL
800/327-0200 Reservations
SIX CONTINENTS CLUB
affiliated with
    Airlines: *American, United, Delta, TWA*
    Rental Cars: *No Car Rental*

Car Rentals

HERTZ
800/227-4653 Reservations
#1 CLUB GOLD
affiliated with
    Airlines: *American, Delta, United, Northwest, USAir*

AVIS
800/331-1212 Reservations
PREFERRED RENTER
affiliated with
    Airlines: *American, Continental, Delta, United*

NATIONAL
800/328-4567 Reservations
EMERALD CLUB
affiliated with
    Airlines: *United, USAir, Northwest, Continental*

BUDGET
800/527-0700 Reservations
AWARDS PLUS
affiliated with
    Airlines: *America West*

APPENDIX C

Organizations and Other Resources

ACCOUNTING

American Institute of Certified Public Accountants: 1211 Avenue of the
Americas, New York, NY 10036

Institute of Management Accountants: 10 Paragon Dr., Montvale, NJ 07645

National Society of Public Accountants and the Accreditation Council for
Accountancy and Taxation: 1010 N. Fairfax St., Alexandria, VA 22314

ADVERTISING

American Association of Advertising Agencies (The 4As): 666 Third Ave.,
13th Floor, New York, NY 10019

The Standard Directory of Advertising Agencies /The Agency Red Book:
(National Register Publishing): 121 Chanlon Rd., New Providence,
NJ 07974

BANKING AND FINANCE

The American Bank Directory (McFadden Business Publications):
6195 Crooked Creek Rd., Norcross, GA 30092

The U.S. Savings and Loan Directory (Rand McNally and Co.):
8255 N. Central Pk., Skokie, IL 60076-2970

Securities Industry Association: 120 Broadway, New York, NY 10271

The Insurance Almanac: Who, What, When, and Where in Insurance:
(The Underwriter Printing and Publishing Co., 50 East Palisade Ave.,
Englewood, NJ 07631)

BROADCASTING AND JOURNALISM

(NAB) National Association of Broadcasters: 1771 N St. NW, Washington,
DC 20036

(RTNDA) Radio-Television News Directors Association: 1717 K St. NW,
Suite 615, Washington, DC 20006

American Newspaper Publishers Association Foundation, The Newspaper
Center: Box 17407, Dulles International Airport, Washington, DC 20041

The Newspaper Guild: 8611 2nd Ave., Silver Spring, MD 20910

National Newspaper Association: 1627 K St. NW, Washington, DC 20006

CONSULTING

The Council of Consulting Organizations: 251 Fifth Ave., New York, NY
10175

ENGINEERING

American Society of Mechanical Engineers: 345 E. 47th St., New York,
NY 10017

American Society of Civil Engineers: 345 E. 47th St., New York, NY 10017

American Institute of Chemical Engineers: 345 E. 47th St., New York,
NY 10017

Institute of Electrical and Electronic Engineers: 345 E. 47th St., New York,
NY 10017

GOVERNMENT

Roll Call: Weekly newspaper in Washington, D.C., which covers what is happening in government. Also includes classifieds.

MERCHANDISING AND RETAIL

National Retail Federation: 100 W. 31st St., New York, NY 10001

PERFORMING ARTS

Screen Actors Guild: 1515 Broadway, New York, NY 10036

Actors' Equity Association: 1560 Broadway, New York, NY 10036

American Federation of Television and Radio Artists (AFTRA): 260 Madison Ave., New York, NY 10016

Society of Stage Directors and Choreographers: 1501 Broadway, New York, NY 10036

Theater Communications Group: 355 Lexington Ave., New York, NY 10017

Associated Actors and Artistes of America: 165 W. 46th St., New York, NY 10036

PUBLIC RELATIONS

Public Relations Society of America (PRSA): 33 Irving Place, New York, NY 10003

SALES AND MARKETING

American Marketing Association: 250 S. Wacker Dr., Chicago, IL 60606

Sales and Marketing Executives International: 458 Statler Office Tower, Cleveland, OH 44115

TEACHING AND EDUCATION

American Federation of Teachers: 555 New Jersey Avenue NW, Washington, DC 20001

National Education Association: 1201 16th Street NW, Washington, DC 20036

The Handbook of Private Schools: An Annual Descriptive Survey of Independent Education. (Porter Sargent Publishers, Inc., 11 Beacon St., Suite 1400, Boston, MA 02108)

Directory of Public School Systems in the U.S. (Association for School, College and University Staffing, Inc., Addison, IL)

THERAPY

American Occupational Therapy Association: P.O. Box 1725, Rockville, MD 20849

VISUAL AND GRAPHIC ARTS

The Society of Illustrators: 128 E. 63rd Street, New York, NY 10021

The American Institute of Graphic Arts: 1059 Third Avenue, New York, NY 10021

APPENDIX D

Suggested Reading

The following is a list of suggested reading. These books cover a wide range of topics, from management to job search techniques to life skills. Some were mentioned earlier in this book. They have all helped me and countless others. I hope that you can benefit from them, as well.

A Passion for Excellence: The Leadership Difference. Thomas J. Peters and Nancy Austin. Warner Books, 1985. Read anything by Tom Peters. Others include *In Search of Excellence, Thriving On Chaos, Liberation Management, The Tom Peters Seminar*. They are all great!

In Search of Excellence: Lessons from America's Bet-Run Companies. Thomas J. Peters, Robert H. Waterman. Warner Books Edition, 1982.

Whack on the Side of the Head: How You Can Be More Creative. Roger von Oech. Warner Books, Inc., 1983.

Swim with the Sharks, Without Being Eaten Alive. Harvey MacKay. Ivy Books, 1988. If you don't read anything else, read this. Read anything you can by Harvey MacKay.

Beware of the Naked Man Who Offers You His Shirt: Do What You Love, Love What You Do and Deliver More Than You Promise. Harvey MacKay. William Morrow and Co., 1990. Down-to-earth, common-sense business skills, and easy to read.

Sharkproof: Get the Job You Want, Keep the Job You Love . . . in Today's Frenzied Job Market. Harvey MacKay. Harper Business, 1993.

The One Minute Manager. Kenneth Blanchard, Ph.D., Spencer Johnson, M.D. Berkeley Books, 1987.

Career Tracking: 26 Success Shortcuts to the Top. Jimmy Calano and Jeff Salzman. Simon and Schuster, 1988.

Do What You Love, The Money Will Follow: Discovering Your Right Livelihood. Marsha Sinetar. Dell Publishing, 1978.

Does Your Résumé Wear Blue Jeans? The Book on Résumé Preparation and Job Search Strategies. C. Edward Good. Ward Store, 1988.

Even Eagles Need a Push: Learning to Soar in a Changing World. David McNally. Delacorte Press, 1990.

Getting to Yes: Negotiating Agreement Without Giving In. Roger Fisher and William Levy. Penguin Books, 1983.

Leadership Secrets of Attila the Hun. Wess Roberts. Warner Books, 1985.

Liar's Poker: Rising Through the Wreckage on Wall Street. Michael Lewis. W.W. Norton and Co., 1989. Entertaining true story of his career on Wall Street.

Lighten Up: Survival Skills for People Under Pressure. C. W. Metcalf and Roma Felible. Addison Wesley Publishing Co., 1992.

Lions Don't Need To Roar: Using the Leadership Power of Professional Presence to Stand Out and Fit In and Move Ahead. D. A. Benton. Warner Books, 1992.

Maximum Achievement: The Proven System of Strategies and Skills That Will Unlock Your Hidden Powers to Succeed. Brian Tracy. Simon and Schuster, 1993.

Power and Influence: Mastering the Art of Persuasion. Robert Dilenschneider. Prentice Hall Press, 1990.

Professional Presence: The Total Program for Gaining that Extra Edge in Business by America's Top Corporate Image Consultant. Susan Bixler. Perigee, 1992.

The Corporate Coach: How to Build a Team of Loyal Customers and Happy Employees. James B. Miller. St. Martin's Press, 1993.

Straight A's Never Made Anybody Rich: Lessons in Personal Achievement. Wess Roberts. HarperCollins Publishers, 1991.

The New Dynamics of Winning: Gain the Mind-set of a Champion for Unlimited Success in Business and Life. Denis Watley. William Morrow and Co., 1993.

The Power of Positive Thinking. Norman Vincent Peale. Fawcett Books, 1952. Great motivation.

The Road Less Traveled: A New Psychology of Love, Traditional Values and Spiritual Growth. M. Scott Peck, MD. Simon and Schuster, 1978. Classic life skills.

The Seven Habits of Highly Effective People: Powerful Lessons in Personal Change. Stephen R. Covey. Simon and Schuster, 1989. Leadership skills.

What Color is Your Parachute? A Practical Manual for Job Hunters and Career Changers. Richard Nelson Bolles. Ten Speed Press, 1988. The classic career search book. Soup to nuts.

13th Gen: Abort, Retry, Ignore, Fail? Neil Howe and Bill Strauss. Vintage Books, 1993. Witty social commentary about our generation.

Unlimited Power. Anthony Robbins. Fawcett Columbine, 1986. Yes, the guy on TV. If you can get over the fact he is on late-night TV, he has some great things to say. Any of his books or tapes are highly recommended.

Unwritten Rules for Your Career: 15 Secrets for Fast-Track Success. George B. Graen. John Wiley and Sons, 1989. A little complex, but a super in-depth guide for getting up to speed in a new organization. Reads like a textbook.

What They Don't Teach You at Harvard Business School: Notes from a Street-Smart Executive. Mark H. McCormack. Bantam Books, 1984. Classic tips.

When Smart People Fail: Rebuilding Yourself for Success. Carole Hyatt and Linda Gottlieb. Penguin Books, 1988.

Lincoln on Leadership. Donald T. Phillips. Warner Books, 1992.

Where Do I Go From Here With My Life? John C. Crystal and Richard N. Bolles. Ten Speed Press, 1974. Workbook to determine what you really want to do.

You Are The Message: Getting What You Want By Being Who You Are. Roger Ailes. Doubleday, 1988. Great tips for communication and presence by former top Republican media consultant and current head of CNBC.